the wine, beer, & spirits handbook

A Guide to Styles and Service

THE INTERNATIONAL CULINARY SCHOOLS℠
at The Art Institutes

Joseph LaVilla, Ph.D., CEC
Photography by Doug Wynn

WILEY

John Wiley & Sons, Inc.

Published by John Wiley & Sons, Inc., Hoboken, New Jersey.

Published simultaneously in Canada.

For general information on our other products and services, or technical support, please contact our Customer
Care Department within the United States at 800–762–2974, outside the United States at 317–572–3993 or fax
317–572–4002.

Wiley also publishes its books in a variety of electronic formats. Some content that appears in print may not be
available in electronic books.

For more information about Wiley products, visit our Web site at http://www.wiley.com.

Library of Congress Cataloging-in-Publication Data:
LaVilla, Joseph
    The wine, beer, and spirits handbook: a guide to styles and service/Joseph LaVilla; photography by
Doug Wynn.
        p.   cm.
    Includes bibliographical references and index.
    ISBN 978-0-470-13884-7 (cloth)
    ISBN 978-0-470-52429-9 (custom)
        1. Wine and wine making.   2. Wine service.   3. Wine—Flavor and odor.   4. Drinking of alcoholic
beverages.   I. LaVilla, Joseph.   II. Wynn, Doug.   III. Title.
    TP548.N45   2010
    641.2'2—dc22

                                                                                    2008042640

Printed in the United States of America

10 9 8 7 6 5 4 3 2 1

the
wine,
beer,
& spirits
handbook

Contents

Preface   vii

Preface

An important aspect of hospitality education is the study of wine and beverages. Beverages have become an important aspect of the industry, not only in the overall dining experience, but also for chefs and restaurateurs who wish to enhance the enjoyment of their food. The recent emphasis on food and wine pairings in print and in menus exemplifies this trend. Two recent trends—emphasizing food, beer and cocktail pairings and the rise of the "bar chef" using savory ingredients—suggest the trend is expanding beyond wine.

Learning about wine can be an imposing challenge and has some obstacles to easy learning. First, unlike teaching culinary arts, the frame of reference for the student is often limited. Students cannot begin their actual wine education until they are twenty-one, yet have eaten all their lives. Discussion of cooking technique and flavors has some familiarity, while wine is often a completely unique experience. Second, wine education is constantly changing. Every year, when a new vintage is released, new wines need to be learned. Considering there are thousands of wineries, each producing multiple types of wine, the task can be overwhelming. It's akin to standing on the 50-yard line at a professional football game and expecting to learn something about every person in the stands. Finally, the instructional organization brings its own challenges. Much of learning about wine begins in France, after whose traditions most wines are produced. However, studying French wine is simply condensing the wine world into a smaller portion. It is still chock full of grapes, styles, techniques, and so on. More advanced classes just delve deeper into the same material. That makes the initial learning curve steep and subsequent learning repetitious.

Audience

The need for a new, comprehensive approach is the motivation behind *The Wine, Beer, and Spirits Handbook*. Most of the wine texts do not address the integration of wine into the hospitality experience. Wine is treated as an isolated subject, occasionally with a reference to basic food and wine pairing. Culinary and hospitality students and professionals will find this book useful for the emphasis on food and wine pairing as a stand-alone topic as well as comments on how grape varietals and wine styles interact with food. For a hospitality student or wine professional, the book focuses not only on the making and flavor profiles of wine, beer, and spirits, but also on the business of wine service. Basic service needs are discussed, as well as management tasks such as inventory control, pricing, menu matching, and storage. Functional skills such as determination of wine faults and understanding the health and legal implications of wine consumption are also addressed. *The Wine, Beer, and Spirits Handbook* is perfect for classes in food and beverage management, wine appreciation, spirits, or advanced restaurant and culinary classes utilizing food and wine pairing.

Organization of the Text

The Wine, Beer, and Spirits Handbook approaches the subject from the modern view of varietal labeling and stylistic similarities. Each part can be used as a stand-alone section to be explored deeply, or the book can be used as a whole to give an overview of the subject and kept as a reference. The material covers both a breadth of topics as well as a depth not found in any other single text. Unique to the text is the inclusion of a large section on food and wine pairing, as well as food and beverage interactions in each part. *The Wine, Beer, and Spirits Handbook* is also not restricted just to wine, but also includes beer and spirits and their interactions with food.

The first part covers the general topic of wine: what makes wines taste different, how they are made, how to taste them, how to store and serve them, how they interact with food, and their implication on health.

The second part focuses on the important grapes in the market today. These are discussed regarding the special circumstances of their growth, wine making, and food interaction. Also discussed are the locations of the best examples of wine from these grapes. Parts three and four look at secondary or up-and-coming grapes (white grapes in part three and red grapes in part four). These are often single-region wines, but they are grouped by style similarities.

After the discussion on table wines, part five is dedicated to specialty wines, namely sparkling wines and fortified wines. In these sections, production is discussed as well as styles and food interactions. Part six focuses on other alcoholic beverages, namely beer and spirits. The spirits are divided into fruit-, grain-, and vegetable-based spirits. The modern beverage program is not focused on just wines or just spirits, but encompasses both in a unified offering. The chef or sommelier must be equally as conscious of beer and spirit choices as they are of wine.

The final part encompasses the business of being a sommelier. The two sides to the job are discussed, the service and the managerial. Service discussion includes how to approach the table and methods of wine sales to customers, while the managerial discussion includes pricing methodology, storage allotment, and product research. Included in these chapters are the development of wine lists, matching lists to menus, and determining faulty wines.

Features for Students

The Wine, Beer, and Spirits Handbook design offers a simple method of learning wine based on grape varietal rather than on region. The grape information includes details on viticulture particular to each varietal and how that influences flavor. Vinification techniques for each varietal are also included. Each major varietal has a detailed description of its tasting profile, as well as individual descriptions of the classic regions of origin and their distinctions. Food and wine pairing guidelines for each varietal and style class are also included. Each major varietal has a summary side bar on basic information as well as flavor profile.

The appendices contain sections that aid the student in deciphering a wine label and local legislation. The maps are designed to give students visual reference for the classic wine regions of the world discussed in the text. Finally, a glossary of the wine- and spirit-related terminology used in the text is included.

Instructor Resources

An Instructor Manual (978–0–470–25407–3) accompanies this text for qualified educators. The manual includes lesson plans, presentation slides, and additional exam questions. Lesson plans, slides, and exam questions are divided by depth of knowledge. An instructor using the text as an introductory course in wine can use the basic level lessons and exams. An instructor teaching a more advanced class has materials that emphasize the depth of knowledge in the text. Lesson plans are developed so that they can be stand-alone lessons. Suggested order of lessons is included, but individual lessons can be used in classes that may not be wine focused. All instructor resources are available electronically at www.wiley.com/go/ai.

Acknowledgments

This text would not have been possible without the help and support of several key individuals and groups. I thank Michael Nenes, Dr. Michael Maki, and EDMC for asking me to write the text, as well as The International Culinary Schools at The Art Institute of Phoenix for supporting me as an author and an instructor. Thanks to Chef Walter Leible, CMC, my food stylist, as well as Chef Eric Watson, CCC, CCE, and each of the members of The International Culinary School The Art Institute of Phoenix faculty. Thanks also to Courtney Schmidt for his assistance to Chef Leible on the photo shoot. I also thank Kobrand Corporation, Palm Bay Imports, Dr. Ann Noble of University at California—Davis, Spaghetti Western Productions, and Lettuce Entertain You Enterprises for contributing pictures and wine lists. Thanks to Doug Wynn and Alicia Martinez for coming up with great photographs, as well as to Tracy Ahvmada, Cristina Nevarez, José Rodrigias, and Corey Lamb for participating in the wine drinking and service photographs at Bomberos Café and Wine Bar in Phoenix. Special thanks to Michael Wray, Metropolitan State College, Denver, and Catherine Rabb, Johnson and Wales University, for their critical review of the text. Thanks also to Julie Kerr, Rachel Livsey, and Richard DeLorenzo at John Wiley & Sons for helping bring this text to reality. We would also like to thank the reviewers who provided feedback on this text in its various stages of development:

Sally Frey, The Art Institute of Pittsburgh, PA

Eyad Joseph, The Art Institute of California, Inland Empire

Joe Raya, The Art Institute of Charleston, SC

Albert Schmid, Sullivan University, KY

Kenneth Mertes, Robert Morris College, IL

PART
ONE

introduction
to **wine**

While wine is simply the fermented juice of grapes, it has gained a place in our psyche as a religious or status symbol. All wine is the same, yet all wines are different. This section expands on the methods of growing grapes and making wine and why all wines do not taste the same. Other basic principles of storage, service, and the interaction of wine with food are also expanded upon, as well as the recent interest in wine's benefits for improving health.

chapter

1

What Makes Wines Taste Different?

Wine is a unique agricultural product. What other food product has aisles upon aisles in stores devoted to it, with so many different varieties and different producers? How can two bottles, labeled with the same grape and from the same region, taste so different? How do you tell the difference or try to decipher what is inside the bottle?

Many factors cause wines to taste different from one another. The most obvious and the most important variable is grape variety. Beside grape variety, grape quality and flavor are affected by the climate, the type of soil, and the agricultural practices (called viticulture) used for growing and harvesting grapes. The wine making process also creates distinctions between wines. All of these factors influence the quality and flavor of the final wine.

Upon completion of this chapter, the student should be able to:

Explain the botanical background of grape varieties
Discuss the life cycle of the vine
Describe when and how to harvest grapes
Discuss the types of climate and their influence on grape growing
Explain how topography influences grape growing
Discuss the influence of soil on grape growing

3

The Grape

Grape plants are part of the family of vining plants Ampelidaceae (or Vitaceae in some references) in the genus Vitis (grape). Within the genus Vitis are many species of grapes that developed around the world, including vinifera, labrusca, rotundafolia, and amurensis, to name a few. While wine can be made from any of these species, *Vitis vinifera* produces the majority of wine as consumers know it. Within vinifera there are several thousand subspecies, called varieties or varietals, which have individual characteristics. Just as a Granny Smith apple differs from a Red Delicious apple, so it is with grape varietals.

Each grape species evolved as woodland vines, climbing trees to reach the sun, and producing tasty, easily pickable fruit that enticed birds to transport the seeds. Depending on the conditions of the area, some vines mutated to better adapt to their surroundings. These mutations led to the differentiation of the grape varieties. As different varieties cross-pollinated, new varieties were created. Vines also propagated via layering, a process by which a vine coming in contact with the forest floor would sprout new roots. If the original branch was severed, then a new plant, identical to the first, would have been created.

NEW GRAPE VARIETIES

Modern nurseries use both the sexual and asexual propagation of grapevines to create new plants. If a nursery wants to create a new variety, it can sexually propagate new vines by physically controlling the pollination of the grape flowers. Pollinating a vinifera variety with a different vinifera variety produces a *cross*. Plant scientists often do this to create a new variety that will hopefully have certain desired characteristics from each parent. The best example of this process can be found in Germany, where many crosses between Rielsing and Sylvaner (referenced as Riesling x Sylvaner) have been created. Because each attempted cross produced a different mix of genes, each cross has different characteristics. In some cases, the cross was successful enough to be recognized as a new varietal, like Muller-Thurgau or Scheurebe.

If a plant scientist breeds vinifera with a different species (such as labrusca) the result is called a *hybrid*. Scientists hybridize grapes in an attempt to create a grape that has the great wine making characteristics of vinifera with the American grape plant resistance to phylloxera, mildew, and cold winters. Initial attempts resulted in poor-quality wines that tasted more like the labrusca than the vinifera (i.e., more like grape juice than wine). Further work has developed hybrids such as Vidal Blanc and Vignoles, which are commonly used for wine production in the eastern United States and Canada due to their increased cold tolerance.

GRAPE VARIATIONS

Whether it is a naturally occurring varietal, a cross, or a hybrid, variations develop within the group. Some plants may thrive better in wetter soil, some may like more sun exposure, or some may have a soil preference. A grower can take advantage of this by propagating the vines that do the best at that site. This asexual propagation produces plants called *clones.* The creation of clones is a controlled version of layering, which grapevines do naturally. Each plant is identical to the parent, so it is just as likely to thrive under the same vineyard conditions. The use of clones is not restricted to single, original sites, but is used by growers who have similar site conditions in other areas of the world. Growers looking to plant in new sites can compare the conditions of their site to those of the clone's origin. They can then order from their nursery the appropriate clone that is adapted to that environment. Not all varietals yield lots of choices. Some grape varieties (such as Pinot Noir) are more sensitive to site selection than others, and therefore yield more clones. If there are multiple clones to choose between, that choice becomes extremely important. A poor clonal selection will result in an inferior wine, while the correct clone can yield a top-quality wine.

GROWTH CYCLE

The growth cycle of the vine is very consistent from year to year. As the springtime temperature reaches about 50°F (10°C), the sap begins to rise in the branches and run through the dormant vine, and new buds begin to swell. These buds will become leaves and new *canes,* or woody stems, from which the fruit will be produced. Grapes are produced only on the new year's growth on a vine. As the temperature reaches 68°F (20°C), *inflorescence,* or flowering, occurs. The flowers are not big and showy, but rather small, typical of wind-pollinated or self-pollinated plants. When the flowers get pollinated, they begin to form berries that will become the grape cluster.

A grower is not concerned with the origin of the pollen so long as the pollination is complete. The seeds that develop will not be used to grow new plants, so their parentage is unimportant. If the weather during flowering is not calm and consistent, the vine has the potential to succumb to shatter or millerandage. *Shatter,* also called *coulure* in France, is the spontaneous dropping of flowers before they have a chance to get pollinated. This will result in a lower yield to the farmer. *Millerandage* is the incomplete pollination and development of the grape cluster. A cluster suffering from millerandage will have both seeded and seedless grapes developing side by side. These do not ripen at the same time and therefore will detrimentally affect the juice at harvest.

Grapevine inflorescence awaiting pollination.

Once pollination has occurred and the clusters have begun to form, the plant will focus on cane and leaf growth. Canes are the woody stems that will hold the developing grape clusters that year. The leaves are the engines producing the sugars that will eventually be transferred to the grapes. In midseason, a noticeable shift occurs and the ripening process, called *veraison,* begins. The beginning of color change that signals that veraison has begun. During the next four to six weeks, the grape clusters will change from small, hard green berries to plump, soft, sweet colored fruit. During this time, the sugar produced by the leaves is transferred to the fruit, the amount of acid in the fruit decreases, and the tannins begin to soften.

HARVEST

Harvest usually occurs four to six weeks after veraison begins, sometimes longer depending on the varietal. As the grapes approach harvest, several factors are analyzed to determine the optimal picking date. Foremost is sugar content, also known as *physiological ripeness.* As the grapes ripen, sugars produced by the leaves are transported to the grapes. Secondly, acid levels are monitored. While unripe, the acids in the grapes are extremely high, but as ripening progresses the acid level decreases. Acid is important in wine, so a grower is looking to balance the sugar level with the acid level. Finally, in the case of red wines, is *phenolic ripeness.* The compounds that characterize red wines, tannins, coloring compounds, and some flavor compounds are from a class of chemical substances called phenols. For some wineries, phenolic ripeness is more important than sugar/acid balance for determining harvest.

A grower, often in conjunction with a wine maker, will use a variety of methods to determine the optimal time to harvest the grapes. For many years, the indicator was taste. The grower would pick random grapes throughout the vineyard, tasting each to determine if the correct balance of flavors had been achieved for wine production. This is still the method to best determine phenolic ripeness. More scientific methods involve the use of pH meters and refractometers. A *refractometer* is a scaled prism attached to a viewing tube. By squeezing juice onto the prism and looking through the viewer, the grower can see how much sugar is in the juice by how the light is refracted. Several different scales are used to measure sugar concentration: Brix in the New World, Baumé in France, and Oechsle in Germany.

Determining Sugar Concentrations

Different scales are used to determine sugar concentration in grape juice. All are related to density—either by measuring specific gravity or concentration of dissolved solids. Below are the three main scales:

- Brix:
  - Most commonly used in North America and by scientists
  - Measures sugar concentration in solution by weight
- Baumé
  - Used in Europe and Australia
  - Measures percentage of concentration of a solution
  - Yields a direct measure of potential alcohol in juice

    °Baumé ~ % alcohol by volume after fermentation

    12.2 °Baumé juice can produce 12.2% alcohol
- Oechsle
  - Used in Germany
  - Measures specific gravity of a solution
  - Directly related to sugar content of juice

Brix and Baumé may be interconverted using:

°Brix = °Baumé * 1.8

After harvest and when the vines have fallen dormant for the winter, they are pruned to prepare the new growth for the next season. There are two main pruning methods, spur pruning and cane pruning. In spur pruning, the canes are removed and only a bud or two are left on the original trunk to form the fruiting canes next year. In cane pruning, all but one or two canes are removed, and these will bud to form the fruiting canes next year. These methods, combined with multiple types of trellising systems, control the quantity and quality of fruit produced by a vine each year. The method of pruning and training must be made when the vineyard is first planted, and will affect the method of harvest.

CONTROLLING GRAPE PRODUCTION

Why would a grape grower be interested in controlling the amount of grapes produced? Wouldn't the vintners want to produce as much as possible, in order to maximize the money they could make? Yes and no. One more factor comes into play when growing grapes, and that is the quality of the grapes produced. In most cases, quality is inversely proportional to quantity. In other words, the more grapes a vine produces, the lower in quality those grapes are. One could consider that a vine has only a set amount of energy, or quality, it can transfer to the grapes. This can be correlated to the amount of sugar the leaves produce via photosynthesis and how it is distributed amongst the grapes. The more grapes that hang on the vine, the more diluted that quality is per grape, the less energy is exerted per bunch to get those grapes ripe, or the less sugar gets placed in each berry. If a vine cannot expend enough energy to ripen a bunch, the grapes will possess vegetal flavors and will not develop the typical aromas needed for quality wine. With this in mind, some growers will conduct a "green harvest" around the time of veraison. A *green harvest* is the clipping of unripe clusters off a vine in order to decrease the yield and allow the vine to focus its energy on the remaining clusters. It is beneficial to the grower because higher-quality grapes will bring a higher price at market.

While all grapevines undergo the same cycle each year, each varietal will display unique physical characteristics. There are obvious differences like skin color (which can vary from pale green to peachy to bluish to almost black) and grape structure (skin thickness, amount of pulp, and size of pips all affect the resultant wine). Some varietals may have the potential to ripen with a lot of sugar content and little acidity, while others may retain high acidity levels. Some lose quality quickly if overcropped, while others can retain their quality at higher yields. As each grape variety is discussed in future chapters, the relationship between vine growth, grape characteristics, and wine flavor will be analyzed.

Phylloxera Vastatrix

The discussion so far has assumed that grapevines can be propagated and planted as any other plant. Unfortunately, in the majority of the wine regions of the world, that is not the case. The reason: a small root louse known as *phylloxera vastatrix*. Phylloxera is native to the eastern United States and Mississippi River Valley and has a very complicated life cycle. Phylloxera can live above ground or below ground, and does not have one distinct series of stages needed to reproduce. Because of the multiple life paths phylloxera can follow, insecticides are useless for eliminating an infestation. The form of phylloxera that destroys vines is a louse that chews on the roots of grapevines. The American vine species that are native to the eastern United States adapted over the years to form calluses around where phylloxera attacked the roots. This adaptation allowed the roots to continue transporting nutrients and water to the vine, and mitigated the damage done by phylloxera.

Initial attempts to plant vinifera in the eastern North American colonies resulted in failure. Most of the failures were blamed on mildew and mold, though the native phylloxera was more likely the culprit. In the middle of the nineteenth century, some American vines were brought to Europe. They carried with them phylloxera as a stowaway. The vitis vinifera, native to Europe, had never been exposed to phylloxera, let alone adapted to it. Instead of forming calluses on the roots, the roots became clogged as the vine tried to block the infestation. Eventually, all the roots would be useless at transporting nutrients to the vine and would die. Thus began a slow devastation of the vineyards of Europe. Several failed solutions were attempted, including flooding and spraying. Eventually the carrier was determined to be the cure. Vinifera cuttings (called scions) were grafted onto American roots (the rootstock). Thus the vineyards were able to be replanted. Much research in hybridization is focused on either developing resistance in vinifera stock or developing new rootstocks. Though is has taken many years to achieve acceptance, the majority of vineyards around the world are grafted vines planted on hybrid rootstocks.

Climate

Another key factor affecting how a wine tastes is the climate where the vineyard is located. The majority of wine growing regions in the world are located in two bands around the globe, between 30° and 50° latitudes north and south of the equator. In the Northern Hemisphere, this band covers most of Europe (southern Germany to North Africa), the United States, southern Canada, northern Mexico, and the Middle East, as well as parts of China. In the Southern Hemisphere, every landmass that falls in the band grows grapes: Australia, New Zealand, Chile, Argentina, and South Africa.

Why in these bands and not elsewhere? These are the temperate zones, with average annual temperatures between 50°F (10°C) and 68°F (20°C). For the most part, these bands also provide the vines with the 1500 hours of sunshine and 27 inches of rain they need each year. The true average temperature, plus the total amount of sunshine and the amount of rain will vary, as a band spanning 20° of latitude cannot have a consistent climate over the whole region. This band also provides a cool enough winter to allow the vines to enter dormancy and rest before the next year's growth.

Other factors affecting the local climate include proximity to water, elevation, and aspect (what direction the vineyard faces). Climate within the band can be broken down into different categories. One method is to classify areas as having maritime, continental, or Mediterranean climates.

MARITIME CLIMATE

A maritime climate occurs in areas within the sphere of influence of an ocean. More specifically, wine regions with the most significant maritime climate are influenced by weather patterns crossing from ocean to land, rather than the other way around. The rain and wind patterns originate over the ocean, and then influence vineyards as they make landfall. Typically, the weather conditions are moderated for the region, with mild winters and warm summers. Water takes longer to heat and longer to release that heat back to the atmosphere. During the summer, a maritime climate is cooler because the ocean is absorbing some of the sun's energy. In winter, that energy is released, making the surrounding area a little warmer than it would be typically. The amount of rainfall may be influenced, depending on the location. An increase in humidity is common due to the proximity to large bodies of water. As a result of the increased humidity, grapes grown in maritime climates often have mold, mildew, and rot issues. Examples of regions with a maritime climate are parts of California, Bordeaux, and parts of Spain and Portugal.

CONTINENTAL CLIMATE

Continental climates have no significant ocean influence, and are subject to the weather patterns as they cross the continent. They are characterized by four distinct seasons. Winter is typically bitterly cold, spring is warm and calm with some rain, summers are hot, and fall is best for the grapes if it is long and protracted. Grapevines growing in continental climates will be affected by frost in the spring (and sometimes fall), hail in the summer, and early rainfall in autumn. , If the winter is extremely cold, vines may be subjected to *winterkill,* or the death of the vine due to freezing. Conversely, hot summers may force the vines to shut down until the temperatures get cooler.

On a daily basis, during the growing season, there will be large fluctuations from the daytime high temperature to the nighttime low temperature. This is called *diurnal variation*. Diurnal variation mimics the weather of a cooler region and allows for a vine to ripen its grapes while still retaining acidity that may normally dissipate quickly, Examples of regions with a continental climate are Burgundy, most of Spain, Argentina, and Eastern Europe.

MEDITERRANEAN CLIMATE

Mediterranean climates are characterized by two apparent "seasons"—rainy and dry. Most of the rainfall occurs during the winter months, while sunlight is profuse in the summer months. There may be temperature moderation from large bodies of water, especially in the summer months. This effect is similar to that seen in a maritime climate, on a smaller scale. Also common is the diurnal variation seen in continental climates. For warmer Mediterranean regions, diurnal variation is important for properly balanced grape components. Examples of regions with a Mediterranean climate include Italy, Napa, the Jerez region of Spain, and parts of Chile.

Cool, Intermediate, and Warm Climates

A region's climate can also be categorized as cool, intermediate, or warm. This method is more directly related to the latitude of the region, and does not consider any influence from weather patterns. Bodies of water, such as lakes and rivers, or altitude may adjust a region's basic climate. This particular terminology is often used in discussing the style and flavor profile of a wine.

Scientists at the University of California-Davis developed a system known as heat summation or *degree days*. This method totals the degrees Fahrenheit above an average temperature of 50°F (10°C) between April 1 and October 31. If the average temperature on April 5 is 52°F (11°C), then 2 degrees are added to the sum. Zones are then classified based on the total number of degrees summed over the period. Zone 1 is any area whose sum is 2500 or below. The zones increase by 500 degree increments to Zone 5, at 4000 degrees or more. It is possible to assign grape varieties to a zone based how much heat the grapes need in order to ripen. This system is used mainly in California. The majority of vinifera grapes are best grown in zones 1 to 3. Zones 4 and 5 are specific to table grape and raisin production. Research is commencing on making degree days more specific to wine grape production, and looking at variations below the zone 1 designation.

Macroclimate, Microclimate, and Mesoclimate

Whether describing a region as cool or maritime, warm or Mediterranean, these descriptions classify the region's macroclimate. Two more specific terms, mesoclimate and microclimate, have differing interpretations, depending on the source. A broad interpretation describes mesoclimate as the climate in a small geographic region, such as a village and its surrounding area. Microclimate is then the climate of a particular vineyard. This suggests that the conditions in a vineyard are uniform with no regard to aspect, slope, drainage, or other similar factors.

A narrower interpretation would state that the macroclimate referred to the village area, the mesoclimate to a particular vineyard, and the microclimate to the area contained within the leaves of a single vine. This interpretation suggests that the conditions at a vine may vary depending on location in the vineyard. It also suggests that the placement and growth of the leaves can influence the "climate" felt by the grapes. This interpretation is used in canopy management.

Canopy management is a method of leaf removal, shoot positioning, and trellising that improves the ripening and flavor of the grapes. Removal of leaves and shoot positioning allow for better air circulation in the vine (preventing mildew and mold issues) and expose the grapes to more sunlight. This aids development of flavor and color. The grower must be careful not to remove too many leaves, as this will adversely affect the amount of sugar produced and may result in sunburn or bleaching of the grapes.

If climate is the general conditions of an area, weather is what happens on a day-to-day basis. Weather can also be seen as the year-to-year variation. It is weather that creates *vintages* in wine. Every year, every growing season, is different. Some may be drier, others wetter. One year may have rain at harvest, while another has a heat wave that changes the flavor of the grapes. In some areas more than others, those annual differences are reflected by the wine in the bottle. Wine regions that are considered marginal (regions near the 50° latitude, or with challenging mesoclimates) often have large vintage variation. The most well known tracking of vintages could be in Bordeaux, where weather can determine if a vintage is considered mediocre or the crop of the century. Other regions, such as parts of Australia or Sicily, have relatively consistent weather and vintage variation is not as dramatic.

TOPOGRAPHICAL VARIATIONS

Topographical variation will also modify a region's climate, actually creating unique mesoclimates. Proximity to water is one feature that modifies the mesoclimate. Just as was seen in a maritime climate, water gains and releases heat more slowly than soil does. Therefore, vineyards near lakes or rivers may see cooler summers and warmer winters than the surrounding region. Anyone who likes to spend a day at the beach, lake, or riverfront is taking advantage of water's moderating effect. It is often cooler at the beach than it may be inland, because of the water's moderating effect. A second beneficial aspect derived from a vineyard's proximity to water (if the vineyard is within sight of the water) is reflected light. Sunlight that falls on the water will be reflected back onto the vineyards, thereby almost doubling the amount of actual sunlight a vineyard would receive. Thus, northerly areas like Germany, which receive only 1300 hours of direct sunlight, can still ripen grapes due to the reflected light. Finally, water can moderate warm climate regions indirectly through the generation of fog. Cool water and warm, moist air combine in these regions to generate ground-level clouds, or fog. This keeps the vineyards cooler during the morning hours until the fog gets burned off.

Elevation has an effect on the mesoclimate, especially in warm regions. The average air temperature is cooler by 3.5°F (1.9°C) for every 1000-foot change in elevation. Planting grapevines at higher elevation not only cools the grapes more than if they were in the valley floor, but also provides for greater diurnal variation. This small temperature difference allows the grapes to ripen more slowly and to retain their acidity while ripening. It is altitude that allows fine wine grapes to be grown in warm regions like Argentina, Spain, and Portugal.

The aspect of a vineyard can also modify its mesoclimate. Many vineyards are planted on hillsides; among other influences, this raises the vines closer to the sun and maximizes the amount of light each vine can receive. Vines can be planted somewhat closer together, as the angle of the slope lifts each row of vines so they are not shaded by the ones below them. Vines on hillsides will be the first to feel the morning sun and the last to see the sun set, depending on which direction the hill faces. In cool climates, vines are planted on the southern- or southeast-facing slopes in order to maximize the amount of sunlight on the vines. In warmer climates, such as Tuscany, vines may be planted on the northern-facing slopes. These vines still get plenty of ambient light, but the north-facing slope is slightly cooler than those facing south, so ripening can be regulated.

Slope becomes particularly important in cool regions, because it acts as a cool air drain. Cool air is denser than warm air, so when the sun sets, the cool air on the vineyard drains to the valley floor. Meanwhile, warm air rises to the level of the vines, slightly warming them during the night. It is common to see frost in the valley regions, while the vines remain safe on the hillsides, avoiding winterkill.

Soil

The third component to wine flavor is the soil in which the grapevines grow. Some growers feel this is *the* factor in wine flavor, while others are not convinced it makes a difference at all. What can be said is that soil is very important to how the vines will grow. Vines, in general, prefer soils that are organically poor, but mineral rich. It is often said grapes grow where no other plant would flourish. The sites for many vineyards are not conducive to highly productive agriculture. They are soils with little organic matter. They are usually, however, high in mineral content. Examples are chalk, iron-rich clays, gravel, and limestone.

In regard to soil, it is not the topsoil most growers are concerned with, but actually the subsoil and its mineral content. The next factor is the position of the water table. The optimum conditions for quality grapes would be deep, varied, mineral-rich subsoil with a deep water table. This forces the vines to send roots deep to find water, and thereby absorb minerals from the subsoil layers. It is believed that if a vine has to struggle to find water or nutrients, a type of survival mechanism activates. The vine then focuses its energy on producing seeds (i.e., grapes), in order to propagate itself on a better site. This is another way that the energy or quality in a vine can be focused on the grapes.

The ability of the soil to drain water well is extremely important. Grapevines do not like "wet feet," meaning that they do not like moist soils. Soils such as clay tend to be moist or heavy, because they retain a fair amount of water. Other soils, like chalk, can hold just enough water to be a humidifier for the vineyard without being too wet for the roots. Each varietal's tolerance for moist, or heavy, soils is different. In future chapters, the soil preference of each varietal will be discussed.

One additional characteristic for some soils is their ability to retain heat and release it back to the atmosphere at night. This follows the same principle as seen in water absorbing and releasing heat, except on a much shorter time scale. Typically, the soil will absorb the sun's energy during the day, and release it back to the atmosphere at night. Vines in cool regions may be trained low to the ground in an attempt to benefit from the heat radiation from the soil. This is seen especially in the galets of Chateauneuf-du-Pape. Galets (sometimes called pudding stones) are large river rocks, some the size of cantaloupes, which cover the ground in this French wine region. The rocks also serve as mulch for the soil, regulating the rate at which the soil dries out after rainfall.

The French have a term that sums up what makes wines taste different: *terroir*. Terroir has been defined by wine writer Matt Kramer as "somewhereness." It is the sense that the soil, the light, the amount of rain, the grapes planted in the next row, the aspect of the slope, the minerals—everything, including the winemaker—contributes to having only that wine able to come from that place. It is the backbone of European wine laws. Many New World winemakers contest there is no such thing as terroir, or that it is not important. They focus more on the expression of the grape itself: its flavor characteristics and how the vintner will express those characteristics in the bottle. In many cases, the specificity of place can be overridden by using grapes from many different areas, or by what could be the most important factor in a wine's flavor—the wine making process itself.

Harvest

Harvest is a very important time in the wine making process. Many factors go into determining the harvest date, and method. Earlier in the chapter, ripeness was discussed, in terms of both sugar and phenols. One corollary to sugar ripeness is acidity. In most fruits, as the sugar level increases, the natural acidity decreases. For wine, it is often not enough to make sure the sugar levels are high enough, but also that the acid levels have not dropped too low. The ratio of sugar to acid changes constantly, so the grapes are continually monitored. Should either the sugar level not be high enough, or the acidity too low, these will have to be treated in the winery.

Weather plays a part in determining harvest as well. The best weather for harvest is a long, warm autumn, which allows the grapes to develop flavor and ripeness slowly. However, that may not be an option if the weather turns bad. Grape growers will forgo perfect ripeness if a rainstorm is imminent. Excess water around harvest will be absorbed by the vine roots, and transported to the grapes. This dilutes the flavors and aromas the grower has struggled so hard to produce. Too much rain will also make the fields muddy—an inconvenience for pickers and an impossibility for machines.

HARVESTING BY HAND

Once the determination to harvest has been made, the grapes need to get from the vine to the winery. This can be a very minor step, or one of seemingly epic proportions. A grower will have decided long before the grapes are planted how they will be harvested. The choice is between hand harvesting and mechanical harvesting. Each has its pros and cons. Hand harvesting allows for individual inspection of each grape cluster, so only the best clusters, partial clusters, or even single grapes are picked. Most grapes are picked in whole clusters, which may or may not be desired for the fermentation process. The grapes are handled delicately, often in small baskets. This keeps the grapes from bruising, and prevents premature *oxidation* (browning of the grapes or juice) or loss of juice. There is also less extraneous stuff (leaves, bugs, stems, and the like) that get mixed in with the grape clusters. The downsides to hand harvesting are labor and time. Often a vineyard will need to be canvassed multiple times (known as *tries*) to get the grapes as they ripen best. This often requires many laborers, often migrant workers. The more acreage that ripens at the same time, the more workers are needed to pick before the grapes get overripe. The same holds for rain. Often, if rain is imminent, everyone available is sent to pick. In warm regions, picking may occur at night, under lights, in order to keep the grapes cool before they head to the winery.

HARVESTING BY MACHINE

Mechanical harvesting does not need the intense labor of hand harvesting. One man and a tractor can harvest an entire field, even at night when the grapes are coolest. Weather, labor, and time no longer are an issue. However, mechanical harvesting is indiscriminate in what it picks. If grapes on the vine are not ripe, they will be picked at the same time as ripe clusters. The grapes are not picked as clusters; the machine shakes the vines to separate the grape berries from their cluster formation. Grapes are now collected that may be bruised or the skin burst, allowing oxidation to commence. Also, there is some accumulation of extraneous materials, mainly leaves but sometimes bugs. Fields that will be harvested mechanically need to be designed as such before the first grapes are planted. The direction of the rows, as well as which trellising systems are to be used, needs to be determined. A great deal of planning and investment is needed to benefit from mechanical harvesting.

One can make some general assumptions about whether a grower has hand-picked or used a tractor. Top-echelon wines, which need high-quality grapes, will get the hand-harvest treatment. The same can be said for hillside vineyards. Mechanical harvesting is common with bulk production, and in vineyards on flat land. This does not mean that quality wines cannot be machine harvested. While harvesting method may affect the grapes at harvest, the real influence is the care taken in handling the grapes overall.

SUMMARY

The French term *terroir* suggests that a wine should taste of a place. Looking at the factors involved in terroir, they mimic all the characteristics that make each wine individual—grape varietal, soil, climate, aspect, weather. Old World winemakers use wine to express single locations, like a Grand Cru vineyard in Burgundy, or a hillside in Germany. While New World winemakers may not believe in "terroir" in the French definition, they make wines that are very reminiscent of place. For example, it is often apparent a wine is Australian because of the jamminess of the fruit. Sun, heat, climate, and weather—many are some of the things that make a wine individual, influencing how the fruit got that way. And while in the New World there may not be overt individual differences based on place, one can definitely determine a "family resemblance."

As with any product, the result is only as good as the ingredients. How the grapes are grown is crucial to the production of wine. Grape growing depends not only on location but also on how the vines are treated in the field. Canopy management, trellising, pruning, and harvesting can all contribute to the quality of the grapes. Perfect ingredients do not guarantee perfect wine, however. That transformation is left in the hands of the winemaker. It is ultimately the wine making process, and the person who guides it, that influences what makes its way into the bottle.

KEY TERMS

Cross

Hybrid

Clone

Vitis vinifera

Cane

Inflorescence

Shatter/coulure

Millerandage

Veraison

Physiological ripeness

Phenolic ripeness

Refractometer

Green harvest

Winterkill

Diurnal variation

Degree days

Canopy management

Vintage

Oxidation

Terroir

Trie

QUESTIONS

1. What species of grape makes quality table wines?
2. Describe the growth cycle of a vine over one year.
3. Describe the two types of ripeness in grapes

4. What is phylloxera, and why is it significant?

5. Why are grapes best grown between 30° and 50° latitude?

6. What is a maritime climate?

7. What is a continental climate?

8. Describe a Mediterranean climate.

9. What does the term *microclimate* describe?

10. How does topography influence grape growing?

11. What type of soil do grapes prefer?

12. What are the advantages and disadvantages of harvesting by hand?

13. What are the advantages and disadvantages of harvesting by machine?

How Wine Is Made

*G*rowing *and harvesting quality grapes are just the first steps in the process of making wine. Turning those grapes into wine, a process called vinification, entails a number of choices by the winemaker. It can be said that some wines make themselves, while others are an expression of the winemaker's philosophy. One way or another, it is certain that the quality of the wine can be only as good as the grapes making it. However, good grapes cannot make up for poor wine making.*

Upon completion of this chapter, the student should be able to:

> *Explain the different styles of wine*
> *Provide an overview of the wine making process*
> *Discuss the difference between red wine making and white wine making*
> *Describe different treatments of the must before fermentation*
> *Describe the fundamentals of fermentation*
> *Discuss how to make sweet wines*
> *Describe the influence of oak on wine*
> *Describe different post-fermentation processes*
> *Provide an overview of different bottle closures*

Preliminary Steps

Upon the grapes' arrival in the winery, the winemaker will often send the grapes through a sorting table. Here, the grapes are checked by hand and any extraneous materials, such as leaves, stems, and wire, are removed. In some cases, the grape quality is also checked, and fruit of poorer quality is removed. This is not a required step, but is typical of high-quality producers and regions. For example, Chateauneuf-du-Pape producers must remove by hand 5 percent of the grapes entering the winery in an effort to improve the overall quality of the wine.

DETERMINING WINE STYLES

The winemaker now has several decisions as to what wine to make. Wine can be classified into four major categories: still table wine, sparkling wine, fortified wine, and aromatized wine. *Still table wine* makes up the largest category of wine. It is defined by the Alcohol and Tobacco Tax and Trade Bureau (TTB) as a wine between 7 and 14 percent alcohol by volume, with no carbonation. *Sparkling wine* is any wine with carbonation, also between 7 and 14 percent alcohol by volume. *Fortified wines* are wines that have had additional alcohol added to them before bottling. These usually range from 15 to 20 percent alcohol by volume, and are taxed at a higher rate than table wines. *Aromatized wines* are wines that have been altered by adding additional natural flavors. Wines that fall into this category are as diverse as vermouth and sangria.

Notice, in the above categories, there is no mention of wine style or color. These are also decisions the winemaker faces. The most general description of style refers to the wine's level of sweetness, determined by the amount of *residual sugar* (unfermented sugar) in the final product. Wines with no apparent sweetness are termed *dry*, and make up a majority of table wines and sparkling wines. Wines with significant residual sugar form the dessert wine category and include ice wines and late-harvest wines. There are also wines of intermediate sweetness, like white zinfandel, that are classified as *off-dry*.

A wine's color can be independent of the color of the original grapes. White grapes can only make white wines, but red grapes can make white, rosé, or red wine. The distinguishing factor is when the grapes are pressed. For white wines, the grapes are pressed before fermentation begins, and only the juice is fermented. For red wine, the grapes are pressed after fermentation, allowing for the skins to color the wine during that process. Rosé wines have shorter skin contact than red wines do, resulting in less color extraction.

Making Wine: General Processes

Wine production typically begins by processing the grapes in a *crusher-destemmer*. This machine plucks the grapes off the stems and gently presses them so they burst. The purpose of the crusher-destemmer is to remove the woody component of the clusters, and also to just break the skin of the grape. This will allow the juice to run freely out of the grape without much effort.

PRESSING THE GRAPES

White wine production separates the juice from the grape pulp early in the process. After leaving the crusher-destemmer, the grapes are placed into a press, where the juice is extracted. Red wine has the must pressed after fermentation.

Three types of presses can be used. The oldest is the basket press, which consists of a basket made of wood slats, into which a flat plunger is lowered by means of a screw mechanism. As the plunger moves downward, the grapes are compressed, and juice flows out between the slats. A horizontal screw press is a modification of the basket press. In this machine, the "basket" is a perforated cylinder mounted horizontally. Instead of using the base as an immobile part of the press, two screw-driven plates are inserted at opposite ends of the cylinder. When the press is activated, the plates converge on the center of the cylinder, pressing the grapes and releasing the juice, which passes through the perforations and can be collected.

An old basket press at Sequoia Grove. Courtesy of Kobrand.

In either a basket or a horizontal screw press, the skin, pulp, and seeds will form a cake in the basket. If further pressing is to occur, this cake needs to be broken up before the next press. For a basket press, this is often done by hand. The technicians will use pitchforks or shovels to turn and loosen the cake before the next press. In a horizontal press, chains often connect the two plates. As the plates are unscrewed and move away from each other, the chains tighten. Having been pressed into the cake as it forms, the chains break apart that cake as they straighten.

The most delicate press is a pneumatic bladder press. This machine has a similar design to the horizontal screw press, with a perforated cylinder serving as the main holding area. This press, though, has a central tube running the length of the cylinder, around which is a rubber bladder (like a big balloon). This bladder gets filled with water, and as it expands, the grapes are pressed against the outside cylinder, releasing their juice. It is very delicate, in that the skins are not scraped and the seeds are left unbroken. This reduces the amount of harsh flavors in the pressed juice.

As noted in the previous chapter, grapes from different vineyards will develop individual characteristics. These can be retained by pressing small batches of grapes and keeping the juice separated, even through fermentation. The different pressings of juice from each batch are also kept separate. The first batch reserved is the free-run juice, that which naturally flows from the grapes after crushing and being subjected to their own weight. After this is collected, the grapes can be pressed up to three times, with each subsequent pressing utilizing more pressure. Each subsequent pressing, as a result of the increased pressure, is lower in quality. The more pressure that is applied to the grapes, the cruder the juice becomes. More pressure extracts tannins from the skin and seeds, along with heavier aromatic and flavor compounds from the skin and pulp. While this fraction of the press may not make up the bulk of wine, it may be used to increase body or to make base wine for distillation.

PRE-FERMENTATION TREATMENTS

In white wine making, once the juice has been extracted from the skins, it is allowed to settle for a period of time. This helps to clarify the juice, and removes any stray pulp and proteins that may result in off-flavors later. In both red and white wine making, the sugar and acid content of the *must* (the pre-fermented juice) is determined, and if allowed, adjustments are made at this time.

Cool Climate Wines

In cool regions, there may not be enough sugar to produce a wine with a minimum of 7 percent alcohol after fermentation. This wine will not be very stable, and it is important that the final product reach at least the 7 percent alcohol level. This is accomplished through a process called *chaptalization* or *enrichment*. Sugar (cane sugar or beet sugar) is added to the must to increase the amount of alcohol that will be produced. Similarly, concentrated grape must (juice from which most of the water has been removed) may also be added. In many countries, this process is illegal. Preventing the addition of sugar enforces the requirement that the grapes are ripe enough to make wine. This process is allowed, though, for lower-quality wines in cool regions like Germany.

If the sugar level is too low, then, concurrently, the acid level will be too high. A common form of treatment to lower the acid level is to add potassium bicarbonate to the juice. The alkalinity of the bicarbonate neutralizes the acidity of the juice. The same principle is behind elementary school volcanoes of baking soda and vinegar. The only by products of this deacidification process are carbon dioxide and insoluble salts.

Warm Climate Wines

Grapes grown in warm climates have the opposite issues of cool-climate grapes. Commonly, when the grapes have ripened fully (for sugar level and, if appropriate, phenolic ripeness), the sugar levels with be extremely high, while the acid levels will be disproportionately low. The high concentration of sugars will produce a wine with high alcohol content. If the concentration predicts an unusually high alcohol level, special yeasts may be needed to ferment the juice to dryness. For many winemakers, high sugar concentration is not seen as a problem to be adjusted but a benefit to be embraced. If the alcohol level will still be too high, the wine can be de-alcoholized later.

Low acid levels, however, pose a problem. If the acid concentration is left low, the resulting wine will also have a low acid level. This creates a wine that is out of balance, with no acid to balance the fruit flavors or the body. Acid provides the structure for a wine. When acidity is lacking, the wine is said to be "flabby." For this reason, wine-makers will typically add tartartic acid to the juice before fermentation, though malic acid and citric acid could also be added. This process is called *acidification*.

Use of Sulfur

Sulfur is involved in several parts of the wine making process. In the form of *sulfur dioxide* (SO_2), it serves as both an antiseptic and an antioxidant. Once sulfur dioxide is introduced to a solution, it reacts with free oxygen, preventing the oxygen from reacting with other compounds.

As an antiseptic, SO_2 is used to clean barrels and tanks after fermentation. This prevents any cross contamination of one yeast strain by another and also deters bacterial infection. Treating the incoming grapes with sulfur dioxide will kill any natural wild yeast strains and bacteria living on the surface of the grape skins. SO_2 can be used to arrest fermentation, as in the case of inexpensive sweet wines.

Sulfur dioxide's greater role as an antioxidant effects the wine directly. Sulfur dioxide treatment of the grapes prevents them from oxidizing while awaiting pressing. If enough SO_2 has been added, the juice is protected as it is exposed to oxygen. Sulfur dioxide will also be added at bottling, to kill any yeasts or bacteria that may infect the wine, and to prevent any oxidation in the bottle from the small amount of oxygen in the headspace.

The quantity of SO_2 used will vary from producer to producer. European wine laws restrict the amount of sulfur used in wine making. Typically, white wine requires more protection from oxidation, since it contains no phenolics that can serve as antioxidants. Additionally, too much SO_2 will bleach some of the color of red wines. Thus, contrary to popular belief, white wines contain more sulfites than red wines.

Excessive use of sulfur dioxide can have a detrimental effect on wine. Sulfur dioxide can be reduced to hydrogen sulfide (H_2S), which will give wine a rotten egg odor. If the H_2S reacts with some of the alcohols in the wine, a class of compounds called mercaptans develops. These have a characteristic odor of a burnt match or cabbage. Any of these odors are considered faults in the wine.

Fermentation

The process of fermentation turns grape juice into wine.

The simple description of the fermentation process is shown below:

$$Yeast + Sugar = Ethanol + CO_2 + Heat$$

Sugars are simple carbohydrates containing carbon, hydrogen, and oxygen. The most abundant sugars in grapes are glucose and fructose. Both of these have a chemical formula of $C_6H_{12}O_6$, but their atoms are configured differently. Sugars, in their many forms, serve as energy storehouses for living things. Cells obtain the energy to live by breaking down sugars into smaller organic compounds. The conversion of grape juice into wine utilizes specialized cells, known as yeast, to break down the sugars.

There are many species of yeast, but the dominant strain in wine production is *Saccharomyces cerevisiae*. Yeasts have two possible mechanisms by which they convert sugar to energy. The difference is the presence or absence of oxygen. In the presence of oxygen (called *aerobic fermentation*), yeasts can fully metabolize the sugars to form water and carbon dioxide as the waste products. This is the form of fermentation seen in bread making. Plenty of oxygen allows all the energy stored in the sugar to be utilized. In the absence of oxygen (*anaerobic fermentation*), the yeast cannot fully extract the energy out of the sugar molecules. The yeast's metabolism is slower, and the waste products are indicative of the incomplete conversion. The waste products for anaerobic fermentation are ethanol and carbon dioxide. This is the form of fermentation seen in wine production.

The process of fermentation, however, is not as simple as the above equation. Many metabolic processes are occurring concurrently during fermentation, with new organic compounds being formed that were previously nonexistent in the juice. Several alcoholic compounds are produced along with ethanol, and these contribute to the final aromatic profile of the wine.

CHOICE OF YEAST

As noted earlier, the predominant yeast used in wine making is Saccharomyces cerevisiae. However, a winemaker has a choice of allowing the wine to undergo fermentation via natural yeasts or cultured yeasts. Natural yeasts are introduced to the juice from the exterior of the grapes themselves. The white, hazy bloom on the outside of the grape skin is a collection of wild yeasts and bacteria. It would be very easy to simply allow the natural yeasts on the grape to ferment the juice into wine. This is called a *wild ferment*. Typically, all the strains of wild yeast present will begin converting sugar to alcohol. At about 3 percent alcohol, however, many of the wild yeasts will die off, since they are not tolerant of the increasing alcohol concentration. At this time, stronger yeasts (S. cerevisiae) can take over and complete the fermentation. The caveat here is that often the fermentation will not be completed to dryness, or that off-flavors will develop from the wild yeasts. In regions with a long-standing tradition of wine making, or in well-used wineries, the population of yeasts has been naturally selected to favor the stronger yeasts.

To avoid the risk of off-flavors in a wine, a winemaker may choose to use *cultured yeasts*. This method entails using yeasts that have been specially selected for their characteristics. The must is then dosed with a small amount of juice harboring a high concentration of active yeast cells. These cells now dominate the fermentation, and prevent other strains and bacteria from multiplying.

TEMPERATURE CONTROL

One of the "waste products" of fermentation is heat. A fermenting vat of wine will produce a great deal of heat. Depending on the type of wine being made, controlling the temperature inside the vat will affect the final product. For white wines, it is important to keep the volatile aromatic compounds in solution, and not allow them to evaporate or bubble away with the carbon dioxide. White wines are typically fermented at cooler temperatures, 50–65°F (10–18°C). Fermenting at even cooler temperatures slows the process (the yeast get sluggish) and produces tropical fruit aromas, such as pineapple or banana. Sluggish fermentation allows extraneous chemical processes that create the esters responsible for the tropical fruit aromas. In the traditional temperature range above, these esters would evaporate and not interfere with the varietal-specific aromas.

Red wines, on the other hand, require warm temperatures to increase color and flavor extraction from the skins. Red wines typically ferment at 75–90°F (24–32°C). Extraction of color is dependent on temperature, just as steeping a tea bag gives better results in hot water than in tepid water. Because the fermentation times are relatively short when compared to the time needed for color and flavor extraction, the natural heat of the fermentation aids in maximizing extraction.

Traditionally, wineries utilized the cool autumn weather and small barrel size to regulate the temperature of the fermentation. Small barrels aid in heat transfer, since they have a significant surface area in relation to the volume of the barrel. The heat is naturally dissipated into the autumn air, maintaining moderate heat levels. Modern, technologically advanced wineries use thermal jacketed stainless steel tanks, which allow easy heating and cooling of the fermenting must.

Temperature also determines the speed of the fermentation. The effect of temperature on fermentation is the same whether the item is grape juice or bread dough. A cooler temperature slows the fermentation, and as a result it takes longer for the process to complete. Warm fermentations are more rapid and therefore take less time. Scientifically, increasing the temperature at which a chemical reaction takes place will affect the rate of the reaction. A difference of 20°F (11°C)—say the difference between 60°F and 80°F (15.5 and 27°C) during the fermentation—will double the rate of the fermentation.

IS IT WINE YET?

The progress of the fermentation is monitored by measuring the density of the must. This involves the use of a *hydrometer*. A small portion of the must is placed in a tube and the hydrometer is floated in the liquid. A scale on the hydrometer is calibrated so that the point where the instrument rises out of the liquid indicates the density. Before fermentation, the mix is denser than water, due to all the sugars in the liquid. Alcohol, on the other hand, is not as dense as water. As the fermentation proceeds, the density will decrease as the sugars are converted to alcohol. When there is no more sugar to convert, the density measurement will stabilize. This indicates that fermentation is complete and the wine is now ready to move to the next stage.

Sometimes during fermentation, the process slows down and/or comes to a halt. This is called a *stuck fermentation*. Fermentations can get stuck if there is a sudden drop in temperature. Stuck fermentations are also more common in wild yeast-fermented batches. There may not be a dominant yeast to take over the fermentation, or the wild yeasts get poisoned by the alcohol that is produced. Getting the yeast to start fermenting again is often easier said than done. In traditional European wineries, this may be cause for "the vigneron's annual bath." The winemaker would jump into the vat and use his legs to find a warm spot, indicative of fermentation taking place. He would then kick his legs to stir the active fermentation into the greater vat. Modern methods may include introducing some oxygen to the vat, which gets the yeast restarted by shifting them to aerobic mode for a time. A sure-fire method to restart a stuck fermentation is to blend it with a different vat that is actively fermenting.

Producing Sweet Wines

Wines that are known to be naturally sweet, such as Sauternes or Port, have not had all the sugar in the must converted to alcohol, resulting in a wine that tastes markedly sweet. These wines can result from natural processes, or through winemaker intervention. If the must has a high level of sugar at the start of fermentation, several factors can combine to hinder the yeast from fermenting the must to dryness. Yeast becomes sluggish in high concentrations of sugar and alcohol due to osmotic pressure. When two liquids of differing concentration are separated by a semi-permeable membrane (like a cell membrane), water diffuses to the area of higher concentration, in an attempt to equalize the concentrations. In the case of sweet wine production, the yeast is the area of lower concentration, so water diffuses out of the yeast and into the must. In other words, the water in the yeast cell will diffuse out, attempting to dilute the sugar in the juice. The yeast cell itself then begins to shrivel from lack of water. This slows the yeast metabolism, thereby slowing fermentation. Additionally, the yeast may use up the other nutrients they need to survive before all the sugar is fermented. This, too, will inhibit fermentation.

Occasionally, the winemaker determines when fermentation will end. Several methods can be employed. Temporary methods to stop fermentation are cooling the must or increasing the pressure of carbon dioxide. As seen earlier, cooling the must slows the metabolism of the yeast. If the temperature is then raised, fermentation will commence again. The yeast can also be inhibited by increasing the concentration of carbon dioxide in the vat. When carbon dioxide pressure rises above seven atmospheres, the yeast are effectively suffocated by their own byproduct. If that pressure is released, the fermentation will continue.

To arrest fermentation completely, the winemaker must either kill or remove the yeast from the must. Inexpensive sweet wines may use sulfur dioxide to kill the yeast at the correct point in the ferment. Simply adding SO_2 to the must kills the yeast, in a method similar to ridding the juice of wild yeast before fermentation. More commonly, the must is pasteurized. The wine will be heated to approximately 220°F (104°C) for one or two seconds. This flash heating kills the yeast but does not cook the wine. A third method of killing the yeast is the addition of alcohol, known as fortification. By adding enough pure alcohol to the must, the concentration is artificially raised above the concentration at which yeast die. This stops the fermentation and allows sugar to remain. (See the discussion on Port production in Chapter 23.)

Physically removing the yeast from the must will cease fermentation. This can be accomplished by using filters designed to prevent the passage of yeast cells, or by centrifuging. The process of centrifuging spins the must at a high rate of speed and separates the liquid from the solids. The yeast-free must can now be racked off the solids. Filtration or centrifuging does not prevent potential future fermentation. If yeast is reintroduced into the sweet wine, fermentation will commence and continue until stopped or until the wine has achieved dryness.

An extremely simple method of making sweet wine, typical of inexpensive dessert wines, is to add sugar or concentrated grape must to dry wine. This is actually an easier process to control, as the yeast will have died off and been removed, and pasteurized sugar can be added to the desired sweetness. Some German wines add juice that was withheld before fermentation, called a sussreserve. This not only sweetens the wine, but also helps balance the high acidity typical of the wines.

Post-Fermentation Treatment

Once fermentation is complete, a series of steps occur that prepare the wine for the bottle. In some cases, the wine has been made in the style desired. In others, another process is needed to create the final style. This second process is called *malolactic fermentation* (also known as M-L or the malo). It is a fermentation in the sense that a more complex organic molecule is broken down into a smaller one plus carbon dioxide. In this case, it is the conversion of malic acid, found naturally in grape must, into lactic acid. This conversion has a softening effect on the acidity of a wine. Malic acid is noticeably tart (think Granny Smith apples), and lactic is tangy, but milder (think yogurt). A significant by product of M-L is diacetyl, the chemical compound responsible for buttery flavors. Diacetyl provides wine with a buttery or creamy component.

Malolactic fermentation is not a yeast-driven process. It is the result of action by a variety of bacteria, most notably Lactobaccillus. These bacteria, once used, are found throughout the winery and in barrels. Therefore, starting the malo process is as simple as placing wine in a barrel that had been used for malo previously. Allowing a wine to undergo malo also protects it from bacterial contamination later. The bacteria performing the malo deplete the nutrients other bacteria would need to survive.

RACKING

Once the fermentation is complete, the wine contains millions of yeast cells. As the cells die, they settle to the bottom of the fermenting vessel. The simplest way of separating the wine from the yeast is a process known as *racking*. The wine is siphoned off the top of the vessel and into a clean vessel, leaving the dead yeast behind. Not all the yeast will settle at the same time, so racking continues several times until no more cells precipitate.

THE USE OF OAK

Many woods have been used throughout the history of wine making. Over time, however, the favored wood for making barrels has become oak. There are three main sources of oak: France, Slovenia, and the United States. French and Slovenian oaks are different species than American oak, which provides one choice for the winemaker. Some winemakers chose oak from specific forests, since each has its own unique flavor characteristics and grain structure.

Oak is the wood of choice for a variety of reasons. First, the forests in Europe are relatively close to the wine making regions that use barrels. Second, the flavor profile provided by oak is complementary to many wines. Oak is a source of vanillin, the flavor compound in vanilla. Third, oak has a grain structure that allows for controlled diffusion of air through the wood. This slow incorporation of air into aging wine aids in the development of mature characteristics. French and Slovenian oak has a very tight grain, and therefore the slowest diffusion of air. American oak is wide-grained and oxygen can play a much bigger role earlier in the aging process.

BARREL MAKING

The long-standing use of oak is in barrel making. Depending on where the barrels are made, the process to get the oak ready to make barrels is different. In France, an oak tree is split along the natural grain of the wood into planks. This keeps many of the cell walls intact in the wood. This wood is then stacked outdoors for one season, and allowed to naturally age in the weather. The exposure to the sun, wind, and rain extracts the bitter tannins out of the wood. The result is French oak that has very subtle flavor influence on the wine, often presenting as baking spices rather than overt vanilla.

American oak is sawn into planks. This exposes more cell structure to the surface. Then the wood is kiln-dried. This does not decrease the harsh tannins. American oak is noted for having a stronger, more forward influence on a wine, usually a strong vanilla or even coconut flavor profile.

Planks, called staves, are then used to form barrels. The first set of staves are placed in metal rings, and adjusted to the wood to form a water-tight seal. Since the staves are straight but a barrel is curved, the unsecured end of the barrel is placed over a firepot, which heats the wood and allows it to be bent. The staves can then be bent to fit into a second set of metal rings. While the fire pot heats the wood, it also toasts the inside of the barrel. The toasting process caramelizes the natural sugars in the barrel, which in turn complements the vanilla and baking spice flavors of the oak itself. The level of toast also determines the influence of the wood. Lighter toasted barrels yield more oak influence in the wine. Heavy toasted barrels actually form a layer of charcoal in the barrel, insulating the wine from the oak.

OTHER METHODS OF OAK INFLUENCE

For many producers, oak barrels are too expensive. For a single tank of wine, the cost for the quantity of barrels needed may approach $50,000. To cut back on this expense, some winemakers have resorted to other methods to put oak flavor into wine. One method is to use just the staves, inserting them into a tank of wine. The cost of staves needed for the same tank described above is around $5000. Other methods include using oak chunks or chips, and even adding oak dust to the grapes before fermentation. With each of these methods, the amount of oak needed is decreased because the contact area between the oak and the wine is increased. Toast levels can be controlled, just as they are in barrels. However, with these faster methods of adding oak to wine, the possibility of putting too much oak into a wine is great. The price of the wine often indicates which method of oak influence was used.

STABILIZATION

Although racking has removed a fair portion of the remnants of fermentation, the wine is still unstable. A common treatment for the wine is *cold stabilization*. In this process, the wine is chilled to just about freezing for a period of eight days. The objective is to cause any excess of tartrates (tartaric acid salts) to precipitate out of solution. Chilling the wine decreases the solubility of the tartrates, and they will crystallize in the tank. The wine can then be racked off of the newly formed crystals. There is no guarantee that chilling the wine in the winery will precipitate tartrates. The crystals may still form after bottling, say if a consumer keeps wine in the refrigerator for an extended period of time. The tartrates will appear as small colorless crystals, either in the bottle or attached to the bottom of the cork that has been in contact with the wine. But winemakers attempt to remove the tartrates because the consumer may view these crystals in a finished wine as a fault.

FINING

After racking, the wine is not clear. There are still pieces of pulp, proteins, and other compounds that are too small to settle to the bottom of the tank. The winemaker will then utilize agents that will "collect" the stray particles and clarify the wine. This process is called *fining*. Most agents used to fine wine are protein based. The oldest method that is still used is egg whites. Other possible fining agents include gelatin, isinglass (obtained from the swim bladder of a sturgeon), and bentonite (a specially mined clay). What each of these agents has in common is some type of electrostatic charge as part of their makeup. For the protein-based items, some of the amino acid constituents have natural positive or negative charges. When placed in solution, the different charges on the proteins and the agent interact through static electricity. The different compounds are attracted to each other and form bigger molecules when stuck together. These larger molecules are now too large to stay in solution, and they settle to the bottom of the barrel. Fining agents are not considered additives, because the amount added is removed later as sediment.

The choice of fining agent depends on what the winemaker is trying to accomplish. Some agents will precipitate proteins in the wine. Others may focus on decreasing tannins. The amount of agent is also important. If the amount of agent is greater than the proteins dissolved, other constituents will be removed. It is possible to overfine a wine, and remove tannin, color, and flavor.

FILTERING

After fining, a wine may undergo *filtration* as a final step to stabilize the wine. Some winemakers feel this is an important step to ensure that the wine is crystal clear and has no impurities. Others feel that filtering removes flavor and aroma, and that the alteration of the wine is too great to take the chance.

There are several methods by which a wine could be filtered. A basic filtration, called sheet filtration, utilizes pads. The wine is passed through a series of fiber pads that collects any impurities. Pads have inconsistent spaces to collect impurities, so some items may still pass through. More specific is plate filtration. In this method, the wine is passed through a series of porous ceramic plates, which mimic the pads but have smaller openings. The most specific is membrane filtration. In this method, a synthetic membrane with a specified pore size is used as the filter. The pore size can be chosen so that anything larger than the pore remains behind. This method is used to filter yeast cells from wines and can also eliminate bacteria.

Lack of selectivity is the issue some winemakers have with filtration. In the case of membrane filtration, anything larger than the pore size is removed from the wine. It is possible to utilize a membrane that could strip a wine of color and tannin. If a filter can do that, it can also remove flavor and aroma. Winemakers who avoid filtration claim their wine is closer to the natural product than one that has been filtered.

Bottling

The final stage in wine production is bottling. Because wine is a food product, it has the possibility of spoilage. Precautions must be taken in bottling to prevent bacterial infection and oxidation of the wine. Infection is prevented through cold sterile bottling. The bottles are sanitized before being filled with wine. Heat is avoided because it would alter the flavor of the wine. The bottle will also get a small amount of sulfur dioxide, to scavenge any oxygen that may have been introduced in the bottling process.

Most wines are bottled in brown or dark green glass. The colored glass is used to absorb ultraviolet light that will degrade the wine. In some areas, such as Germany, the color of the glass is indicative of a specific wine region. White wines are sometimes bottled in clear glass, because they are meant to be consumed soon after bottling.

Bottle shape varies with grape variety. In areas other than France, producers will choose the bottle shape of the French region where a similar wine is produced. A Cabernet Sauvignon will be bottled in a Bordeaux bottle, while Pinot Noir will be bottled in the Burgundy-style bottle. Rieslings are bottled in the flute d'Alsace, which also is the bottle shape of top-quality German wines. With modern glass production methods, color and shape are no longer as characteristic of certain wines as in past years. Many wines are now placed in bottles that serve as marketing tools as well as containers for the wine.

CLOSURES

Once the wine is in the bottle, it must be sealed. The classic seal is cork, derived from the bark of the cork oak. This tree produces a thick bark, which can be peeled off the tree without damaging it. The bark will grow back in 9 to 11 years, and can

The bottling line at a winery.
Courtesy PhotoDisc, Inc.

Some wines, by law, are required to spend time aging in the bottle before release.

Courtesy PhotoDisc, Inc.

yield more cork then, making it a sustainable resource. The bark that has been removed will have plugs punched out of it, and these form the corks for bottles. These are known as colmated corks. Corks are considered the best closure, as they keep the wine in the bottle, but also allow oxygen to diffuse slowly through them to aid in maturing the wine.

In order to preserve the natural resource, other cork products have been developed. A closure that is made of pieces of cork held together by an epoxy is called an agglo cork. It utilizes some of the leftover cork material and synthetically creates a cork closure. A finer style of agglo is an Altec cork, which utilizes smaller cork pieces to form the plug. Some producers use a modification of the agglo, called the one+one cork. This is an agglo core, sandwiched between thin slices of colmated cork. Thus the wine is in contact with solid cork, not epoxy-bound pieces, yet the stability of the agglo is still there.

Being a natural product, cork needs to be sterilized so the wine it comes in contact with does not get infected. Sterilization usually uses a chlorine-based solution, which kills any mold or bacteria in the cork. Depending on the study, it has been shown that 3 to 10 percent of all corks have a mold, which when treated with chlorine produces a compound called trichloro-anisole, or *TCA*. This compound is the source of "corked" wine, or wine that smells of wet cardboard and loses its flavor and aroma. The corks affected are not specific to quality levels, and it is not apparent through inspection which corks will damage a wine. Many winemakers are not willing to lose a portion of their product, and have turned to alternative closures for their wines.

One choice for an alternative closure is a plastic cork. Plastic corks come in two styles: molded and extruded. A molded cork has a smooth plastic surface over the entire cork. They are usually identified by ridges on the ends that identify the

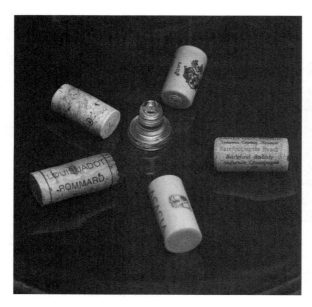

Closures used for wine (clockwise from lower left): colmated cork, one+one agglo cork, molded plastic cork, Altec cork, extruded plastic cork, glass stopper (center).

mold used. Extruded corks have smooth sides and spongy interiors. The smooth side is in contact with the bottle, while the spongy core is in contact with the wine, or the air. While plastic corks have their proponents, there are some negative sides to their use. Plastic corks are difficult to remove from the bottle, and even more difficult to replace if the bottle is not finished. Also, there is no oxygen permeability through a plastic cork, making them ill-suited to aging wine.

A controversial closure currently used is the screw cap, best exemplified by the Stelvin™ closure. The main connotation of a screw cap is cheap wine from the 1970s. Modern wineries use screw caps to ensure that no TCA taints the wine. Oxygen diffusion can be controlled by choosing the appropriate liner. Studies have also shown that the same wine, bottled under both screw cap and cork, is fresher and younger tasting under the screw cap. Opponents to screw caps claim increased "reductive aromas" (i.e., rotten egg smells) in some wines. This may result from oversulfuring combined with lack of oxygen diffusion through the cap.

Another complaint about screw caps could be described as the loss of the romance, or ceremony. To some, the thought of twisting off a cap is not as appealing as hearing the sound of a cork being pulled from a bottle. To this end, a new generation of closures are being produced that combine the best features of the alternative closures. Several, like the Zork™ and a glass stopper with an O-ring, are designed to provide the cleanliness of a screwcap with the sound associated with a cork.

WHITE WINE MAKING

White wine making has a couple unique processes that may be utilized during production. The first involves soaking the skins and seeds in the juice for a short period before pressing. Some winemakers do this, based on varietal, in order to extract more aromatics from the skins.

A more common procedure is *barrel fermentation*. Here, the wine is placed in small oak barrels to undergo the fermentation. The benefits of this include heat dissipation from the small barrels, and better integration of the oak flavors into the wine. The downside of barrel fermentation is the increased cost to provide barrels for both fermentation and aging.

White wine making

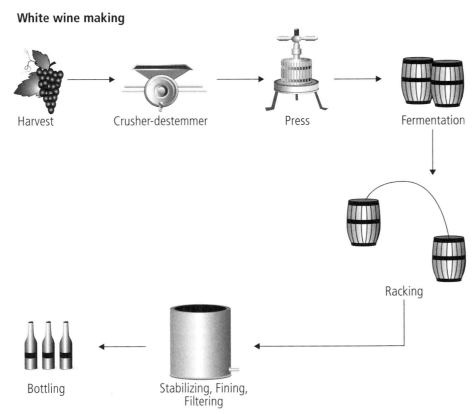

Harvest → Crusher-destemmer → Press → Fermentation

Racking

Bottling ← Stabilizing, Fining, Filtering

The basic steps of white wine production.

If the wine is left on the yeast residue after fermentation, it can pick up other toasty flavors from the decaying cells. To increase the extraction of those flavors, a wine-maker may utilizes *lees stirring* (*battonage* in French). A long rod with an L-shaped end is inserted into the barrel, to stir the sediment back into the wine. This increases the surface area of the yeast in contact with the wine, and extracts more of the flavor from the lees. The result is a wine with more complexity and stronger bread and toast notes.

RED WINE MAKING

The process of red wine making has some additional steps that distinguish it from white wine making. These steps revolve around the skin and the seeds, which are a component of the must during the fermentation process.

Before Fermentation

Some red wines undergo a phase before fermentation known as a *cold soak* or cold maceration. In this phase, the skins and seeds are allowed to steep in the juice

Red wine making

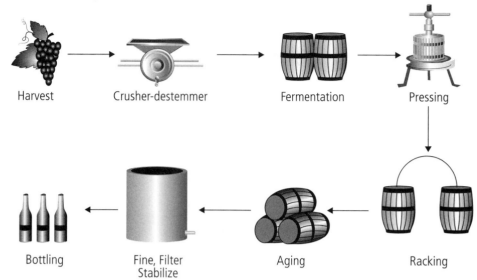

The basic principles of red wine production.

of the grapes before the addition of yeast. This soaking allows time for more water-soluble flavor and color compounds to be extracted from the skins. This cold soak is a fairly standard process for some grape varietals, such as Pinot Noir, which do not have much intrinsic color or tannin. The compounds that are extracted during a cold soak are water-soluble, since fermentation has not yet begun.

During Fermentation

The presence of the skins and the seeds in the fermentation vat changes the dynamic of the process. Instead of carbon dioxide merely bubbling out of solution, the gas gets trapped in and around the solids in the vat. This causes the gas to force the solids up to the top of the vat, forming a cap. Carbon dioxide now collects under the cap and remains trapped in solution, which creates an anaerobic environment for the yeast. Having the solids form the cap also decreases the contact area between the skins and the juice, thereby slowing the extraction of color and tannin.

There are four major methods of *cap management*. The first process, and the simplest, is punching down (*pigeage* in French). This procedure is exactly as it sounds: the cap is pushed back down under the surface of the liquid. The tool used is a flat board attached to a handle (picture a push broom with no bristles). If the fermentation is vigorous, the pressure of the trapped gas may be too great to press back down upon. In this case, the winemakers may jump into the vat and use their leg muscles to push down the cap. This is very dangerous, as the released carbon dioxide could overwhelm and asphyxiate the winemaker, who in turn may fall into the vat and drown. More modern systems used mechanized platforms that push the cap back under the liquid, thus reducing the risk.

A more complex system to manage the cap is called pumping over (*remontage* in French). This process involves removing some of the wine below the cap via a pipe and pumping into a spray nozzle over the cap. The wine can then seep through the layer of skins and seeds, extracting color and tannin along the way. The process is similar to coffee made in a percolator. The spray action of the remontage not only distributes the wine over the entire cap, it also incorporates a little oxygen into the wine. This limited incorporation of oxygen is beneficial because it prevents the development of some off-flavors and aromas in the final product.

A third, more technical method is the use of a *rotary fermenter*. Rotary fermenters are designed to constantly mix the cap back into the wine. Shaped as a large, horizontal cylinder, the fermenter has a screwlike fin inside the chamber. As the wine is fermenting, the chamber spins. This causes the fin constantly to mix the solids back into the wine. When the fermentation is complete, the wine can be drained off, and the rotation of the chamber reversed to collect the skins for pressing.

A new technique used by some Oregon winemakers is called *pneumotage*. In this process, an air distribution system is placed at the bottom of the fermenting tank. As the cap forms, small bursts of air are released into the vat. As they rise, they get larger and flatten in shape until they burst through the cap. The resulting agitation mixes some of the cap back under the surface of the liquid. The burst also splashes some liquid over the top of the cap. The use of ambient air incorporates a small amount of oxygen, similar to remontage, to help eliminate off-flavors and to oxygenate the yeast.

Post-Fermentation

Some winemakers let the fermented wine remain in contact with the skins and the seeds after fermentation, a process called *maceration*. This soaking increases the extraction of alcohol-soluble compounds. Maceration also tends to be varietal specific. Cabernet Sauvignon is typically allowed to macerate, sometimes as long as three weeks or more. The extended maceration tends to extract more tannins from the skins and seeds. However, instead of merely increasing the tannin level of the wine, the increased concentration of phenols starts a polymerization process. Phenols begin to join together to form longer chains, and eventually the resulting polymers are too large to stay dissolved. The polymers precipitate out of solution, leaving a wine with much softer tannins than would have been obtained immediately after fermentation.

MICRO-OXYGENATION

For red wines that use oak chips rather than barrels, another modern replacement for barrel aging has developed. Oak has two influences on wine: flavor and controlled exposure to oxygen. To replace the controlled oxygen exposure, some winemakers utilize micro-oxygenation (MOX). MOX is a process in which controlled amounts of oxygen are dissolved into a vat of wine. The amounts are so small that they are imperceptible to the naked eye (i.e., there are no bubbles). Using this process plus oak chips, a winemaker can reduce the amount of time a wine "ages" from three to four years to nine to eleven months. Additionally, MOX can reduce the vegetal flavors and aromas in a wine, as well as increase its color and mouthfeel.

DE-ALCOHOLIZATION

In warm regions, grapes have no trouble reaching physiological ripeness (i.e., they easily have plenty of sugar). If the winemaker leaves the grapes on the vine to increase phenolic ripeness, there is a danger that the sugar level will increase too much, resulting in a very high level of alcohol in the final product. The solution to this problem is *de-alcoholization*, to reduce the amount of alcohol in the wine.

One simple solution to reducing the alcohol in the final wine is to reduce the concentration of sugar in the grapes. Grapes that have been left on the vine tend to lose water and begin to raisinate. The solution in the winery: add water to the must. This dilutes the sugar levels back to concentrations that will support normal yeast cultures and produce typical table wine.

There are more technological methods to reduce alcohol in a finished wine. The most common is the use of reverse osmosis. In this procedure, the wine is passed through a filter that removes water, alcohol, and some acetic acid. The separated component is then distilled to remove some of the alcohol. The remaining liquid, with the alcohol removed, is then added back to the initial batch. The addition allows the creation of a series of test wines, all separated by 0.1 percent alcohol. The winemaker monitors each test wine to find the best-tasting wine, where the final alcohol concentration has hit a "sweet spot," or a final wine whose alcohol concentration is in perfect balance with the other wine components.

A less common de-alcoholization method involves selective evaporation after the wine is fermented. The technology to accomplish this is a spinning cone column. In order to create a wine with lower alcohol, a portion of the wine is removed from the main batch. This portion is then run through the spinning cone. The first pass removes the volatile flavor components, which are held in reserve. The second pass removes alcohol. The de-alcoholized wine, and the reserved flavor compounds, is then recombined with the main batch. This process effectively decreases the overall alcohol content without sacrificing the volatile flavors and aromas of the wine. This is an expensive proposition and only recently has been increasing in usage.

CARBONIC MACERATION

Some red wines are made in a soft fruity style by a technique known as *carbonic maceration*. In this method of production, whole clusters of grapes are placed into a vat that is blanketed with carbon dioxide and sealed. Enzymes in the grapes begin to break down the sugars in the pulp, in a sort of intracellular fermentation. Eventually the grapes burst, releasing juice into the vat. The wild yeast on the exterior of the grapes then begins fermenting the juice. The lack of oxygen in the vat creates an aroma profile that can be described as banana, bubble gum, or Kool-Aid. Because the grapes have burst and are not crushed, there is little surface area for the tannins and color compounds to be released. These wines, therefore, have low-intensity color and very low tannins. The most famous wine made by this method is Beaujolais Nouveau.

A purely carbonic maceration method is not commonly utilized. Most wines using this method really undergo partial carbonic maceration. The weight of the clusters bursts some of the grapes before the enzymes have a chance to work. Thus, normal fermentation and intracellular fermentation are occurring at the same time. The carbon dioxide released from the normal fermentation fills the vat, providing an anaerobic blanket for the intracellular fermentation. The aroma profile will still possess the artificial fruit notes, but not to the extent of a pure carbonic macerated wine.

While this method is often thought of in regard to the "Nouveau" style wines, its use is becoming more and more common. Wines in the Nouveau style are often served chilled, which decreases the perception of tannins even more. These wines also will not get any oak treatment, so the color will appear purple in the glass. These are wines that are meant to be drunk young, and sometimes within a year of the vintage are already past their prime. More and more mass market wines are utilizing the technique to make the wines more approachable when young. In these cases, the wines have a portion of their grapes "undergo carbonic." The wine from the carbonic grapes is then blended back into the normal batch, increasing the fruitiness and decreasing the tannin levels of the overall batch of wine.

SUMMARY

Wine making is a complex and transformational process. It allows a winemaker to transform the fruit of the vineyard into an alcoholic beverage. Along the way, many decisions are made that will influence the final product. These decisions start with how the grapes are to be processed and end with what type of closure the bottle will get. Every step of the wine making process is a decision point, influencing the product that will find its way into the bottle.

Winemakers around the world differ in preference for technology, their desire for the grapes to express their origin, and the amount of influence they themselves wish to impart into the wine. It is often said that if you like one wine from a given producer, you will probably like their other offerings. In this sense, wine making can be compared to cooking. As with chefs, personal taste determines whether you like their product. How much you like the result is often determined by the methods they use.

For all the choices a winemaker has, ultimately these decisions are nuances that layer onto the flavors of the grape. While these decisions may make the difference between a Cabernet Sauvignon that is meant for aging versus one that is drinkable immediately, the truth is that they are both still Cabernet Sauvignon. It should be remembered that the wine can only be as good as the fruit it was made from, and that the winemaker cannot improve upon Mother Nature. Hopefully, a winemaker can fully realize the potential of the grapes.

KEY TERMS

Still table wine

Sparkling wine

Fortified wine

Aromatized wine

Residual sugar

Dry

Off-dry

Crusher–destemmer

Must

Chaptalization

Enrichment

Acidification

Sulfur dioxide

Saccharomyces cerevisiae

Aerobic fermentation

Anaerobic fermentation

Wild ferment

Cultured yeast

Hydrometer

Stuck fermentation

Malolactic fermentation

Racking

Cold stabilization

Fining

Filtration

TCA

Barrel fermentation

Lees stirring

Cold soak

Cap management

Pigeage

Remontage

Rotary fermenter

Pneumotage

Maceration

De-alcoholization

Carbonic maceration

QUESTIONS

1. Define the following terms:

   Residual sugar

   Off-dry

Aromatized wine

Still table wine

Crusher-destemmer

Basket press

Acidification

Malolactic fermentation

Stuck fermentation

Chaptalization

Must

2. Why is pressing grapes gently so important?

3. What treatment can be applied to cool-climate grapes to make better wine?

4. What treatment is often applied to warm-weather grapes to make better wine?

5. How is sulfur dioxide used in wine making?

6. Why is temperature control important in wine making? How does it differ between red wine making and white wine making?

7. What are the methods of making sweet wines?

8. Describe the effects of malolactic fermentation on a wine.

9. How does oak influence the flavor of a wine?

10. Describe two methods of introducing oak flavor without using a barrel.

11. What are the two steps in clarifying wine?

12. What are the methods of cap management in red wine fermentation?

13. Describe carbonic maceration

14. How does micro-oxygenation affect a wine?

chapter 3

The Science of Wine Tasting

*W*hen the subject of wine tasting arises, the most common response is
"I know how to taste wine; I certainly drink enough of it." But wine drinking and
wine tasting are as similar as eating dinner and trying to replicate a chef's recipe,
ingredient by ingredient. One is for pleasure, the other is for analysis. In the role
of sommelier, it is important to be able to analyze a wine for its attributes and
quality, more than for simple enjoyment, in order to make informed choices for the
customer's pleasure.

Upon completion of this chapter, the student should be able to:

> Explain why analytical wine tasting is important
> Set up a proper wine tasting environment
> Discuss the steps in an analytical wine tasting
> Conduct an analytical wine tasting
> Write a tasting note
> Discuss types of tastings
> Use proper language when discussing wines

Why Do We Taste Wine?

Picture this scenario: you are the sommelier at an upscale, trendy restaurant with very wine savvy customers. You have just returned from a distributor-sponsored tasting event, and you found lots of new favorites. Now, back in the office, you leaf through the book of wines you received at the wine tasting show, trying to remember the ones you liked. Reasonably confident you remember which five Chardonnays were your favorites, you place an order and add them to the wine list. You schedule a training for the staff in the next few days on the new wines. At dinner a couple of nights later, some of your regulars, who happen to love Chardonnay, come in for dinner. You approach the table and begin to talk up the new additions. Their immediate reaction is to ask what makes each wine special, and which you would recommend for their entrees.

How could a controlled, disciplined style of wine tasting have helped in the above scenario? Wine tasting has many purposes, beyond the need of a sommelier to recommend wines. At a large tasting, like the one mentioned above, a wine buyer may taste dozens of wines, sometimes all the same varietal, with the only differences being that the wines are from different places and different producers. Having a systematic way of recording how those wines tasted is extremely valuable. Some wines may stand out, but they may not be appropriate for the current situation. A future menu change may elicit the need to revisit one of those wines. Rather than try to jog your memory, you would have a personal record of the wines you had tasted. Good sommeliers, and some very enthusiastic amateurs, often have a tasting book filled with notes about wines they have tasted—at shows, at dinners, wherever. It is their personal documentation of all the wines they have ever had the pleasure of tasting.

A sommelier will fill the tasting book with very specific notes. The wine is assessed by color, *smell*, and *taste*. There typically is no judgment in the assessments themselves; that is left for a section at the end. The components of the wines are assessed—the acidity, sugar, tannin, fruit, and alcohol content. While these are assessed in the absence of food, it is necessary to record them as they will play a part in determining how the wine will ultimately pair with food.

With tasting notes in hand, the training of the staff becomes easier, and provides a consistent sales approach to the wine. While everyone has his or her own perception of a wine, having a baseline for tastes, flavors, and attributes is a starting point in training. Not only will the servers now have a reference when it comes to sales, but they also will train their palates to taste more analytically. The education they receive in how to taste becomes a tool they can use down the road, either in the hospitality business or when purchasing wine for their own use.

Tasting notes also allow you to convey enthusiasm about a wine to the customer. This is beyond the "it's yummy and goes good with beef" type of enthusiasm. More specific notes allow for more precision in your enthusiasm as to why this particular wine is good, or why it will pair with the chosen entrée. If a customer is then looking for a particular attribute in a wine, say an oaky Chardonnay, then it is easy to recommend several possible wines and explain what makes each of them good. Sommeliers wouldn't place a wine on a list that they were not enthusiastic about; a tasting note helps to convey that enthusiasm.

Finally, tasting notes can be used as snapshots in time. Some wines are meant to be consumed years after they were made and bottled. Determining when the wine is at its optimum can be a guessing game. Tasting notes, taken each time a bottle is opened, provides a view into the wine's development. Comparison of the tasting notes over time will show how the components have changed, and how they are likely to change in the future. It is from watching these changes that a decision is made about the quality of the wine. Then, when the wine is determined to be at peak drinking quality, it can be enjoyed before it begins to decline.

Up until now, there has been no discussion of wine quality versus price. There is no consistent, direct correlation between price and quality. In fact, some wine consumers view the search for a top-quality wine priced under $20 a bottle as a personal challenge. For a restaurant wine buyer, it is doubly important to get the best-quality wine at the best possible price. Because there is no direct correlation between quality and price, it is important to be able to determine quality in the absence of pricing knowledge. A well-written, detailed tasting note can aid in determining the quality of a wine and reveal some unexpected results when compared to a price list.

To achieve a detailed tasting note, it is important to have a systematic method for tasting and for recording those impressions. This means tasting wine in the same way every time. It also means writing the tasting note the same way every time. This consistency allows for later comparison of the tasting notes, either to compare one wine to another, or to compare the development of the same wine over time.

THE TASTING EXPERIENCE

When tasting wine, it is best to have a neutral canvas so the focus is on analyzing the wine. Because sight and smell are important factors to be analyzed, the correct lighting and the absence of ambient odors is vital. The best light is natural sunlight, which shows the colors in the wine at their true quality. Incandescent lights emit light in the warm end of the light spectrum. This means warm colors (yellow and red) are enhanced and cool colors (blue and green) are diminished. The opposite is true for fluorescent lights, which enhance blue and green and diminish yellow. This has an effect on the color perceived in wine. Under fluorescent lighting, a greenish tinge may be enhanced in a young white wine. A young red wine may take on a purplish cast, appearing younger than it is. The opposite is true in incandescent light—making wines look a bit older than they really are.

Neutrality can also be achieved by using a plain background. The preferred background for most wine tasters is a clean, white surface. This could be a white tablecloth or napkin, or it could be a piece of plain white paper. The stark white background not only provides a "colorless" backdrop, but also increases the ability to see small changes in color or hue. Some white wines are practically colorless, yet against a white backdrop the low color intensity is easier to perceive.

Neutrality extends to ambient aromas as well. Many *aromas* in wine are delicate and hard to perceive. Those aromas can range from food-related smells to floral notes. Having either of these types of aromas in the environment when tasting wine may alter what aromas are attributed to the wine. The best method of avoiding these extraneous aromas—don't taste wine in or near a working kitchen. Also, the tasting group should avoid wearing perfume or aftershave, which may be perceived as floral notes. Smokers should make sure they have carefully washed their hands and do not smell of cigarette smoke, which may also alter aroma perception.

Wine tasting takes a great deal of concentration. For many tasters, noise can interfere with that concentration. Therefore, a relatively quiet environment is the rule of thumb for a tasting room. Another factor that reinforces the need for a quiet environment is the power of suggestion. Once a taster expresses his or her perceptions out loud, the other tasters usually cannot help but smell or taste the same thing. This defeats the purpose of individual assessment, and can cloud a taster's judgment if the "suggestion" ends up being false.

The Senses

The term "wine tasting" seems to suggest that only the sense of taste will be used. In actuality, four of the five senses are required to fully analyze a wine. The human sensory system is extremely sensitive, and often can ascertain tastes and aromas that scientific instruments would have difficulty determining. There are two potential drawbacks to the human sensory system, however. First, while it is sensitive, the senses cannot determine the chemical makeup of a taste or aroma. We may be able to taste acidity, but cannot tell exactly if it is malic acid, citric acid, tartaric acid, or any of the other acids in wine that is causing the sensation. The second drawback is where the information gets processed—the brain. Each taster is subjective and, unlike a scientific instrument, not easily calibrated. The experiences and memories of the taster will determine the notes that he or she writes.

Because our perceptions are our own, there are very few right or wrong answers in tasting. One man's cranberry is another woman's unripe strawberry. Some obvious things, like tasting lemon in red wine or tasting raspberries in white wine, are not so much incorrect as they are a misanalysis of the taste or aroma perception.

Each sense has an optimum ability, but many people do not have the ideal, textbook sensory response. Sight can be impaired by color blindness, typically a problem for men. The sense of smell may be attenuated by allergies, medication, or simply decreased sensitivity. The sense of taste among people has been demonstrated to fall into three categories. About 50 percent of the population has what we would term a normal sense of taste. Twenty-five percent have decreased taste perception (they typically eat anything, but have no favorites or are not enthused by food), and 25 percent are known as super tasters. Super tasters have an extremely sensitive palate, because of a large concentration of taste buds, and this attribute often manifests in a sensitivity to bitterness.

Taste and smell are interrelated. Anyone with a cold can attest to not being able to taste food. The tongue can only taste what it is wired to detect—the five tastes of sweet, salt, bitter, sour, and umami or savory. It is in combination with smell that a sense of "taste" develops. A better way to say this is that the five tastes plus smell equals flavor.

Dr. Ann Noble of the University of California–Davis has developed a tool to aid in determining wine aromas. Called the *Wine Aroma Wheel*, this tool breaks down aromas into general categories, and then gets more specific. It is useful for guiding tasters toward more specific descriptions of what they are sensing. The wheel is based on aromas, but often these aromas mirror taste, and the wheel is often used for both. (Copies of the Wine Aroma Wheel can be obtained at www.winearomawheel. com.) One caveat—beginning tasters tend to use the wheel as a crutch, looking up tastes as if to fill in the blanks. Often for new tasters, the wheel serves as the power of suggestion, rather than a guide to elucidate nuances in taste.

THE TASTING PROCESS

The tasting process begins by setting the scene appropriately. Good lighting, white backgrounds, and a quiet environment are all requirements. Next, we need to address the appropriate equipment for tasting—the glassware.

Tasting glassware varies from tasting site to tasting site, but there is an international standard. The ISO (International Standards Organization) specified in the early 1970s a glass of precise dimensions. The glass should be colorless, with no embellishments or facets. The typical tasting glass is has a volume of 7.5 to 8 ounces, and when filled correctly holds about 1.5 ounces of wine. The dimensions of the glass create a wine surface that optimizes the development of aromas. The sides of the glass focus the aromas above the wine, where the nose can perceive them.

APPEARANCE

Start by looking at the wine. Hold the glass by its stem, and tilt the glass away from you at a 45-degree angle. This provides an angle that allows for looking at a thin rim, as well as an intense core. First, assess the *clarity* of the wine. Do not confuse clarity with translucency. A wine may be see-though, yet dull or with particles floating in it. This assessment measures the presence or absence of particles in the wine. Is it clear, dull, cloudy? Is there sediment, tartrate crystals, or other items floating in the wine? Clear wine is the sign of well-made wine. Dull wine or cloudiness may indicate problems with the wine (signs of infection or of poor wine making practices).

Next, assess the color and its intensity. Color and its intensity can tell a lot about a wine. First, color can be indicative of grape varietal. A varietal like Gewürztraminer makes a wine that is peach colored, different from most other white wines. Color can also be indicative of age. In white wines, color intensifies (deepens) with age. Young whites may start out practically colorless, or a light lemon color. Over time that will develop to a rich yellow, to golden and eventually to an antique gold or amber. Red

Observe the wine at a 45-degree angle to determine intensity of color and rim to core variation.

wines decrease in color with age. Young reds can be purplish, and will develop through ruby red, garnet, brick red, and then mahogany. Both reds and whites ultimately arrive at the same tawny brown color over time. Color, particularly in white wines, may also indicate if there is oak influence in a wine. Oak influence, especially from barrels, will increase the depth of color of a wine.

The depth of color of a wine can also be indicative of varietal and age. Some varietals are noted for their color—a light Pinot Noir, an inky Cabernet Sauvignon, a golden Chardonnay. Color intensity also changes over time. An older white wine will have more intense color than a younger one. Red wines tend to lose color over time, becoming less intense. Finally, color intensity may indicate intensity of other attributes, like flavor or aroma. A high level of extract during the wine making process gets reflected by more intense color.

Next, look for any "textures" in the glass. Is there any sediment in the bottom of the glass? Is it possibly tartrate crystals, suggesting no cold stabilization (and thus, less handling by the winemaker)? Are there bubbles? These are often indicative of a young wine, still fresh from fermentation and bottled soon after the vintage (assuming it is not a sparkling wine, obviously). Legs, also called wine trails or tears, sliding down the inside of the glass could suggest alcohol content or residual sugar. The legs are a combination of evaporation and interaction between the wine and the glass. The alcohol in the wine reduces its surface tension, which allows the wine to climb up the side of the glass. As the wine gets closer to the mouth of the glass, the alcohol evaporates, and the remaining water and other constituents are drawn back down into the glass. (To test this observation, cover the mouth of the glass with your hand and the legs will disappear.) Quantitative analysis of the legs is difficult due to the differences in glasses, the change in alcohol level over time, and other factors.

The final "sight" observation is the difference between the rim and the core. All wine will have a thin, colorless ring where the wine meets the glass. This is called the *meniscus*. The rim being referred to is the area inside the meniscus. The core is the area where the wine level is the deepest. It is at the rim where subtle variations can begin to be noticed. Red wines may show brown or orange hints at the rim that are not visible in the core. Young white wines may have a greenish tint that is more visible in the rim as well. This is because the core is where the wine will have its greatest depth of color. The intensity of color at the core often "drowns out" the small variations seen at the rim.

One other observation about the *rim to core variation* concerns the width of the rim itself. As a wine gets older, the width of the rim changes and the size of the core also changes. In white wine, as the wine ages and the depth of color increases, the core gets larger and larger. Conversely, the rim will become narrower. In wine that is approaching its peak, there will be an even gradation of color from core to rim. In wines past their prime, the core color will extend fully to the meniscus. In red wines, the opposite is true. As the wine ages, the color at the core will diminish, increasing the size of the rim. Wines at their peak will also have the same continuous gradation of color from core to rim.

NOSE

Next, you can assess the nose of the wine, or its scents. Sniff the wine before swirling, and then begin to swirl the wine in the glass. If this seems a bit difficult to do in midair, keep the glass on the table and move the base in a circle. Once you are comfortable with this movement, you can easily repeat it in the air. Smelling the wine before swirling often yields different aromas than you may smell after

Swirl the wine to release some of the aromatic compounds.

swirling. Swirling incorporates air into the wine, and helps release some of the aroma compounds.

The first judgment is whether the wine is healthy or not. This is often noted as specifying whether it is clean or unclean. An unclean wine suggests there is something faulty with the wine. This could be cork taint, oxidation, maderization, or volatile acidity, among other things. If a wine is unclean, that does not end the tasting. Often, the other attributes of the wine are still detectable, and the assessment can continue.

Wine Faults

Various *wine faults* may occur. These are problems with a wine that have resulted from poor winemaking, infection, contamination or improper handling.

Cork taint: The product of TCA, or tricholoranisole, in wine from tainted corks, *cork taint* is recognized as the smell of wet cardboard, or a musty old book. On the palate, cork taint characteristics can range from a bitter aftertaste to the total loss of fruit flavors.

Oxidation: *Oxidation* is the result of exposure of the wine to oxygen. This can occur through a compromised (dried out) cork, or from leaving a bottle open too long. Oxidation is indicated by the smell of bruised fruit or nuts.

Maderization: A combination of oxidation and "cooked" wine, *maderization* is the result of high temperature damage to wine, and is indicated by cooked, caramelly fruit smells.

Volatile acidity: Also referred to as VA, *volatile acidity* presents itself in different ways. If the wine has had a bacterial infection and turned to vinegar, the smell will be of acetic acid. If the fault occurred during fermentation, the result is ethyl acetate, or the smell of nail polish.

Sulfur: The heavy-handed use of sulfur dioxide can present itself in many ways. The smell of burnt matches results from too much sulfur dioxide. It will dissipate with aeration or time. While not a fault, it is a detraction. More faulty smells are hydrogen sulfide (rotten eggs) or mercaptans (cabbage or garlic).

As with the appearance, the intensity of the nose is assessed. In this case, intensity refers to the ease or ability to smell the components of the wine's aroma. Many wine tasters use qualitative terms to describe the nose; this is cumbersome at best,

When determining the aromatic traits of a wine, small sniffs are better than one long inhalation.

because there is no scale by which to compare wines. What does a "good nose" mean? A taster should be as quantitative as possible, using terms such as low, medium, or high. A highly intense nose is so pronounced that you don't even have to put your nose in the glass to smell it. Medium intensity means the scents are easily noticeable with your nose in the glass. A low-intensity nose makes you have to work to smell something.

Now the real work comes when assessing the nose. What are the aroma characteristics? If we use the Wine Aroma Wheel as a guide, the simplest descriptions are very broad categories—fruit, floral, vegetal, spice, or other, found at the center of the wheel. With practice, it becomes easier to begin to distinguish between different items. Let's use fruit as an example. The next more specific descriptions would be types of fruit. So we could differentiate between citrus, tree fruit, stone fruit, red berries, black berries, tropical fruits, or dried fruits. This is the middle ring on the wheel. Even more precise, we can specify a particular fruit. The citrus smell could be lemon or lime, fresh juice or zest. These are summarized on the exterior ring of the wheel.

PALATE

Finally, we can assess the *palate* or tastes in the wine. Take a small sip. With the wine still in your mouth, slurp in some air. While many people are self-conscious at this step, or think it's pretentious, the slurping has a purpose. Pulling air through the wine sprays small bits of wine all over the palate, and it also aerates the wine to release more flavors and aromas. Sometimes two sips are required to get the full spectrum of flavors, but do not take them too close in succession. You need time from the first sip to judge length and flavors on the finish.

The first item to assess is sweetness. Most table wines are dry, meaning they have no residual sugar. Sugar is one of the first things the tongue can detect, but sometimes the brain gets in the way. Many New World wines, with their concentrated fruit flavors, trick the brain into thinking they are sweet when they are just very fruity. To confirm sweetness, wait for the finish. A lingering sugary flavor will remain in the finish, enticing you to take another sip. That usually confirms residual sugar. The levels can fall anywhere from dry (no sugar), off-dry (low residual sugar), or medium (like a sweet blush wine) to sweet (dessert wines). Note also that some

A small sip is all that is required to fully assess a wine on the palate.

people are more sensitive to sugar than others are; they have a lower threshold to detect sweetness. These people may label a wine off-dry that most others would say is dry. They may also detect high alcohol levels as sweetness.

The next component to assess is acidity. As before, this trait needs quantitative analysis of low, medium, and high intensity. Wine that has unusually low acidity is termed flabby, because it does not have the structure to hold the other components together. Acidity reacts on the palate by initially being astringent, or drying out the palate. Immediately after that, the saliva glands begin producing and your mouth begins to water. It is the mouthwatering character of acidity that helps to determine its intensity in a wine. In some high-acid wines, another aspect of acidity is textural. Sauvignon Blanc is described as having "sharp" acidity, because it feels as if there is something stabbing in the taster's cheeks (think biting into a lemon wedge). Riesling, on the other hand, has "rounded" acidity. Its acidity builds and then recedes, for a smoother feel on the cheeks (think about eating a tangy orange).

In red wines, the next component to assess is tannin, which has been extracted from the skin and the seeds of the red grapes. Tannin often distorts the judgment of acidity. Tannin (rated as low, medium, or high intensity) dries the mouth out with its astringent quality, and tastes bitter. It is often the tannin level that causes novice tasters to state, "This wine is dry." Acidity and tannin get confused because of the reaction on the palate. Tannin, like acidity, dries out the palate, but the mouth does not water afterward. In an acidic, tannic wine, both are happening at the same time, and the taster must decipher which sensation belongs to which attribute. Once the mouth begins to water, if it still feels astringent, that is from tannin. Tannin also tends to affect areas of the palate that acidity does not, like the gums and cheek linings.

Judging tannin uses the sense of touch, as does judging body. Tannin is often described by how it feels on the palate,—for example, gritty, dusty, or velvety. Body is the weight of the wine on the palate; how mouth coating it feels. The most common analogy is to dairy products. Imagine the mouth-coating ability of skim milk (light body) versus whole milk (full body). Body can be an indicator of alcohol content. However, be wary of using it as a rigid standard because other factors like extraction (amount of flavor compounds) and glycerol content (a by product of fermentation) can affect the weight of the wine.

Now we can get to actual flavors. These flavors also follow the Wine Aroma Wheel categorizations, and can get more specific as you get more comfortable with the flavors. Here is where the slurping comes into play. The increased aromas released by slurping are recognized by the sense of smell. They reach the nose through the sinuses, slipping in the back door, as it were. This process is called retrolfaction. It actually can give more accurate and precise smells because the path through the sinuses is a direct route to the olfactory bulb. It is the aromas obtained through retrolfaction that give us tastes.

Finally, judge the *length*. Do the flavors disappear rather quickly, or do they linger? If they disappear in a couple seconds, that is a short finish. If the flavors last twenty seconds or more, that is a long finish. Also, assess what is happening on the finish. Is one flavor or taste dominating? Do new ones appear? Is the finishing flavor(s) in balance with the rest of the flavors, or does it become a one-note aftertaste? These observations will help distinguish the wine in the notes, but also lead you into the quality and maturity assessments.

QUALITY AND MATURITY

With all the data in hand, it is now possible to assess the quality and maturity of the wine. Based on the aromas and tastes, you should have an idea about the age of the wine. This can be done by assessing the types of aromas and tastes. There are two schools of aroma and taste categorization. The first school describes these attributes as primary, secondary, or tertiary. *Primary odors* are those attributed to the grape varietal itself. For example, Sauvignon Blanc is noted for herbal, grassy aromas. *Secondary aromas* are a result of the wine making process itself. The bubble gum aroma of carbonic maceration and the buttery notes from malolactic fermentation are secondary aromas. *Tertiary aromas* are those that arise with age. These smells can include leather and tobacco in red wines, or cheese in white wines.

The second school of thought merely distinguishes between young wine and aged wine. Youthful wine is said to have aromas, while older wine develops a *bouquet*. Note here that aroma is a specific description of youthful smells, and would include both varietal and wine making smells. Bouquet develops over time, and it is possible to have a wine that displays youthful aromas while developing a bouquet. Some bouquet smells can also be attributed to wine making, namely smells derived from barrel aging. The toasty or spicy notes of oak may be considered a "bouquet" because they have come from aging wine in a barrel. It is often common to cross-utilize the two systems, and talk of aroma and tertiary smells in the same wine.

Maturity comments should focus not only on the current age of the wine, but also on predictions about when it should be consumed. Wine will be judged as needing more time (and often a range of years are quoted), ready to drink, or past its peak. These terms are not necessarily exclusive of one another. It is possible that a wine is ready to drink but could improve with three to five years of aging. Alternatively, a wine may be categorized as "drink now" because it has begun to lose its vibrancy and is on the down slope. This type of maturity assessment helps in purchasing decisions, and in usage decisions of cellared wine.

The more wines you taste, the better feel you will get for what are outstanding wines and what are poor wines. Again, the assessment is quantitative. A wine is either poor quality, acceptable, good, or outstanding. What makes a quality wine? Quality wine starts with quality grapes. Quality is assessed in all the tasting steps and you should be able to ascertain the ripeness level of the grapes, if they were oxidized during handling, and if they were grown properly in the vineyard. Quality grapes can still make poor wine, based on the wine making techniques. Was the wine making process done well? Was lots of sulfur or other enhancement needed to make up for some shortcoming? Finally, was the wine handled properly after it was made?

The other assessment of a quality wine is its balance. Are the components in harmony with one another? Does the acidity match the concentration of other flavors? Is the tannin level appropriate for the style of wine? Have the flavors developed as much as they can? Often if a wine seems out of balance in the glass, it may be because it needs to age. Then the judgment call is whether the wine will be balanced as it ages and the components adjust over time. There is no guarantee that an unbalanced wine in its youth will become balanced with age. Each component changes differently over time, typically decreasing in intensity. Often judgment calls in terms of how much longer a wine should age are based on the premise that the wine will become more balanced with age. If a wine is high in tannin, it would be expected that the *astringency* would soften with age. If there is not a lot of fruit concentration, however, the fruit components may disappear over the same period of time, and the wine will still be unbalanced.

Notice that the quality assessments—whether the wine is balanced, the quality of the fruit, the skill of the wine making—do not mention price. As mentioned previously, good-quality wine does not have to be expensive, and not all expensive wine is good quality. After the quality assessment has been made, it can then be compared to price. This then determines if the wine is a good value. Some sommeliers work backward, and note how much they would pay for a bottle. This is then compared to the actual price for a value comparison.

Tasting Sheet

| **Appearance:** |
| Clarity: |
| Intensity of Color: |
| Color: |
| Rim to core change: |
| Other observations: |
| **Nose:** |
| Health: |
| Intensity: |
| Aromas/bouquet: |
| **Palate:** |
| Dryness: |
| Acid: |
| Tannin: |
| Intensity of flavor |
| Flavor profile: |
| Body: |
| Length: |
| Finish: |
| **Conclusions:** |
| Maturity: |
| Quality: |
| Price: |
| **Details of Wine:** |
| Producer: |
| Vintage: |
| Grape: |
| Country: |
| Region: |
| Price: |
| Alcohol: |

One example of a preformatted tasting sheet.

TASTING SEQUENCE

There is a commonly accepted correct sequence for tasting wines. The wines are poured, or tasted, in the following order:

- White wine before red wine
- Light-bodied wines before fuller-bodied wines
- Sparkling wine before still wine
- Dry before sweet wine
- Younger before older wine

The main reason wines are tasted in this order is to prevent one wine from overpowering the taster's palate before the next wine is tried. In most scenarios, these rules are logical and make for the best tasting experience. Because sparkling wines are often the lightest of all wines, it is logical that they would come first. The one major contention may be with young wines preceding older ones. In some instances, say the tasting of extremely old, delicate wines, older wines would be tasted first. In this scenario, having a younger wine before the older one would overpower the flavors and the aromas of the older wine. Thus, in order to fully appreciate the nuances of the older bottle, it should be tasted first.

Tastings are organized in *flights,* or a series of wines meant to be tasted together. There are two types of flights, vertical and horizontal. A *vertical flight* is a tasting of the same wine over a succession of vintages. For example, a vertical flight of Penfolds Grange may have wines from 2000, 2001, and 2003. A *horizontal flight* is one in which some characteristic of the flight is consistent among the wines. Examples of horizontal flights would be a tasting of Italian Barolos, Merlots from around the world, or a Napa Cabernet tasting.

Cleansing the Palate

Many wine tastings provide bread, water, or even food to cleanse the palate while tasting wine. The assumption is that wines tasted side by side will interfere with the perception of each other. What is forgotten is that the bread, water, and food will also interfere with the wines, probably to a greater extent. The interaction of food and wine will be discussed in more detail in Chapter 5. Water can have two affects. It can "zero out" the palate, making it harder to compare wines directly. Secondly, mineral waters contain salts, which will interact with the wines and alter the perception of acidity and tannin. It is best to avoid "cleansing" between wines, unless you are moving from red wines back to white wines.

Blind Tastings

A *blind tasting* refers to normal tasting process conducted without knowledge of the wine(s) being tasted. It is truly neutral, since there can be no preconceived notion of what attributes the wine "should" have. Often, these tastings include the added challenge of determining what wine is being tasted and where it is from. The best tasters (and there are a few) can identify wines, regions, producers, and vintages. These tasters are extremely skilled, and their ability is a goal to strive for. The only way to get there is practice, practice, practice.

When subject to a blind tasting, it is extremely important to focus on the cues of the tasting note. The tasting note forms the pieces to a puzzle, and the goal is to put the pieces together and solve for the correct wine. The hardest part is prejudging what the wine may be, and then forcing the tasting note to comply. It is best, often, to just do the analysis, gather the data, and then come back and see what the data tell you. It is also important to focus on the major attributes of a wine, not subtle nuance. Many a blind taster has been swayed by a whiff of grass in a Riesling to say it's a Sauvignon Blanc, or by oak in a FuméBlanc and call it Chardonnay.

It is also important to approach the wines when they are at their most expressive. For a white wine, that is while they are still properly chilled. After white wines warm to room temperature, the varietal character of the aromas evaporates, and they all begin to smell and taste alike. For red wines, it is best to let them sit for a few minutes. This allows oxygen to interact with the wine and open up its aromas. It also gives a chance for the heavier aromas of red wine to evaporate and develop. In contrast to white wines, reds can be nosed more than once, and sometimes more expression and character comes out after they have sat longer in the glass.

Foremost, when it comes to blind tastings, it is all about context. Are you at a tasting of French wines, or just white wines? Even if this is not evident, the wines are still in some context with the others in the tasting. This may make it easier to discern varietals or regions more easily. Color intensity can be compared, aromas compared, and acidity levels analyzed. This side-by-side comparison puts all the wines in a context of low-medium-high intensities. Tasting a single wine out of context may not be in sync with your expectations, because anything seems acidic if you were just drinking water.

Language Development

The description of tasting notes thus far appears fairly clinical, and to some extent it needs to be. Each area assessed is judged on a quantitative level. This allows for comparison of notes, no matter when the wine was tasted. It also allows for a point of reference to which future wines can be judged. Finally, consistency of language allows tasters to compare notes between themselves and eliminate personal, subjective preferences.

If tasting notes were left strictly to the clinical style described thus far, it may become very hard to distinguish between wines. In an effort to distinguish wines from one another and to add the "experiential" aspect of wine drinking to the note, it is possible to be more descriptive. Descriptions vary depending on the category. Words used to describe appearance often describe the reflective quality of the wines (silvery, golden, jewel-like). Intensity descriptors often use personality trait modifiers like shy, exuberant, seductive, or forward. Body can be referenced as a physical type—lean, muscular, lithe, flabby. Tannins are often equated to fabric, such as satiny, silky, or velvety. Adding these comments to your tasting note personalizes a wine, and evokes the taste memory better than just a "low-medium-high" comment.

SUMMARY

Just as chefs are regarded for their palate, so sommeliers are also regarded for their tasting ability. Tasting wine is the primary job of the sommelier. It is the basis for being able to describe wines, pair them with food, and assess wines for future purchase and inclusion on the wine list. The process of tasting wine must be methodical. The language used must be quantitative, consistent, and free from personal judgment. Only after a wine has been assessed, and its attributes compared to other wines, can conclusions of origin, quality, and maturity be made. Overall, the sommelier is the testing apparatus as well as the keeper of records in all wine-related things.

KEY TERMS

Smell

Taste

Aroma

Wine Aroma Wheel

Meniscus

Clarity

Rim to core variation

Wine fault

Cork taint

Oxidation

Maderization

Volatile acidity

Palate

Length

Primary aroma

Secondary aroma

Tertiary aroma

Bouquet

Astringency

Flights

Vertical flight

Horizontal flight

Blind tasting

QUESTIONS

1. Describe ideal conditions in a room setup for wine tasting.

2. How are smell and taste related?

3. Outline the steps of an analytical tasting note.

4. What is clarity?

5. What does rim to core variation possibly indicate in a wine?

6. What components are assessed on the palate?

7. Describe each of the three types of tasting flights.

8. Why is having a common language for wine tasting important?

chapter 4

Wine Storage and Service

*K*nowledge about wine is a major portion of a sommelier's job. However, all the knowledge in the world cannot make up for a wine that has been ruined by poor storage or been served improperly. Proper storage is important to maintain quality, and also to preserve the investment of wine that needs aging. Service is not only about the hospitality provided to the customer, but also about setting up the wine to be experienced in its best light.

Upon completion of this chapter, students should be able to:

> *Discuss how aging changes wine*
>
> *Describe the proper conditions for storing wine*
>
> *Discuss the differences between storing wine for the long term versus the short term*
>
> *Describe the tools for proper wine service*
>
> *Describe proper serving temperatures for a variety of wines*
>
> *Explain proper etiquette in wine service*
>
> *Outline white wine service*
>
> *Outline red wine service, including decantation*
>
> *Describe adjustments needed for service of wines with alternative closures or service mishaps.*

Aging Wine

The French have a term for aging wine: *elévage*. Translated, elévage means to raise, as a child. That is the belief toward aging wine. One is allowing the wine to mature, to gain character, complexity, and finesse. Youthful wine is exuberant, forward, and obvious (like children) and an aged wine is demure, nuanced, and layered (like an adult). Not all wines are meant to aged. Some varietals are not conducive to long aging; they are meant to be enjoyed while young. These wines are destined to be drunk within a few years of the vintage in which they were made. In fact, the majority of wine produced falls into this category. Others are designed for the long haul, requiring time to reach their optimum expression.

Wine Storage

Wine is a product that differs from other foodstuffs or commodities. Wine can be viewed as "being alive." It has a lifespan, it can be healthy or not, and it "lives" best in environments that promote its health and longevity. Depending on the source, the average time a wine is held before consumption is said to range from a week to as short as twenty-seven minutes. Whether a wine is meant to be kept twenty minutes or twenty years, the principles of cellaring are essential.

The first principle of storing wine involves the physical handling of the bottle. Wine bottles should be stored on their sides. This allows the wine inside the bottle to remain in contact with the cork, keeping it moist and plump. This is especially necessary if the wine is to be aged for a long period of time, but should be applied to any wine awaiting consumption. There is one exception to that rule; wine with screw caps do not need to be on their sides. The inner seal is not affected by changes in humidity, and does not need wine contact to keep the interface moist.

Why age wine? What happens in the bottle that makes older wine different from young wine? Shouldn't wines be as fresh as possible to get the best flavor? Much of the wine that is aged is red wine, and aging helps to harmonize the wine components. Wine that is aged in the bottle is said to undergo *reductive aging*. This means oxygen is not present in the aging process. This is opposed to barrel aging, which has more oxygen influence and is known as *oxidative aging*. Even though a bottle of wine is undergoing reductive aging, a small amount of oxygen diffuses through the cork. This is just enough oxygen to interact with the tannins and color compounds. The result is that the tannins soften and become less intense. At the same time, color begins to be lost. Where do the tannin and the color go? To the bottom of the bottle. The tannins and color compounds precipitate and form *sediment*. Sediment is a fine solid that settles out of the wine over time. At the same time, new flavors and bouquet are being created. The enjoyment of these new flavors and bouquet, as well as the newly balanced components to the wine, are what make aging worthwhile.

ENVIRONMENTAL FACTORS

What are the environmental factors that influence the health and longevity of a wine? The four key factors are temperature, humidity, vibration, and light. Each of these can affect both the health of a wine and its longevity. Each has an effect on the wine, and proper cellaring manages each factor to the ultimate benefit of the wine.

Temperature

The temperature at which a wine is stored can greatly effect how that wine ages. The evolution of wine is a series of complex chemical reactions, which for the most part happen very slowly. Basic chemistry states that as the temperature is increased, the rate of reaction increases. Therefore, wine stored at warmer temperatures ages faster than wine at lower temperatures. If a wine is too warm, it will begin to cook inside the bottle. The aromas, and particularly the fruit component, will be compromised. Also, different chemical reactions are favored, yielding wines with jammy or cooked flavors that do not appear in wines aged at cooler temperatures. Secondly, increased temperature will cause the wine inside the bottle to expand. Expansion of the liquid presses it against the cork, possibly pushing the cork out of the neck of the bottle. If this happens, the wine will be exposed to oxygen and will spoil quickly.

What is the ideal temperature for cellaring wine? The answer is *cellar temperature* or 55°F (13°C). This is the temperature of caves and old basements that are used to store wine. Modern technology allows dedicated wine refrigerators to hold this temperature fairly constant. Temperature fluctuations are not beneficial to wines being aged, and should be avoided. Having wine go through hot and cold cycles will alter the flavor of the wine more than will holding it at a constant temperature. In fact, it is worse to have the temperature of wine fluctuate than to store it at the wrong temperature.

Humidity

The humidity of the cellar is of extreme importance to aging wine. The humidity relates directly to the health of the cork. The ideal humidity, 75 percent, provides enough moisture to keep the cork pliable. Pliability is necessary to maintain the seal between the cork and the bottle. That seal keeps air out of the bottle, thus preventing oxidation.

What happens at higher humidity? Excess moisture on the outside of the bottle will not directly affect the wine. Instead, the changes occur to the cork and the label. At high humidity, it is now possible for molds and mildew to grow. These can grow on the cork, and they can grow on the label. The label may also begin to peel away from the bottle, if water-based adhesive was used. Or the label may begin to deteriorate as the paper fibers relax in the moist environment. The mold and mildew will not enter the wine, so it is safe. The effect on the label, on the other hand, may have an affect on the wine's value. Wines cellared for investment purposes need intact, legible, even pristine labels to achieve the highest monetary value.

Low humidity has the most detrimental affect on a wine. At low humidity, even as low as 50 percent humidity, the cork will lose moisture. Upon losing moisture, the cork begins to shrink, compromising the seal between the cork and the wine. Now, oxygen may enter the bottle, or wine may leak out. Just as a cut can become infected, a wine can become infected if it is exposed to the air. This infection could be bacterial, which will turn the wine to vinegar. Or it could merely be oxygen, which will react with the alcohol in the wine and create an oxidized, sherry-like, or bruised apple aroma and taste.

Vibration

Chemists understand that to make a reaction increase in speed, the molecules need to bump into each other at a faster rate. Most commonly, this is achieved by increasing the temperature, which stirs up the solution. Another method is ultrasound. High levels of sound waves pulsed through a chemical reaction physically shove molecules into each other. The same is true for vibration and wine. Constant vibration has the same effect as ultrasound; the molecules of the wine are forced into one another at a greater rate. Just as was seen with temperature, increased vibration will accelerate the aging of a wine. It may also "bruise" the wine, or allow the creation of atypical flavors in the bottle.

Vibration, or even sharp movement, can cause a disruption of sediment in red wine. Because sediment is so fine, it can take days for the wine to clarify again. Storing wine on its side not only keeps the cork moist, but prepares the bottle for service. Very little movement is necessary to move a horizontal bottle to a pouring position. If the bottle had been held upright, there is a greater chance of stirring up the sediment on transporting and pouring.

Light

Light is a long-term factor when it comes to aging wine. The color compounds in red wines—anthocyanins—absorb ultraviolet light. Wines need to be protected from UV light, because the rays will cause the anthocyanins to form free radicals. These free radicals will in turn begin to interact with other compounds in the wine, producing off-flavors and aromas. One solution has been to bottle wine in dark brown or green bottles. Very few wines—only those meant to be drunk early or tied to tradition—are bottled in clear bottles. Another solution is to keep cellars dark. Most cellars (above ground or below) have no windows, and only incandescent bulbs or candlelight. This provides the lowest chance of UV radiation, but care must be taken because incandescent bulbs generate a lot of heat.

There is one spot in every home that is the worst place to store wine, yet many people keep it there. The top of the refrigerator is the worst place for wine storage. It is subject to excess heat, as the refrigerator pulls heat out of the interior and vents it out the back. It is subject to excess vibration, as the refrigerator turns on and off. It is also subject to low humidity and to light, since most kitchens have windows. If the object is to create a cooked, possibly oxidized wine, the top of the refrigerator is the place this can be accomplished the fastest.

The Wine Cellar

Wine cellars come in all shapes and sizes. The investment in a wine cellar should be determined by the purpose and length of the storage rather than by the wine. That may seem counterintuitive, but there is a big difference between short-term storage and long-term storage.

Short-term Storage

All restaurants need access to the wines on their wine list. What is not necessary, however, is ready access to every single bottle. Based on sales, a restaurant can predict which wines and which quantities are needed in the near future. These wines are held in short-term storage. The conditions for short-term storage are not as rigorous as for extended aging. The most important factor is accessibility. A server or manager must be able to obtain the wine from the cellar when the customer orders it. Then factors such as temperature, vibration, humidity, and light can be addressed.

Some restaurants use their short-term storage as a marketing tool. The wall of wine bottles as you enter the restaurant often serves as storage space as well as adding ambiance. The downside to this approach is the lack of control over temperature and light. Often the wine wall is near windows and receives a fair amount of sunlight during the day. Being near the door, or even in the dining room, the temperature can fluctuate, which is harmful to wine. Humidity is often a factor as well, since this factor is uncontrollable in a dining room.

Short-term storage must balance the needs of the restaurant. While there should be enough space to hold all the wine needed in the near future, it should not be so large as to take space away from the dining room. After all, the seats in the dining

The short-term storage of a restaurant must primarily address accessibility and sales needs.

room—not floor space of the wine cellar—are what make money. Creative usage of space, such as dividing a bar and dining space with a bank of wine refrigerators, or creating a "wine cellar" private dining room, can successfully combine marketing, space usage, and storage in one.

Long-term Storage

Restaurants and private collectors who have older, more valuable wines, may look to long-term storage for their bottles. Long-term storage is not fancy, but controls all the necessary environmental factors. This could be a special room built in a home, with lighting and temperature/humidity controls, or it could be storage at an off-site location, such as a specially designed wine warehouse. In the case of off-site storage, planning is extremely important, in order to have the wine on hand when required. If the off-site location is near the restaurant, this creates an ideal situation. The wine is kept in the proper environment, but is relatively easy to access. Inside the long-term storage area, organization is important. More commonly retrieved wines should have easier access than those that are being kept for aging or those that are needed less frequently.

Wine Service

THE SOMMELIER

Historically, the *sommelier* was the cellar master of the castle. The word is derived from the French for "where it is kept." The sommelier was in charge of the stores—food, water, and wine—for the lord of the manor. The job also entailed being the

Wine kept for the long term should be stored on its side in temperature- and light-controlled environments.

official taster; the one who ate and drank a portion of the royals' food before they consumed it to ensure it was not poisoned. Over the years, most of those roles disappeared, but some remained in new forms. Nowadays, the sommelier is known for keeping a cellar of wines and being able to taste them for their quality and health.

Of course, the sommelier must perform many tasks, the most visible of which is wine service. Service of wine is the ultimate expression of hospitality and ceremony. There is a formal protocol, which can be adapted to less formal situations. There are variations on protocol depending on whether the wine is a white, young red, old red, sparkling, or dessert wine. All have a common flow, with small alterations based on the wine to be served. The next sections describe formal protocol, followed by comments for more casual settings or for more modern packaging.

TOOLS

The tools for wine service have evolved over the years. In the classical period and the Middle Ages, all that was needed was a jug and some mugs. The invention of the glass bottle with the cork as a stopper required a new tool. Thus, the *corkscrew* was developed. Glasses evolved from ceramic or wooden mugs to crystal stemware, all the better for appreciating the wine's color and clarity.

Corkscrews come in a wide range of styles. Some of these are better suited to restaurant service than others. No matter the style, they all have the same working

Types of corkscrews (clockwise from top left): single pump, screwpull, dual wing, Ah-so, T-pull, and pulltap.

components. The business end of the corkscrew is the *worm,* the curled metal that will be inserted into the cork. Inexpensive corkscrews have worms that resemble a simple screw—a twisting blade of metal around a solid core. These are to be avoided because they may cause an old or poor-quality cork to crumble. The server is then left with a hole through the middle of a cork that is still well secured in the bottle. A better worm is a helix of metal, sometimes with a slight ridge on the side. (A matchstick should be able to be placed into the center of the worm.) This provides a noncontiguous entry into the cork, yielding a better grip to pull the cork from the bottle, and more support within the cork to prevent crumbling.

Corkscrews should also have a lever mechanism, which uses leverage, bracing against the bottle, to extract the cork. This is the area of greatest variation in corkscrews. The simplest is the *T-pull,* a worm attached perpendicularly to a handle. With this corkscrew, the person is the lever and must use strength to pull the cork from the bottle. The T-pull is not appropriate for hospitality service, and should be avoided if possible. The next style is the *screwpull,* which houses the worm in a tube, the bottom of which serves as the point of contact with the bottle. Turning the handle of the worm initially drives the worm into the cork. Once the worm housing is wedged firmly against the bottle, continuing to turn the worm slowly "unscrews" the cork from the bottle. The worm itself is used as the lever to extract the cork. These could work in hospitality, but are often confined to home use since they are bulky.

Next is the *dual-wing opener.* This works similarly to the screwpull, but instead of the worm slowly raising the cork out of the bottle, continuing to turn the handle raises two winglike levers. These levers are then pushed back down toward the bottle, which leverages out the cork. This style could also be used in hospitality, but does not give the versatility needed for older wines.

There are three styles of corkscrews that should be used in a hospitality setting. The most versatile and the most common is called the *waiter's friend,* or *pulltap.* It is a small, compact apparatus that contains a folding worm, lever, and foil cutter. Some waiter's friends can be purchased with bifurcated or hinged double levers. These provide great range of motion for opening bottles with longer corks. Once the foil is cut and the cutter folded back into the apparatus, the worm is unfolded perpendicular to the handle. This is screwed into the cork until one turn of the screw is left showing. The lever is now placed onto the side of the neck of the bottle, and the handle lifted to extract the cork. For longer corks, the worm can then be turned one more revolution, and the lever engaged again to finish the cork extraction. This corkscrew is preferred by wait staff, because it is small, easy to carry, very versatile, and allows bottles to be opened standing upright.

The next style that can be use is the *single pump corkscrew,* most commonly known as a Rabbit™. In this model, the neck of the wine bottle is placed against a cradle under the worm. This may be handheld or mounted to a backbar. The downward action of the lever drives the worm into the cork. Returning the handle to the up position pulls the cork out of the bottle. Remove the bottle, repeat the lever action, and the cork is removed from the worm. This style is most often used in high-volume situations, such as opening a large quantity of bottles for a tasting or for opening bottles for by-the-glass service behind a bar.

The final cork extractor does not use a worm. It is called an *Ah-so,* which reflects what people say when they figure it out (Ah, so that's how it works. . . .). The Ah-so consists of two concave blades perpendicular to the handle. One blade is slightly longer than the other. The longer of the two blades is placed between the cork and the bottle. The Ah-so is then wiggled back and forth as the blades are inserted between the cork and the bottle neck. Once in place, the cork can be removed with a twisting and pulling of the wrist. This style takes some practice to master, but having one around is handy if a cork breaks during extraction with a waiter's friend or other worm-based corkscrew. It is often preferred for bottles with old corks because the cork itself is not punctured.

GLASSWARE

The single most important tool in service of wine, at least from the guest's perspective, is the glassware. Good glassware should be leaded crystal. Crystal glassware is much stronger than regular glass and can withstand handling better. The glassware should also have thin rims, making them seem delicate when placed in the mouth. The glasses must be specially handled, avoiding soaps and harsh chemicals. Because they are delicate, these glasses are often washed in their own machine, or by hand. They are also hand polished, if allowed.

There are companies that make glassware for every type of wine and spirit. It is a matter of debate whether there is truly a difference in the taste of the wine with different glassware. Studies to date have been inconclusive. Certain required styles

Styles of wine glasses (left to right): White wine, port or dessert, water, sparkling flute, sparkling tulip, tasting, and red wine glass.

of glassware should be used in fine dining situations. At a minimum, a restaurant should stock champagne flutes, red wine glasses, white wine glasses, and dessert wine glasses.

Flutes are preferred to coupe-style glasses for sparkling wine. It is a matter of preference if the glass is a flute, tulip, or other tall, thin glass. The tall shape accentuates the bubbles as they ascend in the wine.

Red wine glasses and white wine glasses differ in the shape of the bowl. Red wine glasses are often wider, taking on a balloon shape. This allows for greater surface area to be in contact with the air and also for the wine to be swirled. Both of these abilities provide for more aromas to be released from the wine. White wine glasses, on the other hand, are narrower in the bowl and at the mouth. This allows the delicate aromas to be kept in the glass and enjoyed with each sip.

Dessert glasses, usually much smaller than regular wine glasses, can serve multiple purposes. They can be used in dessert wine and port wine service. They can also be used for Sherries and possibly liqueurs.

Two final comments about glassware: first, the size of the bowl should not be too large. The standard portion size, or pour, for a glass of wine is 5 ounces. If a bowl of a red wine glass is 19 ounces (or larger in some styles), the pour only fills the bowl to 20 percent capacity. In the eyes of the guest, this appears to be a very small glass of wine. While large bowls are beneficial for swirling and allowing aromas to develop, it is best to balance the size of the bowl with the perceived pour size.

Second, some restaurateurs reserve their best glassware for the expensive wine purchases. Again in the eyes of the guest, there is a double standard for those who purchase expensive bottles and those who do not. Any guests would feel well served if they enjoyed their wine in good glassware. Using the same glassware for all wines reduces glassware inventory, but more importantly, makes guests feel well treated.

SERVICE TEMPERATURES

Wine should be served at the temperature that allows the wine to express itself the best. More often than not, however, white wines are served too cold, and red wines are served too warm. Serving a wine too cold will mask its flavors and prevent the aromas from developing in the glass. In the case of red wines, it will also accentuate the tannins and acidity, making the wine seem out of balance. Wine served too warm will accentuate the alcohol content, and does not provide thirst-quenching refreshment during the meal. In the case of white wines, most of the varietal character disappears at warmer temperatures. In sweet wines, the sugar is accentuated, making the wine cloying and unbalanced.

The accompanying table shows the proper temperatures for serving wines. Often service temperature is dictated by storage. White wines are commonly stored in a refrigerator, and therefore arrive at the table around 40°F (4.5°C). Red wines are often stored in displays, thus at room temperature. However, room temperature in Phoenix in July or Chicago in August is much warmer than red wine should be served. Room temperature refers to approximately 72°F (22°C). Keeping the wine cellar at 50–59°F (10–15°C) is ideal for service. White wines stored at this temperature can be placed in an ice bucket on the way to the table, and in 10 minutes will have reached their optimal temperature. Red wines, having been brought to the table without a bucket, will have warmed to about 65°F (18°C) in about 10 minutes, placing them at the ideal service temperature.

Wine Service Temperatures

Champagne and sparkling wines	40–45°F	5–8°C
Dry white wines and rosés	42–54°F	6–12°C
Light-bodied reds	50–54°F	10–12°C
Full-bodied reds	54–66°F	12–18°C
Sweet wines	40–46°F	5–8°C
Dry fortified wines	45–52°F	8–11°C
Sweet fortified wines	72°F	22°C

Each style of wine has a temperature range where the wine is best. Emile Peynaud, a wine making professor at the University of Bordeaux, wrote in his book, *The Taste of Wine*: "the same red wine will taste hot and thin at 70°F, supple and fluid at 64°F and full and astringent at 50°F." The reason is that each of the wine's components (alcohol, aromatics, tannin, and so on) all react differently on the palate at different temperatures. At a temperature that is too cool, only the astringency of the tannin will be perceived. At too high a temperature, the alcohol is very volatile, making the wine seem more alcoholic and thinner than it really is.

ETIQUETTE

The etiquette of wine service has not changed significantly over the years. Initially, the host was the owner of the home (or castle) providing the refreshments. In a show of hospitality, the host checked the wine to be served, but allowed all the guests to be poured first. This tradition continues today, with the person ordering the wine assuming the position of host. This person may change from course to course or wine to wine, so the sommelier must be aware of who is placing the wine order each time. The next tradition is to pour the women first. Very formal protocol requires that the women also be poured in order of age, oldest to youngest. Then the men are poured, also oldest to youngest, with the host (of either sex) poured last. In modern society, this may pose some problems. To avoid having the sommelier pass judgment on the ages of the guests, or to keep from assuming a "border collie" herding feel by circling the table repeatedly, it is best if the pouring commences with the first woman to the left of the host, continues to all the women, and then finishes with the men.

Another very formal protocol is the sommelier tasting. Many sommeliers wear a *tastevin* around their neck for this purpose. A tastevin is a shallow silver cup, often with small impressions in the bottom. The purpose of the tastevin shape is to amplify the color and aroma of a small amount of wine to assess it for the guest. In another scenario, the sommelier would bring a glass to the table in order to assess the wine before the host is given a taste. The purpose of this is to conduct a mini-assessment in front of the guest, ensuring that the wine that was ordered is in perfect condition. Many guests enjoy this level of service. It also prevents wines from being sent back because they are deemed faulty, and also catches faulty wines before they reach the guest. This aspect of wine service is typically reserved for very formal dining rooms, or for very expensive bottles.

Casual operations often do not have a clientele for whom a formal style of service would be desired. These operations will find that special carts for wine opening, sommelier tastings, and formalized decanting do not fit into their style. Wine service should fit the operation, but there are some essentials that all operations can follow to ensure proper service.

WHITE WINE SERVICE

The *mise en place,* or essential equipment, for white wine service is:

The glassware

The wine

A corkscrew

A serviette or napkin

A small side plate and a coaster

An ice bucket and stand

The following is a step-by-step procedure on white wine service.

1. Approach the table with the appropriate glassware, placing it on the right-hand side of the guest, from the right side. The placement of glasses follows the order of pouring the wine, with the host's glass placed last.

2. Place a small plate near the right side of the host, and a coaster in the center of the table.

3. The wine is now brought to the table in a wine bucket draped with a napkin. Place it in view of the table and especially the host, but not encroaching on the table.

4. Remove the wine from the bucket and wipe with the napkin.

5. Cradle the wine in the napkin and present to the host from the right-hand side. Confirm wine, vintage, and producer.

6. After receiving confirmation from the host, return the bottle to the ice bucket. Remove a portion of the foil capsule, cutting under the second lip of the neck with the knife on the corkscrew.

7. Remove the foil cap and inspect for mold or leakage. Place the cap on the small plate or in your pocket (depending on the policy of the restaurant).

8. Wipe the top of the cork and the neck of the bottle with the napkin.

9. Place the tip of the worm in the center of the cork. Slowly twist the worm so that it is inserted into the cork at a slight angle. Continue twisting until one turn of the worm is left outside the cork.

10. Place the lever against the neck of the bottle. Securing the lever with your finger, raise the handle of the corkscrew to leverage the cork out of the bottle. Do not remove the cork completely by raising the handle. Rather, leave a small portion of the cork in the bottle, to be removed by slight tugging by hand.

11. Remove the cork from the worm, without touching the mirror, or the portion of the cork that was in contact with the wine. Inspect the mirror for irregularities. Place the cork on the small plate.

12. Wipe the neck of the bottle inside and out.

13. Remove the bottle from the bucket, wiping the excess moisture from the bottle. Pour a one-ounce taste for the host, holding the bottle so the label is visible.

14. Receive confirmation that the wine is acceptable to be poured.

15. Proceed to pour the wine for the guests. Start with the first woman to the left of the host; proceed to serve all the women, then the men, then the host. Make sure to wipe the neck of the bottle between pours to collect drips.

16. Ask the host if the temperature of the wine is acceptable, and if the host would like it back in the ice bucket or on the coaster to warm slightly.

17. Remove the small plate with the cork and foil as you leave the table.

RED WINE SERVICE

The mise en place for red wine service is:

The glassware

The wine

A corkscrew

A serviette or napkin

A small side plate and a coaster

A small cart or table (optional)

The following is a step-by-step procedure on red wine service.

1. Approach the table with the appropriate glassware, placing it on the right-hand side of the guest, from the right side. The placement of glasses follows the order of pouring the wine, with the host's glass placed last.

2. Place a small plate near the right side of the host, and a coaster in the center of the table.

3. The wine is now brought to the table cradled in a napkin. Present the wine to the host from the right-hand side. Confirm wine, vintage, and producer.

4. After receiving confirmation from the host, place the wine on the table, or on a small cart positioned near the host. (This will be determined by the

restaurant protocol.) Do not attempt to open the bottle while holding it in midair.

5. Remove a portion of the foil capsule, cutting under the second lip of the neck with the knife on the corkscrew.

6. Remove the foil cap and inspect for mold or leakage. Place the cap on the small plate or in your pocket (depending on the policy of the restaurant).

7. Wipe the top of the cork and the neck of the bottle with the napkin.

8. Place the tip of the worm in the center of the cork. Slowly twist the worm so that it is inserted into the cork at a slight angle. Continue twisting until one turn of the worm is left outside the cork.

9. Place the lever against the neck of the bottle. Securing the lever with your finger, raise the handle of the corkscrew to leverage the cork out of the bottle. Do not remove the cork completely by raising the handle. Rather, leave a small portion of the cork in the bottle, to be removed by slight tugging by hand without a sound.

10. Remove the cork from the worm, without touching the mirror, or the portion of the cork that had been in contact with the wine. Inspect the mirror for irregularities. Place the cork on the small plate.

11. Wipe the neck of the bottle inside and out.

12. Pour a one-ounce taste for the host, holding the bottle so the label is visible.

13. Receive confirmation that the wine is acceptable to be poured.

14. Proceed to pour the wine for the guests. Start with the first woman to the left of the host; proceed to serve all the women, then the men, then the host. Make sure to wipe the neck of the bottle between pours to collect drips.

15. Place the bottle on the coaster.

16. Remove the small plate with the cork and foil as you leave the table.

DECANTING

Decantation of red wine may be required for one of two reasons. The first situation arises with a very young wine with high levels of tannin. This calls for a style of decantation known as splash decanting. The bottle is opened normally, and a sample is poured for the host. If the host then wishes, the bottle is poured vigorously into a decanter. This aerates the wine, softening the tannins.

Presentation of the bottle
to the host to confirm wine,
vintage, and producer.

The foil is cut below the
second rim of the neck.

The corkscrew is inserted and
the bottle opened with the label
visible to the customer.

A small portion is poured for the
host to taste and approve before
the table is served.

The mise en place for decanting a red wine (clockwise from upper left): The wine, held in a wine basket, decanter and coaster, pulltap, small plate for cork after removal, candle (center).

The second situation is the more common decantation, the separation of wine from its sediment. The mise en place for a separation decantation is:

The glassware, including an extra tasting glass

The wine, held in a wine basket

A corkscrew

A serviette or napkin

A small side plate and a coaster

A decanter

A lit candle or other light source

A small cart or table

The following is a step-by-step procedure on red wine service.

1. Approach the table with the appropriate glassware, placing it on the right-hand side of the guest, from the right side. The placement of glasses follows the order of pouring the wine, with the host's glass placed last.

2. Place a small plate near the right side of the host, and a coaster in the center of the table.

3. The wine is now brought to the table cradled in a wine basket. Present the wine to the host from the right-hand side. Confirm wine, vintage, and producer.

4. After receiving confirmation from the host, place the wine on the side table, or on a small cart positioned near the host. (This will be determined by the restaurant protocol.)

5. Remove the *entire* foil capsule, cutting a slit up the side of the neck with the knife on the corkscrew, and removing the foil in one piece. This is necessary because the wine must be totally visible while pouring to determine the location of the sediment.

6. Inspect the foil for mold or leakage. Place the foil on the small plate. Wipe the top of the cork and the neck of the bottle with the napkin.

7. Place the tip of the worm in the center of the cork. Slowly twist the worm so that it is inserted into the cork at a slight angle. Continue twisting until one turn of the worm is left outside the cork.

8. Place the lever against the neck of the bottle. Securing the lever with your finger, raise the handle of the corkscrew to leverage the cork out of the bottle. Do not remove the cork completely by raising the handle. Rather, leave a small portion of the cork in the bottle, to be removed by slight tugging by hand.

9. Remove the cork from the worm, without touching the mirror, or the portion of the cork that had been in contact with the wine. Inspect the mirror for irregularities. Place the cork on the small plate.

10. Wipe the neck of the bottle inside and out.

11. Pour a one-ounce taste for the host in the extra tasting glass.

12. Receive confirmation that the wine is acceptable to be poured and that it should be decanted first.

13. Position the light source so that you can see the wine through the neck of the bottle. Holding the decanter in one hand and the wine in the other, slowly begin transferring the wine to the decanter. Allow the wine to pour slowly down the side of the decanter, rather than splash into the center.

14. Continue transferring the wine until the sediment can be observed approaching the shoulder of the bottle. When it appears the sediment is about to enter the neck of the bottle, stop the transfer.

15. Pour another taste for the host and receive confirmation to begin service.

16. Proceed to pour the wine for the guests. Start with the first woman to the left of the host; proceed to serve all the women, then the men, then the host. Make sure to wipe the decanter to collect drips between pours. Pouring from a decanter should involve a straight up and down motion, with no twist to catch a drip.

The wine, in a basket to prevent disturbing the sediment, is presented to the host to confirm it is the wine ordered.

The entire capsule is removed to aid in viewing the progress of the sediment during decantation.

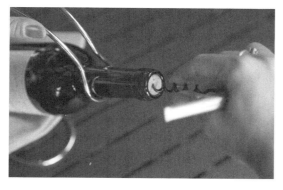

The corkscrew is carefully inserted into the bottle in the basket.

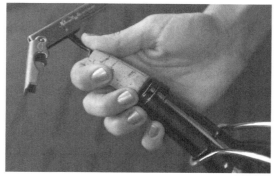

The cork is carefully removed by hand from the bottle, to avoid disturbing the sediment.

The wine is carefully poured into the decanter. The candle aids the server in viewing the progress of the sediment toward the neck of the bottle.

The wine is served from the decanter, with a napkin standing by to catch any drips.

17. Place the decanter on the coaster and place the basket with the bottle in the center of the table.

18. Remove the small plate with the cork and foil as you leave the table.

ALTERNATIVE CLOSURE SERVICE

For most synthetic closures, the procedure for opening the bottle will be the same as it was for a bottle with a standard cork. Bottles with plastic closures open just like bottles with corks with one exception. The plastic closures are often slightly larger than the neck of the bottle. This creates more friction between the closure and the glass neck than with a regular cork. The result is that removing plastic corks takes more effort than removing a regular cork. It is much easier to slip or chip the glass neck if not careful.

Opening a bottle with a screw cap requires a change of procedure. The cap should be treated as if it were a cork. Once the wine is presented to the host, the cap is removed. There are many methods suggested in an attempt to make this process more elegant. The two logical solutions are either to turn the cap itself, or if possible, to turn the lower metal base of the capsule in order to crack the seal. Once the seal is cracked, remove the cap. The cap is placed on the small plate, just as a cork would have been. The remainder of the service stays the same as with a standard cork.

SERVICE MISHAPS

The typical service mishap involves a broken cork. Should this occur, it is best to excuse yourself from the table to remove the cork. This will save the embarrassment of trying to remove the remainder in front of the guests. Away from the table, you have several options. It is possible to remove the cork with the corkscrew, bracing it against the side of the bottleneck. Another option is to use an Ah-so to remove the remaining cork. If all else fails, it may be best to replace the bottle with another. When the bottle is returned to the table, it should again be presented to the host before offering a taste.

If the cork falls into the bottle, it is again appropriate to excuse yourself from the table. Have a cork extractor behind the bar, and use this to remove the cork. Present the wine to the host upon returning to the table.

In both of the scenarios above, the host may request a different bottle. It often may be in the best interest of time (and potential faulty wine) to merely replace the bottle without the host requesting it. This demonstrates that the sommelier is committed to the optimum wine experience for the customer.

CORKAGE

In some locations, it is possible for customers to bring their own wine into the restaurant. This will depend upon the local liquor laws and may or may not occur in a restaurant that sells wine. In either case, it is important for the service staff to understand the proper steps of service. It is equally important that the restaurant possess the proper equipment to serve the customers' wine. It may be as simple as having quality glassware and ice buckets to satisfy the need. In higher-end restaurants, investment in decanters, fine glassware, and chillers will meet the expectations of that clientele. For the service of providing glassware, a restaurant will typically charge a corkage fee.

RESPONSIBLE SERVICE

The sommelier has other responsibilities besides providing guidance and service of wine. The sommelier is also responsible for appropriate alcohol service, as is any other server or bartender. The sommelier should be aware of how much the customers are drinking, how many bottles they order, and the alcohol content of those wines. As with other service staff, the sommelier staff should be trained to note the signs of intoxication, and how to terminate service if appropriate.

It is also important for the sommelier to be aware of the local liquor laws. In some jurisdictions, it may be legal to bring bottles home if they are not completely consumed. If this is allowed, it is usually with stipulations. These requirements may involve the amount of wine in the bottle, or placing the cork back into the neck, flush with the top.

SUMMARY

Wine service is a last reminder of the day when food and drink were presented to the lord of the manor for his acceptance. Nowadays that ceremony is relegated to the presentation of the bottle for confirmation of producer, vintage, and varietal. However, the job of the sommelier has not changed with regard to wine over the years. Besides service, storage and care of wine are still the responsibility of the sommelier.

Proper wine storage is important for the benefit of the restaurant and the customer. In some cases, restaurants take on commitments of aging wine for their clientele, adding to the storage requirements and responsibilities. The proper care of wine, be it short-term or long-term, is about maintaining the health of the wine so it will be in the proper state for service to the customer.

Ultimately, the sale of wine in restaurants is about service. Many people equate part of their enjoyment of wine with the ceremony surrounding opening the bottle. It is the service of wine, from selection to opening to pouring, that remains a quintessential example of hospitality and service.

KEY TERMS

Elévage

Reductive aging

Oxidative aging

Sediment

Cellar temperature

Sommelier

Corkscrew

Worm

T-pull

Screwpull

Dual-wing opener

Pulltap

Single pump corkscrew

Ah-so

Tastevin

Mise en place

QUESTIONS

1. Describe oxidative aging.

2. Where does reductive aging occur?

3. What environmental factors must be controlled when storing wine? Why?

4. What happens if the humidity is too low in a wine cellar?

5. What happens if the temperature is too high in a wine cellar?

6. What is meant by short-term storage?

7. What tools does a sommelier need daily?

8. Outline the service of white wine.

9. Outline the service of decanting a red wine.

10. What is the basic etiquette of wine service?

chapter 5

Food and Wine Pairing

We've all heard them, the rules about choosing a wine with your meal. The mantra that everyone seems to know: white wine with white meat and red wine with red meat. That single mantra is the biggest oversimplification in the world of gastronomy. Yet it is perpetuated because of its simplicity, its ease of use, and for the most part, a modicum of truth. But what about salmon? It is fish but not exactly white meat. Coq au vin is white meat cooked in red wine, but are you supposed to drink white wine with it? And that doesn't even begin to ask: what wine? Should that steak au poivre be served with Pinot Noir or Cabernet Sauvignon? They are both red, but are very different wines.

There is a great deal of self-imposed pressure in food and wine pairing. If the discussion was about what sauce to place with a dish, or whether the flavors of the vegetables complement the main course, most people would not have a second thought about commenting. But make the discussion about wine, and even the most confident may freeze. One reason is the absolute plethora of wines. It is one thing to say a dish is best paired with a Cabernet, but is it this *cabernet, or what about that one? As David Rosengarten and Josh*

Wesson, authors of Red Wine with Fish, *state, the only way to determine the best pairing is to know all the foods in the world, all the wines in the world (including each vintage's character), and to have tried them all against one another. Now that we face an Everest that is impossible to climb, let's ignore it and start fresh.*

Upon completion of this chapter, students should be able to:

> *Explain the reasons behind pairing food and wine*
> *Describe the principles of basic food and wine pairing*
> *Discuss taste interactions and how they influence food and wine pairing*
> *Explain principle of "compare or contrast" in terms of pairings*
> *Make pairing recommendations based on tastes and flavors of foods*
> *Describe classic food and wine pairs and why they work*
> *Explain what are difficult foods and why they are hard to pair with wine*
> *Discuss pairing of wine and cheese*

Why Pair Food with Wine?

Only in parts of the New World is the question of pairing wine and food difficult. For most of Europe, or other countries with a strong wine drinking history, pairing is not even a second thought. Wine *is* food. It is another component of the meal that is almost always on the table. Europeans do not hold some secret knowledge of pairing, nor are they genetically predisposed to be able to pair wine with food. They just do it. Europeans understand that wine is not a "special occasion" item, it's an everyday item. They sit down for lunch with some wine. The key there is the word "some." Do they ignore pairing—are they really that frivolous with all their food and wine combinations? No. It is all a matter of context.

With that said, let's look at the reasons why wine is typically enjoyed with food.

Refreshment. Wine is a beverage and its purpose it to help wash down a meal. It can also serve to reawaken the palate between bites of food. What wine has in common with most other common beverages is acidity. The acidity of wine is both palate cleansing and refreshing.

Taste and Enjoyment. Wine, as shown previously, has its own flavor profile. Many people choose wine as a beverage just because they like the taste. Some prefer the buttery toastiness of Chardonnay, others the spicy kick of Syrah, or the savory quality of Pinot Noir. The choice has nothing to do with the food; really, it's just what they like. Choosing a favorite wine with dinner is no different than choosing iced tea versus lemonade.

Matching. This is where understanding food flavors and wine flavors begin to come into play. The focus now is on finding a wine that suits a particular dish. The enjoyment and refreshment factors are taken for granted at this stage. Now the focus is on harmony between the wine and the food. Another way to look at it: if you can choose food and wine that doesn't taste *bad* together, you are ahead of the game.

Sublimity. The Holy Grail of food and wine pairing. This level means choosing a wine such that the combination with food is greater than the sum of the parts. Many of the classic food and wine pairs fall in this category, such as Port and Stilton or Foie Gras and Sauternes. This stage is difficult to achieve, and sometimes unattainable. The misconception is that somewhere out there is a wine that will transform a meal, or vice versa. That thought creates a lot of stress for most consumers. Achieving sublimity in a pairing is a goal, but it should not be the only measure of success. When it happens, the combination is spectacular. When it doesn't, it means you keep trying (which is not necessarily a bad thing).

Making the Most of Pairing

A successful food and wine pair is based on knowledge of both areas. It is not enough to be a wine expert and successfully match to food without some knowledge of the culinary arts. It is also not possible to be a chef and suggest wines you have never tasted. This is where experience plays the biggest factor. For a sommelier or anyone who serves wine in a restaurant setting, the tasting note not only tracks what wines have been sampled, it also opens the door to determining which food might pair best. Experimentation (and observation) is the key to success.

As in science, observations that are repeatable, and independent of the experimenter, become tenets upon which further experiments are based. Let's look at the tenets of food and wine pairing.

BALANCE THE WEIGHT

Pairing works best when the weight of the wine is matched with the weight of the dish. We observe weight in a wine as light-, medium-, or full-bodied. In this case it is about the mouth-filling character of the wine. Food is very similar when looking at "weight." Sole is a lighter fish than tuna. Veal is lighter than beef or lamb.

Even cooking methods can alter a dish to be lighter or heavier. Poached chicken breast is not as heavy on the palate as fried chicken. Determining the proper pair can be approached from either the food or the wine angle. If a light-bodied wine is chosen, the dish to pair it to should also be light. The same is true if dinner is chosen first.

What if a light-bodied wine is paired with a full-bodied dish? More than likely, the food will overpower the wine. Matching a grilled rib eye steak with a Vinho Verde would not do the wine any justice. It would taste like tangy water, which is effectively what it is in relation to the steak. The same is true if the roles are reversed. A full-bodied, tannic red wine would overpower a delicate beef carpaccio.

MATCH FLAVOR INTENSITIES

As with weight, one can match the intensity of flavor starting with the wine or with the food. A wine's body is independent of the intensity of its flavors. Some delicate wines are chock-full of aroma and flavor. Some examples of this would be a New Zealand Sauvignon Blanc or a French Red Burgundy. The tasting note tracks intensity of flavor and aromas, so there is a reference for every wine you have tasted. It is possible to rank wines based on flavor intensity, which may make it easier to zero in on the right wine. The weight of a dish is also independent of its flavor profile. A delicate chicken piccata is redolent with the flavors of lemon, garlic, and capers (that is, lightweight but full flavor). A tournedo of beef tenderloin, while weighty, has very delicate flavor.

STAY CLOSE TO HOME

When considering food, it is often easiest to pair a wine that comes from the same area. The cuisine of a place evolved at the same time the wine style did. Especially in Europe, this reinforces the notion that the wine is just another food to be enjoyed. The everyday rustic food of the place often pairs best with the everyday, or simpler, wines of the region. More elegant dishes get the special occasion wines. Another clue to this fact is that many of the dishes use the wine of the region. If that is not a setup pairing, nothing is. So coq au vin, chicken stewed in red burgundy, is crying for red burgundy to be paired with it. Same for beef braised in Barolo.

What about New World and ethnic cuisine? In this case, the "local" connection may not play out. Should you search out a Mexican Cabernet to go with your mole? Is there wine from Vietnam? In these cases, it is best to follow some of the other tenets before trying to keep it local. What about "California Cuisine"? Here it is important where the dish's influence comes from; an Asian fusion style dish may not go with Napa Cabernet, even if they are both "Californian." California produces so many styles and types of wines, it is easy to "stay local" but use the other tenets to make a decision.

Cooking Methods

A guide to whether a dish's weight is heavy or light, intense in flavor or delicate, can be determined by looking at the main cooking method utilized to make the dish. A food product can be altered in weight and intensity just by changing how it was cooked. Methods such as poaching, steaming, boiling, and some deep-frying (like tempura) are delicate and produce dishes that are relatively delicate and light. More concentrated methods of cooking, such as sautéing, roasting, and braising, increase the weight and intensity of a dish. These methods intensify flavor by caramelizing sugars, developing umami (savoriness), or simply concentrating the flavor through long, slow cooking. Finally, there is grilling. This method adds the most weight and intensity. In the case of grilling, there are often added flavors from the char of the grill and some of the smoke. This addition takes the weight and intensity above that of simply roasting or sautéing.

SHOULDN'T TASTE BE A FACTOR?

In the discussion so far, no mention has really been made about the flavors of the wine itself. The true test of a food and wine pairing is how the combination of flavors and tastes are perceived. Let's review the basic tastes: salty, sweet, bitter, sour, and umami. These tastes are the only sensations the tongue perceives. Once smell has been added to the mix, the brain interprets that as flavor. Right now, let's focus on the tastes.

All taste buds are sensitive to the five tastes. Each taste bud, however, does not trigger the same response to each taste, making it appear that there are individual taste buds for each taste. This originally led to the "tongue map," or the belief that sweet is tasted on the tip of the tongue, sour on the sides, bitter at the back. In actuality, all flavors are tasted everywhere on the tongue. Each person may have a different distribution of taste buds, reinforcing the fact that a "tongue map" is outdated.

The interaction of tastes then becomes important to food and wine pairing. If we try to analyze all five tastes in wine against all five tastes in food, we would have twenty-five different combinations. Not all of these taste combinations are important, but many have significant interactions that a sommelier needs to be aware of when pairing wine and food.

The following table summarizes the interactions between tastes. Let's take the interaction of an acidic wine, such as Sauvignon Blanc, with various tastes in food

Interaction of Tastes

	Salty food	Sweet food	Sour food	Bitter food	Fatty food	Savory food	Pungent food
Acidic wine	↓ acidity	↑ in wine	↓ in food ↓ in wine		Cuts fattiness of food	↑ acidity	
Tannic wine	↓ tannin in wine	↑ tannin in wine		↑ tannins	↓ tannins	↓ tannin	↑ heat ↑ tannin
Sweet wine	Match well together	↓ sweetness in wine	↑ sweet				↓ heat
Oaky wine		↑ bitter in wine		↑ bitter			↑ heat ↑ bitter in wine

as an example. If pairing an acidic wine with an acidic food, the first thought would be, "That's way too much acid to handle." In actuality, the interaction neutralizes the acidity. The taste buds are overwhelmed by the acid response, and other flavors are now triggered. This is evidenced in the pairing of Sauvignon Blanc with goat cheese. This regional combination from the Loire region of France works because the tang of the goat cheese is neutralized by the acidity of the Sauvignon Blanc. Now the herbal, grassy notes of the cheese can match with the herbal, grassy notes of the wine.

Acid interacts with sweet components by lessening the sensation of sweet, and increasing the sensation of acid. This means that an off-dry wine will taste dry when paired with an acidic dish. On the opposite side, the sensation of sweet will decrease slightly. The sugar will not seem as cloying. This is evident in wine itself, where acidity is needed to balance residual sugar. For the most part in a wine and food pairing sense, the wine will taste overly acidic, while the sweetness of the dish may be little affected.

By studying the table, it is possible to draw a couple of conclusions. First, acid and salt decrease the intensity of a wine. Wine's refreshment comes from acid, and by adding an acidic component to a dish, the wine will seem less acidic and softer that it would on its own. Because salt works via the same receptor pathways in taste buds, salt has the same affect on wine.

Second, sweetness and umami make wines seem stronger. This observation has larger implications when it comes to food and wine pairing. These two categories cover desserts and most entrees. For a wine to be paired best to a dessert, it must have as much or more sweetness than the dessert does. If the dessert is sweeter than the wine, the extra sweetness will make the wine taste stronger (that is, less sweet and more acidic).

Let's look at chocolate and wine as an example. The most common pairing between chocolate and wine involves Port. This sweet dessert wine has enough residual sugar to stand up against a chocolate dessert. Some adventurous diners will pair chocolate with Cabernet Sauvignon. This pair could work or it could be disastrous, depending on the choice of chocolate. Milk chocolate, which has a higher percentage of sugar, would be horrible paired with Cabernet Sauvignon, making the wine taste more acidic and astringent. Dark chocolate, with lower sugar content and a higher proportion of cocoa, would be a better match to the Cabernet.

There are a few implications of these observations. One school, led by Tim Hanni, MW, promotes that any wine can work with any dish, if the tastes are balanced. If a wine is too strong, the addition of some lemon and salt in the dish will tone down umami influence, making the wine more palatable with the pairing. If a wine is too soft, increasing the umami or sweetness content of the food would then improve the wine's taste. The bottom line of this school is that if all food is balanced between sweet, sour, salt, and umami, then any wine can pair well. Therefore, there should be nothing wrong with having a big, tannic Syrah with oysters, or a delicate Riesling with prime rib. While this matching style makes all wines work with all foods, it does not create those sublime combinations that a sommelier may achieve, except by happy accident. This method may be useful where the bottle of wine is the focus, and the food is a secondary, supporting character.

Another interpretation of the effects suggests that the choice of food can be used to alter the perception of the wine. Take a couple who wish to share a bottle of wine. She prefers big, chewy reds while he prefers softer, more supple reds. How, as a sommelier, could you get a bottle that will be a pleasure to both? By guiding their menu choices. The couple both orders steak. Suggesting that the gentleman get crumbled blue cheese on his steak, while the lady gets sautéed mushrooms, the sommelier will make the wine work for both customers. The blue cheese increases the salt component of the man's dish, softening the wine. The mushrooms, on the other hand, are high in umami, and will increase the intensity of the wine. Again, this may be where food is the focus and the wine is a secondary component.

WHAT ABOUT WINE FLAVORS?

When initially planning a food and wine pairing, most people will look at the flavors in the food and try to match it with flavors in the wine. This creates pairs such as a dish with mushrooms paired with Pinot Noir, or a cream sauce with a buttery Chardonnay. While there is nothing wrong with using this approach, it should be secondary to the taste analysis previously described. Remember, flavors are tastes combined with smells, so taste comes first. Flavors play a secondary role on the palate, especially if they are overpowered by a bad interaction of tastes.

There is one surefire method to get this flavor matching method to work, however. Cook the food with the wine that is to be served. Many classic dishes have a built in wine pairing: coq au Riesling, beef braised in Barolo, pears poached in wine. More commonly, wine is often used in the sauce for the dish with which it will be served. For example, serving a Pinot Noir with duck whose sauce contains Pinot Noir will solidify this pairing.

TEXTURE MATCHING

As with food, texture plays a role in wines and wine pairing. The body or weight of the wine has already been discussed and, as stated previously, the weight of the wine should match the weight of the dish. However, there are other textures that are perceived in wine. In writing a wine tasting note, it is the additional explanation of some of the components that gives the textural clue. A Sauvignon Blanc is said to have sharp acidity, because of the way it bites the cheeks and the palate. Chardonnays can be buttery, not only in flavor, but also in the silkiness they evoke. An intensely tannic wine may have chewy tannins, or they may be velvety. Texture, therefore, becomes the third component to a food and wine pairing.

There is one food-based "texture" that has a significant influence on wine: piquant. Spicy foods, mainly those whose heat comes from black pepper or capsaicin, not only interact with wine in special ways, but the wine also affects the way the food tastes. The least successful combination of spicy food is with tannins. Highly tannic wines will seem even more tannic with piquant items. Concurrently, the spice level of the dish will also increase, so the pairing that develops is highly astringent and piquant. A better pair to spicy food is something with residual sugar. Sugar calms the effect of capsaicin. With the heat subsided a bit, the fruit of the wine will help develop the fruity notes in the chiles, often missed due to the piquancy.

COMPARE OR CONTRAST?

The final question a sommelier planning a wine and food pairing must answer concerns how to approach the pair. While all the components are there—texture, flavor, and taste—the real art is putting it all together. One way to accomplish this is to match components. Acidic foods could be paired with acidic wines in order to develop the other flavors, as seen in the Sauvignon Blanc and goat cheese example. The combination of a mushroom dish with Pinot Noir also is a "matching" style because of the flavors in the wine. Putting a buttery Chardonnay with dish containing a cream sauce is another attempt at matching.

The other method, and one that takes practice and experimentation, is contrast. This involves playing one component against another. For example, instead of a buttery Chardonnay with the cream sauce (a comparison), pair a tangy Pinot Grigio with it. Now the acid of the Pinot Grigio cuts through the fat of the cream, providing a contrast. The classic pairing of Port with Stilton is an example of a contrasting match. Here, the sweetness of the Port match (through contrast) with the saltiness of the cheese. This method can be tricky, and often takes trial and error to find the right balance. If the previous interactions of tastes are remembered in the process, that experimentation can be half the fun for the sommelier and the guests.

Making Pairing Determinations

For sommeliers or chefs who have been working with food and wine for a long time, many pairings are second nature. The guidelines described above become an automatic reference point, so "thinking" about the possible partners is not required. For the majority who have not developed this innate ability, it is necessary to process what combinations will work. While not really a step-by-step process, let's look at the methodology of developing food and wine pairing suggestions.

So far, a lot of considerations have been discussed when thinking about food and wine pairing. There is taste interaction, weight of the dish, intensity of flavor, cooking method, flavors and textures. What is most important? Ultimately, the taste interactions will determine if the pairing is a good one. But how often is the pairing to pure sugar, or straight lemon, or unseasoned meat? Not very often. So the place to start is with an evaluation of the dish and its taste components.

In analyzing a dish, it is important to keep the tastes discussed earlier as a guide. Dishes can be sweet, tangy, meaty, or bitter. They can also be smoky, earthy, or fatty. Dishes that are dominant in one type of taste profile make for easy pairing, because they have specific categories of wines that match well.

"SWEET" DISHES

Sweet dishes, in this case, do not imply desserts. It indicates that the ingredients on the plate have a natural sweetness to them. What foods might fall into this category? Shellfish of all kinds are a good example. Shrimp, scallops, mussels, and lobster all have an inherent sweet quality to them. So do other ocean fish like flounder, halibut, and mahi mahi. In terms of vegetables, almost anything that is picked at the height of season falls into this category. Tomatoes, ripe off the vine, are inherently sweet. Some vegetables have high levels of sugar, like sweet corn, sweet potatoes, carrots, and parsnips. Any dish that may have these as dominant components would be "sweet."

Sometimes the cooking technique influences the dish's level of sweetness. Any dish in which caramelizeation occurs, either through sautéing, broiling, or roasting, has inherent sweetness. The caramelization could be overpowered by other components, so this should be considered after the actual product itself. A rib eye steak, no matter how caramelized the exterior is, will always be meatier than anything else. Similarly, roasted beets will be sweet, but they will have a very strong earthy character.

Wine decisions need to be made based on the "sweetness" of the dish. Even though it is not matching residual sugar levels to actual sweetness of a dessert, the diner's brain is convinced it is eating sweet food and therefore it needs a "sweet" wine. In this case, the "sweet" wine, or at least one that fools the brain to thinking sweet, is something that is fruit-forward. Fruit-forward wines, or those whose fruit flavors and aromas are the predominant flavors, are found in the New World. Therefore, the wine that would best pair to a dish with these components should come from outside Europe.

Let's look at how this may work. Take a pan-seared halibut served with sweet potato puree and succotash as an example. The primary ingredient is halibut (naturally sweet) that is pan-seared (caramelized crust on fish) and served with sweet potatoes and succotash (sweet corn with beans and sweet peppers). Obviously the deck is stacked for this to be a sweet dish. The first decision regarding the wine should be New World. The next may consider the weight of the dish (medium) and its intensity of flavor (fairly high overall). The indicators point to a medium- to full-bodied white wine with intense flavor. The first wine that comes to mind is Chardonnay. But not every Chardonnay is the same, and it is by looking at the tasting notes that the right combination of tastes, flavors, and body points the sommelier in the right direction. Is Chardonnay the only answer? Absolutely not. The choices could range from an oaked FuméBlanc to a Viognier and even to a full-bodied Riesling. The nuances of making the dish, as well as the sommelier's taste experience and adventurousness, will help determine the "best" pairing.

EARTHY DISHES

Earthiness is a little harder to define in food and wine. It is not a taste, nor is it a flavor; it is an impression of earth or a fermented character. This is one category where examples explain better than any definition. Items that are earthy are mushrooms, beans, root vegetables, and greens. Proteins that are earthy are mostly game or freshwater fish, such as rabbit, frog's legs, catfish, and escargot. Earthiness can be increased through the process of curing, as in preserving. Cured meats such as prosciutto and salami are earthier than regular pork.

Wines to pair with earthy dishes are found in the Old World. Many of the wines from European countries are not dominant in fruit, but in other flavors. Those flavors are meant to be reflective of the place of origin, or terroir, and are often influenced by soil. These wines are also meant to be drunk with food, so they are not inherently fruity or sweet, as that is not the best match of a wide variety of items.

How would earthy food and wine pair on the table? An example may be a simple wild mushroom risotto. Grains have an earthiness to them, and adding the intense mushroom flavors increases that character. The wine pairing now is up to the diner. If a white wine is the preferred match (depending on the placement of the course in the menu sequence), a good medium- to full-bodied white wine from Italy, France, or Spain may suffice. If a red wine is more to the diner's liking, a light-bodied red or rosé may be the choice. The choice of an Italian wine may solidify the pairing by matching region of origin, but it is not necessary.

ACIDIC FOODS

Most of the time, the acid component of food or wine plays a secondary role in the flavor profile. In cooking, acid is often used as a seasoning, allowing other flavors to be pulled forward and highlighted. Acid tends to balance the richness of a dish, as in the squeeze of lemon that a piece of grilled salmon, or some fish and chips, might receive. Sometimes, however, acid dominates the flavor profile of an item. This could be tangy tomatoes, citrus, olives, a brined fresh cheese like feta, or capers. It could also be a sauce to a dish, like a Carolina barbecue sauce or hollandaise. Any dish with these components would have acid be a major player in a wine pairing.

Remembering what happens when acid in food is paired with acid in wine, the result is diminished acidity and a brightening of all the other flavors. It should also be remembered that fat reduces the influence of acid, and that acid and sugar do not go well together. That said, pairing wine to acidic foods is as simple as finding wines with prominent acidity.

Why worry about the other interactions, if balancing acid with acid enhances the other flavors? It goes back to the fact that taste interactions trump flavor combinations. For example, Carolina barbecue sauce is a vinegar-based sauce that is also sweet. Depending on the ratio of vinegar to sugar, the influence on the wine will be different. A decidedly tangy sauce would pair well with an acidic wine. A sauce with even slightly more sweet influence will tip the scales so that the interaction is now acid with sweet rather than acid with acid. That makes what was a good pair with the tangier sauce a less desirable pair with the sweeter sauce.

MEATY FOODS

Meaty foods are those rich in the taste of umami. While it is obvious that most land-based proteins would be meaty, there are some items that are vegetable based that may have enough umami to qualify. Portobello mushrooms have this distinction.

Though earthy, they also have an inherent meatiness, or savory richness. A well-made stock or demiglace sauce adds a meaty richness to a dish without directly adding meat as a protein. It is that savory richness that needs to be addressed.

Savory richness in food can come from one of two methods. The item can be cooked hot and fast or low and slow. Broiling or searing increase the concentrated flavor of a meat product, much more than roasting or baking would. There is a caramelization of the meat juices due to the high heat, which also concentrates their flavors. Also, braising, stewing, or true barbequing concentrates the flavors in a meat dish. A good braise or stew will have developed a savory richness that is not obtainable any other way. The low, slow cooking develops the gelatin in a meat, creating mouthfilling richness and more umami taste.

For a dominant meaty flavor, the wine pairing should focus on the richness of the wine. Wines with high intensity of flavor and a mouthfilling quality are the order of business. The acidity level of these wines is also important. Acid is needed in the wine to balance its richness, but it is also necessary to cut the richness of the meat. Without acidity, eating after a few bites would become a chore, with the palate being coated by gelatin and umami. Acidity cuts through that richness, cleansing the palate and preparing the diner for the next bite.

Preferred wines for this category are typically European. This is not so much from the earthiness of the wines, but these wine regions are inherently cooler than most in the New World. White wine choices would include the more familiar grape varieties of Chardonnay, Riesling, and Sauvignon Blanc, but also Gewurztraminer. Red wines, such as a northern Rhone Syrah or a Ribera del Duero Tempranillo, have the requisite acidity while still providing a great deal of rich flavor. The northern Rhone Syrah is a particularly good match for many meaty dishes because its flavor profile includes a meaty, bacon fat–like component.

RICH OR FATTY FOODS

If a dish is very rich, or has a high influence of fat (oil or cream) as a component, the fattiness must be addressed in the pairing. What does fat provide a dish? First, it is mouthfilling richness. It also is palate coating, dampening tastes as time progresses. How does fat interact with wine? The most common effect is that it tames acid. It is important to remember that concept when choosing a wine because it will have to have an acidity level high enough to cut through the fat and still be refreshing. Fat interacts with red wines by taming the tannins. This allows for wines with more tannic structure to be used when pairing than may normally be considered.

How can this richness be observed in food? It can happen through ingredients or sauces. Items such as cheese, puff pastry, coconut milk, oils, fatty meats (bacon, salami, and the like), or nut pastes all contribute fatty richness to food. It is even possible to have the influence of a fat, without it making it to the plate. While salmon is a "fatty" fish, it would be considered lean compared to beef. To increase the richness, the salmon could be poached in olive oil. The fatty richness of the oil will imbue the fish with even more richness.

Sauces are an easy method of infusing a dish with fatty richness. Sauces based on oils, butter, or cream will have a strong enough influence on a dish to affect the wine pairing. These sauces are more of the classical French style, such as mayonnaise, beurre blancs, and vinaigrettes. For each of these, the acid component should also be considered when looking at wine pairs.

What wines work best? High acid levels in both red wines and white wines. This typically means wines from cool regions. More specifically to red wine would also be relatively high tannins. This could be from naturally high tannin wines such as Cabernet Sauvignon, but could also mean a younger wine whose tannins have not mellowed yet. Because matching weight of wine to food is important, the wines selected should be full bodied to hold up to the body provided by the fat component.

SMOKE

Some foods have an inherent smokiness, either because of ingredients or from cooking methods. Foods such as mozzarella, tomatoes, salmon, or pork can all be smoked, and retain some of the smoke in their flavor profile. Barbeque is known for the smoke ring, created as the meat is subject to low and slow heat and smoke for a long period of time. On the opposite end of the smoky spectrum is smoked salmon, which has some hint of smoke, but is more about the richness of the meat or the flavors of the cure.

Imparting smoke through a cooking method is relatively easy. Anything grilled will possess some form of smoke or char flavor. The grill marks on meat, the smokiness of a charcoal grilled burger, or the charred smokiness of vegetables that are placed on a grill before removing the skin, all have a hint (or more) of smoke in the final flavor profile. A third method of instilling smoke would be to use a smoked ingredient in the dish. Ingredients can range from chipotle chiles and pimenton (Spanish smoked paprika) to smoked mozzarella or smoked tomatoes.

Pairing a wine to smoke may seem difficult, because the smoke may have a tendency to overpower the wine. In this case, matching intensity of flavor is extremely important to prevent that from happening. It is possible to match the flavor component as well. In white wines, smoke appears in a few cases. Many Rieslings, Gewurztraminers, and Pinot Gris from Alsace have an underlying smoky nuance. Pouilly Fumé is noted for having gunsmoke character, especially if grown on flinty soils. Other ways white wine gets a smoky flavor is through oak treatment. Oaked Chardonnays will have a toasty, smoky character that will pair well with a smoky component in a dish. For red wines, smokiness can be found in some wines. Northern Rhone Syrah, some southern Rhone Grenache-based wines, some Spanish reds, and southern Italian reds all possess a hint (or more) of smoke. Pairing just to smoke is probably not going to yield a high rate of success. The other flavors and tastes in the food and wine should be considered as well in choosing which wine would pair best with a particular dish.

HERBS

Dishes with strong herbs, either fresh or dried, make fairly easy pairings with wine. Fresh herbs have a bright, lively quality that livens up any dish in which they are used. Dried herbs retain a vegetal quality while also providing an earthiness to a dish. It is a common misconception to try to match to the actual herb flavor, such as trying to match dill with a wine that has dill flavors, or tarragon with something with a licorice flavor. It is best to stay more generalized with the fresh versus dry herbal character as the focus for the pairing.

Fresh herbs and their liveliness require a wine that is equally lively. That means medium to high acidity. The wine should definitely fall into the "refreshing" category based on its acidity. That often means white wines or cool-region red wines. The benefit is that these wines often have a vegetal component to them. The simple pairing would be Sauvignon Blanc, notorious for its vegetal quality. Yet wines like Cabernet Franc or Pinot Noir also have a "green" component to them, even at their ripest.

Dried herbs do need a nod to their earthiness, but keeping the vegetal component is important. Again, refreshing acidity is a key requirement. This often leads to some of the same wines used for fresh herbs. European wines from France or northern Italy make great complements to the dried herbal character of these foods, while still providing refreshing acidity.

SPICES

Cooking with spices is inherently different than cooking with herbs. First, almost all spices are dried. Second, most of their flavor components are fat-soluble, meaning there will be a bit of richness involved in the dish. Finally, while herbs are almost always savory, spices are divided into two camps—sweet and savory. Each needs to be treated differently.

Sweet spices include things like cinnamon, nutmeg, allspice, ginger, and cloves. These are reminiscent of sweet things, like fruitcake or holiday desserts. Their use in some styles of cooking implies sweetness, though no sugar may be present. These spices have the ability to fool the brain into thinking sweet. They are also highly aromatic, often identified by smell before the food is eaten. This is the pattern to follow for a wine pairing. Items redolent with these spices need intense aromatic wines. They also need some inherent "sweetness" to balance that of the spices. That "sweetness" does not always mean the wine has residual sugar. It could also mean the fruit-forward style of a New World wine, or the choice of a varietal known for its "spicy" character.

These spices do come in several guises. They could be mild and sweet, like a Chinese Ginger Beef. They can be tangy, like a Mulligatawny soup. They can be piquant, like a Thai Red Curry or Moroccan tagine. Each of these variations causes a small change in the wine style chosen. The mild spice would match with a wine that has a hint of spice in it. Something tangy would require a wine with a higher acidity level (back to the acid to acid comparision). The piquant dish needs true sweetness. Earlier it was demonstrated that sugar tames piquancy. This would suggest a wine with residual sugar, as well as a spicy character to complement the flavors. Low alcohol would also keep the piquant character remaining from becoming overpowering or making the wine taste "hot."

Savory spices are found mostly in ethnic and regional cuisines. Examples of savory spices would include cumin, caraway, paprika, black and white pepper, and aniseed. These often find their way into meat and vegetable dishes. For the most part, the same rules apply as with sweet spices. Mildly spiced dishes would benefit from spicy wines. Tangy dishes like a lime-tortilla soup may need wine with more acidity. Piquant spiciness in a savory dish, however, would not pair best with residual sugar to tame the heat. The wine that would pair best would be a fruity, dry wine with low alcohol. This pair differs because the combination of residual sugar with the other components of the dish may not be as successful, and would not merit its use to cool off the palate.

The Pairing "Process"

When presented with a dish for which a wine is needed, it is important to consider the most important item on the plate. An appetizer of smoked salmon with crème fraiche and caviar should not be paired to the caviar. The leading component here is the smoked salmon. Only after the attributes of the salmon are considered for weight, intensity, and texture, should the crème fraiche and caviar be considered.

Sometimes, the sauce alters the perception of the dominant item. Take a grilled chicken breast, for example. In analyzing the chicken, we could consider a full-bodied white wine, like an oaky Chardonnay. The grilling could also move the chicken into red wine territory, possibly pairing with a light Shiraz or a Pinot Noir. The choice will be made by the sauce. Serving chicken with a mango salsa may solidify a white wine choice, while a wild mushroom sauce screams for Pinot Noir.

Occasionally, a side dish may tweak a pairing one way or another. A sautéed duck breast served with a black pepper blueberry sauce has all the hallmarks of a Syrah pairing. But which Syrah? Styles vary around the world. The deciding factor in this particular case is a side dish of braised red cabbage. When paired with a fruit-forward Australian Shiraz, the wine tastes bitter, and the fruit in the wine seems nonexistent. Changing the wine to a Rhone Syrah makes a much better pair. The earthiness of the Syrah complements the cabbage and allows the fruit in the wine to come forward, complementing the sauce and duck.

Once the main component has been identified, weight and intensity of wine possibilities can be narrowed. Next, determine if a contrasting or a complementing match is in order. A great way to show off pairing skills would be to make both types of matches to a single dish. Finally, flavors can be analyzed to complement or contrast, followed by textures. It is possible to have some parts of the pair contrast while others complement. This creates an especially dynamic pairing, and one that could be very satisfying to the guest.

As can be seen by the "process" of developing a food and wine pairing, it is really about layers of complexity. It is possible, by only assessing one or two layers of taste, weight, and intensity, to come up with a good pairing. As experience (both in food and wine tasting) grows, it becomes more possible to find pairs that approach synergy. Food and wine pairing has a constant learning curve, thanks to chefs who produce new and interesting dishes, and wine changing with each producer and vintage. It is one subject that sommeliers and chefs do not mind studying and doing "research" on.

Classic Pairs

There are some foods that have always gone together. Whether these all work as examples of perfect pairing is in the perception of the taster, but they do outline some of the underlying principles discussed above.

Port and Stilton (or Sauternes and Roquefort). This pair is a study in contrasts. The wine has a high level of residual sugar and can be moderately acidic, and the cheese has developed a tangy, salty character while aging. These two flavor profiles put together in this pairing are a favorite of most people. There is a contrast and a complementary pairing happening at the same time. The complement is the match of the acid in the wine to that in the cheese, reducing the perception of tanginess in both. Then there is the contrast of the sugar and salt. One additional note to the Port/Stilton pairing: some people can perceive the development of a new flavor that is not in the individual items.

Sauternes and Foie Gras. This combination is all about a complementing partnership, with a supporting contrast. Sauternes is a sweet, rich, silky, mouth-filling wine that is full bodied and envelops the palate in luxury. Foie gras, either as sauté or as a terrine, is rich, fatty, mouth-filling luxury. Note that even the luxury component is complemented by this pairing. The slight contrast of the acidity of the wine against the richness of the liver keeps the pair from being cloying or heavy.

Champagne and Caviar. This pair is another example of matching luxury with luxury, but there is a great deal more going on here. Champagne has intense acidity, a definite mineral character, some yeasty or bready notes on the nose, and of course, bubbles. Caviar is briny, fatty, rich, and has a distinct textural character. How do these work together? On a complementary level, the minerality of the wine matches well to the brininess of the caviar. The bready notes provide extra body to match the fattiness of the caviar. Contrasting the fattiness is the acidity and the bubbles of the wine. The acidity cuts through the richness while the carbonation actively cleanses the palate. Those bubbles provide a textural comparison at the same time. Bursting fish eggs on the palate are mimicked by the bubbly carbonation. This pairing is a good example of the multiple layers that food and wine pairing can develop.

Difficult Foods

Some foods are notorious for making food and wine pairing difficult. In most cases the food has certain properties that alter the perception of the wine dramatically. The most notorious are artichokes, asparagus, eggs, and salad.

Artichokes are unique because they contain a chemical called cynarin, which interacts with the taste buds to make anything tasted after it seem sweeter than it is. For this reason, most of the advice is to avoid artichokes and wine altogether. However, pairing a fairly acidic wine to the artichoke will mimic lemon juice, and bring the pair together. The wine does have to be acidic enough that the increased perception of sweetness does not alter the true character of the wine.

Asparagus is another vegetable that scares away wine pairs. The asparagus is often perceived as being too green and its unique flavor is a tough combination to wine. The "answer" to this match is found regionally. Asparagus is a key component to the food in the Loire valley in France, so that suggests the local grapes of Cabernet Franc and Sauvignon Blanc.

Eggs are problematic because of the yolks. Not only are the yolks high in fat, they are intensely mouth-coating, masking other flavors. The method by which the eggs are cooked plays an important part in deciding whether to pair a wine with them. Typically, because the pairing is so hard, it is best to choose a wine that is not extremely nuanced or intense. It is best to stay with modest wines of moderate acidity to help cut the fattiness.

Salads, in and of themselves, are not the true culprit in this pairing; it's the vinegar. Some chefs resort to changing the acid in a vinaigrette in order to be able to match a wine to it. More amenable acids in a vinaigrette would be verjus (unfermented grape juice), lemon juice, or balsamic vinegar. The acidity of the vinaigrette could also be tweaked by changing the acid to oil ratio, making the acidity less intense. In looking at wine, two components help this pairing. A wine should have increased acidity, to balance that of the vinaigrette, but it could also have some residual sweetness, which would also tame the tang.

Pairing Wine to Cheese

The standard belief is that wine and cheese are a perfect match. If we look at that statement, it is so generalized that it really does not provide any guidance for a good cheese and wine pairing. With almost as many cheeses as there are types of wine, the combinations, both good and bad, are limitless.

This text is not meant to serve as a primer on cheese; however, let's look at some cheese basics. Cheese is a fermented milk product, and as a result it changes with milk, fermenting agent, and age. For the purposes of this text, we will break cheeses down into soft or hard, and mold-ripened or not. The major difference between a soft cheese (like mozzarella) and a hard cheese (like Parmesan) is moisture content. Soft cheeses retain much of the moisture in the cheese making process. Hard cheeses, on the other hand, are made in such a way as to remove a great deal of the moisture. They also tend to be aged longer, allowing for more moisture evaporation.

What does a cheese's moisture content have to do with wine pairing? Moisture content should be viewed as a guide to protein and fat concentration of the cheese. With their higher moisture content, soft cheeses have more "dilute" fat and protein in the cheese. Thus, the cheese is lighter in intensity. Mozzarella, cream cheese, Brie, and fresh goat cheese are all examples of soft cheeses that are fairly light and delicate in flavor. Hard cheeses, containing less moisture, have a higher concentration of fat and protein per piece. They also tend to have a higher salt content than soft cheeses. This means the flavor is more intense, and the cheese is "weightier" than a soft cheese.

Cheese can be paired to wine based on flavor and intensity. And the rules of matching weight levels and intensity levels still stand. A soft cheese will be best paired with a lighter wine, most likely a white wine. Red wines will be too heavy, even Pinot Noir and Gamay, and will overpower the delicate flavor of the cheese. Hard cheeses, on the other hand, need red wine, as they would overpower white wines. In fact, the increased fat and protein of a hard cheese helps soften the tannins of red wines. In all cases, it should be remembered that cheese is basically a very fatty product, and that wine with a good balance of acidity is needed to cleanse the palate and not allow the flavors to be muted.

Mold-ripening refers to a cheese that forms a rind on which a mold, such as Penicillin, grows and aids in ripening the cheese. Blue cheeses are also mold-ripened, but from the interior outward, so a rind typically does not form. In pairing wine to a mold-ripened cheese, especially one with a rind, it is best to look at the interior of the cheese as a guide. For example, Brie was classified as a soft cheese earlier in the discussion. That part of the pairing process remains the same. What makes Brie and other moldy-rind cheeses unique is the interaction of flavor between the rind and the wine. Moldy rinds will make tannins taste bitter and metallic. Therefore, it is best to either remove the rind, or serve these cheeses with white wine. Blue cheese is the exception because the increased salt content softens the tannins before the mold interacts with them. Therefore, they do not become overpowering.

Special Wines or Special Dishes

Previously, it was mentioned that a complementary pairing may include luxury with luxury. In the case of a special wine, the definition of luxury should be fairly specific and related to the ultimate complexity of the wine. As an example, you have the great good fortune to drink a bottle of 1961 Chateau Margaux, a much nuanced, aromatic Bordeaux from a great year. The bouquet and flavors will be developing throughout the time the bottle is consumed, displaying a great deal of complexity. You have two choices as to what to have for dinner. First is a delicious Filet Mignon, wrapped in bacon, with rich mushroom sauce that includes truffles. Second is an herb-crusted rack of lamb, with a simple au jus as the sauce. Which is the correct choice? The lamb. The first thought is that the lamb is too simple for that expensive wine. Exactly. The last thing this food pairing should do to the wine is compete. All those flavors on the beef will overpower the delicate flavors of the wine, making it seem not so special anymore.

On the opposite extreme, take a very complex, nuanced dish, with many flavors happening on the plate. What is a good wine pair? Something simple. Does this mean the wine should not be of equal quality? Absolutely not, but the wine should be able to hold its own without competing on a flavor level with the nuanced dish. So, a plate of choucroute garni (smoked pork items cooked with sauerkraut) is often paired with a simple Alsatian Riesling or Gewurztraminer, which complements without overpowering.

Final Notes

Some wines that may be extremely pleasurable to drink may not be well suited to being "food wines." With modern wines, the biggest detriment to being a good pairing wine is alcohol content. Wines high in alcohol, above 13 percent, do not pair well with food. The increased alcohol is perceived as "hot" and will appear even more alcoholic with many food combinations. Also, many fruit-forward wines are not food friendly. While these are enjoyable to drink alone, they will lose some fruitiness paired with food and will not seem as balanced. The most food-friendly wines are Old World (European) wines. One reason is because they were developed to be on the table with the meal. Old World wines are just another component of dinner. Also, fruit flavors are not the most prominent in European wines, a certain earthiness is. When paired with food, that earthiness matches well to the umami in the dish, and then the fruit bursts forward on the palate. Thirdly, Old World wines tend to have higher acidity, which works better at refreshing the palette.

QUESTIONS

1. What are the reasons wine is paired with food?

2. Describe what is meant by "balancing the weights" when talking about food and wine pairing.

3. Give an example of matching flavor intensities in a food and wine pairing.

4. Why do regional pairings work well?

5. How does cooking method affect the choice of wine in a pairing?

6. How does taste differ from flavor?

7. Discuss how sweetness in food interacts with wine. Discuss how umami interacts with wine.

9. Discuss the interaction of piquant spices with tannin in wine.

10. For each of the following categories, discuss a plan for matching a wine to the food:

Ripe, fresh flavors

Acidic foods

Earthy dishes

Protein-dominant foods

Spicy foods

11. Choose one classic food and wine pair, and describe how the pairing works.

12. Why are eggs considered a difficult food to pair with wine? What is a method of approach for pairing a wine?

13. What philosophy guides pairing cheese with wine?

14. How is a complex wine best showcased in terms of food served with it?

chapter

6

The Health Aspects of Alcohol

*T*here has always been a love-hate relationship with alcohol. Temperance movements around the world have decried it as the root of all evil, while immigrants have claimed it is part of their culture. Recently, scientific studies have been used to rationalize having a drink. But science can also reinforce the negative affects of alcohol on the human body.

Upon completion of this chapter, the student should be able to:

Discuss the "French Paradox" and how it changed wine consumption
Discuss resveratrol and its effects on the body
Explain the negative affects of alcohol consumption

History

Alcohol has been around for thousands of years, and with it, opinions about its consumption. The majority of historical references relate to the outward behavioral and social consequences of consuming alcohol. Many Bible references state that it is not the consumption of wine but drunkenness that should be avoided. Islam forbids alcohol consumption, partially based on the behavior when drunk.

In the seventeenth century, temperance movements began to spring up around the world. The movements bashed "demon liquor" and strove to rid society of the evil drink. Cartoons, pamphlets, and speeches all emphasized the harmful affects on the family and society by drunkards. Eventually, the movements won the argument, if for a short while, with the institution of Prohibition.

On the other hand, alcohol was considered a necessity by other parts of society. Artists, writers, and poets claimed wine as a muse for inspiration. Immigrants fought to keep what they considered a foodstuff on the table. They felt that wine was a part of their cultural heritage and should continue as such.

It was in light of all these factors that the wine industry developed in America, and in the New World. Most of the evidence for or against alcohol consumption was based on behavioral observations. With no other reason to drink than to alter one's state of mind, wine was relegated to minority status.

Recent Developments

The world of wine changed on November 17, 1991. Until then, wine was considered by most Americans as a luxury item, drunk on special occasions, or not of any interest at all. Then, on that Sunday evening, *60 Minutes* broadcast a segment called "The French Paradox." Winemakers, especially red wine makers, had a new ally.

The television segment explored an unusual observation. The French, especially those who lived in the southwest regions of the country, seemed to have very low heart attack rates. This was despite a diet full of artery-clogging fats, unfiltered cigarettes, and minimal exercise. Americans, by contrast had a similar diet regime, but had some of the highest heart attack rates in the world. The most likely reason was the daily, moderate consumption of red wine by the French.

Over the next fifteen years, numerous studies were conducted to study not only the effect of red wine on health, but also alcohol in general. The findings of many studies suggested that while moderate consumption of alcohol had some heart health benefits, red wine was specifically better. In 1992, Harvard researchers stated that moderate alcohol consumption was one of "eight proven ways to reduce coronary heart disease risk."

Research into red wine suggested it contained something that provided even better benefits in reducing heart disease. It is the flavonoids, the color- and tannin-related compounds in red wine, that seem to have antioxidant properties. These flavonoids reduce heart disease risk in three ways:

- Reducing the production of low-density lipoprotein (LDL or "bad") cholesterol
- Boosting the production of high-density lipoprotein (HDL or "good") cholesterol
- Reducing blood clotting

Additionally, in a Dutch study published in 2007, a group of men were studied starting in 1960 to see the effect of drinking wine. It was shown that men who had one drink a week lived an average of four years longer than men who did not.

Resveratrol

Upon further research, it has been shown that the antioxidant resveratrol, which is prevalent in the skins of grapes, has many health benefits. Resveratrol not only has the effect of lowering LDL and raising HDL cholesterol, it has the ability to prevent blood platelets from sticking together. This slows the formation of arterial plaque, a major cause of heart attacks and strokes. Resveratrol has also been shown to regulate nitric oxide. Nitric oxide is a gas that causes smooth muscle tissue to relax. Blood vessels are made from smooth muscle tissue, so the presence of nitric oxide causes them to relax, reducing hypertension and allowing blood to flow smoothly through the vessels.

Aside from heart health, resveratrol has been shown to inhibit tumor development by causing certain cancer cells to self-destruct. This has been demonstrated with breast cancer, skin cancer, and leukemia. Resveratrol has also been shown to inhibit colon and prostate cancer growth. Resveratrol is also known as a phytoestrogen, meaning that it is a plant-based compound that mimics estrogen in the human body. Because of this, resveratrol may protect against estrogen depletion in the body.

Other Antioxidants

Resveratrol is not the only antioxidant found in grapes. Another flavonoid, saponin, is found in red wine as well as in olive oil and soybeans. Saponin has been shown to protect against heart disease by reducing levels of LDL cholesterol. Another antioxidant, quercetin, is being studied for its value in preventing lung cancer.

How to Get the Best Effect

Resveratrol and other antioxidants are in the skins and seeds of all grapes. However, white wine has small amounts of these antioxidants because the juice is separated from the skins early in the process, preventing adequate extraction of the antioxidants. Therefore, red wine is the best source. Resveratrol levels vary with the grape varietal. It appears that the antioxidants in the skin are there to protect against mildew and fungus infections. These are common in cool-weather grapes, so cool-weather reds, such as Pinot Noir, appear to have the highest levels of resveratrol. Cabernet Sauvignon and Petit Sirah also have high levels, most likely due to the thickness of their skins rather than to any cool-weather effect. Wines such as Merlot and Zinfandel have some of the lowest levels of resveratrol for red wines. Recent research has shown the native American grape, Muscadine, has more resveratrol than any red grape. This may indicate grapes from humid climates, as well as cool, may serve as a good source of resveratrol.

Moderation is also key. Moderate consumption for a man is one or two four-ounce glasses of wine a day. For a woman, the recommended consumption is one four-ounce glass daily. Increasing the consumption over the moderate level did not show a marked improvement in heart health, but rather, began to show the detrimental effects of increased alcohol consumption.

NEGATIVE AFFECTS OF ALCOHOL CONSUMPTION

In general, high consumption levels of alcohol (of any form) increase health issues. Those who consumed three or more drinks per day risked elevated serum triglyceride (fat) in the blood stream. Long-term, excessive consumption can damage the liver, pancreas, and nerve cells.

Allergies

Allergies affect many wine drinkers. The most common complaint is that consumers are allergic to sulfites. This is often the rationale for people who get headaches drinking red wine. As discussed previously, the level of sulfites is actually lower in red wine than it is in white wine. If the consumer can eat dried fruit, or bagged, processed salad greens (both of which contain more sulfites than wine), the issue is probably not sulfites.

One cause of headaches from red wine consumption is a class of compounds known as phenols. These compounds include the color and tannin components of red wine. In some people, the flavonoids in the wine inhibit an enzyme in the gastrointestinal tract. The function of the enzyme is to break down phenols before they enter the blood stream. If the enzyme is inhibited, the phenols are absorbed, and the result is headaches. Young, tannic wines are more likely to cause headaches in those whose enzymes are inhibited. Older wines, whose phenols have decreased due to aging, are less likely to cause problems.

NASA scientists have used space technology to narrow down the suspects even more in the red wine headache debate. Using a device meant to search for life on Mars, scientists have found that red wine contains high levels of biogenic amines, such as histamine, that is most likely the culprit for causing headaches. Those drinkers who are susceptible to getting headaches from red wine often have a lower level of diamine oxidase, which is the enzyme that breaks down biogenic amines in the intestines.

Finally, there is a percentage of the population, mainly of Asian descent, that does not have an enzyme needed to break down alcohol in the liver. If this enzyme is not present, acetaldehyde builds up in the person's system. The symptoms of this are facial flushing, headaches, nausea, and rapid heart rate. The symptoms arise so quickly that many who are afflicted cannot have even a single drink.

Alcoholism

Excessive consumption of alcohol can lead to serious health issues. Liver cirrhosis, high blood pressure, and ulcers are just some of the diseases for which excessive drinkers are at risk. Excessive drinkers are also at risk for alcoholism.

Alcoholism can be classified as either abuse or dependence. Abuse is the excessive consumption of alcohol, often as a result of societal pressure or emotional causes. Dependence begins when the body begins to adapt to high consumption levels of alcohol. It appears that the body changes in brain chemistry and in endocrine functions. The drinker builds a tolerance for alcohol, and needs more in order to obtain the effect that fewer drinks used to provide. The body may change to the point where alcohol is craved, and the drinker spends most of his or her time drinking or trying to get a drink.

There is a debate in the medical community as to whether alcoholism is a societally based issue or a genetic one. It has been shown that the propensity for becoming an alcoholic runs in families. It is also true that people make a choice to drink in order to relieve social pressure. In either case, alcoholism is a form of drug abuse, and results in severe health issues for the victim.

SUMMARY

Alcohol consumption can be beneficial to the human body, if kept in moderation. It has been shown that moderate consumption of red wine has benefits for cancer prevention and preventing heart disease. Scientists and doctors are constantly uncovering more of the benefits of alcohol, particularly red wine consumption. On the other hand, some members of the population are not as tolerant of alcohol consumption as others. Also, alcohol abuse is detrimental to the drinker's well-being and overall health.

KEY TERMS

Flavonoid

Resveratrol

Phenol

French Paradox

QUESTIONS

1. What is resveratrol?

2. What is the "French Paradox"?

3. What health conditions has red wine been shown to influence?

4. Discuss some of the negative effects of alcohol consumption.

PART TWO

wines
from **international grapes**

There are over three thousand varieties of grapes in vitis vinifera, but only a handful make good wine. Of those that make good wine, eight are known to make great wine and have spread across the globe. These eight are the backbone of the wine industry and are the most familiar and most commercially successful varietals. Each has unique attributes and requirements, which is reflected in the top-quality wines that they make.

chapter

7

Chardonnay

*I*f there is one wine that made the leap from grape varietal to "brand," it is Chardonnay. The word has become synonymous with white wine in many American restaurants, and elicits reactions from all wine drinkers (though not all the comments may be favorable). Chardonnay is accessible to everyone—consumers and growers alike. It is the ultimate blank canvas that allows for expression of the site, or the skills of the winemaker. No other grape is as adaptable and malleable as Chardonnay.

Upon completion of this chapter, the student should be able to:

> *Describe the vineyard conditions preferred by Chardonnay*
> *Describe unique characteristics of making Chardonnay wines*
> *Discuss ageability of Chardonnay wines*
> *Outline classic regions for quality Chardonnay*
> *Describe styles of Chardonnay wines*
> *Outline typical food pairings with Chardonnay*

In the Vineyard

Any up-and-coming wine region that wants to get recognized has a friend in Chardonnay. The grape is relatively easy to grow, and is very adaptable to climate and soil. Unlike many other grape varietals, Chardonnay is a cool-weather grape that can also perform well in warm weather. It is no surprise, then, to see Chardonnay grown in the chilly fields of Champagne, as well as in the blistering heat of South Australia. It also springs up in nontraditional wine regions of India, China, Thailand, and England.

Chardonnay's origins are in the Burgundy region of France, and it is thought to be named after the village where it was first grown. Initial determination of Chardonnay's lineage was based on ampelographic analysis and stated that Chardonnay was one of the many mutations of Pinot Noir. Visually, Chardonnay is very similar to Pinot Blanc (also a mutation of Pinot Noir), and in parts of Burgundy its supposed heritage was acknowledged in the name Pinot Chardonnay. Only recently have some Italian winemakers determined that they actually have Chardonnay and not Pinot Blanc. Genetic analysis indicates that Chardonnay is not a mutation of Pinot Noir, but rather, an offspring. Chardonnay has been shown to be a cross between Pinot Noir and Gouais Blanc, a local "throwaway" grape.

Chardonnay is not considered "soil-specific." It can grow in almost any soil, with the exception of wet soils or those that are rich in organic matter. Because Chardonnay is a relative blank slate in terms of its own flavor and aroma profile, it is easily a medium by which to express terroir. Soils high in limestone, such as those in Champagne and Chablis, are expressed as steely and minerally wines. Chardonnay planted on other soil types are often vinified in a way that expresses the winemaker more than the vineyard.

The vine is an early budding variety and an early ripening variety. Early budding puts the vines in danger from spring frosts, which can wipe out new buds and flowers. The grower has a choice of methods to mitigate the problems from early budding. Some choose to use *chaufferettes,* or small oil burners, to raise the ambient temperature when frost is imminent. More often, growers use an aspersion technique, which sprays the vines with water while the temperature drops. The newly formed buds are coated in ice, but not the sharp crystals produced by frost. The buds are protected by the ice from any further drop in temperature below freezing, and do not freeze themselves due to the internal sap movement.

Chardonnay is prone to uneven fruit set, especially if the weather during inflorescence is cool and wet. With an early budding variety in a cool region, this is a very likely possibility. Some growers will prune the vines later in the season, which can delay flowering for up to two weeks. That may be just enough time for the weather to warm, and for better fruit set.

European versus American measurements

1 hectoliter (hl) = 26.4 gallons

1 hectare (ha) = 2.47 acres

During growth, Chardonnay is a very vigorous vine. Unless deterred, more energy and nutrients will go into shoot formation and foliage growth than ripening the grapes. This may result in vegetative flavors in the grapes rather than full fruit flavors. The French slow the growth of Chardonnay in Burgundy and Champagne by employing high-density plantings (on the order of 3,000 vines per acre). In California and Australia, the vines are spaced farther apart (about 400 per acre), and growth control comes from aggressive pruning and leaf plucking.

While vigorous vegetative growth can hinder ripening, apparently the quantity of fruit produced by a Chardonnay vine does not greatly affect its quality. The "homeland" of Chardonnay, Burgundy, typically produces 35–40 hectoliters per hectare, while in Champagne and New Zealand, equally good quality wines come from 100 hectoliters per hectare production.

Chardonnay's ripening ability is a blessing and a curse for many growers. The ability to achieve high sugar levels is a great benefit to many winemakers. However, while it achieves high sugar, the acid level drops very quickly upon ripening. Deciding upon when to harvest is often determined not by sugar level but by watching the acid level to avoid a flabby wine.

There are several different clones to choose from when planting Chardonnay. Several of the New World wine regions (areas of California, Australia, and South Africa in particular) were initially planted with inferior clones, because at the time that was all that was available or all that was propagated. Clonal selection is preferred over field-selected vines because it guarantees the vines will be virus-free. Virus-infected vines have a much shorter lifespan than noninfected vines. Newer clones developed in Burgundy, known as Dijon clones, are replacing inferior vines in cooler regions, and as a result are improving the quality of the wines produced there.

In the Winery

Winemakers small and large, bulk and boutique, all love Chardonnay. The grape makes wine that has been described as adaptable and consistent, and has been derided as "formulaic." Chardonnay makes wine that is inherently drinkable, which appeals to every budding winemaker. Whether the vineyard is in England or India, Hunter Valley or Napa, making a Chardonnay puts the winery into the marketplace. Making Chardonnay serves as the training wheels many new regions need before they find their stride with signature varietals and top-level wines.

Chardonnay is a relatively neutral grape, and as such can be manipulated to create a variety of wines. While the varietal character alone can be difficult to determine, the grape has attributes that can be enhanced or diminished, depending on the winemaker's preferences. Whether from a cool climate or a warm climate, Chardonnay will provide plenty of sugar to make a high-alcohol wine, as well as plenty of extract to provide body. More than any other varietal, Chardonnay has the ability to reflect the differences between cool and warm regions. In cool regions Chardonnays tend to be lean, steely, and acidic. In warm regions the tendency is toward melony flavors and low acidity (unless picked early, in which case there is less flavor and extract).

When the grapes arrive at the winery, the winemaker has a multitude of choices with Chardonnay. Treatment of the grapes and juice influence the fermentation and the flavor profile. Typically, the grapes are crushed and pressed immediately, yielding clean juice. Occasionally, when a large quantity of grapes enters the winery, they are crushed but not pressed immediately. The skins macerate in the juice and can result in higher extraction of flavor and color. The deep golden Chardonnays of years past often had the skins briefly macerated after crushing.

Fermentation can take place in temperature-controlled stainless steel vats, or can be in oak barrels. Enhancements to the juice depend on where the grapes were grown. In Burgundy and Champagne, chaptalization is allowed to increase the potential alcohol content of the wine. In the Mâcon, wines are chaptalized to compensate for early picking, in an attempt to save the acid in the grapes. Warmer regions like California and Australia resort to acidification of the juice.

The decisions around fermentation are often based on the wine style the winemaker is trying to produce. If classic Burgundian techniques, such as barrel fermentation, malolactic fermentation, and battonage, are employed, the buttery, toasty attributes of the wine are elicited. If stainless steel tanks and minimal aging are employed, a lean, steely, crisp Chardonnay results. If New World techniques are favored (skin maceration, low-temperature fermentation, and ultra-hygiene), lush, fruit-forward wines result. The technique of choice is no longer determined by region or tradition. It is just as common to find New World techniques in Europe as it is to find Burgundian techniques in Australia.

Classic Regions

Chardonnay is grown around the world, but some areas are known for historically producing great wines. The homeland of Chardonnay is Burgundy. Except for one or two areas, the best white wine from Burgundy legally must be made from Chardonnay. The top white Burgundies in the world, Montrachet and Meursault, are the model around which the majority of Chardonnay production around the world has been built. The best white Burgundies come from a subregion of the Cote d'Or, known as the Cote du Beaune. This region has a prominent band of limestone that anchors the soil and provides perfect vineyard sites for Chardonnay production. The aspect of the vineyards chosen for Chardonnay allow for sun exposure from dawn to at least midafternoon.

The cooler region of Chablis makes crisp, clean, steely wines from Chardonnay, in contrast to those from the Cote d'Or or the Maconnais. The area is known for its unique soil, the sedimentary remnants of an old ocean bed composed mainly of fossilized oyster shells. The soil, first analyzed in England, is called Kimmeridgean soil. It is the chalk of the White Cliffs of Dover, but also appears in Sancerre and in Champagne. This calcium-rich soil, and the northerly latitude, contributes to the Chablis style of Chardonnay.

Champagne is an important region for Chardonnay production, in particular the Cotes des Blancs area. Here, Chardonnay is the only white grape used in the production of Champagne. The soil in the region is similar to Chablis, but being farther north, it is more difficult to ripen the grapes. Hence, they have very high acidity and just enough sugar to create a stable wine. The juice from Chardonnay is typically blended with that of Pinot Noir and Pinot Meunier to broaden the flavor profile of the wines.

In the New World, there are two areas that produce noted Chardonnays, Australia and California. With their ripe flavors, easy drinkability, and splash of oak, the Australian Chardonnays helped to create Chardonnay into the "brand" it is today. The key regions are the Hunter Valley, Victoria, and Margaret River. All these regions are cool for Australia, especially Victoria, which is the southernmost region. Each of these areas have slightly different styles, but the ripeness of the fruit makes them unmistakably Australian.

California also set its fortune with Chardonnay. In looking at California Chardonnay over the past thirty years, it appears to have had an identity crisis. Initial Chardonnay production was aimed at creating a New World equivalent of Montrachet. This is evidenced with Chateau Montelena being chosen as the best Chardonnay in the Judgment of Paris in 1976. However, producers soon began overplaying the oak, so that wines began to taste more and more of oak and less and less of Chardonnay. A consumer backlash resulted. The trend then became to produce very clean, precise "recipe" wines. Many winemakers, having been educated at University of California-Davis, had a formula for creating wine. The wines in this era were technically correct, but often lacked any personality or "soul." The modern style that has developed is a balance between the two styles.

California producers use technology and innovation to create well-crafted wines, while embracing the ideas of single-vineyard wines, small-batch production, and/or unique expression of a California style.

Wine Styles

Chardonnay's malleability allows winemakers to choose the style they want to create. Chardonnay is typically found in sparkling and still wines, but can even be made into dessert wines. What drives a winemaker to choose one style over another is climate and soil.

COOL-CLIMATE CHARDONNAY

Chardonnays grown in cool climates—Chablis, Champagne, New Zealand, Carneros—are inherently acidic and lean. One wine style that benefits from these attributes is sparkling wine. Chardonnay is commonly used as a blending grape in Champagne, but it makes a classic sparkling wine known as blanc de blancs ("white from whites"). Blanc de blancs is 100 percent sparkling Chardonnay. The wine is crisp, lean, with the fruit profile expected of a cool-weather white—apple and citrus. Of course, there are the quintessential Champagne notes as well of toast and biscuits (see Chapter 22).

Still table wine made from cool-weather Chardonnay is often made as expression of terroir. Chablis is noted for its steely minerality and high acidity. New Zealand Chardonnays are more fruit-forward and buttery, the result of malolactic fermentation, and are often unoaked. The signature of a cool-weather Chardonnay is the acidity. Often these wines do not have the extraction or ripeness to create full-bodied wines, and as a result are not subjected to oak treatment. In recent years, with warmer vintages occurring in Chablis, some vintners are experimenting with oak influence.

Chardonnays from the Cote d'Or or Macon in Burgundy are fuller bodied and have been influenced by oak. The wines of Montrachet and Meursault are the ideal to which many winemakers, New World and Old World alike, aspire. Meursault produces a Chardonnay noted for toasty hazelnut flavors along with a buttery creaminess. The wines from Montrachet are the most expensive and the most long-lived Chardonnays in the world. These wines are much leaner and steelier than Meursault, gaining notes of honey and smoke with age.

WARM-CLIMATE CHARDONNAYS

The New World style of Chardonnay is about accessibility, approachability, and drinkability. Australian Chardonnays are prime examples of this style. The wine is very fruit-forward, with lots of butter, cream, and vanilla from American oak influence. Some wines can taste like a liquid version of buttered popcorn. The idea is not to create another Montrachet, but to have a wine that is easy to drink, enjoyable, and flavorful. Because these wines are so approachable for new drinkers, they can be considered the "entry-level" wine for many consumers. With their intense buttery and toasty components, however, these wines are not the most food friendly.

Not all New World Chardonnays fall into the New World category. Many try to emulate Montrachet, just as many European wines are fruit-forward and approachable. That is one characteristic of Chardonnay: the wines' styles are no longer restricted to the region from which they come. Toasty, oaky Chardonnays can now be found in Chablis, and lean, minerally Chardonnays in California. The style all depends upon the producer.

CELLARING CHARDONNAY

The intent and skill of the producer determines when Chardonnay is best drunk. Some New World producers make a wine that is meant for quick consumption, within a year or two of the vintage. Regions that produce more concentrated fruit or cooler regions with their increased acidity may generate wines that are best drunk five to ten years after the vintage. The epitome of aged Chardonnay, the Grand Cru white Burgundies, are often not even ready for ten years and can last as long as thirty years. The simplest rule is to drink warm-weather Chardonnays now, and reserve the cool-weather ones for later.

Food and Wine Pairing

How to pair a Chardonnay with food depends on the extent of oak treatment the wine has seen. A light, unoaked Chardonnay is the perfect match for seafood. Chablis and oysters is a classic food and wine pairing. As the seafood dishes become richer or more intensely flavored, lightly oaked Chardonnay is an excellent pairing. The buttery creaminess of malolactic fermentation in Chardonnay makes these wines great complements to cream-based sauces or cream- and cheese-based dishes. Very richly oaked Chardonnays could substitute for a light red in some cases, matching very well with a simple grilled filet mignon. The slightly sweet, oaked Chardonnays could be used with sweeter Asian food, so long as tannins from the wood are not noticeable in the wine.

Basics for Chardonnay (shar-doh-NAY)

Climate	Very adaptable to climate
	Makes great wine in cool or warm regions
Soil	Prefers limestone and chalk
Disease susceptibility	Uneven fruit set in cool, wet weather
Growth habit	Very vigorous
Characteristics	Rapid ripening causes fast drop in acidity
	Yields vegetal flavors if canopy not controlled
	Early budding and early ripening
Average yield	35 hl/ha in France, up to 100 hl/ha for mass commercial production
Fermentation quirks	Very open to winemaker influence
Classic region	Burgundy (Montrachet, Meursault, Cote de Beaune)
	California (Sonoma and Napa)
	Australia (Victoria, Margaret River, Hunter Valley)
	Common worldwide

Cool-Climate Chardonnay Tasting Note

Appearance	Pale straw fading to watery rim, sometimes with hint of green
Nose	Minerality: chalk, steel, rocks
	Tart fruit: green apple, citrus, pear or peach in ripe vintages
Palate	High acidity
	Drying minerality, chalkiness
	Tart fruit: green apples, citrus, pear
	Sometimes butter or cream (New Zealand)
	Light to medium bodied, medium finish
Ageability	Ability to age for 5 to 10 years

Warm-Climate Chardonnay Tasting Note

Appearance	Yellow to gold with slight decrease in color toward rim
Nose	Vanilla, toast, biscotti, pie crust, popcorn
	Warm, ripe fruits: peach, tropical fruits, melon
	Vegetal if underripe or large leaf canopy: creamed corn
	Thread of minerality
Palate	Low to medium acidity
	Possibly light tannins from oak barrels
	Ripe yellow fruits, tropical fruit
	Vanilla, toast, popcorn, biscuits
	Full bodied, long finish
Ageability	Ability to age for decades
	More commercial versions: drink within two years of vintage

QUESTIONS

1. Discuss the challenges of growing Chardonnay in cool climates.

2. What adjustments need to be made to Chardonnay when grown in warm climates?

3. Discuss the differences in wine styles between cool-climate and warm-climate Chardonnay.

4. Why does Chardonnay have a high affinity for oak?

5. What are the soil affinities for Chardonnay?

6. What techniques are used in Burgundy to ensure ripe Chardonnay grapes?

7. What are the important regions for making Chardonnay?

8. Describe the differences between Old World Chardonnay and New World Chardonnay.

9. How does malolactic fermentation affect the flavor of Chardonnay?

10. Write a tasting note for a barrel-fermented New World Chardonnay.

11. Write a tasting note for a Chablis.

12. Discuss the food and wine pairing options for Chardonnay.

chapter *8*

Pinot Noir

*I*f a grape variety could take on a mythical mystique, Pinot Noir would be the one. It has been called the Holy Grail of vines and of wines. Before the 2004 film Sideways, *before the French invested in Oregon, there was the aura and mystique of Burgundy. What monks and terroir created over three hundred years, the New World and other European countries have tried to reproduce in merely thirty years. Whether the subject is an established Pinot Noir producer or a new startup, one thing is certain: Pinot's charm will always be captivating and elusive.*

Upon completion of this chapter, the student should be able to:

> *Describe the vineyard conditions preferred by Pinot Noir*
> *Describe unique characteristics of making Pinot Noir wines*
> *Discuss ageability of Pinot Noir wines*
> *Outline classic regions for quality Pinot Noir*
> *Describe styles of Pinot Noir wines*
> *Outline typical food pairings with Pinot Noir*

In the Vineyard

Pinot Noir, as a varietal, is very old. This is evidenced by its frailty, which translates into its ability to mutate easily. The Roman writer Columella mentions Pinot Noir growing in northeastern Gaul (modern France) in the first century B.C.E. It appears Pinot Noir was grown in that region of Gaul before the Roman invasion. A great deal is written about Pinot Noir after the fall of the Roman Empire, in the vine growing and wine making texts of the Benedictine monks based at Cluny, and the Cistercian monks throughout northeastern France.

Recent genetic analysis suggests that Pinot Noir may be the offspring of a cross with Pinot Meunier, which had previously been thought to be a mutation. Whichever turns out to be true, it seems Pinot Meunier is at least as old as Pinot Noir. Another possible parent of Pinot Noir is the Austrian red grape, St. Laurent. One determination was consistent in all the testing: the other parent of Pinot Noir is Gewurztraminer.

Pinot Noir has a preference for calcium-rich soils. Some of the more notable regions for Pinot Noir are areas of chalk, limestone, or calcareous marl. The common component of these soils is calcium. In its mineral forms, calcium is a cationic (positively charged) ion that forms a salt. It is through cation-exchange that nutrients cross the root cell barriers and enter the plant. The plant, in effect, exchanges one positively charged ion for another. The roots will exchange sodium or potassium for the calcium in the chalky soil. Once the calcium is freed from being a salt in the soil, it can be absorbed by the roots.

Other preferences include shallow soils, those that drain well, and those that are low in fertility. While these are the preferred soils for Pinot Noir, variations from these do not preclude good grapes from being grown. Pinot Noir is noted for its ability to show off the nuances of the soil profile. In Burgundy, a high level of limestone in the soil tends to yield wines with a lot of aromatic components. Pinot Noir grown in more iron-rich clay tends to yield more tannic, bigger wines.

Pinot Noir is considered a cool-climate red varietal. It is both an early budding and an early ripening variety. While early ripening is a benefit in a cool climate, the early budding can result in a host of problems for Pinot. Budding early in a cool region leaves the vine susceptible to frost. In Pinot Noir's case, the secondary growth after frost damage is very slow, and will curtail production that year. If the buds make it through without a frost, the next danger is at flowering. Cool climates in spring have notoriously changeable weather, and a bout of cool weather at flowering can result in coulure in Pinot Noir.

Though Pinot Noir is a cool-weather grape, it needs plenty of sunshine. The vineyards where Pinot is planted often have the best exposure to the sun for the grapes in the region. The grapes should be exposed to the sun from dawn until as late in the day as possible. The aspect should also allow for the temperature to cool during the nighttime. This continued cooling each night allows the aromatic compounds to develop in the grapes.

Growth during the season in Pinot has challenges of its own. Because Pinot Noir is a relatively thin-skinned grape, it is therefore even more susceptible to rot. Pinot clusters are very tight. The lack of air circulation in the clusters, combined with a cool, possibly moist climate, is a recipe for rot and mold. The shape of the vine as it grows is greatly influenced by how it was pruned over winter. Vines pruned too short will form bushes, and the grapes will not receive enough sun to ripen. Some producers leave longer canes but trim the buds in order to create ample air circulation through the growing canopy later.

Crop thinning, or green harvest, is common among many producers. The goal is to keep the vine in balance. This thinning typically occurs after veraison so any green berries can be removed at the same time. Pinot Noir is known to lose a great deal of aromatic complexity if overcropped. The ideal yield is thought to be about 35 hectolitres per hectare. Some of the top producers, such as Domaine de la Romanée Conti, decrease yields through crop thinning even further to around 24 hl/ha.

Pinot Noir does have other disease susceptibilities. As with most cool-climate grapes, mildews can be a problem during the growing season. Vines are also susceptible to viruses, particularly those that cause fanleaf disease and leaf roll. In each of these cases, the deformation of the leaves lowers the amount of photosynthesis that can take place, and the grapes have difficulty ripening properly. A final, and extreme, disease the Pinot Noir seems prone to is Pierce's Disease, which is an infection by the bacterium *Xylella fastidiosa*, transmitted by the glassy winged sharpshooter. The bacterium clogs the xylem of the vines, stopping water and nutrient flow and eventually choking the vine. Because Pierce's Disease is restricted to portions of the United States with mild winters, it is only Pinot in these areas that is affected.

The final issue most growers contend with regarding Pinot Noir is the short lifespan. The vines begin to die off around the thirty-year mark, making them some of the shortest-lived varieties of vitis vinifera. Considering that the first six years of a vine's production are not particularly useful for fine wine making, a vintner has only about twenty years of production before the vines need to be replaced.

If there is one grape varietal that is impossible to generalize, it is Pinot Noir. Being such an "old vine," it is extremely susceptible to mutation. Besides new varietals, such as Pinot Gris or Pinot Blanc, that have arisen from such mutations, there is a large collection of clones that have developed. Some growers claim as many as

250 different clones of Pinot Noir, others more accurately state there are at least 1000 clones. In Burgundy, 35 clones are recognized legally for production.

The choice of clone is extremely important in growing Pinot Noir. Some clones yield grapes that barely make a wine that would pass as a rosé, others produce big, jammy flavors and dark color. Some clones are more elegant and perfumed, others are chunky. Some yield small crops of fruit, others large quantities. Newer clones, the Dijon clones, have been developed in recent years to improve the choices for growing Pinot Noir. While these newer clones have better varietal characteristics, and are virus free, they also produce lots of grapes, which detract from quality.

Newer vineyard techniques, besides the use of the Dijon clones, include planting multiple clones of Pinot Noir, and harvesting separately. The clones are then vinified separately to utilize only the best of the group. Other producers do not replant with purchased clones. They take field cuttings of healthy vines, called massal selection, and replant using vines that produce well in their particular meso-climate. These producers believe that the complexity of the wine comes from a complex mix of vines.

In the Winery

If there is a wine whose vinification procedures are more akin to art than science, it is Pinot Noir. For Pinot Noir, the wine making is just as finicky, exasperating, and satisfying as the grape growing. For a winemaker to succeed in obtaining the "Holy Grail," the first step is determining which Grail to pursue. Pinot can be light and refreshing, aromatic and earthy, or deep and long-lived. None is really the archetypal Pinot Noir, and they all are the archetype. More than any other wine, the "goal" in making Pinot Noir is perfection, but a perfection that is impossible to define or achieve.

Production of still, red table wine from Pinot Noir grapes requires extra effort to extract color, tannin, and flavor. Because Pinot is a thin-skinned grape, there is not the concentration of flavor and color compounds typically seen in red grapes. In contrast, Pinot Noir is high in aromatic compounds compared to other red grapes.

In order to get as much extraction out of the grapes in a short period of time, two different techniques can be used. One technique involves warming the must to promote extraction. If the grapes are viewed as being similar to a tea bag, the warmer the liquid, the more color and flavor is extracted from the grapes. Therefore, especially in cool climates, it is beneficial to warm the must until the fermentation can generate enough heat of its own. The second method is to use a rotary fermenter. The constant mixing of the grape skins into the fermenting juice facilitates better extraction of color and flavor.

AGING

Pinot Noir is typically aged in wood, but often the barrels have already been used for previous vintages. This eliminates any predominant oak influence, which would obscure any varietally based aromatics. What old oak barrels do allow is controlled oxidation, or oxidative aging. Therefore, Pinot Noir is allowed to mature in barrel with minute oxygen exposure before bottling. Only in some of the top *crus* of Burgundy might there be oak influence, and if so, extremely subtly.

SPARKLING WINE PRODUCTION

Pinot Noir is a major component of Champagne production, and its treatment differs significantly from the production of still red wine. The method for making sparkling wines is discussed in a later chapter, so the focus here is the treatment of Pinot Noir in the sparkling winery. The objective for using Pinot to make a sparking wine is to prevent color and tannin extraction. The grapes are handled very delicately, so as to avoid any bursting of the grape berry, causing accidental extraction of color and tannin. The grapes are pressed soon after picking, often while still out in the fields. The colorless juice is then transported back to the winery for the remainder of the process.

CLASSIC REGIONS

The homeland of great Pinot Noir is Burgundy, specifically the Cote de Nuits in the northern part of the Cote d'Or. Pinot Noir here is used as a vehicle to taste the soil in the glass. It is said the Cistercian monks, after clearing a vineyard site, tasted the soil before they planted grapes to determine which grape variety to plant. Top Pinots from the Cote d'Or still reflect the variation in the soils.

The quintessential Pinot Noir is from Vosne-Romanee. These wines are described as being "an iron fist in a velvet glove." It is powerful, intense and rich, yet it is also velvety and smooth. Other wines which are great reflections of Pinot Noir are the premier and grand crus of Gevrey-Chambertain, Aloxe-Corton and Chambolle-Musigny.

An indication of the ability of Pinot Noir to translate terroir into wine can be seen in Pommard and Volnay. These two communes are neighboring villages in the northern part of the Cote de Beaune. Volnay is the softer and more nuanced of the two, while Pommard is firmer and more robust. The French would describe Volnay as feminine and Pommard as masculine wines. The difference lies in the soil. Volnay has more limestone influence, which develops more aromatics in the grape. Pommard has more clay and iron in the soil and therefore the grapes are expressed with more tannins and color.

There is only one other major French area for Pinot Noir production and that is Champagne. As stated previously, Pinot Noir is one of two red grapes that form the backbone of the sparkling wine, Champagne. Here the goal is not ripeness per se; it is the retention of acidity for the base wine. Pinot Noir accounts for over one-third of the grapes planted in Champagne, and only in the areas such as Montagne de Reims and Ay that have warmer microclimates.

In the rest of Europe, the plantings of Pinot Noir are slim, if not bordering on barely experimental. In Germany, Spätburgunder, as Pinot Noir is known, accounts for most of the red wine produced in the country. In Switzerland, Pinot Noir is used as one of the blending grapes to make Dôle. In Italy, mainly in Lombardy and Oltrepo Pavese, Pinot Noir is used for sparkling wine production.

In the New World, Pinot has gained some classic regions, as well as being planted in new, marginally cool regions. The synonym for Pinot Noir in the United States is Oregon. The Willamette Valley has developed into a key area for Pinot Noir. Oregon gained its reputation after David Lett of Eyrie Vineyards took second place in a French-sponsored wine tasting in 1979. After that showing, even top Burgundy producers, such as Joseph Drouhin, began investment in Oregon.

A close second to Oregon are the cooler areas of Napa, Sonoma, and the south central coast in California. The Carneros region was originally planted to include Pinot, and much of it is used in the California sparkling wine industry. Other regions of note are the Russian River and Santa Barbara. Each of these areas has significant influence from fog off the Pacific Ocean, which keep the regions cool.

New Zealand is staking their claim as a region for Pinot Noir production. Most of the vineyards planted to Pinot are on the country's South Island. The original plantings were in the region of Central Otago, though the more commercially familiar Marlborough is providing the majority of the exports.

Each area described for Pinot Noir is a quintessential cool region. The areas in Burgundy utilize aspect to give the grapes enough sun to ripen while developing aromatics. In the New World, it is fog or latitude that creates the cool weather needed to create the aromatics for which Pinot Noir is famous.

Wine Styles

In reference to Pinot Noir, style really depends on which "Holy Grail" the winemaker is trying to achieve. The choice to make a refreshing wine, or a long-lived wine, or one that is aromatic all comes from the ideal the winemaker has for Pinot Noir. Some generalizations can be made, though not all wines will reflect every characteristic.

Pinot Noir is a lightly colored wine. In fact, for this and other reasons, it is often described as "a white wine masquerading as a red wine." It is often a ruby or garnet red, if young, and will age to a light mahogany. The intensity of color is such that it is often transparent, and can be so light as to resemble a rosé.

Where Pinot really begins to shine is on the nose. It is one of the more aromatic of the red wines, and has a complex mix of aromas. The nose can be described in terms of red berries, or other red fruits like cherries. But Pinot Noir has distinct nonfruit aromas. These have been described as being vegetal like mushrooms or beetroot, gamy like barnyard or a petting zoo, earthy like leather or *sous bois* (French for undergrowth), and floral like violets. Words that are heard most commonly in descriptors of Pinot Noir are funk and ethereal. These terms are hard to define, though funk usually is an indication of something earthy and slightly out of place. Ethereal often refers to the aromas of Pinot Noir and their light, wispy, fleeting character.

The palate of Pinot Noir confirms it is a wine of low extraction and of unique flavor components. There are low to medium levels of acidity, and low levels of tannin. In top wines meant for extended aging, tannin and color levels will be higher than average. Flavors on the palate reflect those on the nose, again with savory characteristics. Fruit, earth, vegetal, and savory all combine to create a complex and intriguing blend of flavors.

There was a time when the smell of manure was considered the hallmark of a good Pinot Noir. It has since been discovered that wines evoking this characteristic were the result of a fermentation infection by a strain of yeast known as Brettanomyces, or Brett. Clean, sterile wine making eliminated the "country air" but took with it the nuance and intrigue of Pinot Noir. Currently, the testament to good wine making is not the rote perfection of the wine, but the small errors in technique that give the wine its character.

Vintage variation is a factor when discussing Pinot Noir. Because of the penchant for Pinot Noir to express its terroir, weather is part of that system. Wet weather may change the flavors one year, while a cool year may mute some aromatics. New World winemakers have more consistent weather, keeping their wines somewhat more consistent about the soil and place. French winemakers, though, can look to Pinot Noir not only as an expression of place, but one which can track each year's growing season.

CELLARING PINOT NOIR

Most Pinot Noir is meant for drinking while young. To enjoy the fruit and aromatics, Pinot can typically be drunk in the first two to five years after bottling.

Most Pinot will begin to decline after about eight years, though there are producers in Burgundy whose wine can last upward of fifteen or twenty years. As the wine transitions from youthful fruit to mature savoriness, Pinot can get disjointed. This period typically lasts a couple years, so tasting and evaluating the wine is extremely important. A lot depends on the producer and the style of wine that they make to determine whether a wine is meant for early consumption or extended storage.

It is the complexity of Pinot Noir that keeps growers, vintners, and drinkers coming back. The interweaving of fruit and earth with game and savory constantly changes. A good glass of Pinot Noir is constantly evolving, and constantly changing how it presents itself to the world.

Food and Wine Pairing

Pinot Noir is one of the most food-friendly wines available. It is often described as a white wine in disguise. This suggests that Pinot has the ability to work as well with lighter dishes as it does with more full-bodied ones. This is true in the cuisine of Burgundy, where Pinot Noir is served with rabbit in mustard sauce, coq au vin, and beef bourguignon. To enjoy Pinot Noir's subtlety may lean toward pairing to simpler dishes, while the wines complexity can also complement richer and more complex dishes. In Oregon, the classic pair is Pinot Noir with wild salmon, again emphasizing the richness and also the delicacy of the wine.

Basics for Pinot Noir (pee-NOH NWAHR)

Climate	Loves cool weather
Soil	Calcium rich, shallow, and well-draining soil
	Limestone yields aromatic wines
	Iron rich clay yields more tannic wine
Disease susceptibility	Coulure
	Rot
	Fanleaf disease
	Leaf roll virus
	Pierce's Disease
Growth habit	Short lived compared to other vines
Characteristics	Large selection of clones
	Thin skinned, hard to extract color and tannin
	Early budding and early ripening

Average Yield	27 to 40 hl/ha
Fermentation quirks	Some favored aromatic may be due to dirty wine making
Classic region	Burgundy
	Champagne
	Oregon
	Carneros, California
	New Zealand

Pinot Noir Tasting Note

Appearance	Light intensity ruby with fading to the rim
Nose	Bright red fruit: cherries, cranberry, raspberry
	Mushrooms, beets
	Animal, barnyard
	Earthy, sous bois
Palate	Low to medium acidity
	Typically low to medium, soft tannins (higher in Grand Cru Burgundy)
	Cherry, cranberry, raspberry
	Earthy, beets, soy sauce, dill, mushroom
	Medium alcohol, medium finish
Ageability	Most is meant for drinking within 2 to 5 years of the vintage.
	Top Burgundy can last upward of 20 years

QUESTIONS

1. Describe the preferred soils for Pinot Noir.

2. What is the preferred climate for Pinot Noir?

3. What are some of the challenges growers face when tending Pinot Noir?

4. What are the challenges for the winemakers?

5. Why is clonal selection important in growing Pinot Noir?

6. What are the classic regions for Pinot Noir production?

7. Write a tasting note for a Burgundian Pinot Noir.

8. Write a tasting note for a New World Pinot Noir.

9. What are the food pairing options for Pinot Noir?

▲ French vines trained in gobolet or head trained manner. *Courtesy PhotoDisc, Inc.*

▲ Vineyard planted for trellised vines. *Courtesy PhotoDisc, Inc.*

▶ Hand-harvesting requires more labor but is a more delicate method of handling the grapes. *Courtesy PhotoDisc, Inc.*

▶ Hand-harvested grapes
are treated carefully all the
way to the winery. *Courtesy
PhotoDisc, Inc.*

▼ Recently hand-harvested
Pinot Noir has little extraneous
material among the grapes.
Courtesy PhotoDisc, Inc.

▲ Mechanical harvesting allows for rapid and low cost grape harvesting but with little selection. *Courtesy Digital Vision.*

▼ Stainless fermentation tanks at Cakebread Cellars. *Courtesy of Kobrand Corporation—www.kobrandwineandspirits.com.*

◀ Making barrels at Cadus Tonnellerie. *Courtesy of Kobrand Corporation—www.kobrandwineandspirits.com.*

▼ Toasting the formed barrels. *Courtesy of Kobrand Corporation—www.kobrandwineandspirits.com.*

▶ Aging room of small oak barrels at Cakebread Cellars. *Courtesy of Kobrand Corporation—www.kobrand wineandspirits.com.*

▲ Traditional large oak barrels for aging wine. *Courtesy of Kobrand Corporation—*
www.kobrandwineandspirits.com.

▲ Note the differences between the low intensity of color in the white wine on the left and the high intensity color of the wine on the right.

▲ Note the differences between the low color intensity in the red wine on the left and the high color intensity in the wine on the right.

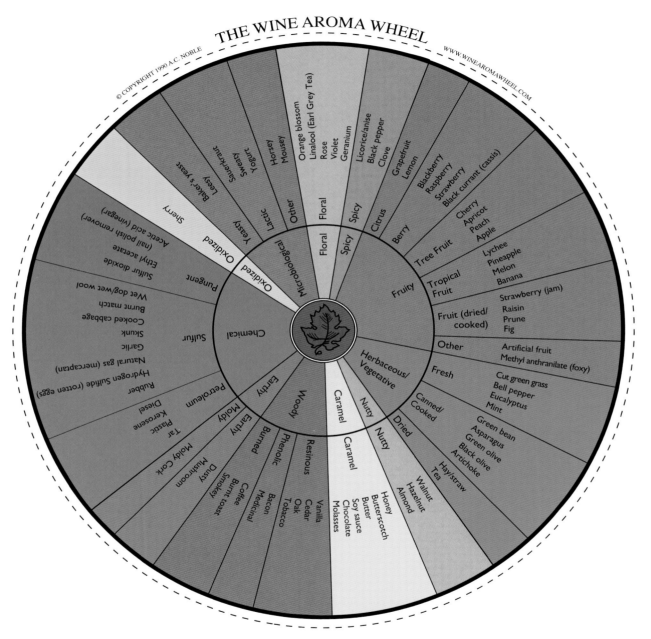

▲ Wine aroma wheel. ©1990 A. C. Noble 1990, 2002.
www.winearomawheel.com

▶ White asparagus from the Loire and Sancerre exemplify a classic regional pairing.

▼ Artichokes make wine taste sweet. A high acid wine like Pinot Grigio would balance the added sweetness.

Caviar and Champagne match texture, richness, and minerality. The salmon's richness is countered by the Champagne's acidity, and the blinis mimic its yeastiness.

▲ No white wine with fish here, a hearty preparation like cioppino calls for a fuller bodied rosé.

▲ A creamy cheesecake is contrasted with a fruity vin doux naturale, Muscat Beaumes-de-Venise.

▶ A simple fruit tart is delicious with a late harvest Riesling.

▲ This simple preparation of rack of lamb would be the perfect food for a Grand Cru Classe Bordeaux (Cabernet Sauvignon).

▶ Tangy and sweet, this lemon tart works best with a Tokaji Azsu.

▲ Chablis is a crisp and light pairing with a variety of seafood and shellfish.

▼ Briny olives, salty ham and Marcona almonds all have flavors which match Fino sherry.

▲ Nebbiolo has been described as truffles in a glass, so what better pairing than anything made with truffles.

▼ The aromas and flavors characteristic of Chardonnay are toast, butter, apple, pear, and vanilla.

▼ Fresh halibut and ripe vegetables need the luscious ripeness of a New World Chardonnay.

▲ Rich, crisp crab cakes are complimented by a buttery white Burgundy.

▼ The aromas and flavors characteristic of Pinot Noir are cherries, berries, mushrooms, beets, and soy.

▲ Another classic regional pairing of escargot in red wine sauce paired with a simple red Burgundy.

▲ Burgers do not always need beer, this truffle burger is asking for an Oregon Pinot Noir.

▶ The aromas and flavors characteristic of Cabernet Sauvignon are berries, plums, pencil shavings, gravel, and mint.

chapter *9*

Cabernet Sauvignon

*T*o most of the wine-consuming public, Cabernet Sauvignon has grown to be synonymous for "red wine." That makes it appealing to growers, who know they can sell their grapes, and to vintners, who know the public will buy anything that says Cabernet Sauvignon on the label. From accidental beginnings, Cabernet Sauvignon has grown to take the wine world by storm—grower, vintner, consumer, and critic.

Upon completion of this chapter, the student should be able to:

> Describe the vineyard conditions preferred by Cabernet Sauvignon
> Describe unique characteristics of making Cabernet Sauvignon wines
> Discuss ageability of Cabernet Sauvignon wines
> Outline classic regions for quality Cabernet Sauvignon
> Describe styles of Cabernet Sauvignon wines
> Outline typical food pairings with Cabernet Sauvignon

In the Vineyard

Records from growers and producers barely mention Cabernet Sauvignon until the late 1700s. Many people attempted to create a mythical beginning for the grape. Was it found in the wild, and given the name "sauvignon" because it was "sauvage"? Was it an ancient Roman grape whose name had evolved over the years and then been renamed? None of these myths gained support, and once genetic testing identified the parents, it seems the answer was in front of everyone all along. It turns out that Cabernet Sauvignon is actually an accidental cross between Cabernet Franc and Sauvignon Blanc, which first occurred somewhere in Bordeaux, probably in Graves.

Cabernet Sauvignon has few requirements when it comes to soil. It needs a soil that is well draining, low in organic matter (thereby reducing vigor), and warm. In the homeland of Cabernet Sauvignon, Bordeaux, these requirements are met by gravel. The gravel soils of the Médoc, Graves, and Pessac-Leognan heat up quickly and retain that heat, transferring it to the vines in the cool, maritime climate. These soils are also deep. The mounds of gravel drain well, with the help of some drainage pipes in some vineyards, and the vine roots are forced to search deeper and deeper for the water table. Cabernet Sauvignon does not like "wet feet," meaning that the vine prefers to search out water rather than have the roots sit in moist soil. A gravel soil is the perfect match. Finally, when you are planting in a bed of gravel, there is not a lot of topsoil to provide nourishment for the vines. Again, the roots must search out pockets of clay or loam in the gravel beds in order to find more nutrients.

In warmer regions, like Australia or California, the warmth factor is provided by the climate rather than the soil. In these places, Cabernet is grown on a range of soils (terra rossa topsoil on limestone in South Australia and alluvial silt in California). The drainage ability and the low organic matter concentration become more important in these areas.

Warmth is a key requirement for Cabernet Sauvignon. As a late-budding variety, it needs some warmer temperatures to get the buds to break. It is also a late-ripening variety, and needs warmth to get the grapes to ripen properly. Not only is Cabernet late ripening, it is also slow ripening. This makes Cabernet susceptible to early onset of winter, or rainy seasons.

Cabernet Sauvignon inherited a good deal of hardiness from its parent Cabernet Franc. But it is fairly susceptible to one vine disease, powdery mildew. Its susceptibility is demonstrated by the tendency of the grapes to succumb to mildew, even though the bunches themselves are loose and allow plenty of airflow around the clusters. In the mid-1800s, powdery mildew devastated the vineyards in Bordeaux. A treatment of copper sulfate and lime, known as Bordeaux mixture, was created to treat the vines before any mildew appeared. Clever vintners noted that roses also were susceptible to powdery mildew, and presented the symptoms before the grape vines did. Now many vines have rosebushes at the head of the row to serve as mildew barometers.

The characteristics of Cabernet Sauvignon wine are directly related to the anatomy of the grape berry itself. Cabernet has a very thick skin and very large seeds, yet the overall berry size is small. The result is a high ratio of skin and seeds to pulp. The skins contain large quantities of tannins and color compounds (phenolics), in addition to the tannins found in the seeds. The high level of phenolics dissolve into a relatively small quantity of juice, increasing the influence of the skin and seeds.

The yield of grapes from Cabernet Sauvignon has traditionally been low. Newer clones introduced, first in the 1970s and then more recently, have dramatically increased the yields of the vines, but not to the benefit of the wines. Higher yields make it more difficult for the vines to ripen properly, and often the fruit is not to complete ripeness. Many growers do a green harvest at veraison to reduce the yield and increase the quality. Other wineries deal with the lack of concentration in the winery.

In the Winery

Like anything with a thick skin, Cabernet Sauvignon can take some abuse. The high phenolic content of the skin and seeds allows Cabernet to withstand fairly vigorous treatment. The first treatment is often a cold soak. Allowing the crushed grapes to sit undisturbed for up to several days extracts a good deal of color and softer tannins from the skin and seeds.

Fermentation for Cabernet is often one of the warmest. Typically, Cabernet will ferment at 85–90°F (29–32°C). This is a fairly high temperature, and extracts even more color and tannin. While some producers utilize gravity feeds and other gentle measures for moving wine, Cabernet can withstand the abuse given by mechanical pumps or repeated punching down.

Finally, the skins and seeds are often allowed to macerate in the finished wine. In regions where a light, easy drinking style is desired, this maceration may only last a couple days. Traditionally in Bordeaux, the maceration period approached three weeks. It was this long maceration time that allowed the tannins needed for extended aging to be extracted.

The body and tannin of the final wine can also be regulated by blending different fractions of the pressings. After maceration, the wine is drained off the pomace, and this free-run wine will make up the majority of the bottlings. The pomace is then pressed to remove more wine, called the *vin de presse*. This will contain more color and more tannins that have been extracted from the skin and seeds. If the wine does not have the body and tannin structure desired, some of the vin de presse can be blended back into the free run wine to increase its structure.

AGING

Cabernet Sauvignon and oak is a match made in heaven. The black fruit profile of Cabernet Sauvignon (black currants, plums, and the like) is only enhanced by the vanilla and baking spice notes that are infused by the oak. Which species of oak is preferred? That depends on the producer. Many curtail the amount of American oak they use so as not to overpower the basic Cabernet flavors. Quality producers will use a blend of French and American oak in their aging cellars.

Cabernet Sauvignon, made with intense concentration and extraction, can last for decades. The benchmark of aged Cabernet is one of the Cru Classé from the Médoc in a good vintage. These wines will only begin to be approachable at ten years of age, and often last for up to three decades. In "best-of-the-century" vintages, the wines can last even longer. Top older vintages being drunk now are 1945, 1961, 1964, and 1966. The 1970 vintage can still be held before drinking.

New World winemakers can also produce wines that can age. However, these wines tend not to have the longevity that the Bordeaux wines have. Napa Cabernet is typically best between five and fifteen years of age, while Australian Coonawarra Cabernet is best before it becomes a teenager. What many New World winemakers more commonly produce is easy drinking Cabernet that can be consumed within a year or two of release.

CLASSIC REGIONS

Cabernet Sauvignon is grown all over the world. Depending on the style of the wine, some regions make more classic representations of Cabernet Sauvignon than others. We will focus on these regions here.

The homeland to Cabernet Sauvignon is Bordeaux in southwest France. More precisely, the region known as the Left Bank or the Médoc is the heartland of Cabernet. It is here that the Dutch drained the swampy marshes along the Gironde estuary and exposed wide swaths of deep gravel banks. These outcroppings of gravel form the main vineyard area in the Médoc.

Wines of the Médoc are blends, with Cabernet Sauvignon being the largest component. Other components include Merlot, Cabernet Franc, and to a lesser extent, Petit Verdot and Malbec. Blending is a result of the growing practices of the region. Soils are varied, and vines are planted on the soils they are best suited to.

Multiple varieties are also practical in such a large region. If all the grapes ripened at the same time, there would not be enough labor to pick them all. Multiple varieties have staggered ripening times, allowing better distribution of labor. Finally, there is the insurance factor. If something should happen to wipe out part of the crop, or a single varietal, in any year, there are still other grapes to make wine from.

The wines of the Médoc are considered the benchmark for Cabernet, not only because of their complexity and longevity, but because of their historical significance. The moment Médoc became important was 1855. The French were to have the World's Fair in Paris in 1856, and wished to show off their agricultural bounty. Part of that was to be the wines of the Médoc. Initially, the producers were not willing to rate themselves, so the task fell to the Bordeaux Chamber of Commerce. They researched prices and history back one hundred years, and chose sixty-one chateaux that were considered the best. These sixty-one were further categorized into five "growths," or cru classé. This classification of 1855 became the standard by which Bordeaux wines were judged. Only one change has been made to the original classification, when in 1973 Chateau Mouton-Rothschild was elevated from Second Growth to First Growth.

The wines of Bordeaux are still a major player in the wine world. Their wines are sold as futures, years before they are actually bottled and released. Every year, speculation arises as to the quality of the vintage and the longevity of the wines. Bordeaux, and especially the Médoc, are constantly under scrutiny and always a reference point for Cabernet Sauvignon.

In the United States, the words "Cabernet Sauvignon" are often preceded by the location of Napa. The wines of Napa Valley were originally patterned after those of the Médoc, but have developed a style all their own over the years. Because Napa is warmer than Bordeaux, choice of soil is not as important. Napa has many types of soil throughout the valley, but some of the best wines come from the areas of Rutherford, Oakville, and Stag's Leap. The soil in these areas is classified as alluvial fan, or the silt of ancient rivers. The fans form a geological feature called a bench, and the Rutherford Bench is considered one of the prime areas in California for Cabernet Sauvignon.

One other significant note for Napa is the use of mountain fruit or valley fruit. Many parts of the valley are converted farmland, and therefore somewhat more fertile than what quality grape vines need. The mountainside vineyards have poorer soils and better drainage, resulting in grapes that often have more concentration than those on the valley floor.

Depending upon the location on the mountainside, another difference is the effect of fog. Part of Napa, from the south northward about 15 miles inland, is covered by fog from San Pedro Bay in the mornings. This keeps valley fruit cool during the day, but also cuts some of the sunlight and slows ripening. Mountain fruit, on the other hand, is above the fog line. It benefits from larger diurnal variations to maintain acidity, but receives constant sunlight, and ripens more completely.

California made its impression on the world at the Judgment of Paris in 1976. As mentioned with Chardonnay, the Cabernets of Bordeaux and California were tasted blind and judged. The French judges commented on the complexity and richness of some of the wines, judging them to be the better ones (and obviously French). When the results were tallied, Stag's Leap Wine Cellars was the winner. This victory, along with the Chardonnay victory for Chateau Montelena, kick-started the American wine industry and the California industry in particular.

The third classic region for Cabernet Sauvignon is Australia. Cabernet was initially planted here to promote export sales, because it was the grape consumers were asking for. It was found to make exceptional wines that could age, especially in the region of Coonawarra in South Australia. Coonawarra is unique in that the soil is a red, known locally as terra rossa, but is relatively thin. The terra rossa sits on bedrock of limestone, providing the good drainage that Cabernet Sauvignon prefers. Coonawarra has consistent cloud cover, making it slightly cooler than the surrounding region. Though not as cool as Bordeaux, Coonawarra is cool enough to allow the grapes to retain acidity during the ripening process.

Cabernet Sauvignon is making its mark in other areas of world, not as the premier grape, but as a blending partner. Cabernet is a major component of many of the blends known as Super Tuscans, from Italy. It is also used in some blends, and as a single varietal, in Spain. Other New World regions to note are Margaret River in Western Australia, Chile, and the North Island of New Zealand.

Wine Styles

Cabernet Sauvignon is said to be the most "transportable" grape. Unlike other grape varieties that change or express themselves differently in new places, Cabernet Sauvignon pretty much tastes the same no matter where it is planted. It is the quintessential "international" grape not only because it is planted everywhere, but also because it tastes the same everywhere. For many up-and-coming wine regions, they are guaranteed that if they plant and make Cabernet Sauvignon, it will be recognizable to the buying public around the world.

Of course, fine wine makers do not want their wine to taste like everyone else's. They want the wine to taste of place, of "somewhereness," of terroir. Cabernet Sauvignon has the ability to do just that. The lower, more production-oriented wines retain a common Cabernet thread that appeals to consumers. Higher-quality, boutique wines made with low yields and from single vineyards can express location elegantly, while still retaining the Cabernet character.

The profile of young Cabernet Sauvignon is fairly distinctive. The wines are deeply colored when young, often described as inky. On the nose, the dominant fruits are black: black currants, plums, and black cherry. Other aromas include something woody, often described in older wines as pencil shavings, cigar box, or cedar. Finally, there is some vegetal component, giving Cabernet a characteristic "black-green thing." The vegetal components vary by place but can be the scent of crushed blackberry leaves, mint, or, in underripe Cabernets, green bell peppers. On the palate, the fruit and cedar return, along with the vanilla and spices of oak treatment. What characterizes Cabernet on the palate, however, is big, gripping tannins. These tannins typically soften with age, but in young wines they can dominate the palate. Cabernet with no blending partners does have one shortfall: it lacks a "middle palate." The flavor starts strong, then disappears, only to return for a strong, long-lasting finish. The reason Cabernet is often blended is to smooth the tannins and to fill in the middle palate.

Location can be determined in quality Cabernet, both on the nose and on the palate. Bordeaux wines are more about austerity than they are about vibrant fruit. The top chateau will make inky wines, while those of lower classification will make wines that are medium intensity in color. These are the basis for the English term for Bordeaux: claret. Initially on the nose, the notes of pencil shavings, gravel, and earth are more predominant. Only under these aromas does the scent of cassis come through, often presenting as "jam on hot rocks." Occasionally, an earthy funk can be found in Bordeaux wines. This has been termed the "Gironde stink" and is reminiscent of marshland. The vegetal component tends more to the mint and possibly bell pepper. On the palate, the tannins can be large, but ripe. The style on the palate is also about austerity, rather than rich, ripe, juicy fruit.

Even within Bordeaux, location can be determined by a discernable sommelier. The four main communes (from north to south) of St. Estephe, Pauillac, St. Julien, and Margaux have differing terroir that can be determined in the glass. St. Estephe has the most clay in the soil, and therefore retains more water. The wines from this commune tend to be more tannic and a bit fuller bodied, with higher acidity. Pauillac has the classic Bordeaux structure and style. Margaux has the most limestone in the soil, which makes its wines the most delicate, fragrant, floral, and polished of the communes. St Julien, sandwiched between Pauillac and Margaux, exhibits a little of each commune's style.

Napa Cabernet is typically inky in color intensity. On the nose, black plum and blackberries predominate, with a vegetal component of sweetgrass, sweet hay, or alfalfa typically present. There is still a cedar/pencil shavings aroma, but to a lesser degree than Bordeaux. On the palate, the tannins are gritty and chewy. In Rutherford, the tannins are fine, and often described as "Rutherford dust."

Coonawarra Cabernet is initially distinguished on the nose. The fruit is predominant, but rather than being the ripe, juicy fruit of Napa, it is more like stewed fruit, fruit leather, or jam. The nose also contains a distinguishing eucalyptus component. On the palate, the wine may have residual sugar, increasing the approachability but also taming some of the tannins. Coonawarra Cabernet is the most full bodied of these three Cabernets, and can be very mouthfilling.

AGED CABERNETS

Older Cabernet will present very differently from young Cabernet. The color will decrease to a brickish red, thinning at the rim. On the nose, new bouquet elements of tobacco, leather, dried fruit, strong cedar notes, and possibly smoke and spices appears. The palate will seem delicate or fragile, with similar flavors as the nose, but less fruit. The older the wine, the more difficult it is for the fruit to hold on. Great vintages are those with all the old wine notes, but still a thread of fragile fruit lingering.

Food and Wine Pairing

Many food and wine pairs work with Cabernet Sauvignon. Classically, the match would be a simple roast or grilled meat. In Bordeaux, that is simple roast lamb. In Italy it is Bistecca alla Fiorentina. Cabernet is definitely a red meat wine, but those could include duck, goose, or even roasted turkey. If the wine is aged, it is even more important that the food be kept simple, so as not to overpower the nuances in the wine. Old World versions of Cabernet Sauvignon would best match with items with a little more richness and/or a bit of earthiness in the food. New World styles, with lower acidity and higher fruit concentration, would match better with simpler and even a bit lighter fare.

Basics for Cabernet Sauvignon (ka-behr-NAY soh-vin-YAWN)

Climate	Needs warmth because it is late ripening
Soil	Loves gravel (France), terra rossa (South Australia), and alluvial fan (Napa)
Disease susceptibility	Very susceptible to powdery mildew
Growth habit	Vigorous growth, but not unwieldy
Characteristics	Berries have high skin/seed to pulp ratio (small berries, thick skin, big seeds) Late budding, late ripening

Average Yield	35 hl/ha, though newer clones higher
Fermentation quirks	Very warm fermentation temperatures
	Long maceration after fermentation to extract color and tannin
	Separation of free run and pressed wine
Classic region	Bordeaux (Left bank)
	Napa
	Coonawarra
	Common worldwide

Cabernet Sauvignon Tasting Note

Appearance	Inky ruby with little to no rim variation
Nose	Black fruit: cassis, plum, black cherry
	Wood: cedar, pencil shavings, cigar box
	Vegetal: Green pepper (underripe), mint (Bordeaux), hay (Napa), eucalyptus (Australia), bramble
	Earthy (French): gravel, earth
Palate	Medium acidity
	Firm, intensely gripping tannins, sometimes chewy or dusty
	Black fruit: berries in Bordeaux, ripe juicy fruit in Napa, stewed, jammy fruit in Australia
	Cedar, gravel (France), vanilla or spice (oak dependent)
	Lacks middle palate if pure varietal
	Full bodied, long finish
Ageability	Ability to age for decades

Aged Cabernet Sauvignon Tasting Note

Appearance	Brickish red with thinning to rim
Nose	Tobacco, leather, dried fruit, smoke, cedar
Palate	Fragile fruit is less prominent
	Medium acidity
	Soft tannins
	Tobacco, leather, dried fruit, smoke
	Long finish
Ageability	Great vintages can last into their 50s

QUESTIONS

1. What are the preferred soil conditions for Cabernet Sauvignon?

2. How does the structure of the Cabernet Sauvignon berry affect the resulting wine?

3. Discuss how the body and tannin of Cabernet Sauvignon wine can be adjusted in the wine making process.

4. What is the significance of Cabernet Sauvignon from Bordeaux?

5. What are the important regions for Cabernet Sauvignon?

6. Write a tasting note for a young, approachable Cabernet Sauvignon.

7. Write a tasting note for an aged Cabernet Sauvignon.

8. What are the significant differences in style between a New World and an Old World Cabernet Sauvignon?

9. Discuss the food and wine pairing options for Cabernet Sauvignon.

chapter **10**

Merlot

*M*erlot has always played second fiddle to its fellow red wine grapes. *Even though it makes some of the world's best, long-lived wines, it is more often relegated to being a blending grape. Even its big break, after the airing of the 60 Minutes "French Paradox" segment, was because it is a red wine that doesn't taste like other red wines. Then its sales plummeted based on the rantings of a movie character in the film* Sideways. *Even vintners focused on top-quality wines have difficulty with Merlot, because there is no agreed upon benchmark to emulate.*

Upon completion of this chapter, the student should be able to:

> *Describe the vineyard conditions preferred by Merlot*
> *Describe unique characteristics of making Merlot wines*
> *Discuss ageability of Merlot wines*
> *Outline classic regions for quality Merlot*
> *Describe styles of Merlot wines*
> *Outline typical food pairings with Merlot*

In the Vineyard

The origins of Merlot seem to be centered in Bordeaux. Not much is mentioned about Merlot until 1784, when it is mentioned as being the best grape to plant in the Libournais, or Right Bank, in Bordeaux. Genetic testing has suggested that Merlot could be another offspring of Cabernet Franc, though the second parent is unknown.

Merlot is well suited to the Right Bank of Bordeaux because of the soil types there. The best sites for Merlot are clay based. The moister soil is cooler than other soils, and can slow ripening of the grapes. Clay is also responsible for fuller-bodied and more structured wines. While Merlot likes clay, it also is sensitive to drainage. Dry soil is very poor for growing Merlot. The soil needs to be moist but not wet and clay is able to retain the moisture through the dry summer months. Merlot planted on other soils also does well. In limestone soils, Merlot is more perfumed and elegant.

The Merlot vine is early budding and early ripening. The early ripening suggests it can handle cooler locations. The early budding of Merlot does not help if the weather is changeable at flowering, and also makes the vine susceptible to frost damage. Merlot is very susceptible to coulure (flower drop). This, among other maladies, can reduce Merlot yields by half.

While Merlot likes cool soils, it is not a truly cool climate grape like Pinot Noir. Merlot actually likes the climate warm, though not as hot as for Cabernet Sauvignon. The cool soils help to temper the warmth of the location.

One could say Merlot likes the climate warm with ample humidity. Unfortunately, that humidity can trigger a series of ailments for Merlot. The vines are particularly susceptible to powdery and downy mildew and to grey rot. Merlot has relatively thin skins for a red grape, so an instance of rot can have the grapes swell and burst within a day or two of a rain.

The early ripening of Merlot is a benefit to many cooler-region growers. Merlot ripens nearly two weeks earlier than Cabernet Sauvignon, and in a cooler region may ripen where Cabernet never would. The timing of ripening is the key to making a good wine. Picked too early, the wines will have a prominent herbaceous quality. The wines would taste of green peppers and leaves rather than fruit. Once Merlot ripens, it must be picked right away. The transition to overripeness and loss of acidity can happen in a matter of days.

While there are a modest number of Merlot clones on the market, it is thought that there are really only two or three good ones. Unfortunately, most vineyards are planted with inferior clones. Clonal selection can also be modified by choice of rootstock, which is important in Merlot. The vine is fairly vigorous and will produce high yields if allowed. Correct choice of rootstock allows the foliage growth, as well as the size of the yield, to be controlled.

Yield is a major consideration with Merlot. In many Merlot vineyards around the world, the yields are extremely high. The resulting wines are easy drinking and "light"; they are also often underripe. Grapes that are destined to make high-quality, long-lasting wines are those from lower-yielding plants, with proper canopy management and not too warm a location. The famed wine consultant Michel Rolland says, "The picking date is vital. Get that wrong and everything else will be wrong; you lose 80 percent of the potential."

In the Winery

Merlot is noted for its variability in style. Many winemakers create easy drinking, approachable wines. This is partially due to the types of grapes they use—those of high-yielding vines. Another reason is the thin skin of the Merlot grape. Thinner skins have less tannin, and therefore make wines that are approachable earlier, and age earlier, than wines made from Cabernet Sauvignon. For fuller-bodied, ageable wines, Merlot is often subjected to a cold soak with pumping over, before fermentation, in order to extract the color and tannin. This gives a chance for water-soluble color and tannin compounds to soak into the juice before the introduction of yeast.

In the New World, Merlot is often made as a single varietal. More often than not, however, it is used as an "improving grape," meaning a grape blended with other varietal to improve them. That is the main function of Merlot in Bordeaux, and in some other regions around the world. Even though Merlot is the most planted grape in Bordeaux, most of the grapes are used as the softer component of a blend. The exception to this is the Libournais, or the Right Bank of Bordeaux. Here, Merlot is the major, and sometimes almost exclusive, grape that makes the wine.

AGING

Merlot is a wine that can be drunk within a year or two of the vintage, but can also last for up to a decade or more. In either case, it is often aged in oak, to impart the vanilla and spice character that complements the natural varietal character. The majority of Merlot, if aged, would last on the order of four to five years.

CLASSIC REGIONS

The homeland for Merlot is Bordeaux. It is the most widely planted grape in both the Right and Left banks. On the Left bank, Merlot accounts for 25 to 50 percent of the blend. It only makes up a majority of the blend in Right bank wines, where it can be up to 95 percent of the blend. The two communes that make the most notable Merlots are St Emilion and Pomerol. Both communes have out-croppings of gravel, but Pomerol has a subsoil of iron-rich clay, which lends more structure to the wines. Chateau Petrus, considered the top Merlot-based wine from Pomerol, sits on top of a lens of the clay that is very close to the surface.

Another major area for high-quality Merlot is California. It can be found in some of the cooler regions of Napa, like Stag's Leap, Oakville, and Carneros. Other areas include the Russian River, Dry Creek Valley, and Monterey. The hallmark of California Merlot is higher alcohol and low acidity. That is because the New World producers leave Merlot on the vine longer than their counterparts in Bordeaux. The extended hang time allows the Merlot to ripen more and develop more plummy-type fruit. It also makes the tannins even silkier than in Bordeaux, and the result is a fuller-bodied, fruitier style of wine.

Merlot is an important grape elsewhere in the world. It is becoming more preva-lent in Italy. In northern Italy it is being made as a varietal wine, but one that is meant to be easy drinking and very approachable. It is also used as a blending grape, taking advantage of its lower acidity (compared to the local grapes) and soft tannins. Further south in Italy, in Tuscany, Merlot plays a more important role. Here it is often used as a blending grape with Sangiovese to make what have been called Super Tuscan wines. Again, Merlot is used to increase body and flavor without becoming dominant.

In Chile, Merlot had been an important wine throughout the years, but it was never quite the same as other expressions around the world. DNA testing showed that the majority of Merlot planted in Chile's vineyards was actually Carmenere, the lost grape of Bordeaux and a possible sibling to Merlot. Most of the vines have been identified, and Merlot now makes up less of a percentage of exported wine from Chile than previously noted.

Wine Styles

In describing Merlot to a novice wine drinker, it would sound like the perfect, generic red wine. The color is often a bright ruby, with a medium to high intensity. On the nose, it may have a wide variety of black fruits, from cherry to plum and even fig and prune, depending on the region and the ripeness of the fruit. Other indicators include the aroma of baking spices (such as clove, nutmeg, cinnamon) or of chocolate or cocoa powder. Merlot can also take on an herbaceous quality if the grapes were not totally ripe. On the palate, the same flavor profiles match. Acidity is medium; length and body are also typically medium.

The indicator on the palate is texture. Specifically, the texture refers to the tannins. Merlot is known for silky tannins. Overoaked or overextracted Merlot will have coarser tannins, similar to Cabernet Sauvignon, but the real measure of a good Merlot is velvety, smooth tannins. In fact, because the tannins are so soft, the term "smooth" is used to best describe Merlot. It is this quality that makes it a great blending grape for more tannic grapes, as it automatically helps smooth the blend, and helps it to be more approachable earlier. This is also the quality that makes Merlot a good entry into red wine for many novice wine drinkers.

Food and Wine Pairing

Food pairs with Merlot will depend on the style in which the Merlot was made. For the most part, the moderate acidity allows for pairing with many types of food. Starting with "regional pairing," anything similar to the cuisine of Bordeaux would make a good pairing. This includes duck, goose, game, lamb, and pâtés. The moderate tannins allow Merlot to be a good pair for well-spiced foods, like not-too-fiery curries, tandoor, Middle Eastern cuisine, and some Asian dishes. Its implied sweetness from the fruit and baking spice aromatics lends itself to savory dishes also with a hint of sweetness, or with sweet/savory dishes.

Basics for Merlot (mer-LOH)

Climate	Warm with cool attributes and humidity
Soil	Clay
Disease susceptibility	Coulure Powdery and downy mildew Grey rot
Growth habit	Very vigorous
Characteristics	Ripens two weeks earlier than Cabernet Sauvignon Choice of rootstock is important Very dependent on harvest time Early budding and early ripening
Average yield	27 to 40 hl/ha
Fermentation quirks	Cold soak employed to increase color and tannin extraction
Classic region	France (Bordeaux Right bank) California

Merlot Tasting Note

Appearance	Medium intensity ruby with slight variation to rim
Nose	Bright black fruit: cherries, plums, prune
	Baking spices, cocoa, chocolate
	Roses
Palate	Medium acidity
	Silky, velvety tannins
	Plum, fig, black cherry
	Spices or chocolate
	Medium alcohol, medium finish
Ageability	Less than Cabernet Sauvignon
	California 4 to 8 years
	Pomerol 10 to 40 years

QUESTIONS

1. What are the soil preferences of Merlot?

2. Describe the type of climate Merlot prefers.

3. What are the important regions for growing Merlot?

4. What is the most important characteristic of Merlot?

5. Write a tasting note for Merlot.

6. What are the food and wine pairing options for Merlot?

chapter *11*

Sauvignon Blanc

*T*he moniker "classic grape" typically means that the wine made from those grapes has the ability to age and develop. Sauvignon Blanc is the exception to the rule. Sauvignon Blanc has the distinction of being a classic grape because it is a difficult grape to make perfectly. It makes many wines that are acceptable and pleasant, but to reach the pinnacle of varietal expression and potential ageability is not so easy.

Upon completion of this chapter, the student should be able to:

Describe the vineyard conditions preferred by Sauvignon Blanc
Describe unique characteristics of making Sauvignon Blanc wines
Discuss ageability of Sauvignon Blanc wines
Outline classic regions for quality Sauvignon Blanc
Describe styles of Sauvignon Blanc wines
Outline typical food pairings with Sauvignon Blanc

In the Vineyard

Sauvignon Blanc is an old variety, identified as one of the parents of Cabernet Sauvignon. It has many cousins, including Sauvignon Vert, Rosé, Noir, Rouge, and Violet. While its own parentage has not been determined, the existence of multiple permutations of the grape suggests a long enough history to allow mutations to occur.

Soil preference in relation to Sauvignon Blanc is more a matter relating to the ripeness and flavor profile than to specific soil-related flavors. Sauvignon Blanc planted in sandy, alluvial, or otherwise well-draining soils ripens earlier, and yields more herbaceous flavors. Vines planted on heavier soils, like clays, will ripen later and yield riper, fuller fruit flavors.

The French regions of Sancerre and Pouilly-Fumé focus on the expression of soil through the Sauvignon Blanc grape. There is a variety of soils between these two villages, each influencing the flavors and aromas of the wines. The vines that are planted on Kimmeridgean chalk, a type of chalk similar to the White Cliffs of Dover and the soils of Chablis, produce the richest and most balanced wines. More compact chalk, called caillotte, produces lighter, more elegant wines with increased perfume. The vines planted on flint, or silex, yield lively wines with a flinty, gun-smoke aroma. These wines also tend to be the longest lasting.

Sauvignon Blanc is late budding and early ripening. This suggests it is the perfect cool-climate varietal. For the most part, this is true; Sauvignon Blanc does not like the heat. However, the grapes do need a lot of sunlight. Grapes that do not receive enough sunlight will yield very high herbal and vegetal notes, low levels of fruit aromas, and unbalanced acidity. This is also true for grapes that have not had the advantage of a slow ripening process.

Sauvignon Blanc gets its name from the term *sauvage*, or wild. This could relate to the fact it was a wild vine that was tamed. It also still relates to vigorous vegetative growth of the vine. Many growers make a strong effort to keep the vine in check, so that the focus is on the grape and not on producing more leaves. To provide more sunlight to the developing bunches, leaf picking is often employed to reduce the vegetative growth and to expose the grapes.

Yield is an extremely important factor in wine quality. Most of the Sauvignon Blanc grown has a fairly high yield. While this does not totally diminish the quality of the grapes, it does make a lighter, less concentrated, earlier drinking wine. This style is the most common and the most familiar to consumers. Vines that have their yields reduced can create wines concentrated enough to withstand oak treatment, and which can age for several years. These are less familiar to consumers, though not necessarily less important.

Sauvignon Blanc vines are vulnerable to a variety of growth issues. The excessive vegetal growth can dominate the vine's energy, even during flowering and fruit set, resulting in some vines displaying lower grape production from coulure. The grapes themselves are thin-skinned. This, along with the cool-climate environment, makes the grapes particularly susceptible to powdery mildew, black rot, and grey rot. In the case of grey rot (botrytis), if the conditions are ideal, the infection may be a blessing and not a curse. It is botrytis that creates dehydrated grapes that make the world's best sweet dessert wines. In some areas of Sauvignon Blanc production, the botrytis infection is anticipated and appreciated rather than curtailed.

In the Winery

Production of wine from Sauvignon Blanc grapes is a straightforward process. There are a few twists the winemaker can choose from that will alter the final style of the wine. The first of these, and probably the most important, is fermentation temperature. Wines in the New World are more often than not fermented in stainless steel tanks, with temperature regulation. These wines are often fermented at very cool temperatures, which results in wines with lush fruit, often with a strong tropical fruit component. Warmer fermentation temperatures, approximately 60–65°F (15.5–18.3°C), tend to neutralize the varietal aroma profile and allows the minerality and site terroir to be highlighted. Finally, barrel fermentation, which can reach temperatures of 80°F (26.7°C), makes wines that are richer in style and retain some of the varietal character.

Another twist to a Sauvignon Blanc fermentation may be extended skin contact before pressing. Many producers avoid allowing extended skin contact, partly because of the belief that it reduces the ageability of a wine. Other producers use a short skin contact, twenty-four hours or less, in order to increase the fruit aromas and flavors in the wine.

Oak treatment is not common among single-varietal Sauvignon Blanc. Some is being produced in the Loire Valley of France, with wines that are made from low-yielding vines. The more common place to find oak-treated Sauvignon Blanc is in the Fumé Blanc style of California. Fumé Blanc is a marketing term developed by Robert Mondavi to highlight a style of Sauvignon Blanc that was different than what was currently on the market. Mondavi borrowed the term from the French village of Pouilly-Fumé, whose wines are said to have a smoky character. This term now refers to any New World Sauvignon Blanc that has received new oak treatment.

Other options from which the winemaker can choose include aging on the lees, batonnage, and malolactic fermentation. Aging on the lees, particularly in barrel, moderates the influence of the wood. Batonnage increases the weight of the wine. Malolactic fermentation provides a buttery tone layered onto the varietal character. While these are choices, they often create wines that are not "the usual" for Sauvignon Blanc.

One path that a whole region of winemakers chose to follow was to create blended wines from Sauvignon Blanc. Bordeaux winemakers use Sauvignon Blanc blended with Semillon. Adding Semillon to the mix increases the body of the wine and also tames some of Sauvignon Blanc's acidity. White Bordeaux is commonly treated with oak. Old style White Bordeaux often had a tired, oxidized character, but recently producers have begun investing in making more modern, stylized wines.

AGING

The majority of Sauvignon Blanc produced is meant for early consumption. While its aromas and acidity are intense, the body and extract is usually low to medium. Without the benefit of oak treatment, the wines are at their best in the first year or two after the vintage. Wines that have undergone oak treatment mature later and can last longer, often needing five to eight years to develop and lasting on the order of ten to fifteen years.

CLASSIC REGIONS

The homeland of Sauvignon Blanc is two appellations in the Loire Valley of France, Sancerre and Pouilly-Fumé. In both of these appellations, the focus is on the soil. Sancerre is noted for having an outcropping of chalk, similar to Chablis and Champagne. Pouilly-Fumé has a great deal of flint-based soils, known as silex, which are said to give the wines from this village a gunflint aroma. While the region has been noted for single varietal Sauvignon Blanc, the wines are typically French in their expression of terroir over varietal character of grass and minerality.

The Marlborough region of New Zealand is the new classic when discussing Sauvignon Blanc. The region has a cool, maritime climate, but with a lot of sunshine. This combines to produce wines with great clarity and purity of varietal character. While the trademark Sauvignon Blanc character is present, there is a great deal more fruit and vibrancy than is typically found in Sancerre.

A third region of note for single-varietal Sauvignon Blanc is Chile. Chile is notorious not for the purity of character or a singular style, but for a labeling mistake. It seems that much of the Sauvignon Blanc planted prior to 1995 may or may not be true Sauvignon Blanc. Only in the mid-1990s was it determined that the majority of plantings were Sauvignonasse (also known as Sauvignon Vert), a cousin to Sauvignon Blanc. Chilean Sauvignon Blanc does have the distinction of lower acidity than that from New Zealand. The location of Chile's vineyards closer to the equator increases the amount of sunlight they receive, and provides for long ripening seasons.

California is noted for a particular style of Sauvignon Blanc, originally created and marketed by Robert Mondavi in the 1970s. Fumé Blanc is Sauvignon Blanc that has been treated with oak. The oak treatment is an answer to the American consumer, who found the aromas and acidity of Sauvignon Blanc too overpowering. Oak tames the acidity, and also layers new familiar aromas onto the riper melon and peach notes of ripe Sauvignon Blanc.

A classic region for using Sauvignon Blanc is Bordeaux. Here the grape is blended with Semillon, and occasionally a drop of Muscadelle. Dry White Bordeaux is now made in fresher style, often fermented in stainless steel and/or with temperature control. In general, the wine is less aromatic and less acidic than in the Loire. This is partially due to the increased ripeness the Sauvignon Blanc can achieve in a warmer climate, but also because of the addition of the fuller-bodied, lower-acid Semillon. Because of the increased body, White Bordeaux from Pessac-Leognan or Graves is often fermented and aged in new oak.

Sauvignon Blanc is also a major component of the sweet wines of Bordeaux, in particular, Sauternes and Barsac. Two factors contribute to the inclusion of Sauvignon Blanc to make these sweet wines. First, the thin skins make the grapes susceptible to botrytis, thereby dehydrating the grapes and increasing the sugar content. Second, the high acidity remains even in botrytis-infected grapes. This sets up the juice to be a combination of extra-high sugar content, as well as high acidity. The final wines will have elevated levels of residual sugar, yet the acidity balances the sweetness so it is not cloying. The increased sugar and high acidity allow this wine to age for long periods, upward of a hundred years in the top chateaux of Sauternes.

Wine Styles

Sauvignon Blanc is a very distinctive wine, immediately noted for its piercing aromas and high acidity. The appearance of most Sauvignon Blancs is pale straw, sometimes bordering on water-white, but often with a greenish cast. The first true indicator of Sauvignon Blanc is on the nose. The nose is often high intensity, with very characteristic aromas. Common descriptors for the fruit aromas of Sauvignon Blanc are gooseberry, grapefruit, and lime. For riper grapes, the fruit aromas may lean more to peach and melon than the citrus fruits. For New Zealand Sauvignon Blancs, the fruit aromas also include tropical fruits such as guava and passion fruit.

There is also a distinct greenness in the aromas. These are often described as cut grass, canned asparagus, jalapeno, green bean, boxwood, or tomato bush and even (in less appealing terms) cat urine. Finally, for Sauvignon Blanc from the Loire, there is a flint or mineral component to the aromas as well.

On the palate, the most notable trait for Sauvignon Blanc is the acidity. It is often described as sharp or piercing acidity, because of the perception at the back of the palate. In general, the wine is light in body, dry, and has no perceptible tannins. As for fruit character, many of the items in the aroma profile are also noted on the palate. These include grapefruit and lime zest for fruit notes, asparagus or grass for the green component, and something minerally or flinty.

The notes of a Sauvignon Blanc dessert wine, such as a Sauternes, have some of the same characteristics, but the major aroma and palate notes are dominated by the effect of botrytis. Most prevalent are the aromas and tastes of dried apricots and of honey, both of which are classic indicators of botrytis.

Food and Wine Pairing

There are two considerations when pairing food with Sauvignon Blanc. First, the acidity needs to be addressed, and second, the vegetal flavor profile. The acidity of the wine can be viewed as a substitute for the acidity of lemon with seafood. In fact, Sauvignon Blanc is an excellent match with all types of seafood, from raw oysters to rich, cream-based seafood dishes.

The classic pairing for Sauvignon Blanc is goat cheese. The match of the tangy cheese and the tangy wine neutralizes that aspect and the vegetal and herbal flavors of both wine and cheese then marry. It is also an excellent wine for asparagus (actually a "regional pairing") and as a wine for a salad course. Other items for which Sauvignon Blanc is a match are tomato-based dishes. The wine's acidity can play off the tomatoes, and the herbal component of the wine can complement the fruitiness of the dish.

Basics for Sauvignon Blanc (SOH-vee-nyawn BLAHN(GK))

Climate	Cool-weather grape
Soil	Chalk, silex
Disease susceptibility	Powdery mildew Grey rot Black rot

Growth habit	Extremely vigorous
Characteristics	Needs a lot of sunlight
	Vegetation must be trimmed to ripen fruit
	Late budding and early ripening
Average yield	30 to 80 hl/ha
Fermentation quirks	Wine dependent on quality of grapes
	Rare oak treatment (Fumé Blanc)
Classic region	Sancerre and Pouilly Fumé
	Bordeaux (Graves and Sauternes)
	New Zealand
	California

Sauvignon Blanc Tasting Note

Appearance	Low intensity straw yellow with fading to the rim, possible greenish tint
Nose	Gooseberry, grapefruit, lime
	Apple, pear, stone fruit, melon
	Cut grass, tomato bush, jalapeno, cat pee
	Flint or mineral
Palate	High, piercing acidity
	Lime zest, grapefruit
	Asparagus or grass
	Minerality
	Low alcohol, short finish
Ageability	Most dry Sauvignon Blancs are early drinking

Sauternes Tasting Note

Appearance	High-intensity yellow gold
Nose	Apricot, honey
	Apple, pear, stone fruit
Palate	Intense sweetness
	High acidity
	Apricot, honey, citrus
	Medium alcohol, long finish
Ageability	Can age and improve for decades

QUESTIONS

1. Describe Sauvignon Blanc in the vineyard.

2. What soils are important for Sauvignon Blanc?

3. What differences are there between New World and Old World wine making with Sauvignon Blanc?

4. What type of climate does Sauvignon Blanc prefer?

5. What are the classic regions for growing Sauvignon Blanc?

6. Write a tasting note for a New Zealand Sauvignon Blanc.

7. What are the food pairing options for Sauvignon Blanc?

chapter 12

Riesling

*A*t one time, Rieslings commanded the respect in the wine world that Cabernet Sauvignon does today. It was (and is) a wine that can be enjoyable when young, but also develops a complexity with age that makes it all the more intriguing. Unfortunately, Riesling has fallen victim to the "guilt by association" syndrome, and its reputation has decreased because of bulk commercial sweet wines that are poor imitations of the great grape.

Upon completion of this chapter, the student should be able to:

> *Describe the vineyard conditions preferred by Riesling*
> *Describe unique characteristics of making Riesling wines*
> *Discuss ageability of Riesling wines*
> *Outline classic regions for quality Riesling*
> *Describe styles of Riesling wines*
> *Outline typical food pairings with Riesling*

In the Vineyard

Riesling is a very old grape, probably having been domesticated directly from wild vines in Germany. It is believed that Riesling was first systematically planted by the Romans as they moved up the Rhine Valley. The first written record with a name resembling Riesling comes from the mid-fifteenth century. It seems to have always been regarded as a top-quality grape, as it soon traveled throughout the German wine regions, and was soon the sole grape planted in many vineyards.

Riesling is not too finicky with regard to soil. In low-yielding vineyards, it can be a vehicle for demonstrating the terroir of a vineyard. There is a correlation with poorer soils and better quality. Riesling is planted on everything from slate screed to sandy loam. The requirement for any soil is that it is well draining. There can be some influence on ripening time based on soil, with cooler soils like clay lengthening the time it takes to ripen the grapes. This can be used to an advantage in regions that seem warm for growing Riesling.

Riesling is a "cool-climate" grape. The suggestion that that is a loose description is accurate. It is possible in some areas, such as Australia, to grow Riesling in what would be classified as a warm climate. What these areas have that distinguish them as a Riesling region is cool nights. The Riesling vine is very cold-hardy, making it a good choice for very marginal regions (such as Germany and Canada). It can survive a hard freeze that other vines (even crosses based on Riesling) cannot endure.

Riesling is also considered an early ripening grape. This is another benefit for a vine that is typically planted in cool regions. Fortunately, Riesling does not rush rapidly to overripeness and loss of acidity like other grapes do. In fact, while Riesling is early ripening, it prefers long, drawn-out ripening conditions. An extended ripening season does not significantly decrease the acidity in the grape, making late-harvest wines an option because the natural acidity will balance the residual sugar.

The Riesling vine does have some viticultural issues, however. As with many cool-climate grapes, Riesling is susceptible to changes in weather during flowering and can succumb to coulure. While the skin of the grape berry is moderately thick, it is possible for the vines to become infected with grey rot. Of course, in its beneficial form grey rot is botrytis, or noble rot, and Riesling can occasionally contract botrytis infections that result in excellent dessert wines.

The yield of a Riesling vineyard is usually placed in a medium-yield category. Yields can be curtailed by coulure in the spring. On the other hand, it is generally accepted that high yields do not totally compromise quality. This is reflected in several of the wine laws regarding Riesling production. In Alsace, it is legal to yield 80 hectoliters/hectare (most of the rest of French law stipulates around 37–40 hl/ha). In Germany, sometimes the yields are even higher than in Alsace. In the extreme high yield category, there is definitely a dilution of taste, and many producers keep yields around 50–70 hl/ha.

The Riesling vine is not particularly difficult to grow. What it possesses is the combination of top-quality grapes that make ageable wines, while also being cold hardy and early ripening. This has led to Riesling being the subject of a great deal of research in the German viticultural community. Riesling has "fathered" a great variety of grapes, most commonly crosses have produced Muller-Thurgau and Scheurebe. Riesling has even been crossed with the red grape Trollinger to yield Kerner. There are so many Riesling crosses that some have not even been named.

With all that research on crossing Riesling, clones have been developed. There are approximately fifty clones of Riesling currently in use around the world. Unlike other varieties, however, it does not seem that the choice of clone is a make-or-break decision when it comes to the ultimate wine production.

There are also Rieslings in name only. Throughout Europe, there are grapes that have (or have had) Riesling as part of their name, but that are completely unrelated to the classic grape. Welschriesling is a very common wannabe, often called Olasz Riesling, Riesling Italico, or Laszki Riesling. While it has a similar profile, it is much lighter and less aromatic than true Riesling. Synonyms for the real Riesling include Johannesburg Riesling (actually named for a notable German village), White Riesling, and Rhine Riesling.

In the Winery

Riesling is a grape variety whose wine "makes itself." The grape is really not amenable to winemaker intervention—it is what it is. Since that is the case, the quality of the grapes is what determines the quality of the end product.

Of course, there are still some choices left to the winemaker. The most obvious are of fermentation and of aging vessels. For fermentation, the winemaker can choose between stainless steel and old inert oak. Stainless gives a clarity to the fruit character and makes the wine pristine. Oak, on the other hand, allows for oxygen to infiltrate. During aging, this will soften the wine and allow greater complexity to develop. The choice is really about what style of Riesling the winemaker is striving for.

New oak is almost never used with Riesling. In most cases, the wine is not extracted enough to handle oak treatment. In other words, the intensity of flavors extracted from the grapes is not very concentrated. The unique varietal character of Riesling, its acidity and floral aromas, are overpowered by new oak. In fact, new oak tends to suffocate the delicacy of the aromas and flavor nuances in Riesling.

Rieslings can be made in a variety of styles. Several regions of production make dry Riesling. Others leave some residual sugar after fermentation and create off-dry Riesling. In good years, it may be possible to create a syrupy, sweet dessert wine style. And finally, some producers create a sparkling wine out of Riesling. Discussion of the different styles of Riesling and their characteristics appear in the Wine Styles section later in this chapter.

AGING

Most Riesling is meant to be drunk early, within a year or two of the vintage. Some Rieslings—those with high extract and concentration from a good long ripening season—are often left to age. Unlike other wines, the concentration and extract evident immediately after release is not an indicator of ageworthiness in Riesling.

Often the light, delicate, crisp wine seems like it would dissolve away into nothing if allowed to age. However, Riesling gains a great deal of complexity and nuance with bottle age. As discussed above, Riesling is not subjected to new oak, and occasionally sees time in old oak. Where most of the magic happens, however, is in the bottle. The reductive aging process in the bottle turns the light, delicate aromas of young Riesling into complex, heady, nuanced wines with age. This does not develop smoothly. There is typically a period of three to five years during which the wine seems clumsy. After this period, the bouquet begins to develop, and aged Riesling can then be enjoyed for a number of years.

CLASSIC REGIONS

Riesling is the champion grape of Germany. Of the thirteen wine growing regions in Germany, Riesling makes its greatest impression in the wines of the Mosel-Saar-Ruwer and from Rheingau. The wines of these regions have different styles based on climate (see below), but both regions make Riesling that is approachable young, but can also age for years.

The area of the Mosel River and its tributaries, the Saar and the Ruwer, are some of the northernmost vineyards in the world. Here, the vineyards are located on south-facing slopes along the twisting rivers. Only in the areas where the sun shines the longest is it possible to ripen Riesling enough to make a quality wine. The soil of this river system is slate, and a very loose, shallow slate at that. Also, the slopes are very steep, on the order of a 60-degree gradient in some places. To work these vineyards it is necessary to have strong ankles and good rock climbing skills.

The configuration of the vineyards in the Mosel serves a purpose. Vines grown on such steep slopes are raised closer to the sun. They are at such a steep angle that they do not shade the vines around them. Finally, the slope allows cold air to settle into the valley at night, allowing the rising warm air to increase the ambient temperature around the vines.

The slate soils of the Mosel also serve dual purposes. As merely soil, the slate is well draining and provides minerality to the wines produced in these vineyards. Expert tasters can distinguish between the red, blue, and gray slates of the region. These stones also serve as heat reservoirs. As the sun beats down on the hillside, the slate absorbs the energy of the sun and heats up. At night, that heat can then be released back to the vines, increasing the ambient temperature. One other characteristic of slate is the crystalline structure. There are small reflective crystals in slate, and this allows sunlight to reflect off the soil and up into the canopy of the vine, thereby increasing the effective amount of sunlight.

Also serving to increase the effective amount of sunlight that the vines receive is the river itself. The river serves as a giant mirror, reflecting light up onto the hillside and the vines. The river also serves as a heat reservoir, but for a longer time span. As discussed in an earlier chapter, the water slowly absorbs heat from the sun over the course of the summer, and releases it back slowly to the environment in the fall.

The Rheingau is an area similar to the Mosel. Many of the characteristics of the Mosel discussed above also describe Rheingau. In this region, the Rhine River makes a 13-mile curve from flowing northwesterly to southwesterly, before it turns north again. This is a natural sun trap and is so well regarded as a region that one vineyard and town, Johannesburg, has become synonymous with Riesling.

In nearby France, Riesling is grown in one region, Alsace. Unlike its German counterparts, Alsace makes dry Riesling. This area of France is one of the driest, due to a rain-shadow effect from the Vosges Mountains. This effect allows for a long, slow, dry ripening season to allow Riesling to get fully ripe, and therefore create high-alcohol wines. Riesling in Alsace is more about the aspect of the vineyard than it is about the soil, though that does contribute to the wine being fuller bodied and longer lived than German Riesling.

Outside Europe, Riesling is beginning to make a stronghold in the New World. Several regions are up-and-comers, including Victoria State in Australia, the Pacific Northwest in the United States, and the Finger Lakes region of Upstate New York. Each of these areas is seeing investment and research, and are all beginning to produce signature styles of Riesling.

The one New World area that has already made its mark is Canada. The two main grape growing regions in Canada, the Niagara Peninsula in Ontario and the Okanagan Valley in British Columbia, both produce fine Rieslings. Their claim to fame, however, is in a unique style known as Ice Wine (*Eiswein* in German). These regions are one of the perfect areas in the world to produce this signature style (see below).

Wine Styles

As mentioned earlier, Riesling can be made into a variety of styles ranging from dry to off-dry to sweet dessert wines and sparkling wines. The discussion of sparkling Riesling will be reserved for the chapter on sparkling wine. This section will elucidate the different styles, their characteristics, and any regional variation in their production.

German wines range in style based on the ripeness of the fruit at harvest. Growers study the vineyards and measure the grape sugar concentration using a refractometer. When certain benchmark levels of sugar are reached, then picking the grapes to make that level of wine is allowed. It is possible to ferment the wine and classify it as a lower level, but it is not possible to classify it upward. The choice is always to pick the grapes at a level that is reliable, or to wait and hope the weather allows the grapes to reach the next stage of ripeness. In good years, some grapes will be picked initially, while some are left on the vine to develop further.

The top level of quality wine in Germany is called *Qualitatswein mit Pradikat*, or QmP. These wines are then subcategorized into Kabinett, Spätlese, Auslese, Beerenauslese, Eiswein, or Trockenbeerenauslese. Kabinett wines (the name describes wines that can be stored) use grapes that have just ripened. Spätlese wines are classified as late harvest. These grapes have been allowed to get very ripe before picking. Auslese wines utilize specially selected bunches to make the wine. These bunches are extremely ripe, and may or may not have botrytis influence.

The wines in these first three levels can be vinified dry or off-dry. Here the winemaker has two choices: stop the fermentation before all the sugar is consumed, or vinify the wine to dryness, then add back sweetness. The sweetness is typically added back in the form of a *süssreserve*, or a portion of the grape juice held back from fermentation. The use of a süssreserve does not dilute the flavors of the wine because it is the original juice from which it is fermented. There is a difference to be noted between these two sweetening methods. During the fermentation process, yeast is consuming all the sugars in the juice. Some, like glucose, are consumed more rapidly than others, like fructose. As a result, wines whose fermentation has been stopped will have a high ratio of fructose remaining, which in turn tastes fruitier. Süssreserve wines have the initial balance of glucose to fructose and will not taste as complex, just sweet.

As the grapes increase in ripeness from Kabinett level to Auslese, several things change in the wine. First, the acids become "riper." That is to say, the high levels of malic acid in Kabinett wines decreases with increasing ripeness, and is replaced by higher levels of tartaric acid. Tartaric acid is not as sharp as malic acid, and the resulting wine will taste more balanced and have fruitier acidity.

On inspection, these three levels of wine may appear the same. They will be pale straw in color. Some young wines may have a greenish tint, and wines from riper grapes may have more color than those from less ripe grapes. That refers not only to grapes of differing ripeness levels from the same region (Kabinett versus Spätlese), but also grapes from different regions at the same level (Rheingau versus Mosel). On the nose, there is a definite combination of stone fruit (peach, apricot) and citrus. Citrus will predominate in Kabinett or Mosel wines, while riper or warmer climate grapes lean more to the stone fruit. Floral notes are present, in the form of jasmine, honeysuckle, or orange blossoms. A slate minerality is also apparent on the nose. Finally, there can be a hint of kerosene as well. As these wines age, bouquet will develop into a stronger kerosene nose, along with marzipan (almond) and honey. On the palate, the acidity would be noted as high, but it differs from Sauvignon Blanc. While Sauvignon Blanc's acidity is sharp, that of Riesling is "rounded." The acidity builds, but feels full and fruity instead of biting and strong. The sweetness level will not determine quality level. As stated earlier, it is possible to make a dry Auslese. It doesn't happen often, but it is possible. Riesling's body is light, it is low in alcohol, but it has a lingering finish for a light wine.

In two of the dessert wine levels, Beerenauslese (BA) and Trockenbeerenauslese (TBA), the grapes have been infected with botrytis. Beerenauslese refers to berry-selected grapes. Each grape is picked separately for use in making this style. It is not made every year in Germany, only in good years when harvest has been lucky enough to last that long. Trockenbeerenauslese is the rarest of wines. It refers to dried berry-selected grapes, meaning that not only are the grapes botrytis infected, but they have shriveled up as well. These wines only happen a few times a decade, and are considered so expensive to make that some wineries actually lose money when all the labor and effort is calculated into the price.

These wines have a definite botrytis profile. Their color is intense golden, which will become more amber with age. The nose is that of its younger counterparts, but more concentrated, sweet and heady. Often these wines take on the nose of raisins or baked apples. On the palate, these are definitely sweet wines, but with a strong thread of acidity to keep the sugar in balance and make them refreshing. The influence of botrytis is also evident in the dried apricot and honey tones.

Eiswein is a category unto itself. There are now worldwide regulations governing the production of Eiswein, or Ice Wine. First, the grapes cannot be harvested until the temperature reaches 16°F (−8°C). At this temperature, the water inside the grape is frozen, and when pressed immediately after picking, only syrupy grape nectar flows out. The ice crystals that were in the grape remain behind in the press. Then the wine is fermented. This wine differs from the other botrytis-infected wines in that botrytis is often not present, and the flavor profile is much fresher and has brighter fruit flavors than do the wines from raisinated grapes.

There is a subclass of wines made in the Rheingau, known as Charta wines. These are producers who formed an association in 1983, and have agreed to produce dry Riesling from the Rheingau. There is no vineyard designation on the bottles, but they must come from top vineyard sites. The Charta logo is displayed and is a sign that the wine will be dry, no matter what the quality level designation.

Alsace is the second home to Riesling. Alsatian Riesling is always dry. It is often from the best vineyard sites—those that receive the most sun and are the most sheltered. Because Alsace is farther south than most German vineyards, and it has a long ripening season due to the Vosges Mountain rain shadow, it is possible to get high sugar levels in the grapes. This, in turn, creates wines with more body than their German counterparts. The wines have a similar flavor profile to the German wines, the notable differences being that the wine is dry and that it is fuller bodied with greater concentration. The high acidity is now balanced by that concentration of flavor rather than sweetness.

The Alsatians also produce wines that are the equivalent of Beerenauslese and Trockenbeerenauslese. These are Vendage Tardive and Selections de Grains Noble. Vendage Tardive wines are late harvest. They can be sweet or dry, and are often made in good years with long ripening seasons. Selections de Grains Noble refers to wine made from botrytis-infected grapes. This will be a rich dessert wine, and is rare because the conditions for botrytis are not as good in Alsace as they are in parts of Germany.

The Australians have developed a style of dry Riesling for which they are becoming noted. The difference between an Alsatian Riesling and that of Australia is in the fruit profile. Australian Riesling is much more fruit forward, and often has a scent of lime zest or lime gummy candy. As with Alsace, Australian Riesling is higher in alcohol content, because the grapes can get riper.

Food and Wine Pairing

To pair a Riesling with food really means you have to understand the wine. The wines range from bone dry to syrupy sweet, with every level in between. The only way in most cases to know the sweetness level of the wine is to taste it before planning a food pairing.

Riesling does have high acidity, no matter the sweetness level. This allows Rieslings to pair well with very rich foods, like duck, goose, pate, or cream sauces. Increasing sweetness levels from dry to German Spatlese would be good with spicy foods, like Thai and spicy Chinese. Anything with a sweetness over Auslese should be treated as a dessert wine. Because some of these are table wines and not true dessert wines, it is best to pair them with only lightly sweet desserts, or with a cheese course.

Basics for Riesling (REEZ-ling)

Climate	Cool-weather grape
Soil	Slate
Disease susceptibility	Coulure Grey rot (and noble rot) Bunch rot
Growth habit	Very vigorous
Characteristics	Develops high sugar levels Easy to grow Clones available but not critical Early budding and late ripening
Average yield	30 to 80 hl/ha
Fermentation quirks	Wine dependent on quality of grapes
Classic region	Germany (Mosel, Rhine Valley) Alsace Australia Canada

Riesling Tasting Note

Appearance	Low-intensity straw yellow with fading to the rim, possible greenish tint
Nose	Citrus, lime zest
	Apple, pear, stone fruit
	Jasmine, honeysuckle
	Kerosene (mainly in German)
Palate	High, rounded acidity
	Citrus zest, stone fruit, apples, and pears
	Slate, minerality
	Potentially off dry, depending on style and region
	Low alcohol, short finish
Ageability	Up to 15 years for German and Alsatian; ready to drink elsewhere

QUESTIONS

1. What is the preferred soil for Riesling?

2. What styles of wine can Riesling make?

3. Describe the growing characteristics of Riesling.

4. What happens to Riesling if it is aged?

5. What are the classic regions known for growing Riesling?

6. Write a tasting note for a German Kabinett Riesling.

7. What are the food pairing options for Riesling?

chapter 13

Syrah/Shiraz

*S*yrah is an ancient varietal that, until recently, was well regarded but not very popular. Its historic home was not on major trade routes, like Bordeaux, and it was often used to help improve other wines. It took a modern-day makeover as Australian Shiraz to open the eyes of the wine-consuming public and reawaken interest in this classic grape.

Upon completion of this chapter, the student should be able to:

Describe the vineyard conditions preferred by Syrah
Describe unique characteristics of making Syrah wines
Discuss ageability of Syrah wines
Outline classic regions for quality Syrah
Describe styles of Syrah wines
Outline typical food pairings with Syrah

In the Vineyard

Most of the theories surrounding Syrah's origin have some form of exotic twist. The name Shiraz suggested to some that the grape originated in the Persian (now Iranian) city of the same name. Others believed the grape came to France from Egypt, via the city of Syracuse (Siracusa) in Sicily, and the name is a reflection of the stopover. Yet another theory gives the honors to Gaspard de Sterimberg, who returned from the Crusades with the vine and became a hermit in a small chapel in what is now Hermitage. Unromantically, the real origin is as a wild vine from the Rhône, cultivated since Roman times.

Syrah's flavor profile can be influenced by the soil. In general, Syrah prefers shallow, well-drained soils. The most intense and perfumed Syrahs come from granite- or schist-based soils. In the New World, soil can vary from sandy to clay, with corresponding variation in tannin structure and concentration.

The best way to describe Syrah's preferred climate is to say that Syrah is Goldilocks—not too warm, not too cool, but just right. As a late budder and early ripener, a short growing season is not a problem for Syrah. However, too much heat and the grape will shoot straight to being overripe, and will lose many of its delicate aromatic components. Regions that tend to be cooler can take advantage of the vineyard aspect to increase the ripening potential of Syrah. These wines often demonstrate the most perfume of all Syrahs. Warmer regions need cool nights to slow the ripening process, and produce wines bursting with cooked and jammy fruit.

Syrah's growth is vigorous when compared to many other grapes. Its canes also have a tendency to be droopy, resulting in trellising of one form or another. The trellising also helps getting sunlight to the grapes so that they ripen properly. Another vine characteristic is its hardiness to disease. Only grey rot and bunch rot take a toll on Syrah, and then only under certain conditions.

Yields from Syrah vines ultimately determine quality. Many producers believe good-quality wines result from yields in the 36–40 hl/ha range. There is a belief that proper canopy management can increase the yield without compromising quality. The results of these tests have not been released yet.

Clonal selection for Syrah is fairly limited to ten or fewer clones. The Australian Shiraz is considered a new clone, though it originated in France. Most clonal selection in the vineyard is to provide flavor nuances to the wine, rather than due to preferred growing conditions. What all Syrahs do have, though, is a high concentration of compounds known as glycosyl-glucoses. These compounds, essentially glucose attached to esters and other metabolites, are believed to be precursors to the aromatic compounds released during fermentation. There is currently a great deal of research in Australia to determine if analysis of the glycosyl-glucose levels is a good indicator of physiological ripeness.

In the Winery

Making Syrah is fairly straightforward. Many French producers used to ferment whole clusters of grapes. This produced extremely tannic wines, and a good dose of those tannins were green and stemmy. More modern styles either eschew stems altogether or the stems that are included are riper, because the fruit has been allowed to ripen more before picking.

Syrah grapes have a great deal of color in the skins. Winemakers vary on how long a maceration the grapes receive before fermentation begins. Some producers only macerate for a few days, while others may allow the grapes and juice to sit for three weeks. In either case, once fermentation begins, it is typically a hot fermentation. The standard temperature for a Syrah fermentation is 90–100°F (32–38°C).

Fermentation used to be, and in some places still is, conducted in large, open wood barrels. More typical are closed stainless steel tanks. In some areas of Australia, shallow fermenters open to the air are being utilized. The shallow fermenter allows for greater area of contact between the wine and the cap during fermentation. This makes extraction easier without increased punching down or pumping over.

Once the wine is fermented, it is aged in oak. The French vary in the size of the oak barrels they use, with the small barriques becoming more popular. Also, the French tend to use old oak, so as not to overpower the natural aromas in Syrah. The Australians, on the other hand, will finish the fermentation process in new American oak barrels. This allows the oak flavors to be integrated into the wine more effectively and helps to stabilize the color. The use of new oak should be monitored carefully, however, as it can outshine the intriguing Syrah aromas.

One common practice in the Rhône has been to blend Syrah with the white grape Viognier. It is thought that blending the two provides more floral character to the wine, and helps to temper the tannins. However, this blend is not merely mixing a white and a red wine together. The blend happens at the fermentation tank, where both grapes are crushed together and fermented with the skins. Originally this occurred because the grapes were a "field blend," meaning that Syrah and Viognier were grown side by side and picked at the same time. It is now believed that there is something about that combination that extracts more color from the skins of the Syrah and also serves to stabilize the color. Further research is being conducted to see if there are other possible symbiotic relationships beside that of Syrah and Viognier.

AGING

Until the 1970s, Syrah in France used to be bottled upon demand, rather than at the optimum time of cask age. This resulted in large variations in the ageability of the wines. French Syrah is among the longest lived, not really opening up until at least five or ten years after the vintage, then lasting until they are in their twenties. Australian Shiraz lasts longer than Californian—six to fifteen years compared to four to ten years. Syrah does increase in complexity with age, as we will see in the Wine Styles section.

CLASSIC REGIONS

The home to Syrah is the Rhône, in particular the northern Rhône. Here the regions of Côte Rôtie, Hermitage, and Cornas produce some of the biggest and most elegant Syrahs. Syrah is the only red grape grown in the northern Rhône.

Côte Rôtie comprises very steep slopes above the Rhône River. As the name suggests, these "roasted slopes" face south and southeast, and get a great deal of sun that warms them up relative to the rest of the region. The slopes are so steep that many have been terraced over the years, and often the soil must be collected in buckets at the bottom of the slope and returned to the higher elevations.

The Côte Rôtie is divided into several *lieux-dits,* or named plots of land. The most famous are the Côte Brune and the Côte Blonde. The Côte Brune is high in iron and clay, which creates wines that are fuller and longer lived. The Côte Blonde has more limestone in the soil, and the wines from these grapes tend to be more aromatic and delicate. Other *lieux-dits* in the Côte Rôtie are La Mouline, La Landonne, and La Turque.

Hermitage is a granitic hill that juts out into the Rhône River. Depending upon the soil of a particular lieu-dit, the wines can vary from soft and supple to tough and concentrated. Notable lieux-dits in Hermitage are l'Hermite, le Méal, and les Bessards. At one point in history, these wines were considered the best in France. The wine from here was often exported to Bordeaux in order to enrich the wines there.

Cornas is a natural sun trap, facing south and sheltered from the wind. The wines are the most tannic and deepest in color, because the grapes can ripen so well. However, Cornas Syrah tends not to be as aromatic or as nuanced as those from Hermitage or Côte Rôtie.

The wind is the dominant climatic issue in the northern Rhône. It influences the grapes from flowering (hindering self-pollination) to harvest. The wind is the Mistral, a cold wind that originates in Switzerland and rushes down the narrow Rhône valley to the Mediterranean. The wind is beneficial in that it cools the grapes as they are being blasted by the sun. On the other hand, the wind roars through at up to 90 miles per hour, and has the ability to rip the vines right from the soil. Syrah vines are therefore staked, sometimes with one stake (Hermitage) and sometimes with as many as three stakes (Côte Rôtie).

The southern Rhône is also home to Syrah, but here it is a mere player and not the star of the show. That title is reserved for Grenache (see the following chapter). Syrah in the southern Rhône often is planted on secondary sites, even north facing slopes. This slows its ripening, which can happen too quickly in the warmer south.

Australian Shiraz, especially that from the Hunter and Barossa Valleys, was not planted based on soil, but rather on the understanding that Shiraz could handle the heat in those regions. The producers then made everything from light, fruity wines to big, chewy reds to Port-like wines to sparkling wine. The vines were originally from the Rhône, as was the wine making philosophy, which was handed down over the years. Many of the vines in Barossa are ungrafted, and were planted in the mid-1800s, producing amazingly concentrated and rich grapes.

California is one of the top new places for Syrah, even though it has been around since the 1970s when planted by a group known as the Rhône Rangers. California Syrah is still looking for the best locations in terms of climate, as well as a style. One tip to the style in the bottle is the grape name displayed on the label. "Shiraz" denotes a wine made in an Australian style, whereas "Syrah" refers to a more French style.

Wine Styles

Having just referred to an Australian style and a French style, exactly what are the differences? First, let's discuss what is similar about types of Syrah and then note what distinguishes Australia and France.

Observation of Syrah in the glass will show a deep garnet red (depending upon age), with some variation as the color approaches the rim. On the nose comes the first indication this is no ordinary red wine. One of the first aromas is that of flowers—violets and carnations. There are black fruits like blackberries and plums. There is an herbal component, but not the green herbs of Cabernet Sauvignon. These herbs are more like the *garrigue* (a type of scrubland vegetation found on limestone soils) of southern France—the scent of wild rosemary, lavender, and thyme, along with black pepper. There is also something meaty about the aromas; this may best be described as salami or bacon fat. Smoke, licorice, game, and earth all intertwine with those other aromas. As the wine ages, more notes of leather and chocolate may appear.

On the palate, Syrah will have bright black fruit, the black pepper bite, and balanced tannins. The acidity will be medium, but just enough to balance the richness of flavor or the concentration of fruit. Depending on the alcohol level, the wine may be more dominated by peppery notes (lower alcohol) or by fruit (higher alcohol).

Australian Shiraz distinguishes itself by the vanilla of the new American oak, but also by the jammy or stewed fruit qualities on the nose and on the palate. French Syrah will taste ripe, but never as cooked as Australian Shiraz. French Syrah will also be more perfumed than its Australian cousin, and have more meat and herbal notes as well.

Food and Wine Pairing

Syrah is a wine that is intensely flavored. This is the key component to matching a dish to Syrah. The grape can be made in a variety of weights, which allows the pairings to range from full-flavored chicken dishes to game, beef, and even barbeque. The key is to choose a wine equal in weight, but make sure the dish has plenty of flavor. Syrah is not the best match for Asian dishes, since it often overwhelms them and does not pair well with the slightly sweet character of some of the items.

Basics for Syrah (see-RAH) / Shiraz (shee-RAHZ)

Climate	Not too warm, not too cool
Soil	Shallow and well drained, preferably granite or schist
Disease susceptibility	Resistant to many diseases, except grey and bunch rot
Growth habit	Droopy vines need trellising
	One of the largest berry sizes among vinifera varietals
Characteristics	Few clones to choose from
	Needs physiological ripeness to achieve best aromatics
	Late budding, early ripening
Average Yield	36–40 hl/ha
Fermentation quirks	Fermentation with Viognier helps stabilize color and tannin
	Restrained use of oak in France, liberal use of new American oak common in Australia

Classic region	Northern Rhone
	Australia
	California
	Southern Rhone

Syrah Tasting Note

Appearance	Deep garnet red with some variation to rim
Nose	Violets and carnations
	Black fruits (blackberry and plum)
	Garrigue and black pepper
	Game, smoke, bacon fat, salami
Palate	Medium acidity
	Balanced tannins
	Black pepper, wild herbs, iron, meaty, game, black fruit
	Medium length
Ageability	Ability to age up to and beyond 20 years; development observable after 5 to 10 years

Shiraz Tasting Note

Appearance	Deep garnet red with some variation to rim
Nose	Very ripe black fruits (blackberry and plum)
	Violets and carnations
	Black pepper
	Vanilla
Palate	Medium acidity
	Balanced tannins
	Jammy or stewed black fruits, meaty, black pepper, vanilla
	Medium length
Ageability	Australian: 6 to 15 years
	Californian: 4 to 10 years

QUESTIONS

1. What type of climate is preferred by Syrah?

2. What unique characteristics of Syrah production are found in the Côte Rôtie?

3. What are the classic regions for Syrah?

4. Write a tasting note for a Rhone Syrah.

5. Write a tasting note for an Australian Shiraz.

6. What are the major differences in the Old World and New World styles of Syrah?

7. What are the food pairing options for Syrah?

chapter *14*

Grenache/ Garnacha

*A*ny other grape that is only used in blending or to make rosés or dessert wines would not be considered a classic, international varietal. But not so with Grenache. While the grape does not make a single varietally labeled wine, it is the most widely planted in the world and responsible for some of the most intriguing and interesting wines being made. Grenache (or Garnacha, as the Spanish call it) is a world traveler, and has adapted to be the melody off which other grapes in the blend harmonize.

Upon completion of this chapter, the student should be able to:

Describe the vineyard conditions preferred by Grenache
Describe unique characteristics of making Grenache wines
Discuss ageability of Grenache wines
Outline classic regions for quality Grenache
Describe styles of Grenache wines
Outline typical food pairings with Grenache

In the Vineyard

It seems that Grenache is originally a Spanish grape, probably from the region of Aragon. From there it spread to Rioja and Cataluña in Spain. Political control led to its spread to the Roussillon region of France, and is also the most likely avenue for Grenache finding its way to Sardinia, where it is known as Cannonau. What do all these regions have in common? Climate.

Garnacha/Grenache is most adapted to hot, arid conditions. The vine itself is drought resistant (of course, that is also necessary of its rootstock for it to be useful). The vine likes it warm, and even a bit windy. It prefers soils that are poor and well drained, most typically these are rocky soils.

Grenache is an early budder and a late ripener, and loves hot weather to get the grapes to ripen. It is very vigorous in its growth, and is extremely prolific if all the conditions are right. Of course, there are some times when they are not right. Grenache is susceptible to coulure, and can lose a significant portion of flowers, thereby reducing yield. It is also susceptible to powdery mildew and to bunch rot of its fairly tightly packed clusters. If ripening gets a bit moist toward harvest, much of the crop could be lost to rot.

These disease susceptibilities are a balance to the prolific nature of Grenache. In very hot regions, with no control of growth, Grenache can produce upwards of 50+ hl/ha. However, this is not good-quality Grenache. For that, the yields need to be much lower, often 27 hl/ha or less.

Yield is probably the controlling factor in growing quality Grenache. It is the perfect example of how the quantity of quality is limited in a vine, and the yield determines how well that is distributed. Grenache has some inherent characteristics—it is naturally low in malic acid and it has very little color and tannin because of the thin skins. If yields are very high, the grapes will express themselves with little acidity and such little color that they may appear pink rather than red. Low-yield Grenache, however, retains its acidity better, and concentrates the tannin and color into the few grapes that remain.

Harvest timing also controls the ultimate character of the grapes. It would seem reasonable that to retain acidity, a grower may pick the grapes slightly underripe. This only results in very green character and very little color. Leaving Grenache on the vine until physiological ripeness is reached exposes one of Grenache's other characteristics—the ability to ripen with high sugar levels. Ripe Grenache will make a wine typically around 15 percent alcohol by volume with little trouble, and have been known to reach 18 percent without the addition of extra alcohol.

If planting a new Grenache vineyard, the grower should consider two options: location and clone. The location should be chosen with two thoughts in mind.

First, the vineyard should be in a place with cool evening temperatures. This will aid the grapes in retaining what little acidity they have. Second should be stress. The vines that produce the best fruit and therefore the best wines are often the most stressed. This stress could take the form of hilltops exposed to the weather, little water, or if all else fails, vigorous pruning.

Clonal selection depends on the style of wine the grapes in the vineyard will produce. There are about 360 clones of Grenache. Some of these clones are very productive, some less. Some of them retain color better than others. Finally, some produce a lot of sugar, best for making dessert wines.

In the Winery

Grenache is a red grape that needs great care in the winery. It is not like Pinot Noir, which loses its aromas and complexity, but rather Grenache loses its more basic characteristic: color. Because of the low amount of color and tannin in the grapes, it is essential that Grenache be handled properly to maximize its potential.

Grenache oxidizes very easily. This is partially due to the low tannin levels found in the grapes. In most red wines, the tannin levels are high enough (or the color concentrated enough) that it acts as a natural anti-oxidant. True, some tannin level is lost, or some color is lost, but in the overall scheme, it is not noticed. In Grenache, every little change is noticed. It is extremely important to keep oxygen out of the wine making process. This includes taking care in pressing and fermentation, as well as very little racking of the wines after fermentation is complete.

In order to extract more tannins, a higher proportion of stems in often allowed in the fermentation. Unfortunately, more often than not this results in strengthening the already strong tendency to green and stemmy flavors in the wine. Harsher pressings or hotter fermentations tend to accentuate the bitterness and astringency of the tannins. The best mix of methods includes long, slow fermentations followed by a long maceration to finish extracting tannins.

Old World producers tend to use old oak to age the wines. New oak is becoming more popular, but the flavors of new oak do not necessarily enhance the wines being made. New oak can, however, help stabilize the color and prevent oxidation. This is probably an area that will see change and experimentation over the next several years.

The final wine profile will not be single-varietal Grenache. Typically, other grapes are often added to increase color, tannin, or acidity, but the result has shown to be better than the sum of the parts. Blending partners (see Classic Regions for who uses what) include Tempranillo, Cabernet Sauvignon, Mourvèdre, and Syrah.

Classic Regions

More than any other wine, the region of production determines the style in which Grenache is produced. There are red table wines, rosé table wines, and sweet fortified wines. The most common wines made and the ones with the most regard are the red table wines.

The best wine from the homeland of Grenache comes from Priorato, a small, once forgotten back corner of Cataluña. The soils here are known as Llicorella, a local name that describes the layers of slate and quartzite that form the base of the soil mix. The vines are typically held to extremely low yields, on the order of 5–7 hl/ha. This results in wine that is black and concentrated. New wave producers will blend Grenache with Cabernet Sauvignon, Merlot, or Syrah to soften and provide aroma. Old school producers stick to making wines that may take twenty years to soften.

In France, the gamut of Grenache style can be seen in the red wines of the Southern Rhône. In its less-concentrated form, Grenache forms the backbone of the wide-ranging Côtes du Rhône blend. The pinnacle of Grenache, however, is Châteauneuf-du-Pape. Châteauneuf-du-Pape is classically a blend of thirteen grape varieties (both red and white) whose backbone is Grenache. The other major players in this blend are Syrah and Mourvèdre. Legally, anywhere from 50 to 70 percent of the blend will be Grenache. Typically, lesser wines will contain more Grenache. Other top regions in the southern Rhone include Gigondas and Vacqueyras, which make similar wines to Châteauneuf-du-Pape, though with a higher proportion of Grenache and less of other varietals.

Châteauneuf-du-Pape is noted for its galets, or pudding stones, in many of the vineyards. These stones absorb heat during the day and radiate it back to the vines at night. They also serve as mulch to the soil, preventing it from drying out completely under the force of the Mistral wind. Whether these stones actually influence the flavor of the wines is up for interpretation.

Australia is noted for making Grenache fashionable again. The grape was on the downswing, and vines were even being pulled in favor of Cabernet Sauvignon and Chardonnay. Then the winemakers created their version of Châteauneuf-du-Pape: GSM, which stands for Grenache-Shiraz-Mourvèdre, in order of percentage in the bottle. These wines are typical Australian reds—jammy, spicy, and fruit forward. While not the caliber of Priorato wines, these are a new style that has revived the interest in Grenache.

Two regions for rosé wines are Navarra in Spain and Tavel in France. Both of these regions make a dry pink wine that is easy drinking and fruity. These wines are best drunk young, soon after the vintage.

Finally, Grenache is made into a fortified dessert wine in southern France. Known as *vins doux naturels*, these wines are the result of partial fermentation of the Grenache juice and the addition of brandy to stop the fermentation (see the method for making Port). The wines can be aged normally to produce dark, fruity wines, or they can be made in a *rancio* style. Rancio wines are left to age in the hot sun, either in wood barrels or glass containers, open to the air for long periods of time. This gives the wines a nutty, raisiny, cooked flavor similar to Madeira. The best regions of note are Banyuls, Rivesaltes, and Maury.

Wine Styles

As noted above, the styles of Grenache wines depend on the region in which they are produced. For our purposes, this section will focus on the red table wines.

On the whole, Grenache-based wines are best drunk young, because of the propensity to oxidize easily and their low acidity. Upon examining a glass of Grenache-based wine, the color and its intensity will tip the hand of what to expect. If the wine is ruby, with a medium intensity, the wine will be of the standard "drink it young" style, like Côtes du Rhône. If the intensity is deep, this may be a higher-quality version, resulting from low yields, like a Priorato. One other indicator of Grenache is a possible orange hint to the rim. This comes from the propensity to oxidize easily. That oxidation may have happened in the winery or in the bottle, but in the glass the color may indicate a wine that appears to be older than it really is.

On the nose is where Grenache begins to stand out. Bright red fruit forms the backbone for some of the more unique combinations of aromas—nuts, baking spices, leather, white pepper, coffee, and licorice. As the wine ages, the fruit will begin to vanish, replaced by more leather and tar. Wine produced from higher-yielding grapes will have less complexity on the nose. On the palate, the aromas are duplicated in flavors. A tasting note would have strawberry and raspberry fruit, white pepper on the finish, and a thread of licorice or anise through the whole palate. Most noticeable would be the high alcohol, which is sometimes balanced by the flavors on the palate and sometimes not. The alcohol may even appear as a residual sweetness rather than a hot burn on the back of the throat.

In terms of aging these wines, Grenache-based wines do not tend to last as long as other red grape varietals. The newer styled Prioratos are best between five and fifteen years old, where Châteauneuf-du-Pape is on the order of six to twelve years. Even the best vins doux naturels only are at their best five to ten years after the vintage.

Food and Wine Pairing

Pairing Grenache with food will depend on the wine making style. A Priorato Garnacha would not work with the same foods as a light Côtes du Rhône. Lighter Grenache is best for foods that have a bit of heat, due to their low tannin level. The low acidity keeps Grenache in this style from being a good match for rich meats, but it would work with light game dishes, simple grilled meats, and even vegetarian dishes. The more full-bodied and tannic styles of Grenache are better with roast beef, lamb, and some richer meats. Grenache in its rosé form is the classic pair with bouillabaisse. These rosés are great bridges for what would be considered dishes that are a little too full bodied for white wine.

Basics for Grenache (gruh-NAHSH)

Climate	Loves hot, arid weather
Soil	Llicorella, galets
Disease susceptibility	Coulure Powdery mildew Bunch rot
Growth habit	Very vigorous
Characteristics	Rapid ripening causes fast drop in acidity Develops high sugar levels Little color and tannin in skins, prone to oxidation Early budding and late ripening
Average yield	27 to 50+ hl/ha
Fermentation quirks	Easily oxidizes while fermenting
Classic region	Spain (Priorato, Navarra) France (Southern Rhône, Roussillon) Sardinia Australia

Grenache Tasting Note

Appearance	Medium-intensity ruby with slight orange tinge to rim
Nose	Bright red fruit: cherries, berries White pepper, baking spices, nuts Coffee, licorice Leather

Palate	Low acidity
	Strawberry and raspberry
	Licorice or anise
	White pepper on finish
	High alcohol, medium finish
Ageability	Up to 15 years, depending on style

QUESTIONS

1. What type of climate is preferred by Grenache?
2. Describe the reasons Grenache needs special care in the winery.
3. What grapes are often mixed with Grenache?
4. What are the classic regions for growing Grenache?
5. What are the soil preferences for Grenache?
6. Write a tasting note for a Grenache-based wine.
7. What are the food and wine options for Grenache?

PART THREE

wines
from **white grapes**

White grapes can be classified into several categories based on the style of the wine produced. Some grapes make wines that are very aromatic, which is their dominant characteristic. Other white wines are known for being light and crisp, with refreshing acidity and delicacy. At the other end of the spectrum are the full and fat wines. These are plump, mouth-filling wines that are rich and complex. The grapes discussed in these chapters exemplify the spectrum of white wine styles.

Chapter 15 **The Aromatics**

Chapter 16 **Light and Crisp White Wines**

Chapter 17 **Fat and Full**

The Aromatics

*T*here is a group of white grapes that are somewhat unique to the world of wine. All wines have aroma characteristics; some are even considered to be intensely aromatic for their styles. And then there are the Aromatics: Viognier, Muscat, Gewurztraminer, Torrontes, Albariño, and Verdejo. These white grapes are, for lack of better terminology, very intensely aromatic. The aromas are not just increased to an exceptionally prolific level; they are often unique smells as well, evoking perfume or a garden in bloom. In all, the most important aspect of these wines is their aromaticity, and preserving that is the most important job of the grower and the winemaker. The most difficult aspect of these wines is often getting it right.

Upon completion of this chapter, the student should be able to:

    Describe the different aromatic white grapes
    Outline the styles of wine made from aromatic white grapes
    Discuss the typical locations for sourcing aromatic wines

Viognier

What is known of Viognier is based on a small appellation in the northern Rhône region of France. The appellation of Condrieu and the smaller Chateau Grillet has been the home to Viognier for centuries. In fact, Viognier has been in the Rhône at least since the Romans. Until about the 1980s, this region was the only place to find Viognier and its exotic expression as wine. Much of what we know about the grape has been from the experiments of winemakers in France, California, and Australia.

Viognier as a quality wine is determined in the vineyard. There are factors that must be satisfied for the grape to produce its signature, and sometimes elusive, aromas. First and foremost is ripening. Viognier's aromatics ripen after the grape appears to be sugar ripe. The vines need heat in order for the aromatics to develop completely. It is often the last grape harvested. This gives ample time for the aromas to develop and the sugar to skyrocket, ultimately to produce a wine with 13 percent alcohol or more.

Soil may have an effect on the grape. In Condrieu, the soil is a deep sandy topsoil, and the wines are subsequently very aromatic. In other regions of the world, the soils are varied, though examples in deep loam in Australia have shown to also be quite aromatic.

One reason why the verdict on soil is still out relates to vine age as a key factor. Quality Viognier is made from vines that are at least fifteen to twenty years old. Many of the vines in the New World are just beginning to approach that age. Those in Condrieu are on the order of seventy years old, which would produce very different wines.

Yield is also a factor for Viognier. In Condrieu, the growers noted that any production over 30 hl/ha has difficulty developing the flavor and lusciousness that quality Viognier is known for. The grower has many factors to balance that influence the yield of Viognier particularly. First, it tends to have poor fruit set. Many bunches are affected by millerandage, or having unripe, seedless grapes on the same cluster as ripe, juicy grapes. Second, leaf roll virus is a problem, affecting photosynthesis and ultimately ripeness. Finally, many shoots do not produce quality grapes on their first buds (where most other varietals produce their best). Pruning and trellising systems must take this into account, so bunches produced further down the cane can be harvested.

In the winery, Vigonier is most commonly left to itself. Some producers experiment with skin contact, though this can extract more oily phenolics that are less than desirable in the wine. Fermentation is straightforward, usually at cooler temperatures to preserve the aromatics. After-fermentation measures vary from producer to producer. Viognier has naturally low acidity (partially due to the overripeness when picked) so malolactic fermentation is really for increased weight rather than de-acidification. In fact, in the New World, the opposite—acidification—may take place just to replace some of the refreshing acidity in the wine. Finally, some producers allow the wine to rest *sur lie* and employ batonnage until the wine is ready for bottling.

Why go to so much effort to produce a wine from a finicky vine whose grapes have to be just perfectly ripe to make great wine? The wine. Great Viognier hits you on the nose like walking into a florist. Good Viognier has components of honeysuckle, apricots, musk, jasmine, and candied orange peel. This could all be cloying and perfumish if not for the full-bodied creaminess on the palate. This combination makes a good Viognier a glass of sensuality.

Old Viognier is an oxymoron. Viognier should be drunk young, the younger the better. As it ages, the aromas are lost and it loses some of its sensuality. Even the best Viogniers from Condrieu are expected to be at their best before their fourth birthday. Some can last for ten years, but these wines are few and far between, not to mention that which ones they are is not readily apparent upon release.

There are three major areas of production in the world: France, Australia, and California. As noted earlier, the main appellation in France for Viognier is Condrieu in the Rhône region. Within this already small appellation is a single owner appellation, Chateau Grillet. These wines of Chateau Grillet often demonstrate higher acidity than Condrieu, but often are not of the concentration or aromaticity of its neighbor. Nearby in the Côte Rotie, Viognier is used in the fermentation with Syrah. Up to 20 percent Viognier is allowed in the mix, yet often the amount is much less than that. It is believed that some of the compounds found in Viognier help to set the color and tannins of Syrah, ultimately producing a darker, bigger wine than would have been made without the aid of the white grapes.

In the New World, Australia began its relationship with Viognier in the late 1970s. There are Viognier vines scattered throughout South Australia and Victoria. As in France, determining the time to harvest is the hardest part of growing Viognier. California has the largest plantings of Viognier in the world, almost double that of France. California planted Viognier as a potential replacement for cult Chardonnay. Unfortunately, Viognier is not as amenable to variation of soil or vinification technique as Chardonnay. Also, it is unclear whether the locations of plantings are the best suited to the grape. As the grapevines mature in both Australia and California, a better indication of the quality of the Viognier from these regions will become apparent.

Viognier Notes

- Regions: Condrieu, California, Australia
- Characteristics: low acidity, floral, honeyed, creamy
- Feature: added to Syrah fermentation to fix color and tannin

Muscat

Muscat is one of the oldest grapes grown. It is can be traced back to the Greeks and Romans, who used it for table grapes as well as wine grapes. It is thought the grape found its way to France through one of these two groups, and had spread to Germany by the twelfth century.

One indication of the longevity of the vine is the number of mutations it has. Muscat has many derivatives and many names, depending on the region. The two most common versions are Muscat Blanc à Petits Grains and Muscat of Alexandria. Muscat Blanc is probably the parent vine, with Muscat of Alexandria first appearing in Egypt and being spread by the Romans. A third vine, Muscat Ottonel, was developed in the mid–1800s in France's Loire region from Chasselas and a very unimpressive Muscat de Saumur. It has risen to be the third most utilized Muscat for wine making.

Muscat grapes have varied requirements based on which vine is being discussed. In general, the soils vary from loam in Alsace to chalk in Piedmont to clay in Frontignan. The one generalization that can be made of all Muscats is that they like it warm. Petit Grains has the longest growing season and is very susceptible to diseases of the cold and damp—mildew and mold. Alexandria and Ottonel are both susceptible to coulure if it is too damp at flowering, and both need warmth to ripen fully. Alexandria has adapted to drought, so it is happy in hot, dry climates. Ottonel, typically found in Alsace, needs the warmest sites with good sun exposure for its ripening to succeed.

One unique quality of Muscat Blanc à Petits Grains is its unpredictability. The Petit Grains can be an "unstable" vine. Some vines are known to produce grapes that vary in color from white to deep pink. This variation can happen from year to year on a single vine, and throughout vines in a vineyard. Not all Petit Grains do this, and it may be that there are two strains, one with color stability and one without.

Muscat, especially Muscat Blanc à Petits Grains, is all about the aroma and the sugar. It can yield good-quality grapes at about 30 hl/ha. When this quantity is doubled, which the vine can easily do, the sugar drops in the clusters and the aromaticity disappears. Thus, bulk-produced Muscats are often less complex and less intense than their more quality-oriented cousins.

Muscat can make every style of wine—dry to sweet, still to sparkling. Each region that grows a Muscat makes its own unique style. Muscat Blanc à Petit Grains used to be the grape of choice in Alsace, but cool-weather-adapted Muscat Ottonel is the predominant varietal. While it is considered one of the four Grand Cru grapes (the others being Riesling, Gewurztraminer, and Pinot Gris), it accounts for less than 10 percent of the plantings. The style of Muscat in Alsace is dry, still table wine. Alsatian Muscat does not have the aroma typically associated with the varietal. This may be due to the lack of sugar, but more than likely it is due to the poor aromaticity of the subvarietal itself.

Muscat Blanc à Petits Grains in Italy is found primarily in Asti. where it makes two styles of sparkling wines, Moscato d'Asti and Asti Spumante. While the method of production of these two wines is covered in the sparkling wine chapter, there are differences based on the grapes. Asti Spumante has a much larger production, on the order of ten times more than Moscato d'Asti. For that reason, the best grapes are typically used in Moscato, and those that are overcropped or picked before fully ripe go into Asti Spumante.

Muscat Blanc is also responsible for the sweet dessert wines of Beaumes-de-Venise in France and Rutherglen in Australia. In Beaumes-de-Venise, it is made by *mutage* or stopping the fermentation with addition of neutral spirits. Rutherglen, on the other hand, makes wines from grapes that are considered late harvest, sometimes to the point of becoming raisins.

Muscat of Alexandria, called Zibibbo, is the grape of choice on the island of Pantellaria. This is a sweet dessert wine, made from grapes that have been dried in the sun before fermentation. It is also the grape that produces wines in Greece, Portugal, and Spain.

Muscat's nose is full of flowers and fruit. It is redolent of orange blossoms, citrus, roses, and grapes. On the palate, the acidity can be low, due to the excessive ripeness of the grapes, but the fruitiness balances any residual sugar. If Muscat has been made into an aged dessert wine, the bouquet will turn to figs, prunes, nuts, and coffee.

When discussing age, the only wines that really can last a long time are the sweet dessert wines of Rutherglen, or similar wines. Table wines are best within two to three years of the vintage. Even the vins doux naturels are not long lived, also best before their third birthday. The advantage of Rutherglen is that the change from year one to year fifteen is very minute, so the wines are almost always at their best.

Muscat Notes

- Regions: Alsace, Piedmont, Sicily; Beaumes-de-Venise, Rutherglen
- Pseudonyms: Muscat Blanc à Petits Grains, Muscat of Alexandria, Muscat Ottonel, Zibibbo, Brown Muscat
- Characteristics: more aromatic when sweet style, aromas of roses, citrus flowers, grapes
- Features: used as a table grape throughout the Mediterranean

Gewurztraminer

Gewurztraminer can best be described as a niche grape. But it is *the* example of an aromatic wine. Of all the grape varietals, Gewurztraminer has some of the most unique aromas and a characteristic palate that dispels any question of what wine is in the glass.

The name Gewurztraminer comes from the German *Gewurz* ("spicy") and the location from where the grape originated—Tramin or Termeno in Alto-Adige, Italy. The name Traminer is sometimes used interchangeably with Gewurztraminer, most often in Australia, while other countries reserve the term for a less aromatic form of the grape.

Gewurztraminer grapes seem to prefer climate over soil. The vines ripen in mid-season but need cool temperatures in order not to completely lose acidity and aromatics. The vines also need plenty of sun in order to achieve that ripeness. Soil, on the other hand, is up for debate. Growers in the same region will argue whether the vine does best on limestone or clay. It is probably true that the soil does affect acidity, skin color, and even aromaticity, but which result is better is still hotly debated.

Gewurztraminer viticulture poses some problems for growers. The vine is relatively vigorous, but with that comes yield issues and problems of unbalanced flavors. It seems anything cropped at over 40 hl/ha will have loss of aromatics. While it is easy to get the potential alcohol into the 14 percent range, if the aromatics are not present, then it will still seem to be of lesser quality. Heavy cropping increases the risk of stem rot, to which the vine is naturally prone. Effectively, the vine punishes the grower for overcropping the grapes. The final issue comes with ripening itself. Gewurztraminer ripens unevenly, with fully ripe grapes and green berries next to each other on the same cluster. This makes good vinification difficult because the balance of the cluster is out of whack.

How the vinification is conducted depends on the style of the wine the vintner is trying to create. Because the aromatics and flavors are concentrated in the skins, some vintners either allow the skins to sit on the juice after crushing, or press slowly, mimicking maceration. Fermentations often start out cool, in the belief that this will retain the aromatics and varietal character. Some vintners, especially in Alsace, allow warm fermentations (on the order of 78–80°F/25.5–26.6°C), which they believe increases the body of the wine. Whether the fermentation is cool or warm, Gewurztraminer can reach high alcohol fairly rapidly. Because of the natural low acidity, malolactic fermentation is often avoided, though it has been known to occur occasionally.

The first distinction of Gewurztraminer in a tasting is the color. For a white wine, the color is often described as brassy. It tends toward the golden color of oak influence (without the oak, of course), but with a slightly peach or pink tone. This is usually evidence of skin contact, as Gewurztraminer grapes are pink to light purple. On the nose are the telltale aromas of Gewurztraminer—roses, cold cream, and lychees. This is an intensely scented wine, and often the spicy notes that give the grape its name are buried under the floral and exotic tones. The spices typical of Gewurztraminer are candied ginger, nutmeg, and sometimes cinnamon or clove. If the nose is confusing, the palate should give the wine away. There will be low acid and a medium to full body, almost making the wine seem thick for the heady aromas it has. In many cases there is also high alcohol. While there is low acidity, it is often the high alcohol that compensates to make the wine seem balanced.

Aged Gewurztraminer is not common. Most of the wines produced are meant to be drunk young, within four years of the vintage. Where ageable wines can be found is in the Grand Cru or Vendage Tardive wines of Alsace. The dry Grand Cru wines have a longer lifespan than the simple versions from the New World. These wines start being their best after four years, and can live as long as ten. Vendage Tardive wines, with the added sugar, can develop longer. These wines can typically be laid down for up to fifteen years.

Even with a German name and an Italian heritage, the main region for Gewurztraminer is Alsace in France. Here Gewurztraminer is considered one of the four Grand Cru grapes, capable of making top-level wines. The Alsatian style of Gewurztraminer is dry, with high alcohol. The best wines are the Grand Crus, and simple Alsace AOC wines can be hit or miss, due to yield issues. Some producers will make a late harvest version, or Vendage Tardive, where the sugar complements the floral and exotic fruit character. With such thick skins, it is extremely rare to see a Gewurtraminer that has been influenced by botrytis.

In the rest of Europe, Gewurztraminer is considered a secondary grape. In Germany it can be found in the southern regions of Pfalz and Baden. In Austria

Gewurztraminer Notes

- Regions: Alsace, northern Italy, Germany, California
- Pseudonyms: Traminer, Traminer Aromatico
- Characteristics: Low acid, exotic aromas of lychees, sweet spices, and roses with brassy color
- Features: Dry Gewurztraminer is often high in alcohol

(as Traminer), it can be bone dry like Alsace, or made into a sweet dessert wine. In its homeland of Italy (where it is known as Traminer Aromatico), Gewurztraminer is limited to its home in Alto Adige. The Italian style is often less aromatic than its other European counterparts.

In the New World, there are plantings of Gewurztraminer almost everywhere. The problem is that it has not become economically feasible to expand plantings, so many are small and experimental. The main areas are California and New Zealand. In both areas, dry and off-dry styles are produced, with an occasional dessert wine. Places with potential for good Gewurztraminer include Canada, New York, and Tasmania.

Torrontes

This varietal has only recently emerged as a successful, commercial wine, thanks to the work of Argentinean winemakers. There are several sub varietals in Argentina, with varying degrees of aromaticity. Of the Argentinean subvarietals, the most aromatic comes from the region of La Rioja—Torrontes Riojano (no connection to the Spanish region of the same name). Lesser aromatic subvarietals include the grapes from the San Juan region (Torrontes Sanjuanino), and also a variety planted in Rio Negro (Torrontes Mendocino). The origins of Torrontes are undetermined. Some have stated that it is a native Argentinean varietal, while others believe it may be a version of the Spanish varietal of the same name. Both theories have been difficult to substantiate, as we know vitis vinifera is of European descent, and the Spanish version is not as aromatic as the Argentinean. DNA testing indicates that all the Argentinean varietals are progeny of Muscat of Alexandria.

Good Torrontes should be somewhat reminiscent of Gewurztraminer or Muscat. It is more floral than Gewurztraminer, with a strong inclination to be perfumelike. It is also high in acid, making it a seemingly more refreshing wine. Casual tasting notes often reveal that the wine will present as a sweet wine on the nose, but will be dry on the palate. This is a result of highly floral and fruity aromatics confusing the brain to think sweet. If made incorrectly or with excessively high yields, Torrontes loses its aromatics and becomes just another high-alcohol white wine, sometimes with a bitter finish. Either way, Torrontes is a wine meant to be enjoyed soon after the vintage is released.

Albariño

Albariño is a grape that straddles two countries, and two styles. It is a white grape with thick skins and a very vigorous habit. If the grape is grown in Portugal, in the region of Vinho Verde, it is known as Alvarinho. Here, many growers still stick to the traditional style of growing, either figuratively or literally. The vines are grown on tall pergolas, and produce very large crops that when ripe can only reach 8 to 8.5 percent alcohol. Some farmers still follow the old dictate of poly-culture—growing their vines up trees to maximize usage of the land.

With the lack of ripeness in Portugal also comes lack of aromaticity and high, refreshing acidity. White Vinho Verde is typified by very light body (low alcohol) and bright, refreshing acidity. Also, there is usually a spritz of carbonation. This traditionally came because the wine was not totally through fermenting when consumed, but now is mimicked by a dose of carbon dioxide on the bottling line.

The Rias Baixes region of Galicia, across the border in Spain, takes advantage of the thick skins of Albariño to produce highly aromatic wines. These wines have more body than Vinho Verde, but are still considered light-bodied wines. The nose is very similar to Viognier—apricots and peaches with a bit of floral added. The palate, at least from a component standpoint, is different. Albariño retains its acidity, unlike Viognier, and also has a lighter body. In Rias Baixes, the vines are also grown on pergolas (this time wire-trained) but are trimmed to reduce yields, resulting in wines of 12–12.5 percent alcohol.

Many who try Albariño claim it is the perfect food wine. That can mean it needs food to bring out its flavors or that it has just the right balance to go with many dishes. That claim is often made about the simply fermented, unaged, unoaked versions of the wine. Some producers are experimenting with aging their Albariño, and also with oak influence. Oak seems to lessen the aromaticity of the wine and tame the acidity, but also add to the weight, making it a fuller, richer style.

Verdejo

Verdejo is a native vine to the Rueda region of Spain. Phylloxera devastation and poor wine making brought the grape to the brink of extinction, but it was saved in the mid-1980s. Today, Rueda white wine must contain a minimum of 50 percent Verdejo, often blended with Viura or Sauvignon Blanc.

Verdejo is a crisp white, with very herbaceous aromas (think bay leaves). It has considerable extract, which can be enhanced by skin contact before fermentation. It can oxidize easily, so care must be taken if barrel fermentation or barrel aging is to take place. Because of its weight, balance, and structure, Verdejo can age several years, developing a distinct nutty character.

Food and Wine Considerations

These wines range from light bodied for Verdejo to full bodied for Gewürztraminer and Viognier. Their flavor concentrations also vary similarly. Keeping in mind that body and flavor concentration should match between food and wine, the next main consideration for these wines is their aromaticity.

Viognier can be thought of as a Chardonnay substitute. Instead of the implied sweetness from oak, though, Viognier's sweetness comes from its honeyed character. The honey and floral character lends itself to pairing with slightly sweet dishes as well as slightly spicy ones. Viognier is an excellent match with Indian dishes, with complementary exotic spiciness.

Gewürztraminer is often touted as one of the best pairs for Asian cuisine. The exotic fruit character, as well as the low alcohol, make it a great wine to serve with a spicy Asian dish, like Szechuan cuisine or a Japanese dish with wasabi. Southeast Asian cuisine, with ginger, lemongrass, and cilantro, works with the sweet herbal and spice character of the wine. The richness of Gewürztraminer is what allows it to be paired with rich Alsatian cuisine like pâté and roast pork and duck.

Albariño is described as a perfect food wine. It is full bodied enough to work with many dishes, while it has an earthy minerality that complements food. Its acidity and hint of bitterness on the finish also are perfect with food. The acidity is refreshing while the bitterness cleanses the palate for another morsel.

Muscat takes a bit more effort to pair with food. The dry Muscats of Alsace are rich but not as aromatic. They are still good pairs with some of the foods as Gewürztraminer. Sweet Muscat, on the other hand, can be a fine dessert partner. Muscat stickies from Australia are good with spice cake, carrot cake, and other rich, intensely flavored desserts.

SUMMARY

The aromatic white wines are some of the most intriguing and misunderstood wines. Their complex aromas often disguise their dryness. As a group, the grapes can be challenging to make into wine well. Incomplete ripening dumbs down the aromatics and makes them poor representatives of the class. Yet well-made versions are intriguing, delicate, layered, and refreshing. As a group they work well with spiced foods and often have the body to handle very rich items as well.

QUESTIONS

1. What are the aromatic white grapes?

2. Describe the aromatic and flavor profile for Viognier.

3. Describe the aromatic and flavor profile of Muscat.

4. Describe the aromatic and flavor profile of Gewurztraminer.

5. Where are the key areas for growing each of the aromatic grapes?

6. Describe the types of food that pair best with aromatic white wines.

chapter 16

Light and Crisp White Wines

*W*hen most wine consumers think of white wine other than Chardonnay, they think of a light, refreshing beverage that is more utilitarian than memorable. While mass production of some of these wines may be responsible for such a reputation, it is probably more the result of changes in fashion. Delicate, subtle, acidic wines are not the best cocktail party wines, though they can be fantastic when used in a meal. Often underappreciated, the light and crisp white wines are delicious alternatives and make excellent matches for food.

Upon completion of this chapter, the student should be able to:

Describe the grapes that make light and crisp white wines
Discuss how growing region influences the wine style
Explain the different styles of Chenin Blanc and how they are made
Describe the type of foods that best pair with light and crisp wines

Pinot Blanc

Pinot Blanc is a mutation derived from Pinot Noir that has developed into a varietal with its own merits. With such a distinctive pedigree, one would expect that Pinot Blanc would be considered on a level with its black-colored forebear. That is not the case, as most of the wine making world relegates Pinot Blanc to being the wine made for "fun" or "artistic expression" rather than commercial interest.

Part of the issue lies with Pinot Blanc itself. It is a relatively neutral grape, which can be manipulated in different ways. In that respect, it is like Chardonnay. Given the commercial viability of Chardonnay versus Pinot Blanc, it is obvious why winemakers and growers choose the former over the later. In the vineyard, Pinot Blanc looks like a less highly prized grape called Auxerrois. Pinot Blanc is often mistaken for Auxerrois, and if not, then blended with it—not the treatment of a varietal that is considered top notch.

Pinot Blanc is beginning to get some recognition. In general, Pinot Blanc has a ripe pear or apple fruitiness, with just a hint of spice. Top-quality Pinot Blanc shows riper fruits of peach and pineapple. Similar to top Chardonnay, the best will possess a bit of hazelnut as well. Where Pinot Blanc's strength lies is in its crisp acidity and balanced flavors. The wine possesses enough body in warm areas to handle more aggressive treatment, while in cool regions its refreshing crispness is the hallmark.

The styles made vary more as a regional preference rather than a winemaker one. In northern Italy, the style is light and mild. In Germany it is often aged in oak barrels. In Austria Pinot Blanc makes botrytized dessert wines.

In the New World, the most interest in Pinot Blanc is in North America. California Pinot Blancs can be doubly confusing. First, some of the vines have been mislabeled, with their actual lineage being Melon de Bourgogne. Second, those that are making true Pinot Blanc make a wide variety of styles. It is worthwhile to determine which producers make bigger, more Chardonnay-like wines, and which make lighter, more delicate wines. Better examples come from Oregon,

Pinot Blanc Notes

- Regions: Alsace, California, Oregon, Canada
- Characteristics: crisp acidity, peach, pineapple, pear notes with nutty character
- Features: often confused or mixed with lesser grapes

which has a love affair with anything in the Pinot family, and Canada (in particular, British Columbia).

Pinot Grigio

This member of the Pinot family is noted for its pinkish skin, hence the Italian *grigio* or the French *gris,* both meaning gray. It is more aromatic than Pinot Blanc, and depending on the style, could be considered as aromatic as Viognier or Riesling.

The style of the wine is the real driver of the "varietal name." While an Italian may refer to Pinot Noir as Pinot Negro, the basic wine style is relatively the same. In the case of Pinot Grigio/Gris, the two styles are very different. It has now become common around the world to label the wine based on the style in the bottle, rather than a preference for Italian or French.

As of the mid-2000s, Pinot Grigio has more of a recognition factor with the public than does Pinot Gris. Thanks to the marketing of Italian winemakers, and the thirst for anything new besides Chardonnay, the production and consumption of Pinot Grigio has increased significantly. The appeal of Pinot Grigio is a light, crisp, refreshing white wine. It is a wine that is as easy to drink alone as it is to have with food.

In the vineyard, Pinot Grigio is adaptable to many climates and soils. Its preference for soils leans toward those that are deep and warm. The soil to try to avoid is one with high clay content. The vine is not overly vigorous, so training methods are often determined by tradition or by economics (mechanical harvesting).

It is ultimately climate that determines the style "Pinot Grigio." The style is born of the cool climate of the Alto-Adige in Italy. The vineyards are in the foothills of the Dolomite Alps, and have very short growing seasons. The onset of an early winter is always a possibility, and the farmers prefer to harvest the grapes earlier rather than later. The grapes are not fully ripe and therefore have not developed all their aromatic compounds. What is lost in aromaticity is regained in acidity. If left on the vine to ripen completely, Pinot Grigio yields a low acid varietal. By picking the grapes early, the wine that is produced displays more minerality, a lighter body, and more acidity than the fully ripe version (see Pinot Gris in the next chapter).

A tasting note would reveal some other key differences between the early harvested Pinot Grigio and its fully ripe version. The appearance is a light straw color, because the color in the skins does not have a chance to develop fully. The nose is very light, with hints of apple and pear, some citrus and minerals. The nose is not

Pinot Grigio Notes

- Regions: Italy, California, Oregon, Canada
- Characteristics: light wine with hints of apple, pear, and minerals
- Features: harvested early to retain acidity but sacrifice in flavor

intensely aromatic since those compounds have not developed either. The palate reflects the high acidity, light body, and moderate alcohol of an early harvested wine. The flavors are often light in intensity as well. In the case of poorly made wine, this can be seen as bland or uninteresting. This neutrality is what seems to make Pinot Grigio a very popular wine for sipping or food pairing.

The premier region for Pinot Grigio is Italy, namely the province of Trentino-Alto Adige. This is where a majority of production of this varietal occurs. Because of the rise in popularity, some other regions in Italy are planting Pinot Grigio and making wine, including the Veneto and Friuli. Elsewhere, this style of wine is produced in Germany, Switzerland, Oregon, and Canada, though many of these areas favor the riper Pinot Gris style.

Trebbiano

As the name implies, this varietal is of Italian origin. It is the ubiquitous white wine grape in Italy, but its influence is not confined to the Italian peninsula alone. Trebbiano has the distinction of being the most productive white wine grape in the world. Its influence, good or bad, reaches almost every country producing wine today.

The main viticultural characteristic of Trebbiano is the ability to produce copious amounts of grapes. In Italy, it is not uncommon to produce between 150 and 200 hl/ha a vintage. It is fairly late ripening, often being picked sometime in October in warm regions. In cooler regions, the combination of high yield and early picking yields grapes that make a very neutral, bland wine.

In fact, a tasting note of any Trebbiano-based wine would not be particularly inspiring. A pale appearance, low-intensity nose, and palate of lemon tartness and low body form a typical description of even the best examples. Much of the production is as a *vino da tavola*, or base table wine. It is sold in carafes as white wine, often just to wash down the meal at a trattoria.

The bland tasting note of the table wine is a clue to the wine's best usage—as the base for distillation. Most of the Trebbiano plantings around the world are used for the production of brandy. In many areas, the name of the grape is the French Ugni Blanc rather than the Italian. Trebbiano was brought to France when the Avignon popes were in power, and its presence has remained strong in southern France while it has continued to spread. As Ugni Blanc, it is responsible for the majority of the base wine in Cognac and Armagnac production as well as brandy in the United States, Spain, and Eastern Europe.

There are several clones of Trebbiano. The most aromatic and flavorful is Trebbiano di Soave. It is often included as a blending grape with Garganega in the production of Soave. The most prolific is Trebbiano Toscano. This grape is responsible for wines such as Orvieto, Frascati, and Est! Est!! Est!!!, while also being the ubiquitous blending grape for many Italian white wines. It is so prolific that its inclusion in the original blending recipe for Chianti, a red wine, shows the prevalence in Italian wine production.

Verdicchio

Verdicchio is another Italian white grape that makes fairly neutral wines. Its name comes from the slightly yellow-green skins. The wines are often very pale and lacking in aroma. They are light and crisp, and those with low yields produce wine that has both lemony and nutty notes. Better versions are being made with each vintage. The improved Verdicchio would be described as light, but not neutral. Its aroma can be described as a blend of pine resin, green apples, and herbs. It is naturally high in acidity, and the herbal component gives it a distinctive savory character. The finish is typically Italian; a bitterness that is described as almond skins.

The home of Verdicchio is the Marche region of Italy. Here, Verdicchio is made into two main wines. Verdicchio dei Jesi, which is a highly common export, can be a quality expression of the grape. It is the largest of the two DOCs. The style from Jesi is relatively lush, with some producers considering oak aging or even barrel fermentation. Verdicchio di Matelica, which comes from a hillside region farther inland, makes wine with somewhat more body. The wines from Matelica are more aromatic and more acidic. The harvest in Matelica is at least a week later than in Jesi, giving the wines more body and structure.

Garganega

Upon initial examination, this grape variety may not appear to be familiar. Yet, anyone who drank wine in the 1970s and 1980s is familiar with the wine it produces. This wine is named after the region of production, Soave, rather than the grape variety. And for many of these wine drinkers, "Soave" is followed by "Bolla" (a major producer).

The wine is a typical Italian white, light in color, neutral on the nose, and fairly bland on the palate. It is not, however, a single varietal wine. It is mainly Garganega, around 70 percent by law, but it is blended with other grapes. The most common blending grape is Trebbiano di Soave, though Chardonnay and Pinot Bianco have been creeping in to try to impart more flavor.

During the imposition of wine laws into Italy, many famous regions were expanded to take advantage of the name. The wines that came from these expanded areas was often a poor reflection of what made the original famous. Such is the case with Soave. Much of the wine bearing the name is industrial, literally and figuratively. Large corporations like Bolla, Folonari, and others make wine under the Soave name, but it is barely above lemon-water quality. The best wines come from the Classico region. Here in the original area of production, producers focus on low grape yields and quality. The wines that typically come from the Classico region resemble a modest unoaked Chardonnay, often with a hint of almonds on the nose and more minerality on the palate. Well-made Soave (from fully ripe grapes with low yields) increases in aromaticity and offers hints of melon, pear, and flowers, with a richer body than most white wines.

Another style of wine can be made with Garganega, Recioto di Soave. This is a wine made in the *passito* method of drying the grapes on mats. It is very similar to Recioto della Valpolicella, which is described in detail in the next section. Recioto di Soave is the Veneto's version of Sauternes. It is rich and honeyed, while the acidity of the Garganega helps keep the wine from being syrupy. While often used as a dessert wine, its concentration of flavor is often lost when paired with a sweet dessert. This wine is best with a cheese platter.

Arneis

This varietal was saved from extinction in the 1970s and is becoming one of Italy's more interesting white wines. It had only been used as a softener for Nebbiolo when making Barolo. Its second purpose was more as a sacrificial vine. It would be planted alongside Nebbiolo, and the sweet grapes would attract birds. The birds would then eat the Arneis, rather than the more expensive and labor-intensive Nebbiolo.

Arneis is not the typical Italian white. It produces a wine with a light yellow, almost pale golden color and is fairly aromatic. The nose has a particular smell of almonds and peaches, with something vegetal in the background. The palate of a simple Arneis may be low in acid, as is typical of the grape. Those that are pro-duced in the chalky soils of the Roero region retain their acidity and maintain some structure. It is a light- to medium-bodied wine, and with grapefruit and apple flavors along with nutty, marzipan undertones it is complementary to many food items.

Arneis may have difficulty leaping to the forefront of Italian wines. It is a bit of a finicky vine, and is susceptible to mildew. It does have a natural tendency to produce low yields and the requisite increased flavor, but the grapes can oxidize easily. It is a grape that needs careful treatment, but can produce a uniquely refresh-ing wine.

Melon de Bourgogne, or Muscadet

This varietal has become so associated with its region of production that the names have become interchangeable. Melon de Bourgogne is actually native to Burgundy, as the name implies. However, in its homeland, the grape was outlawed by Phillip the Bold because it did not make good enough wine. The grape was brought to the Nantais region of the Loire Valley by Benedictine monks, where it served as one of many grapes for a long time. Two key events influenced the Nantais to make this their primary grape. First was the influence of the Dutch, who were influential traders along the Atlantic coast. Once they determined that brandy could be made from wine that was light and neutral, they influenced the outposts along some of France's rivers to plant those grapes and sell them to the Dutch. The Loire was a major trading river for the Dutch, and having wine made from Melon de Bourgogne near the coast was an economical source of brandy material. The second event was a massive freeze in the winter of 1709. This freeze was so intense, it is said to have frozen the sea. It did freeze all the vines in the Nantais. Because Melon is reputed to have good cold hardiness, it was planted extensively to prepare for any other cold winters.

The grape is grown almost exclusively in the Muscadet regions of the Nantais, giving Melon the other name by which it is known. Most of the Muscadet regions produce thin, neutral wines without much flavor or body, but with high acidity. The common descriptor is that the wine is "great with the local shellfish," meaning it does not compete for flavor. A disadvantage of the grape that only exacerbates the neutrality of the wine is its susceptibility to mildews and rot. On the humid Atlantic coast, many growers will pick the grapes before they are fully ripe in order to avoid issues with molds. This does not help the flavor profile of the subsequent wines.

Melon de Bourgogne Notes

- Regions: Muscadet
- Pseudonyms: Muscadet
- Characteristics: very light, crisp wine often treated sur lie
- Features: legally must be below 12 percent alcohol

In order to increase the impact of the wine, producers resort to some vinification techniques that can influence the final flavor profile. The most common of these is maturing the wine *sur lie,* or on the lees. Hand in hand with this is often barrel fermentation (in old barrels) and batonnage (lees stirring). The wines are typically left on their lees until March 1 after the harvest date (approximately six months), when bottling begins. This method is recognized by the French authorities and has its own legal designation on the bottles. Aging the wine sur lie gives more body and richness to the wine. It does not increase the alcohol to increase the body; that must be kept below 12 percent alcohol by volume by law. The added complexity from the yeast autolysis adds more apparent weight to the wine.

Muscadet is a wine that is typically drunk young. While it is aged sur lie, that typically does not give it the body or concentration that would be expected of an ageable wine. However, that does not mean it cannot be done. In fact, aged Muscadet (on the order of five to six years) can have quite interesting development. While a fresh Muscadet will be minerally, lemony, and light, aged Muscadets tend to smell of lemon meringue pie. More of the bready tones develop from the lees influence, and a creamy caramelized scent develops. This should be done with only top-producer Muscadet, as their wines typically have a bit more concentration to start with.

Chenin Blanc

While Chenin Blanc is not one of the most planted grapes in the world, most of the world's consumers have experienced it at one point or another. This is not so much a comment on the wide-ranging palate of today's wine drinker, but rather on the dichotomy of Chenin Blanc in the world. Chenin Blanc can make some of the world's most long-lived wines, ones that do not fully develop into varietal character until they are adults—in human years. On the other hand, much of the world's bulk white wine (think boxes with spigots and generic labels) is made from Chenin Blanc. Even more so than with other grape varieties, quality all comes down to yield, climate, soil, and the winemaker.

The most controllable factor in growing Chenin Blanc is the yield. Given its own devices, Chenin Blanc can crop at 150–200 hl/ha. That is an incredible amount of wine. However, when cropping is that high, all that remains is lots of acid, very little aroma, and barely any flavor—perfect for bulk wine at a low price. But when cropping is low, say on the order of 25–35 hl/ha, it is then that the quality increases dramatically. In order to achieve these low yields, extensive pruning and training must occur. Also, it is common for a "green harvest" to occur immediately after veraison.

If yields are kept low, the wine is next influenced by its region of production. Bulk wines are typical of warm, almost hot, regions. Parts of South Africa, and especially California's Central Valley, are planted to Chenin Blanc for the express purpose of making lots of wine. The grapes ripen early and quickly, producing that characteristic bland wine. It is in the cool, northerly regions, or at altitude, that Chenin finds the best development. In its homeland of the Loire Valley, Chenin Blancs vary from year to year, all because of what the weather was that vintage.

It is only with low yields and cool climate that Chenin Blanc can express the soil upon which it is planted. As was seen with other soils, there are some standard trends in the wines based on the soil types. Clay soils tend to give fuller bodied wines with more concentration. The coolness of the soil also lends itself to botrytis infection. Limestone soils are lighter and more prone to retain their acidity. Calcareous clay is the best of both worlds, yielding Chenin Blanc with weight and acid. Finally, sandy soils yield lighter wines, those that are meant to be drunk early and not to age. All of these soils are present in the Loire, which partially explains the range of Chenin Blanc styles in the region.

More so than with any other variety, the winemaker determines which Chenin Blanc will be made. That seems like an obvious statement, but for Chenin Blanc that decision changes on a daily basis. Those decisions are made based on the harvest. Harvesting Chenin Blanc is tricky in the Loire. With so many different soils, the harvest times will vary based on the soil type. Even then, it is not typical to harvest whole clusters right away. Most vineyards are harvested in *tries,* or in several passes through the vineyard. Each time through the vineyard, the pickers only choose the grapes with the perfect ripeness. Sometimes they pick single berries, other times the whole cluster, or large portions of it. As the harvest comes in daily, the winemaker is observing the crop. If botrytis is beginning to form on some of the clusters, it may be decided that the wine this year will be a sweet dessert wine, rather than an off-dry wine or maybe a bone-dry one. It may be that both dry and sweet wines can be made, based on which trie the grapes were harvested in.

Chenin Blanc made in the Central Valley or in a lot of South Africa is not worth writing a tasting note for. Good Chenin Blanc, on the other hand, can be quite interesting and challenging to a taster. The challenge comes because Chenin Blanc can present itself like Riesling. Appearance of a Chenin Blanc is light straw, possibly leaning toward yellow. Sweet versions will take on a decidedly golden hue. On the nose, Chenin Blanc is one of the few wines that can be described as smelling sweet. The nose will be medium intensity, with some herbal or grassy component, fruits like melon, green plums, pear, and quince, and something chemical, typically described as wet wool or lanolin. Sweet versions, especially those infected with botrytis, will possess the characteristic honey and apricot aromas. On the palate, the dryness level can be anywhere. Wines range from bone dry to fully sweet. Some "dry" wines retain a little residual sugar to balance the acidity. This is a high acid wine (except in those hot regions), and it is a rounded acidity similar to Riesling. There is also minerality that is derived from the soil. Chenin Blanc is a medium-weight wine, even when they are fully sweet.

It is in the nuance of the above note that the difference between Chenin Blanc and Riesling is found. Is it medium intensity or just muted? Is it lanolin, or would that be petrol? There is pear and ripe melon, but am I smelling quince (and what even is quince)? Is this a really ripe Rheingau Riesling, hence the medium body, or not? It is all about determining the true essence that will help differentiate a Chenin Blanc from a Riesling.

As referenced earlier, the home of Chenin Blanc is the Loire Valley in France, particularly the regions of Anjou and Touraine. In Anjou, Chenin Blanc is made in the extremes—bone dry or botrytised sweetness. In Touraine, the full range of Chenin Blanc can be found in one appellation.

In Anjou, the dry style of Chenin Blanc can be found in the region of Savennieres. Here, the wines are always fermented to dryness, yet they retain a honeyed sweetness on the nose. The wines of Coulee-de-Serrant by Nicholas Joly are beautiful examples of biodynamic farming. In terms of aging, a good Savenierres will be drinkable after six years, but really be at its best from fifteen to twenty-five years old. Across the river are the sweet wine appellations. Here, the mists rise up the hillsides and create the perfect environment for botrytis. The wines resemble their counterparts in Sauternes, but lighter in body and with more acidity. The regions of Bonnezeaux, Quarts de Chaume, and Coteaux de Layon are the top regions for sweet Chenin Blanc. These wines can age for many years, being at their best from five to twenty years after the vintage.

Moving to Touraine, the key Chenin Blanc appellation is Vouvray. Vouvray can be a challenge because the wines will vary from year to year. The variation is not about quality, but about sweetness. In a cool year, the grapes may be used to make dry wines, or even sparkling. In better years, the sweetness level will rise. It used

Chenin Blanc Notes

- Regions: Loire Valley, South Africa, California
- Pseudonyms: Steen
- Characteristics: makes all styles of wine from dry to botrytised dessert wine, aromas of melon, quince, and lanolin
- Features: used as bulk jug wine as well as fine wine

to be that producers would not label their bottles with the level of sweetness. The consumer had to know the vintage and the style the producer liked to make. More recently, producers make multiple styles, and the contents of the bottle are noted on the label.

Outside France, the next most important region for Chenin Blanc is South Africa. Though much of it is used to make bulk wine or as a starter for brandy, there are some top-quality wines being produced. The local name for Chenin Blanc is Steen, which still appears on some labels. The South Africans are still developing their style, but it does seem different from the French. South African winemakers seem to be focusing more on tropical fruit flavors and an early approachability to the wine as opposed to the terroir driven, age-worthy wines of the Loire.

Food and Wine Considerations

Light, crisp white wines have few pairing options. They are often too light for most substantial dishes, and are considered too delicate compared to the current trend of big, brash flavors in food. They are excellent pairs, however, with two things in particular: seafood and creamy dishes. Light, crisp wines partner well with fish and shellfish. The briny character of oysters complements the minerality of Muscadet. Many of these wines are great for a fish appetizer, especially if it contains a touch of cream or butter. The acidity of these wines can cut through the richness of a creamy sauce or beurre blanc. It can also serve as a foil for a salad course. For example, the ripe fruit and hint of herbal flavor in Arneis matches well with a Vietnamese shrimp summer salad roll. Though often relegated to aperitif status, these wines make great openers on a menu.

The sweet versions work well with both savory and sweet dishes. Sweet versions of Chenin Blanc are classic pairs for foie gras, pâté, and pork dishes in the Loire Valley. They also serve as either dessert wines or pair well with blue cheeses.

SUMMARY

Light and crisp white wines are noteworthy for their delicacy and acidity. Less aromatic than some white wines, they still possess floral and fresh fruit notes, often with a hint of nuttiness. The crisp acidity of the wines allows them to pair with rich dishes as well as seafood. For the most part, these wines are restricted only to one or two areas of origin. Many of them have a history of poor production, reinforcing their small role in the wine world.

QUESTIONS

1. What grapes make light and fresh white wines?
2. What determines the style in which Pinot Blanc is made?
3. Discuss the influence of harvest time on the style of Pinot Grigio.
4. What are the main uses for Trebbiano?
5. Describe the two styles of wine made by Garganega.
6. Discuss sur lie and its effect on Muscadet.
7. Outline the styles of wine made by Chenin Blanc.
8. What are the key regions that make light, fresh white wines?
9. Describe the food pairings for light, fresh wines.

chapter

Fat and Full

*N*ot all white wine varieties are light and crisp. Several varieties produce
rich, full-bodied wines. Sometimes this is the effect of residual sugar in the wine,
because the grapes can ripen tremendously. Other times it is just that the fully ripe
grape yields a great deal of extract, creating a wine that is full and rich. In either
case, Pinto Gris, Semillon, and Malvasia are the heavy hitters of white wines. With
their richness and body, each of these wines could easily substitute for a red wine
in some food pairings.

Upon completion of this chapter, the student should be able to:

    Discuss the grapes that make fat and full-bodied wines
    Describe the characteristics that make wines fat and full bodied
    Explain how ripeness changes the expression of Pinot Gris
    Outline the styles of wine made using Semillon
    Discuss the use of Malvasia in current winemaking
    Describe foods that pair with fat and full white wines

Pinot Gris

The vine Pinot Gris was discussed in the previous chapter, though the focus there was on the "Pinot Grigio" style. Here, we will discuss the "Pinot Gris" style. Pinot Gris on a label indicates that the wine is made in a fuller, richer style. The acidity will be lower than that of a Pinot Grigio and the wine will also be more aromatic.

The best examples of Pinot Gris in the world come from Alsace. Here, the extended autumn allows Pinot Gris to ripen fully. The grape is so prized it is considered one of Alsace's four noble grapes (along with Riesling, Gewurztraminer, and Muscat). Long hang times for ripening result in a low-acid, highly aromatic wine. This is the most important factor for Pinot Gris. If the grapes do not have the potential to make at least 12.5 percent alcohol, there will not be enough character. To achieve this, Alsatian growers will keep yields in the 40–60 hl/ha range. The hallmark of ripe Pinot Gris is the amount of extraction that can be obtained from the grapes. It is that concentrated extract that provides the body and the intense aroma of Pinot Gris.

One advantage of long hang time in Alsace is the possibility of getting botrytis infection on the grapes. Pinot Gris is particularly susceptible to botrytis. Hence, it is not difficult to presume that sweet wines are made from Pinot Gris, and indeed they are. Pinot Gris is produced in a myriad of rich styles—dry, off-dry, Vendage Tardive, or Selection de Grains Nobles. All these styles have a common thread: low acid and intense aromaticity.

Dry Alsatian Pinot Gris is pale yellow, with an extremely powerful nose. The aromas range from nuts to honey, exotic flowers to something musky or unclean. Interlaced with this is the high alcohol content, making each of these aromas even more lifted and heady. The palate is full and rich, with many of the same flavors. The long-lasting flavor also includes something spicy and is balanced by the high alcohol rather than acidity. In this respect, it resembles one of the parents of the Pinot family, Gewurztraminer. Sweet Pinot Gris keeps many of the same attributes as the dry style. The color changes to a more golden hue, and the alcohol remains high. The flavor balance does change slightly, preferring the honeyed and apricot flavors from botrytis.

Other parts of the world make Pinot Gris in this full-throttle style. Germany, where the grape is called Rulander or Grauburgunder, makes styles very similar to Alsace. Romania makes excellent sweet Pinot Gris. In the New World, the focus is in Oregon, Australia, New Zealand, and Canada. Each is finding its own version of the full-bodied style. In Oregon, the focus is on the honeyed character of the wine. In New Zealand, it is pear and apple fruitiness and honeysuckle blossoms. In Canada, Pinot Gris may be barrel fermented to yield vanilla along with the honey flavors.

Pinot Gris Notes

- Regions: Alsace, Oregon
- Pseudonyms: Rulander, Grauburgunder
- Characteristics: low acidity, rich texture, strong aromas
- Features: can be made in botrytised style

Semillon

There are grape varieties that can travel the world and remain consistent. There are grape varieties that express themselves based on the locale in which they are grown. There are ones that do not travel well, and only make good wines where they are originally cultivated. Then there is Semillon. Semillon makes thin, generic white wine in lots of places, but in two it makes world-class wine. The question is how that differs from others, because for these two areas, the styles could not be more different or apparently reproducible elsewhere.

Semillon is a bit of a grape anomaly. It is thin skinned and can have large berries, which often is characteristic of producing light, acidic wines. However, extract is usually high for Semillon, and it is noted for low acidity and aroma. The key to achieving quality wine is low yield, as has been demonstrated with every other varietal.

Because Semillon has two areas that make world-class wines and those wines do not resemble each other in the least, the best approach is to look at Semillon from a regional bias. The two regions that make noteworthy wines are Bordeaux and the Hunter Valley in Australia.

In Bordeaux, Semillon is a blending grape. Sometimes it dominates the blend; at other times it plays the supporting role to its partner, Sauvignon Blanc. A good deal of dry white Bordeaux is made from this blend. Until the late 1990s, white Bordeaux was a deservedly dying breed. The wines were often tired and oxidized, or reeked of sulfur dioxide to avoid the oxidation. In the 1990s more modern techniques entered the wineries of white Bordeaux makers, and the style changed to medium bodied, fresh, and approachable. Semillon contributes enough weight and concentration to the blend that the wine can now be oak aged, very atypical for Sauvignon Blanc.

Where Semillon really shines in Bordeaux is in the sweet dessert wine region of Sauternes and its neighboring appellations. Sauternes is situated at the confluence

Semillon Notes

- Regions: Bordeaux, Hunter Valley
- Pseudonyms: Hunter Valley Riesling
- Characteristics: thin-skinned grapes make rich, low-acid, highly extracted wines
- Features: best wines in Bordeaux are from botrytis-infected grapes; those from Hunter Valley improve with age

of the Ciron River as it empties into the Garonne. The water of the Ciron is particularly cold, especially compared to the Garonne. That, combined with the humidity in the area, creates fog banks that shroud the grapes in the morning and burn off in the afternoon. This combination of phenomena is the perfect environment for botrytis to thrive. And it is the botrytis–affected wines of Sauternes that are world renowned.

In Sauternes, as in Alsace with Pinot Gris, the botrytis-infected grapes are picked in tries, with anywhere from four to more passes through the vineyard. What gets picked varies with each pass. The final wine should have a potential alcohol of around 21 percent. In order to keep this balance, some trie are to pick healthy grapes to balance the sugar content of the shriveled grapes. Finally, the wine is made, reaching approximately 13 percent, with plenty of residual sugar and acidity to create a wine that can last upward of two decades, or even more in great years.

Sauternes is considered one of the world's truly great wines. When young it appears bright yellow gold and has a heady aroma of honey, apricots, and ripe peaches. On the palate, it is definitively sweet, but with an acidity that keeps the wine from being cloying. The flavors replicate the palate, with honey and apricots predominating, along with marzipan and orange. As the wine ages, the color will take on an intense gold and may even progress to amber. Its aroma and palate will also develop with more nuance and subtlety. Quality Sauternes is at its best around twenty years old, though it is just as enjoyable young.

The other region of note is the Hunter Valley in Australia. Probably the only similarity between the two regions is humidity, though it has not an influence in promoting botrytis in the Hunter. The region is hot, and often, just as harvest time arrives, tropical storms lash the vineyards. When thinking of Semillon in the Hunter, it is best to be counterintuitive. Young Semillon is all acid and no flavor.

The wines, which seem to possess no salvageable qualities, come into their own after about ten years. It is then that they develop silkiness and the flavors of honey and toast. Only if the grapes are able to get fully ripe (without any rain) will the wine be oaked. Then the ripe fruit flavors of green plums and mango will blend with the vanilla of the wood to create a wine that approaches a white Burgundy in body and taste. These wines are fuller and richer than their white Bordeaux counterparts, partly because they are all Semillon, with no Sauvignon Blanc to lighten them up.

Malvasia

This varietal is one of the oldest cultivated wine grapes. Its name has been used to describe a whole range of grapes in France that are not even related (Malvoisie). The true Malvasia is really a large collection of subvarieties, which are white, pink, or red, and are common to the Mediterranean basin.

Malvasia is a grape that makes wine that is full bodied, often well colored, high in extract, and fragrant. In a few regions, these attributes are used to their fullest to make dry wines, but more importantly Malvasia makes excellent sweet wines. When not used as a single varietal wine, Malvasia is a blending partner to many varieties described in the light and crisp chapter. By blending Malvasia with light wines, the body is increased as well as the richness of flavor. The benefit to Malvasia is that its tendency to low acid flabbiness is nullified.

Malvasia is native to Italy and Spain. It actually was originally from Asia Minor, and was a widely produced Greek wine. The Greeks took it around the Mediterranean. In modern times, most of Malvasia is found in Italy and Spain. Even so, the number of vines planted is decreasing, and Malvasia is becoming a rare wine to find.

In Italy, Malvasia was a major grape in Tuscany. It used to be one of the allowed grapes in the recipe for Chianti. Even though it is a higher-quality grape, Malvasia has found itself pushed to the side by Trebbiano. The last holdouts of Malvasia in Italy are in Puglia and on the islands around Sicily. In fact, one of the most famous wines Malvasia makes is Malvasia delle Lipari, from the Lipari Islands of the north shore of Sicily. Both the Apulian and the Lipari wines are made in the passito method, where the grapes are dried to a raisinlike state before vinification.

In Spain, Malvasia has seen the same fate as in Tuscany. It used to be the blending partner of Viura in white Rioja. Malvasia is still used to some extent to flesh out the light Viura, but more and more of the wines are focusing on a lighter, fresher quality.

Malvasia Notes

- Region: Italy, Spain, Madeira
- Characteristics: rich, full-bodied wine used as blending partner
- Features: easily oxidizes, making it a good prospect for fortified wines

Malvasia brings both positive and negative qualities to the varietal wine or as a blending partner. On the positive side, its body and richness give weight to lighter wines. Lighter-colored Malvasia brings an almost Muscat-like quality to a wine, with aromas of peaches and apricots. For darker Malvasia, the aroma and flavor is more grapey, but with a chocolatey bent. On the negative side, Malvasia is prone to oxidize easily. This is definitely a negative if it is being blended with something light like Viura. The best example of making a "silk purse from a sow's ear" is in Madeira. We will save the in-depth discussion of Madeira for a later chapter, but Malvasia makes the sweetest version, called Malmsey, which is both fortified and deliberately oxidized.

Food and Wine Considerations

The full and fat wines are some of the best for pairing with more full-bodied dishes. Semillon and Pinot Gris could partner with meat-based cuisine as well as if not better than with fish. The low acidity keeps these wines from being perfect pairs with cream-based dishes, though they go well with cheeses, especially in their sweet versions. Wines made with higher acidity are excellent with seafood, and can handle dishes that are more intensely prepared in both flavor and body.

SUMMARY

The wines that make up the fat and full group make some of the richest white wines. They tend to be low in acid, and that feature along with their full body makes them ideal blending partners with lighter, crisper wines. The grapes tend to make good table wines, but are often best noted for their late harvest or botrytis-infected wines. These wines can often age for decades, partly due to the high extract initially obtained from the grapes.

QUESTIONS

1. How does time of harvest influence the style of Pinot Gris?

2. What styles of wine are made by Semillon?

3. How is Malvasia currently used to make wine?

4. What are the key regions for fat and full wines?

5. How does Semillon differ between Bordeaux and Australia?

6. Discuss food pairing options for fat and full wines.

wines
from **black grapes**

Black and red grapes create a broad spectrum of wine styles and flavor profiles. Some grapes are known for being light and fresh tasting, with acidity levels that beg to be paired with food. Other varieties make soft and juicy wines, with moderate tannins and ripe fruitiness. Some grapes are more heavy hitters, the full and tannic wines that give a punch of flavor and body along with a big, gripping tannic structure. Finally, there are grapes more noted for their flavor profile of rich, exotic flavors and inherent spiciness. Each of the red wine styles offers different flavors and different food pairing possibilities.

chapter *18*

Light and Fresh

The wines in this category can be some of the most underutilized wines on the market. When most people think red wine, they think big and chewy tannins, deep, rich color, and high alcohol to make a bruiser of a wine. Big red wines are the fashion currently, and have left Cabernet Franc, Gamay, Corvina, Sangiovese, Barbera, and Dolcetto behind. These are the everyday wines; the workhorses of the table in regions where big, bold reds are sent off to export. They marry well with food, they quench your thirst, and they bridge the gap between full-bodied white wines and their bigger red counterparts. But don't be too lulled into thinking these are mere lightweights; some of these grapes can be as big and bold as their more popular cousins.

Upon completion of this chapter, the student should be able to:

> *Describe the characteristics of light and fresh red wines*
> *Outline important regions for production of light and fresh wines*
> *Discuss attributes of grapes*
> *Outline unique production techniques of these wines*
> *Explain food and wine considerations for these wines*

Cabernet Franc

This varietal has been relegated to the shadow of its offspring, Cabernet Sauvignon. There is a great deal of similarity between the two, and for those who enjoy Cabernet Sauvignon but want something lighter, Cabernet Franc is the answer.

This grape has more in common with its offspring in the glass rather than in the vineyard. Unlike Cabernet Sauvignon, Cabernet Franc is noted as a cool-weather grape and one that likes wet soils. It buds earlier than its offspring, but also ripens earlier. The yield is naturally controlled due to the early frost or weather issues of a cool-weather grape. The vine is resistant to almost all vineyard maladies, which is beneficial for a grape suited to cool climates, though it is susceptible to mildew.

In the glass, it is possible to see the origin of some of Cabernet Sauvignon's flavors. Cabernet Franc is naturally herbaceous, with hints of green pepper, mint, and crushed berry leaves. It is also very fruity, leaning to the red berry profile and, in particular, raspberries. Finally, it has a distinct pencil shaving aroma—also described in Cabernet Sauvignon—and some floral components. On the palate, Cabernet Franc is lower in tannin and extract compared to its offspring. Cabernet Franc is a more approachable wine, though it is often used not as a single varietal offering but rather as a blending grape. It is also not expected to create wines for aging, though there are exceptions to the rule.

Cabernet Franc is one of the main *cepage ameliorateurs,* or blending grapes, in Bordeaux. Its main usage is on the Right Bank, in the Libournais region of St Emilion. Here, Cabernet Franc is typically the main blending grape for Merlot. Cabernet Sauvignon is rare on this side, because there is not enough heat or gravel to allow it to reach full ripeness. But for many Libournais producers, adding Cabernet Franc to the blend gives Merlot the structure and fruitiness to round out the flavor profile. Two producers in St Emilion view Cabernet Franc as a primary varietal. Chateau Ausone, named for the Roman wine writer Ausonius, typically makes a blend that is 50/50 Merlot and Cabernet Franc. The other, Chateau Cheval-Blanc, makes a wine that is primarily Cabernet Franc, on the order of 70 percent of the blend. These two wineries are considered the best in St Emilion and create wines that last for decades.

Single-varietal Cabernet Franc can be found in the Loire Valley, in particular the regions of Anjou and Touraine. Here, Cabernet Franc is made into a multitude of single-varietal wines with regional names. With a more northern and therefore cooler climate, Cabernet Franc tends to ripen with a bit less concentration and with higher acidity. This makes the wines labeled Saumur, Anjou, or Touraine very approachable, easy drinking red wines. The "heavyweights" of the region, or those appellations whose wines are considered the best examples of Cabernet Franc are Chinon, Bourgueil, and St-Nicolas-de-Bourgueil.

Cabernet Franc Notes

- ■ Regions: Right Bank Bordeaux, Loire Valley, Canada
- ■ Characteristics: similar to Cabernet Sauvignon, berries, green peppers, mint
- ■ Feature: mostly a blending grape, except in certain areas in Libournais

Cabernet Franc grown in the Loire will often be low extract and high acidity. This allows the production of a style that is uncommon for the Cabernet family—the rosé. Some Cabernet Franc is not made into red wine, but rather made into an easy-to-drink, and sometimes off-dry, rosé wine. The official designation of this style is Cabernet d'Anjou. This should not be confused with Rose d'Anjou, which is typically made from other grape varieties and does not have the sophistication of the Cabernet.

Gamay

If there is one grape that is tied not only to a specific region of production but also to a specific process, it is Gamay. In fact, more people know the region name, Beaujolais, than they do the grape that is grown there.

Looking at Gamay in its home region, it would appear to be a grape that could be successful elsewhere, given the right conditions. It could be considered a cool-weather grape, and it has a very high preference for granite soils. Much of the traditional gobolet, or head training, is giving way to guyot, or wire training, for the purpose of using mechanical harvesting. In fact, in Burgundy (of which Beaujolais is considered a district), Gamay makes up almost two-thirds of the production of *all* wine. For many, that level of production is actually a signal as to why Gamay is not a fine grape.

Much, if not most, of the wine from Beaujolais is produced by the carbonic maceration method of fermentation. As discussed previously, carbonic maceration uses the natural enzymes of the harvested grape to begin the sugar conversion to alcohol. This enzymatic reaction, as well as the subsequent fermentation, takes place in an oxygen-free environment, under a blanket of carbon dioxide. The process creates a wine that is drinkable within six weeks of harvest. This style is called Beaujolais Nouveau. Until recently, Nouveau production was upward of half of all the wine produced in Beaujolais. Because it is an easy-drinking wine that can't really age more than six months, it has not been considered a "serious" wine, and has besmirched Gamay as a grape along the way.

Gamay Notes

- Region: Beaujolais, small amount in Loire Valley
- Characteristics: high acid, low tannin, flavors of cherries and granite
- Feature: most common descriptors associated with carbonic maceration rather than grape itself

Aside from the Nouveau style, the best expression of Gamay is in the *cru* bottlings. There are ten villages in Beaujolais that sit on highly granitic soil, and produce wines that contain no carbonically macerated juice, and that can age for three to five years. These wines are noted by the name of the village on the label rather than any designation of Beaujolais. For many critics who believe that Gamay is an inferior grape that is saved by carbonic maceration, these *cru* wines are the counterargument that these critics are misguided.

Gamay makes wines that are the antithesis of what most drinkers look for in a red wine, even on the *cru* level. It is light purple, low in tannin, high in acidity, and highly aromatic. Nouveau wines have the characteristic nose of carbonic maceration—banana, bubblegum, Jolly Ranchers, or as the English say, peardrops. The palate is very light, with practically no tannin (as expected from the whole-berry fermentation). Nouveau is one of the fruitiest wines from the Old World, but still has an underlying earthiness, much like the granite on which some of it is grown. *Cru* Beaujolais has higher extract than its Nouveau counterpart, but it is still noticeably purple. The nose combines the red berry fruitiness with a dusty, rocky earthiness. That is also reflected on the palate, along with somewhat higher tannins due to more traditional wine making methods. Both of these wines, however, are best served chilled, partly to tame their high acidity but also to enhance that acidity's refreshing quality.

Corvina

Most wine drinkers would be hard pressed to recognize a wine that was labeled Corvina. However, label that same wine with one of its regions of origin in northeastern Italy—Bardolino or Valpolicella—and those same wine drinkers would immediately understand what was in the bottle.

In fact, Corvina is merely the main component of the wines of Bardolino and Valpolicella. By Italian law, Corvina must make up at least 70 percent of the blend, and is complemented by two other minor grapes, Rondinella and Molinara. As demonstrated by basic Bardolino, Corvina makes wine that is light in color and low in tannin. Valpolicella has slightly more of both, but would still fall into the light and fresh category. What Corvina does have is aroma and acidity. The nose of a good Valpolicella would be reminiscent of cherries and flowers with a hint of almonds. Much of the Bardolino and Valpolicella that is currently produced is commercial, and not the best example of the aromatic quality of Corvina. But when the wine is produced by small producers, from volcanic or chalky soils, it begins to show more complexity and depth.

In Valpolicella, not all of the Corvina goes to make a light, fresh wine. Some is taken and processed using the *passito* or drying method. Traditionally, the small lobes to the sides of each cluster would be taken to be used for the passito method. These sides, known as the ears or *recio* in Italian, obtain the most sun and therefore are the sweetest of the grapes. The wines that are made are anything but light and fresh.

The traditional wine made via the passito method is called Recioto della Valpolicella. The ears of the grape clusters are separated from the rest of the cluster, and placed on straw mats. These straw mats are then stacked in well-ventilated areas for the course of the winter. Most wineries still use the attics of the wineries, with their open windows, as the storage area for the drying grapes. This method has the potential to yield rotting grapes if the air does not circulate enough or if there is too much moisture present. More and more producers are changing to dedicated drying rooms with low humidity and high air circulation. The grapes are left to dry over the winter months. By the spring, the grapes have dried and are noticeably shriveled, though far from becoming raisins.

The dried grapes are then used to make wine. The reduced moisture in the grapes concentrates the flavors and sugars, and will yield wines with increased color, body and alcohol content. Recioto della Valpolicella is a sweet wine. Its history dates back to the Venetian traders, who knew that wine with some sugar and higher alcohol content was more stable for shipping. The resulting product is inky black in color, approaching 16 percent alcohol, and definitely sweet. Even though it is dense and imposing, Recioto is fairly approachable young, because of the sugar. It is a wine that gets better with age, often upward of twenty years or more.

Recioto Dolce, or sweet, was the traditional wine up until the end of World War II. At that time, dry wines became the favored style around the world, and Recioto amarone (from *amaro*, the Italian word for bitter) became more desired. Amarone, as it is known, is a wine that was often made by accident. Occasionally, a winemaker would be heard to say "Il vino mi scappa," or "The wine is escaping me." What the winemaker was referring to was the continuation of the fermentation past the point for Recioto Dolce. The yeast would continue to ferment the sugars

Corvina Notes

- Region: northeast Italy
- Characteristics: in basic form, notes of cherries and almonds with low tannins; Amarone has high tannin, full body, and high alcohol
- Feature: multiple wine styles with varying levels of body

to dryness, creating Recioto Amarone. These wines need to be aged a minimum of five years before they are released, and often need a decade or two to develop. Amarone is a *vino da meditazione,* or meditation wine, one to sip and contemplate, because of the density, the layering, and the multidimensions it has after some aging. While a Recioto Dolce is reminiscent of plums, black cherries, and cinnamon, the Amarone will include licorice and tar, plus vanilla from aging in small oak barrels.

An intermediate style of wine, called Ripasso, has been developed by Masi (who has also trademarked the term). This wine is a marriage of the regular Valpolicella process and Amarone production. What results is a wine with more body, more flavor, and more tannin that the simple Valpolicella, but is more approachable earlier than an Amarone.

The process involves collecting the must from Amarone production and placing it in a vat. Next, a simple Valpolicella is added to the vat, and the wine is allowed to macerate with the pressed skins and seeds. Two things happen, in effect. First, the wine gets "bigger." It obtains more color and tannin from the skins and seeds. It also extracts flavors from the dried grapes that were not present in the original wine, along with additional alcohol. Second, the wine undergoes a very crude malolactic fermentation. The effect of the spent grapes is to modify the acid of the fresh wine. This makes the wine a bit more approachable, and a bit more balanced with the new, increased flavors and body.

Sangiovese

One of the most planted grapes in Italy is Sangiovese. It is the backbone of many everyday blends, but is also the grape behind the best of Tuscan wines. It is also one of the oldest vines in Italy, first cultivated by the Etruscans and then by the Romans. It is the Romans who likely named the grape Sanguis Jove (blood of Jupiter), based on its juice.

Similar to Pinot Noir, an ancient grape like Sangiovese has developed a multitude of subvarieties. Two distinctive versions are Sangiovese Grosso and Piccolo. Grosso tend to be earlier ripening, with bigger grapes that are held in looser bunches and with thicker skins. Even that statement is a gross simplification, because so many microclimate and clonal variations have developed over time that it is difficult to categorize which subvariety is better (or even dominant, for that matter).

Sangiovese does not have a dominant preferred soil; rather, it likes soils that drain well, and has a small preference for those with calcium in them. It is a paradoxical grape in terms of climate. In Chianti it prefers south-facing slopes in order to ripen well, while in Montalcino it can be planted on the north side of the hills. It does better if there is a more continental climate, yet the areas along the Mediterranean produce excellent, age-worthy wines.

Sangiovese is not a grape that travels well. While it has been planted around the world, most notably in California and Australia, Sangiovese so far has only made top-notch wines in Italy, and in particular, Tuscany. Only a couple of regions around the world even approach making wines worth their investment, yet what seems to hold them back is that they are *not* Tuscany.

In its simplest form, Sangiovese is a wine with which everyone is familiar, even if they do not drink wine. It is the straw-wrapped flask, called a *fiasco,* that has held cheap Chianti and often serves as a candlestick holder. This wine is often made in bulk, using the classic recipe developed in the 1700s. That recipe is a blend of up to six grape varieties, some of them white grapes. What resulted was a red wine barely classified above rosé, with little flavor, low tannin, but lots of acidity. It is the massive production of this style of Chianti that almost ruined its reputation.

Why blend Sangiovese? Part of the reason is the composition of the grape itself. While Sangiovese Grosso has a thick skin and can produce a wine of high tannin, it is lacking in a particular group of compounds that give red wine a rich, deep color. Many producers through the years had blended other varietals into their Sangiovese just to give it some color. Sometimes those grapes came from the local vineyards, and other times they came from Southern Italy.

When the influence of Cabernet Sauvignon began to rise, Tuscan producers wanted to add that grape to their Sangiovese. In the late 1960s, the wine Carmignano was legally allowed to blend Cabernet Sauvignon into its Sangiovese. By the 1970s producers such as Antinori were breaking with DOC regulations and creating magnificent Sangiovese-Cabernet Sauvignon blends they categorized as *vino da tavola* (table wine). It was a slap in the face of the governmental authorities that the top-selling (and most expensive) wines from the region could only legally be called table wine.

In typical Italian fashion, the government adapted so that the rule-breakers would still be under government regulation—they simply changed the rules. One change was to create the category Indicazione Geografica Tipica (IGT), which indicated a wine that was in a style typical to a region. The other change was to the recipe of Chianti itself. Previously, up to 30 percent other grapes could be added to the Sangiovese. Now, it is possible to add up to 15 percent Cabernet Sauvignon in the blend, or even have a pure single-varietal Sangiovese.

The different expressions of Sangiovese in Tuscany are explicitly based on locale (and DOC/DOCG regulation) and more subtly on producer. Any discussion of a regional wine must always take into consideration that individual producers will vary their recipes within the legal guidelines. The most common place to see this play out is in Chianti. Some producers still follow a version of the older recipe, mixing the traditional grapes into the blend. Other, more modernist winemakers, have changed to using Cabernet Sauvignon or making single-varietal wines. This makes any generalization about Chianti difficult. The safest area for generalizing is in the high-end Chiantis. The Chianti region was expanded to cover a wide swath of Tuscany, and then subdivided based on the sublocale. The best Chianti comes from the original Chianti region, designated by the term "Classico" on the label. A more rarified version, Chianti Classico Riserva, reflects wines made in a style where extra aging was conducted at the winery, and implying that the wines will age longer in the bottle.

The profile of a Chianti Classico is fairly typical of Sangiovese. In the glass, the wine will have a garnet core, but the rim may take on an orange tint. This is the result of the lack of deep color compounds in Sangiovese, and therefore its tendency to oxidize easily. On the nose, the wine is a blend of dusty earth, sour cherries, black tea, herbs, and spice. The producers that have adopted the modern usage of small-barrel aging also see some vanilla notes in the wine. Chianti shows a mouthwatering acidity, moderate tannins, and a slightly bitter finish, all in a medium-bodied wine. Most Chiantis are meant to be drunk within a few years of the vintage, but Riservas can last around a decade or so.

The other famous Sangiovese-based wine in Tuscany is Brunello di Montalcino. Created by the Biondi-Santi family, this wine is solely made from a clone of Sangiovese known as Brunello. The wines take five years of aging in small barrels before they are released, and can continue aging for another fifteen to twenty years. For those who cannot wait that long (or can't afford a Brunello), the same producers often make a Rosso di Montalcino, which is a lighter, younger version of the wine that is more affordable.

Other regional Sangiovese-based wines include Vino Nobile di Montepulciano and Morellino di Scansano. Vino Nobile wine is very similar in structure and flavor to Chianti, and often is a more affordable option. On the downside, it also can be of more variable quality than Chianti. Vino Nobile is noted for using the Prugnolo

Sangiovese Notes

- Region: Tuscany, central and southern Italy, California
- Characteristics: sour cherries and black tea on the nose; tannin levels vary depending on region and producer
- Feature: most widely planted Italian grape; expect wide variation in quality

clone of Sangiovese Grosso. Morellino di Scansano is uses the Morellino clone and is a lighter, more refreshing Sangiovese with a pronounced sour cherry fruitiness.

The final group of (sometimes) Sangiovese-based wines fall into a category formerly known as the Super-Tuscans. These were the wines made from nontraditional blends of grapes, some of which included Sangiovese and some which did not, that came on the scene in the 1980s. Those that contained Sangiovese in their blends spurred the changes seen throughout the rest of Tuscany, and in Chianti in particular. It is difficult to generalize about the Super Tuscans, as many are blends of international grapes, but their significance in modernizing and revitalizing Italian wine production cannot be underrated.

Barbera

The wine that most Italians have on a day-to-day basis is Barbera. In its most common expression, Barbera is an easy-drinking and thirst-quenching wine that pairs with multiple types of food.

Barbera is originally from the Piedmont region in northwest Italy. While this region still produces the best examples, Barbera has spread to all of Italy, along with the New World regions of California and Argentina. Why the prolific spread of Barbera? It's all in the characteristics of the grapes. Barbera is an early ripening grape, making it the grape of choice for vineyards too cool for Nebbiolo. It also retains its acidity upon ripening, which makes it attractive to growers in warmer regions. Finally, it has a good concentration of color. Combined with the acidity, the color makes Barbera a preferred blending grape. In fact, Barbera is the most widely planted grape in Italy, most of it going for blending.

The classic Barbera style does not see any wood influence. It has a bright purple color, which transitions to a pink rim. On the nose it is cherries and a modest earthiness, and on the palate, cherries, high acidity, low to moderate tannins, and a

Barbera Notes

- Region: Piedmont in northwest Italy
- Characteristics: high acidity, low tannins, sour cherry taste, bitter finish
- Feature: everyday wine of most Piedmontese

sour cherry-bitter finish that is typical of Italian wine. It is easy to see why this is an appealing, easy-drinking wine. Modernists in Piedmont are experimenting with small oak barrels. This gives Barbera more heft, and yields plum flavors with a hint of spice from the wood.

In California and Argentina, the acreage dedicated to Barbera is growing. Both regions trace their Barbera plantings back to Italian immigrants who started making wine. California was set back by Prohibition, but the plantings and popularity are making a comeback. Until recently, Barbera was mainly used in blending. The high acidity helped to ameliorate the overripeness of many grapes used for bulk wines and reduce their flabbiness. Now, as in Argentina, Barbera is finding new popularity as a single varietal wine.

Dolcetto

Dolcetto is another everyday wine in the Piedmont. Its name means "little sweet one," but that should not suggest that the grape is overly sugar-rich, or that the wine is particularly sweet. It most likely refers to the fondness the Piedmontese have for this little grape.

Dolcetto is an early ripener—two weeks before Barbera and a month before Nebbiolo. Therefore, it is planted in the cooler pockets of the Piedmont. It is often made into a simple, early drinking wine, which typically is of decent quality. It is pretty easy to grow, so most growers plant it and forget it. Top-notch Dolcetto is rare, because the effort required to grow the grapes is "better spent" on Nebbiolo (the money maker).

Dolcetto has a lot of color compounds in the skin; it is practically a black grape. That means very little maceration is needed to extract color—much less maceration, in fact, than is needed to extract tannin. Dolcettos are very deep purple in color, but possess low tannins and moderate acidity. They are reminiscent of cherries and plums, maybe with a little licorice added. The best Dolcettos will have a

Dolcetto Notes

- Region: Piedmont
- Characteristics: low tannin, moderate acidity, plum and cherry flavors
- Feature: easy to grow, but considered only for places Nebbiolo won't ripen

beautiful perfume as well. In most cases, Dolcettos are meant to be drunk within a couple years of the vintage. Some producers extract more tannins from Dolcetto, and combined with oak aging, create wines that are suitable for long-term aging.

Dolcetto can be found elsewhere in the world. Some of the oldest vines, dating to the 1800s, can be found in Australia. In California, the grape is sometimes called Charbono, and makes wines with more intensity and an almost chocolatey character to them.

Food and Wine Considerations

The light and fresh red wines are the workhorse wines for everyday food. Even in their regions of origin, these wines are on the table every day, while the expensive wines are sent for export. They have a natural medium to high acidity that works well with most foods. They are light enough to handle dishes made with chicken and pork, yet are still full flavored enough to work with beef or heartier dishes. The best example of how these are everyday wines is the image of a Chianti bottle in an Italian restaurant. The image of pasta with tomato sauce and a bottle of tangy Sangiovese is what these wines are about.

SUMMARY

The grapes that make light and fresh red wines evolved with the cuisines in their regions of origin. These are everyday wines. They are light enough in body to handle most dishes, while at the same time they can be made in styles that handle more full-bodied foods. Because they are the everyday wines of their home areas, they are often overlooked. They have not shown they can make good wine in other regions, nor do they have the layers of complexity that many of the international varieties contain. However, these are refreshing, drinkable wines that fill a niche in the wine lexicon.

QUESTIONS

1. What grape characteristics make these wines light and fresh?

2. What are the key regions for growing grapes that make light and fresh red wines?

3. Discuss the differences between Cabernet Franc in the Loire and in Bordeaux.

4. Describe the common technique for making wine from Gamay.

5. Describe the passito method of making Amarone.

6. What distinguishes Recioto from Amarone?

7. Write a tasting note for Amarone.

8. Write a tasting note for Chianti Classico.

9. Describe the variations between the different expressions of Sangiovese.

10. What are the key regions for the grapes that make light and fresh wines?

11. Outline the food pairing options for red wines that are light and fresh.

chapter 19

Soft and Juicy

There is a term commonly used by winemakers to describe a style of wine that will be favored by the majority of consumers—approachable. What does that truly mean? Often for red wine it means acidity that is not too tangy, tannins that are relatively soft or nonastringent, and recognizable fruit flavors. In other words, they want their wine to taste like ripe fruit, soft and juicy. The quintessential grape that fits this category is Merlot, but many of these secondary grapes—Tempranillo, Malbec, Pinotage, and Carménère—meet the profile and can be interesting alternatives to Merlot.

Upon completion of this chapter, the student should be able to:

- *Describe the characteristics of soft and juicy red wines*
- *Outline important regions for production of soft and juicy wines*
- *Discuss attributes of grapes*
- *Outline unique production techniques of these wines*
- *Explain food and wine considerations for these wines*

Tempranillo

Tempranillo is a grape with an identity crisis. It's not Tempranillo's fault; it has produced wines that fall in the soft and juicy category for centuries. The issue is with the labeling. The homeland of Tempranillo, Spain, chose long ago to follow the French model of naming wines—by region. Layer on top of that a very amalgamated culture that keeps its local traditions (read: lots of local names for the same grape variety). What results is great wine that is next to impossible to decipher the grape variety.

Tempranillo is a self-contradictory grape. It needs heat to ripen fully and develop thick skins for color and tannin. It needs cool weather in order to develop aromatics and retain acidity. Tempranillo is a late budding vine that is also early ripening (getting its name from *temprano,* "early" in Spanish). It is also a grape that can adapt to different soil types and express their terroir. On clay soils, the wines develop more complexity and body, while on chalky soils the grape retains more acidity.

There is only one way to satisfy the two faces of Tempranillo—plant at high altitude in a hot region. This is the approach on the Iberian peninsula, where the regions of Rioja, Ribera del Duero, Douro, and others all fit the topographical requirements. Why high altitude in a hot region? The answer is diurnal variation, or the difference in temperature between the daytime high and the nighttime low. In these regions, that variation can be on the order of 30–40°F (17–22°C). The daytime high provides the heat to develop the sugar and tannins in the grapes, while the evening low can slow down the ripening and help retain the acidity of the fruit.

Most Tempranillo is experienced as a Spanish wine. Depending on the region of origin, the treatment of the grape can be very different. The French influence on wine making can be seen in Rioja. Here, the wines are traditionally made in a softer, *clarete* style (similar to the claret of Bordeaux). This version of Tempranillo is the most familiar. It typically involves extended wood aging, often in American oak, and is meant to be ready-to-drink upon release.

Rioja is actually a blended wine. The main component is Tempranillo, but it is often mixed with Garnacha as well as a well-regarded local grape, Graciano. Depending on the amount of aging, each level of Rioja provides a somewhat different experience. Crianza, the shortest length of wood aging, often retain a fair amount of fruit character, along with a good dose of vanilla from the American oak barrels. There is also a characteristic Spanish dustiness to the tannins, and often a hint of leather or tobacco from the aging. Riservas are aged slightly longer (not always in wood, sometimes the extra age is bottle age). The fruit is a little more fragile in these wines, and is often buried under the more dominant oak and

Tempranillo Notes

- Region: Rioja, Ribera del Duero
- Characteristics: light body, medium tannins, strawberry fruit for clarete style, inky color, plumy fruit and chewy tannins for tinto style
- Features: Rioja noted for American oak influence that many confuse for Tempranillo character

age flavors. Finally, in the best years, Gran Riservas show the traditional style of extended age, with more developed bouquets and oak influence dominating the flavor profile.

The second style of Tempranillo is epitomized in Ribera del Duero. Here, the style is more about making big, bold, meaty 100 percent Tempranillos. This style is known as *tinto,* to indicate the inky character of the wines. The most famous of this style are Vega Sicilia and Pesquera. While Vega Sicilia has been around for years, it is the newer Pesquera that sparked the new interest and new development of Tempranillo. The *tinto* style usually uses less American oak in favor of French oak. The result is a wine that is less strawberry and more plum and blackcurrant, and which develops distinct tobacco, black olive, prune, and cocoa with age.

Malbec

Malbec is a grape that found a new life on the other side of the world. Originally from Cahors, and a bit from along the Gironde, in Bordeaux, it was never a stand-out grape. Malbec was, at best, a blending grape with the same usefulness as Merlot. Closer to the Gironde, Malbec produced soft, juicy wines relatively low in acid that tempered Cabernet Sauvignon. But a bad frost allowed Merlot to take over that role, and Malbec was relegated (barely) to its home further inland in Cahors.

In Cahors, with its higher elevation and warmer temperatures, Malbec is known as the "black wine." Malbec develops thicker skins and more tannin and color in Cahors, and is the major component of the local blend. Looks alone would predict Malbec in Cahors is a chewy, long-lived wine. Taste reveals that the grape has kept its blackberry fruitiness, and the tannins are soft and ripe.

As early as the mid-1800s saw Malbec transported to Argentina. Over the years, the two "homes" of Malbec developed differently. In Argentina, Malbec became more refined, more focused as a grape. Malbec became the "Argentinean wine"

Malbec Notes

- Region: Cahors and Bordeaux in France, Argentina
- Characteristics: plum and mulberry fruit, moderate to big tannins, deep color
- Feature: a blending grape in France; a single varietal in Argentina

when it hit the market in the mid-1990s, showing more elegance than it ever did in Cahors.

Malbec from Argentina is grown at high altitude in the foothills to the Andes. The plentiful sun, irrigation from snowmelt, and temperature variation due to altitude create wines that retain their acidity, yet are full, ripe in fruit and tannin, and aromatic. Young Malbec can smell of plums, mulberries, and violets, which may develop into tobacco, leather, tar, and raisins with age. Most aging is done in old oak, just to prevent overpowering the lush fruitiness with oak flavors.

Pinotage

In the New World, it is often the hallmark of a country or region to have a "signature" grape. That grape is associated with the place, either because of the unique quality the region brings to the production, or because that region is the only one where the wine is made with high quality. In the case of South Africa, Pinotage is not only its "signature" grape, it is also its "native" grape.

Pinotage is native to South Africa because it was created at Stellenbosch University by Professor Perold in 1925. Perold crossed Pinot Noir and Cinsault (called Hermitage in South Africa) to produce Pinotage. It was just another interesting grape until it won a gold medal at a Cape Wine competition in 1959. That competition was Pinotage's debut on the world stage.

There exists a love-hate relationship in the wine world with Pinotage. Part of the reason is the way Pinotage has been made in the past. When made well, the wine is a fruity blend of mulberry and raspberry with a touch of plum. Layered on that is a toasty, creamy sweetness. In poorly made Pinotage, typically the result of overcropping or poor wine making, the flavors are more rustic, with increased volatile acidity that has been described as everything from raspberry vinegar to paint to drain cleaner. Other descriptors of Pinotage's unique character include burnt rubber or baked bananas. Depending on which style was your introduction to Pinotage, that typically determined which camp you joined.

Pinotage Notes

- Region: South Africa
- Characteristics: medium body, light tannins, mulberry and raspberry fruit
- Feature: young Pinotage has high levels of volatile acidity that turn off many drinkers

One note on Pinotage in terms of approachability: it seems always to be ready to drink. Young Pinotage has strong tannins, yet when made well they are fine and ripe. As Pinotage ages, it shows more of the traits of its Pinot Noir parentage. Old Pinotage is very reminiscent of aged Pinot Noir, especially because the estery volatile acidity is long gone.

Carménère

Carménère is a grape that has found new life. It was a dominant, often preferred, grape in the blends of Bordeaux. Then came the devastation of mildew and phylloxera. As the vineyards were being replanted, it was decided that Carménère was too much trouble: it suffered from coulure, had variable yields, and did not like grafting. So it was replaced by Cabernet Sauvignon. Meanwhile, on the other side of the world in Chile, Claudio Gay had returned to Santiago in the 1830s with plants from Europe for a botanical garden. These cutting became the source of the vineyards in Chile. Over the years, as production increased, it seemed as if there were two variations of Merlot in the vineyards. Finally, in 1997, DNA analysis confirmed that one of those variations was really Carménère.

Carménère is an excellent example of a grape that needs specific growing conditions or the wine will be unsatisfactory. It dislikes too much water while growing and prefers (practically demands) soils that are enriched and can retain some water without irrigation. The grapes themselves must be exposed to the sun during the final ripening stages. It needs a long ripening season, so the sugars do not increase too much before the tannins are ripe. Without these conditions, the result is a strong green bell pepper vegetal character that dominates.

When Carménère is grown properly, the result is that the green bell pepper character turns into a savory layer under the prevalent fruit. The wine will taste of black fruits like blackberries and plums, and will have a hint of spice. The tannins

Carménère Notes

- Region: Chile
- Characteristics: blackberry fruit, low acidity, vegetal/savory component, hint of baking spices
- Feature: was (and is) confused with Merlot, but savory component is the difference

are full and round, and the low acidity accentuates the apparent sweetness from the fruit. The savory character seems to be roasted red peppers, celery, and soy, perhaps with roasted meat added. The wine is very mouth filling as well as rich, fruity, and juicy.

Food and Wine Considerations

The easy method of matching the soft, juicy red wines is to consider them like Merlot, and pair accordingly. While approaching the wine from the point of soft tannins, moderate acidity, and ripe fruit is proper, it loses the nuance of each of these wines. For example, not all Tempranillo can be treated the same. A clarete style from Rioja will pair differently than a tinto from Ribera del Duero. The moderate tannins and hint of spice in most of these wines allows for pairing with spiced dishes, even some that may have a bit of heat to them. A pairing of Carménère with curried red lentils highlights the savory notes in the wine, while highlighting the earthiness of the lentils. Even the volatile acidity in Pinotage can be matched with grilled or barbequed meats.

SUMMARY

The soft and juicy red wines are often thought of as Merlot lookalikes or substitutes. Yet these wines are anything but poor imitations of Merlot. They each have their own nuances, but all are easy on the palate in terms of tannins and all exhibit fresh berry and plum fruit character. The wine is easy to drink and at times seems more like juice than alcohol. Each grape has its quirks, from Pinotage's volatile acidity to Carménère's savory red bell peppers. They are drinkable on their own, but serve as great refreshing wines with food.

QUESTIONS

1. What are the two styles in which Tempranillo is made?

2. Describe the difference between Malbec in France and Malbec in Argentina.

3. What are the origins of Pinotage?

4. Describe the resurgence of Carménère in Chile.

5. What are the key regions for growing grapes that make soft and juicy wines?

6. Which grape characteristics are responsible for making soft and juicy wines?

7. Outline the food pairing options for soft and juicy wines.

chapter *20*

Full and Tannic

*F*or most wine drinkers, the first experience with a big, full-bodied red wine is Cabernet Sauvignon. While this experience is an introduction to the world of full, tannic wines, it is by no means the complete picture. There is a world of wines that are more full bodied and more tannic than Cabernet Sauvignon. Most of these wines are also complex and aromatic. They are wines for aging, which develop deep complexity over time as the tannins soften.

Upon completion of this chapter, the student should be able to:

Describe the characteristics of full and tannic red wines
Outline important regions for production of full and tannic wines
Discuss attributes of grapes
Outline unique production techniques of these wines
Explain food and wine considerations for these wines

Nebbiolo

Considered the grape behind one of Italy's top wines, Nebbiolo is a challenging grape—for growers, for vintners, and for consumers. It is also on the front lines of the future of Italian winemaking, with strong traditionalists maintaining the old ways in the face of increasing modernism.

Nebbiolo is found in the Piedmont region of Italy. It is a grape with a long growing season, being an early budder and a very late ripener. In fact, the name of the grape is probably derived from *nebbia,* or fog, which fills the vineyards before harvest. Being a late-ripening grape, it is necessary to give Nebbiolo the warmest sites with the best exposure. Most of the vineyards face south or southeast, to give the grapes the most exposure to the sun. The best vineyards are also found in the warmest mesoclimates, another effort to get Nebbiolo to ripen fully. It is extremely important that Nebbiolo be fully ripened; it is a grape naturally high in acid, and if the grapes are not fully ripe, the acidity is overbearing.

In the winery, the differences between the traditionalists and the modernists are evident. Traditionally, Nebbiolo is harvested in late October to November. At this time, the cellars are quite cold and getting fermentation to start is a difficult process. It may take a couple weeks before any evidence of fermentation is apparent. This allows for the skins to macerate in the juice for an extended time. Once fermentation starts, its rise in temperature can be rapid, often resulting in the loss of fruit or aromatics. But the cellars are still cool, and fermentation (after its initial spike in temperature) can drag on for months. This extends the time the skins are in contact with the juice, extracting even more tannins. The wine then goes into large old casks in an effort to have slow oxidation temper the powerful tannins. Traditional Nebbiolo wines will then take extended periods in bottle to age to become drinkable, if they ever become drinkable at all.

Modernists treat Nebbiolo with more precision rather than the traditional "let nature take its course" attitude. Modern vintners use shorter maceration times, shorter (and temperature-controlled) fermentations and, most notably, small oak barriques to age the wine. The wine is also allowed to undergo malolactic fermentation, in an attempt to curtail the acid structure. These wines age in barriques for around two to three years, and are more approachable when bottled.

The area of Northern Italy is home to Nebbiolo, in particular the Piedmont region. Within Piedmont there are two zones where Nebbiolo is the major grape. The most well-regarded region is the Langhe hills, which contains the regions of Barolo and Barbaresco, both considered to be excellent examples of Nebbiolo. Farther to the northeast are the Novara hills, home to Ghemme and Gattinara and a region where Nebbiolo's local name is Spanna. Because these hills are further north and have somewhat different soils, the wines tend to be more rustic and

Nebbiolo Notes

- Region: Piedmont, Italy (Barolo, Barbaresco, Ghemme, Gattinara)
- Pseudonyms: Spanna, Chiavennasca
- Characteristics: light color, high acid, high tannins

earthy than those of the Langhe. Nebbiolo can also be found (as Chiavennasca) in the Valtellina region of Lombardy.

Barolo is thought by many to be Italy's best wine. When young, it is dark, potentially with an orangey rim from oxidation. On the nose, Barolo shows its individuality. The nose is full of layers of aromas: plums, roses, violets, tar (sometimes perceived as latex gloves or bandages), mushrooms (or truffles), cherries, plums and mulberries, licorice, cloves, and dried herbs. On the palate, the acidity is high, the tannins are firm and gripping, and the wine is full bodied with a flavor profile that mimics the fruit and herbal components of the nose.

Upon aging, Barolo will lose a fair amount of color. It will often become as light colored as a Pinot Noir, which often fools the consumer to thinking this is a light wine. The aromas remain, however, developing more with age. The palate also remains similar, gaining the aged wine flavors of tobacco and leather, while often not losing any acidity or tannin. Barolos from a good year can last from ten to thirty years. Barolos that are not made to the best standards will never reach their peak.

Barbaresco is a recent development in Piedmont wine making. Also made from 100 percent Nebbiolo, it is considered the queen to Barolo's king. It is somewhat more delicate, aromatic, and lighter than Barolo. For many tasters, that is actually hard to determine, with more variation being found in Barolos alone than between Barolo and Barbaresco. Barbarescos do age faster than Barolos, though, often reaching their peak after about seven years and aging for up to fifteen years.

Touriga Nacional

Touriga Nacional is a wine with two identities. The first, its main mission in the wine world, is one of the top six grapes used to make red Porto. The second is as a red table wine grape. Discussion of Porto will be deferred to a later chapter, and the focus now is on Touriga Nacional as a red wine.

Touriga Nacional as a wine is evocative of the grapes themselves. Touriga grapes are extremely small, making the ratio of skin and seed to pulp very high.

That results in lots of color and also lots of tannin for the amount of juice. Typically Touriga will be blended with other local Portuguese grapes to soften the tannins.

Touriga Nacional is not a highly productive grape. When replanting after phyloxera, a great number of producers reduced their planting of Touriga. In the 1990s, that trend reversed, with more producers planting the variety. It is not just restricted to the Douro Valley in Portugal, it is also required in blends in Dão and Bairrada.

Touriga Nacional is similar to Cabernet Sauvignon in the amount of extract and the amount of tannins. The flavor and aroma profile is also similar to Cabernet Sauvignon. The fruit component is dark black fruit, like blackberries and dark black plums. There is also a hint of leafiness mixed with a light floral character. All these components develop into tobacco and even richer, sweeter fruit.

Aglianico

One of the oldest varieties on the Italian peninsula, Aglianico is thought to have been originally brought to the region around Naples by the Greeks. Its name is a derivative from the Roman word for Greek, *hellenico*, and the wine was enjoyed by the Romans as red Falerno. There is also a theory that Aglianico is really a native grape, only named by the Greeks. In either case, its origins are ancient and its cultivation on the Italian peninsula longstanding.

Aglianico is an intense red wine. The best regions in southern Italy (its home and, currently, only residence) are at altitude, either in the lower Apennines in Campania or on Mount Vulture in Basilicata. In Campania, the best example is Taurasi, and the more generically named Aglianico Irpinia.

Both Taurasi and Aglianico del Vulture are big yet elegant wines. While many modern wines are sleek and elegant like the Guggenheim Museum, Aglianico is like St Patrick's Cathedral—big, imposing, elegant with many details and layers. Two components to Aglianico are massive, the tannins and the fruit. Most Aglianicos are wood aged to help temper the tannins, yet they often still need more time in bottle before being fully approachable. The fruit flavor is complex and layered. Deep, dark fruits like plum, blackberry, and blueberry are layered with coffee, mint, licorice, tar, tobacco, leather, and meat. Aglianico is not a fainthearted wine. It is rich and complex, with more and more interest from producers who see great potential in the Taurasis and Aglianicos del Vulture currently being produced.

Tannat

Tannat is a grape looking for its big break. As the sound of the name implies, its main attribute is tannin. It can be wild and rough, but more and more producers are developing more refined versions.

Tannat is originally from the Madiran region of France, in the southwest of the country. Here it is known for its highly tannic yet blackberry-ish fruit profile. It has been taken on by Uruguay as its signature grape. Most Tannat, whether it is an American producer like Bonny Doon making Tannat in France, or Uruguayan producers, has an Old World earthiness to it. The best examples in France have a definite terroir of clay and tar along with strong tannins. Uruguayan examples have finer tannins, but retain the more refined fruit profile of the Old World style.

Food and Wine Considerations

These wines are full of tannin. They need protein and fat to help balance that astringency. Classical pairing with Nebbiolo is the rich cuisine of the Italian Piedmont region. Here, cream and cheese are large components of the dishes. The classic Beef in Barolo is a braised roast, which utilizes the rich proteins of the beef to temper the aggressive tannins of the wine.

The flavor profile of these wines makes them better partners with complexly flavored dishes. Nebbiolo, with its truffle character, matches well with mushroom dishes, or those with more earthiness. Aglianico has a licorice-like character. It can be paired with some Asian dishes, like Red Cooked Chicken. The braising of the chicken in soy increases the umami character, which tempers the astringency, and the star anise in the dish is a great match to Aglianico's licorice.

SUMMARY

The full and tannic red wines are complex, aromatic wines that rise above the everyday expectations of full-bodied wines. They are unique to their regions, often having been developed alongside their cuisines. They are also underappreciated, because their complexity is often overwhelming for the consumer. Their aggressive tannins need foods that can handle the astringency and allow the rest of the wine to shine.

QUESTIONS

1. What aspect of the local climate gives Nebbiolo its name?

2. Where are the top producing regions for Nebbiolo?

3. Write a tasting note for Nebbiolo.

4. What wine is Touriga Nacional most known for making?

5. Where is Aglianico typically produced?

6. Write a tasting note for Aglianico.

7. What two regions are known for growing Tannat?

8. Discuss the food pairing implications of serving a full, tannic wine.

chapter 21

Rich and Spicy

*S*ome red wines are known for their juicy freshness and some for their big, chewy tannins. The wines in this section are known for their richness. Some have prominent fruit or spice flavors, others a meatier richness. In all cases the wines are full bodied and full flavored.

Upon completion of this chapter, the student should be able to:

    Describe the characteristics of rich and spicy red wines
    Outline important regions for production of rich and spicy wines
    Discuss attributes of grapes
    Outline unique production techniques of these wines
    Explain food and wine considerations for these wines

Zinfandel

Known as "the American grape," Zinfandel's origin was in question until recent DNA analysis. Zinfandel first came to prominence in the New England states, where it was grown in greenhouses and sold as a table grape. It migrated from there to northern California, making wine for gold prospectors, and to California's hot Central Valley to be used for raisin production. Later it was grown to produce bulk wines, forming the base of many jug wines from the 1950s to 1970s.

In the mid-1980s, many Zinfandel grapes were uprooted and replaced by Cabernet Sauvignon. What saved the vines was a new, blush style of Zinfandel called White Zinfandel. Sutter Home Winery started the White Zinfandel craze in the United States as a fresh, light, fruity, easy-drinking wine. It also saved many of the fifty-plus-year-old vines that were to be uprooted. Zinfandel as a more conventional style of fine table wine is credited to Ridge Vineyards, which saw the potential in the old vines and has created wines that are rich and complex.

Zinfandel is a grape that has more climatic requirements than soil in order to make a great wine. Zinfandel likes warm regions, but not too hot or the grapes will shoot past ripeness and quickly turn to raisins. What slows the grapes from speeding past ripeness is cool temperatures at night. This retards the ripening process and also retains the acidity that is needed to balance the wine.

Depending upon its ripeness when picked, Zinfandel can express different fruit characteristics. Just-ripened berries will yield cranberry- or raspberry-type freshness. More-ripened grapes yield plum and blackberry flavors. Very ripe, or even raisinated, grapes taste of prune, date, and raisin. What makes Zinfandel intriguing to many vintners is that all three characteristics of the grape could be on the same cluster.

In the winery, the vintner has several style options depending on how they handle the grapes. If the grapes are pressed early and fermented with some residual sugar at cool temperatures, the result is the pinkish White Zinfandel. This style is usually made from highly cropped grapes or ones that are just ripe. Having a significant proportion of barely ripe grapes keeps the flavor profile berry-like and the flavor fresh.

Making Zinfandel grapes into red wine can result in differing styles as well, depending on how the grapes are processed. Whole-cluster fermentation will keep the wine light and fruit. This will be a wine that is lighter in body and has a greater proportion of berry and plum flavors. Long maceration of the skins will extract more color and tannin to create a bigger wine, capable of oak influence. The oak most commonly used is American, bringing vanilla and toast essences to the rich fruit profile, though some producers are using imported French oak.

The final style is a late-harvest Zinfandel or a Zinfandel port. The grapes for making this style are typically highly raisinated. However, not all late-harvest Zinfandels are sweet; some are fermented to dryness and often produce wines that approach 17 percent alcohol. Those that do retain sugar in the Port style benefit from the date and raisin flavor profile provided by the grapes.

Upon pouring a glass of Zinfandel, it is apparent that this is an intense wine. It is often inky black, with little change near the rim. On the nose, the fruitiness is often accompanied by black pepper spiciness and a good dose of black tea. On the palate, many Zinfandels are not overly tannic. The tannins are often firm but ripe, and strong enough to balance the concentration of fruit flavor. The acidity level will vary, depending upon the region of origin. Zinfandels from the central coast of California are often lower in acidity than their northern cousins from Sonoma or the Sierra Foothills. Most of these wines will benefit from some aging after bottling, but are their best within four to seven years of the vintage. Wines with no oak influence are best even younger.

One of the most intriguing stories behind Zinfandel has been its origin. It migrated from the East Coast to California, but where did it come from originally? It is thought to have been brought over to New York's Long Island in a suitcase by some immigrants from Vienna, Austria. Meanwhile vine scientists looked at the vine and saw similarities to a vine in southern Italy. DNA analysis finally demonstrated that the Primitivo vine in Puglia (the heel of the Italian Peninsula) was the same as Zinfandel. So how does Vienna fit in? Further analysis shows that both vines are related to the Croatian vine Plavic Mali, and those are all related back to an even rarer Croatian vine. It seems that Zinfandel was taken in two directions—one to southern Italy and the other to Vienna, from whence it came to America.

With that in mind, some producers have turned to Puglia to create another style of Zinfandel: Primitivo. The top-quality region in Puglia that produces Primitivo is Primitivo di Manduria. This region is known for making dry table wine, as well as making sweet, fortified versions, similar to Port.

Monastrell/Mourvèdre

Monastrell, or as it is known by its more familiar French name Mourvèdre, is another in a long list of idiosyncratic grapes. Not often a single varietal, Mourvèdre plays the supporting role in blends around the world.

How is Mourvèdre idiosyncratic? It needs warm temperatures to ripen, and even then needs south-facing slopes and warm sites. On the other hand, it needs cool clay soils to slow down the vines' vigor and the grapes' ripening. It must ripen to produce at least 13 percent alcohol, or no real flavor will develop. In addition, the window to pick the grapes is small, or the resulting wine will taste more like prune juice.

Mourvèdre has a rich, complex profile. It is full of blackberry fruit, with a dose of wild herbs and lots of tannin. What is most characteristic, however, is its meaty, sometimes barnyard-like, character. For many drinkers, this character is too strong, bordering on being a fault. However, either blended with more fruit-centered wines or given enough age, the wine expresses that meatiness as a mature leather characteristic.

The main production areas for Mourvèdre are Spain and France. In the southern Spanish region of Murcia (with its smaller regions of Yecla or Jumilla), Monastrell, as it is known in Spain, makes an intense, rich wine. Improvements in harvest timing and wine making are taming the barnyard character of Monastrell and making wines more approachable to the consumer. In France, Mourvèdre is a contributor to the Châteauneuf-du-Pape blend, as well as making single varietal wines along the Provence, Languedoc, and Roussillon coast.

Australia is another place where Mourvèdre has made a claim. Locally, the grape is called Mataro, but it often is referred to by the French name on exported bottles. Here, it is a major component of the GSM blend—Grenache-Shiraz- Mourvèdre. This blend, used to make easy-drinking wines as well as long-lasting age-worthy ones, is modeled after Châteauneuf-du-Pape. For many of these blends, it is the Mourvèdre that adds the heft and weight as well as some ageability to the mix.

Negroamaro

Negroamaro is an Italian grape localized to the southern portion of the country, most notably along the heel of the boot in Puglia. It is a unique wine, as can be seen by its translated name "black bitter." As a single varietal, Negroamaro is strong. It has a combination of light floral character mixed with barnyard and medicinal characteristics. It is inherently bitter edged, both from its tannins and from the basic profile of the grape. It is a thick-skinned grape, which contributes to its depth of color and intensity of tannins. As with many southern Italian red wines, the flavor of licorice or anise is apparent, but also that of coffee and tobacco. The wine is earthy, but also retains a crisp acidity for a wine made in such a warm climate.

Negroamaro is often mixed with other grapes, such as Malvasia Nera, in order to temper some of its varietal character. When blended, it creates some of the best wines in Puglia, most notably Salice Salentino. Then the wine becomes rich and spicy, the barnyard turns to meatiness, and the bitterness mellows to a finish that is asking to be paired with food.

Nero d'Avola

This grape is a Sicilian native, and exemplifies the sun-baked quality of that island. It is a thin-skinned grape, and therefore susceptible to rot, if it weren't grown in such dry conditions. It is also very late to ripen, one of the latest among vinifera varietals. The wines it produces are deep and dark, but with tannins that are soft and ripe, yet still can age. The flavor profile is reminiscent of black fruits and black pepper, but with an increased richness.

The flavor profile and the texture of the tannins suggest to some tasters that Nero d'Avola may be related to Syrah. One of the theories of Syrah's origins places it in Sicily, so there may be some merit to this theory. In fact, depending on the soils in which Nero d'Avola is planted, the result can be reminiscent of a French Syrah or an Australian Shiraz.

Nero d'Avola is a grape that is just finding its feet. In the past, the wines were uninspiring, but with modern winemaking (and more interest), producers are making better and better versions. If the trend continues, Nero d'Avola is a wine to watch. Currently, the types of wines being produced are either 100 percent Nero d'Avola, or a blend of Nero d'Avola and international varietals like Cabernet Sauvignon, Merlot, and Syrah (similar to Super Tuscan production). There is plenty of room for improvement with Nero d'Avola, from the clonal selection to the wine making itself.

Food and Wine Considerations

The hallmark of these wines is their spicy character. Each of these has intense tannins and need fairly full-bodied foods to match. The key to pairing is the spiciness. In almost each case, there is some influence of black pepper, giving a savory quality to the wines. Enhancing that in Mourvèdre and Negroamaro is the meaty character to the wine. These are wines that work well with basic foods and flavors.

Zinfandel is probably the best known of this category. Because it can be made in so many different styles, it is difficult to state exactly how the wine would match with food. White Zinfandel, in light of all its detractors, is still a great match for piquant flavors like Thai, Mexican, or Szechuan foods. Light and fruity Zinfandels match well with simple cuisines, and also with ripe, fresh flavors. More full-bodied Zinfandels are good with fuller-bodied meats, especially if some pepper is a key component in the dish. Finally Zinfandel Ports are excellent substitutes for Porto, but also good matches with cheese and chocolate.

The other grapes discussed have a stronger earthy character than Zinfandel does. These are for full-bodied dishes with lots of spice. Game meats are great pairs, because their preparation often utilizes lots of spices, but also because of the earthiness of the meat itself. That does not mean that a good Salice Salentino is not appropriate for pasta or pizza as well. These wines are open to experimenting with a favorite dish, and their price allows that to be possible.

SUMMARY

The wines that are categorized as rich and spicy get that designation because of their flavor profiles. These wines are not only earthy, but also carry a meatiness that gives them depth and body. The meatiness is not overpowering because of a spiciness that carries through these wines as well. Most common is a black pepper character, but also anise and licorice play important roles in these wines. Their food matching is based on the spice and the meatiness. They are wines meant for big flavors and full-bodied food.

QUESTIONS

1. Describe the three major wine styles made by Zinfandel.
2. Discuss how the grapes ripen and its affect on the flavor profile of Zinfandel.
3. Write a tasting note for a red Zinfandel table wine.
4. Write a tasting note for Mourvèdre.
5. What are the regions of origin for Negroamaro and Nero d'Avola?
6. What are the food and wine pairing suggestions for rich, spicy wines?

PART
FIVE

sparkling and fortified
wines

Sparkling and fortified wines have a unique place among beverages. Both utilize unique production methods as well has having distinctive profiles and food pairing possibilities. Sparkling wine production methods contribute to the flavor profiles and the food matching possibilities. Fortified wines are influenced by their methods of aging, which distinguishes one class of wines from another. Each of these special wines also requires special storage and service procedures to enhance their enjoyment.

Sparkling Wines and How They Are Made

*I*f there is a single style of wine that is equated with celebration, romance, luxury, and decadence, it is sparkling wine. Originally considered a wine fault, the sparkling aspect actually came to be accepted as a special, delightful characteristic. It takes extra effort to make sparkling wine, and that effort is rewarded by the wine's place of prestige in the consumers' eyes.

Upon completion of this chapter, the student should be able to:

Outline the four methods of sparkling wine production

Discuss the modern improvement to methode traditionelle wine making

Explain different styles of sparkling wines

Explain the differences between sparkling wine styles in different countries

History

Sparkling wine as we know it today is really based on several Old World wines, most notably Champagne. The extent to which sparkling wine is associated with Champagne is evident in the use of the name Champagne as a generic descriptor. However, sparkle in Champagne has only been a significant feature since the eighteenth century.

Before the seventeenth century in France, sparkling wine was considered faulty. In the winery, the juice was fermented immediately after harvest in the autumn. In cool regions, this poses a problem. The cellars are cool, and the yeast does not work quickly at low temperature. Eventually, as the cellars cooled more with the oncoming winter, fermentation would stop. Upon the return of spring, the cellars would begin to warm and fermentation would restart as the yeast were reactivated and began processing the remaining sugar. At the time, there was no understanding of yeast or the mechanism of fermentation, so the resulting bubbles from restarted fermentation appeared as a fault.

Sparkle was not considered a fault everywhere. In England in the mid-1600s, sparkling wine was extremely popular. Often, multiple casks of wine were bought and shipped to England, in order to satisfy the craving for "brisk" wine. It was the sales abroad, rather than French taste, that eventually made wine from Champagne mean sparkling wine.

DOM PERIGNON

The first great contributor to the Champagne story is Dom Perignon, who was commissioned by his monastic order to go to the village of Hautvillers in Champagne. He is believed to be the creator of much of the Champagne tradition, even though he thought bubbles were a fault.

Perignon took what was grown in the region and tried to make the best wine from those resources. The area around Hautvillers, and much of the Champagne region, grew Pinot Noir. The tradition of growing Pinot Noir dated back to the thirteenth century, when the villages of Champagne tried to compete for the Dutch wine trade by underselling Burgundy. The Champenois felt they could make wine that could compete with Burgundy, but since the region is closer to the Netherlands than Burgundy is, their wine could be sold cheaper. It was believed that white grapes made inferior wines, because they had a greater tendency to have sparkle in the spring.

Perignon developed several rules to making top-quality wine. First was the restriction to use solely Pinot Noir. Second, the vines were pruned very small, and yields were kept low. Third, harvest had to be very delicate. The grapes were not to be bruised or the skins broken in any way. Finally, the grapes were not to be tread to press the juice, nor were the skins to remain in contact with the juice. There was to be no extraction of color. Essentially, the wine made was a white wine from the juice of red grapes.

Perignon is noted for creating certain methods for making Champagne. He developed blending to make a more consistent, flavorful product. When the grapes were to be pressed, the juice from the grapes of different vineyards was kept separate. Also, the juice of different pressings of the same grapes was kept separated. Perignon also felt that cask aging of the wine made it "tired" and reduced the aromas.

No matter how hard he tried, Perignon could not eliminate the sparkle from the wine, nor could he prevent the market from demanding more each year. Eventually, the wine was placed into bottles in the winter, and the corks wired into place to prevent them from being pushed out of the bottle. The old chalk caves of Champagne, long abandoned since the Romans stopped using the chalk for building, became storehouses for the wine. It was determined that the constant cool temperature was the best cellars for the wine. Using bottles was not without risk. Bottle making at that time was achieved through hand blowing individual bottles. Each bottle was different, and had minor flaws. Once pressure built inside the bottle, if a flaw failed, the bottle would explode. That often created a domino effect, with flying glass shards shattering the bottles nearby. There were vintages where 90 percent of the bottles exploded. It made being cellar master in Champagne a most dangerous job.

VEUVE CLICQUOT

The sales of Champagne increased throughout the eighteenth century, as the first owners of Champagne "houses," or producers, courted the royalty of France and England to embrace the sparkling wine. The development of bottles also improved, making the glass stronger and clearer. However, the wine still had not become the mainstay of the region. Most of the regional wine production was still cheap red wine. The reason was that Champagne vintages were inconsistent. Anyone who had tasted a good bottle knew the heights the wine could achieve, but those bottles were few and far between, not to mention expensive. If the wine was light, it had good sparkle, but was often very acidic. The amount of bubbles in each bottle was often erratic and inconsistent. And finally there was the issue of the "reappearing grape skins." It was believed that somehow, some of the grape skins must disappear during wine making, then reappear later in the bottle as the bubbles were formed. (Remember, the winemakers were unaware of yeast and lees at this point in history.) It was only when these problems were solved that Champagne became the dominant wine.

The person responsible for taking Champagne to the next level is Madame Veuve Clicquot. She inherited the winery at age twenty-seven, when her husband passed away. She also inherited methods and systems that had been in place for years. She was a very astute businesswoman, and proceeded to introduce changes to the making of Champagne that would revolutionize the industry.

The issue at the time was sediment. Every bottle of Champagne contained sediment. This needed to be removed before the wine could be sold. If the winery tried to make a wine that was more appealing to the consumer (that is, sweeter), it just resulted in more sediment. The prevailing methodology involved tapping and twisting the bottles occasionally to try to collect the sediment in the smallest area possible, a dangerous prospect as bottles still had a strong tendency to explode. Once the sediment was satisfactorily collected, the bottle would be opened and the wine decanted into a new bottle. This was laborious, time consuming, and also caused much of the sparkle to be lost from the wine.

In the early 1800s, in the cellars of Veuve Clicquot, a new system was developed. In this system, rather than collect the sediment in the smallest area on the side of the bottle, the sediment was directed to settle on the cork. This involved twisting and tapping the bottles, with the sediment slowly being directed to the neck of the bottle. It was done using a table with holes cut in it, so the bottles could move from the horizontal to the vertical position. Once the sediment was at the neck of the bottle, the small portion of the neck could be frozen and the cork and sediment removed in one step. This greatly decreased the labor involved in getting the sediment out of the bottle, as it could be turned into a production line.

Several more factors contributed to the rise of Champagne. In September 1815, the fields of Champagne were host to a Russian army almost half a million strong. This event was an impetus to get the Congress of Vienna to determine France's fate after Napoleon fell. Politically, it was a show of strength and a subtle push to keep France as a player on the world stage. Economically, it was a captive audience for Champagne. The "houses," and in particular Veuve Clicquot, were very generous with their product. Much of the Russian officer corps were treated to copious amounts of sweet, sparkling wine. The Champagne producers hoped that the Russian elite would have a taste for the wine when they returned home, and would continue to purchase cases to be shipped to them. At the time, however, there was an embargo on French goods in Russia. As the troops left to return home, Veuve Clicquot commissioned one of her salesmen to travel to Russia with a ship loaded with as much Champagne as it could carry. By the time the troops had gotten home, the embargo was lifted, and the ship pulled into port with no competition for miles around.

The move to make Champagne a dry wine is credited to the English palate. An English merchant tasted the unsweetened vintage at Perrier-Jouet and found it to be delicious. He reasoned that the English had enough sweet liquor, with Port and Cream Sherry, and that sweet Champagne would never compete. However, dry Champagne, especially of the quality of the Perrier-Jouet, would become extremely popular. It also reinforced that the wine was high quality, since sweetness can cover many poor viticultural and wine making practices. Slowly, the sweetening done before export to various countries began to be curtailed, as more and more foreigners came to prefer dry Champagne.

How Is Champagne Made?

The process to make Champagne has not changed much since Dom Perignon and Veuve Clicquot perfected some of the procedures. The procedure, known as *methode traditionelle,* has been accepted around the world as the method for making top-quality sparkling wine. Some viticultural practices may differ around the world, but the wine making technique is the same.

Methode Champenoise or Methode Traditionelle?

Methode Champenoise was the original term used to describe the Champagne making methodology. The shift away from its usage began with the protection of the name Champagne. Because of its popularity, Champagne was often used to describe any sparkling wine, no matter the quality. The French professed that only sparking wine from the Champagne region should be called Champagne. As the use of Champagne to describe a particular wine became a more accepted practice, the French insisted that even the name of the process should be restricted to the Champagne region as well. In deference to the traditions of Champagne, wines now made by the method use names reflecting the tradition without naming the region of origin. Wines made in this manner are labeled:

- Metodo Classico (Italy)
- Metodo Tradicional (Spain)
- Traditional Method (United States and Australia)
- Fermented in this bottle (United States)

VITICULTURE

The grapes used to make Champagne are a combination of black grapes and white grapes. The black grapes are Pinot Noir and Pinot Meunier. The white grape is Chardonnay. In Champagne, the growing of these grapes tends to be split into smaller regions. Chardonnay is grown mainly in the Côtes des Blancs, while the Pinots are grown in the Vallée de la Marne (mostly Pinot Meunier) and Montagne de Reims (mostly Pinot Noir).

The vineyards themselves are classified. Over 300 villages in the region have their vineyards classified on the quality of the soil and fruit. The scale ranges from 80 to 100 percent. If the vineyard is considered the best (that is, a Grand Cru), then the rating is 100 percent. There are 17 villages that have this rating. The Grand Cru villages are special because of their soil. They sit on banks of chalk that is the remains of fossilized oyster shells. The next level, Premier Cru, is designated for 44 villages, and spans the range of 90–99 percent. These sit on chalky soils of different fossilized oysters and shellfish, and also are lower on the slopes than the Grand Cru villages. By law in these villages, any vineyard that possesses a rating of 95 percent or higher cannot plant Pinot Meunier.

Champagne houses do not grow the majority of their own grapes. Rather, the houses depend on the approximately 19,000 growers to tend the grapes, and from whom they buy the grapes. Historically, if your grapes came from a Grand Cru vineyard, you were guaranteed the highest price for your crop. This began to pose a problem for the Champagne houses, because some growers took advantage of the top dollar they were guaranteed and did not produce the best-quality fruit. This price fixing was abolished in 1990. Nowadays quality is also an important part of determining grape prices, along with classification of the vineyards. Houses have set up contracts with growers to guarantee the fruit will not only be purchased, but that it will be at top quality.

Harvest is done by hand. With the tight spacing of the vines, it may take 500–550 man-hours to harvest one hectare of land. Typically, Champagne sees its population grow by 10,000 workers during the two-week harvest period. The grapes are treated very delicately. They are placed in shallow baskets and moved by hand, to prevent any tearing of the skin or bruising of the fruit. This also keeps the weight of the grapes themselves from pressing on one another too much.

The grapes are taken to press houses that have been set up in each village. It would be too dangerous to attempt to take the grapes back to the Champagne houses for processing. Rather, batches of grapes are pressed in the closest village and the resulting juice is then sent by tanker truck to the appropriate producer.

VINIFICATION

Pressing

The first step of the vinification process is the pressing of the juice. The grapes are pressed in wide, shallow basket presses, though sometimes pneumatic presses have been used. Extracting the juice from the grapes is conducted over several pressings, each with increasing pressure. The first extraction of juice is the free-run juice, which comes from just the pressure of the grapes due to gravity. This juice is considered to be too light to use for making Champagne. The next press is called the *cuvée*. Between each pressing, the grapes are loosened and turned with pitchforks. The third press is the *taille*. A fourth press may occur, but this juice is not used for Champagne either, as it is considered too rough and harsh for the delicate wine.

The yield of grapes is controlled for the growers, but more importantly the amount of juice from the grapes is strictly regulated. To ensure the best juice is obtained, only 102 liters of juice may be obtained from 160 kilograms of grapes. This is obtained in the cuvée and the taille press. A basket press can hold 4000 kg of grapes, which would yield 2550 liters of juice per basket.

The juice is then allowed to settle and clarify. This step separates some of the pulp and proteins that are also extracted during the pressing. Having the juice be clear produces a better final wine. The added proteins or extraneous flavors from the pulp are not acted upon by the yeast, and therefore cannot produce off flavors.

Fermentation

Fermentation of the juice is a tedious process. Each grape variety is fermented separately. Each vineyard is fermented separately. Each pressing is fermented separately. This will provide each Champagne house a variety of wines that will be used to create the blend later on.

Fermentation methodology will depend on the Champagne house. This begins the process of distinguishing the house's style. Some producers use stainless steel tanks, while others still use large old oak barrels. Occasionally, a producer will use small oak barrels, but not new ones. Fresh barrels are often rinsed with wine made from the last pressing, before it is sent off for distillation. Only after three years of processing like this is the barrel ready for use. Fermentation will typically take place at relatively low temperatures, 65–68°F (18–20°C), and can take anywhere from six days to four weeks. Sometimes malolactic fermentation is allowed, while other houses may discourage it.

Assemblage

This step is the key to a Champagne house's consistency. *Assemblage,* or blending, is the job of the chef des caves, or blender. The chef is responsible for mixing different wines together to create a wine that matches the house style. The wines include the current vintage (separated by vineyard and grape variety) as well as older reserve wines from good years. The chef must take into consideration not only the balance of the wine when blended, but how it will taste after the second fermentation. The skill required is honorable. Not only must the blender make a wine that is well balanced, but must anticipate what aging will do to the wine in order for it to be identical to previously released wines. Once this blend is made, the wine is fined and sometimes filtered before being readied for bottling.

Second Fermentation

Before the wine is placed in bottles, it needs to be prepared in order to undergo a secondary fermentation. Some of the wine is separated from the main batch and blended with sugar and yeast. It is then blended back together, inoculating the whole batch of wine with yeast and food. This is called the *liqueur de tirage.* The amount of sugar needs to be very precise, and usually amounts to raising the alcohol level of the wine by 1.2–1.3 percent. This is also enough to create a minimum of 6 atmospheres of pressure (about 90–96 pounds per square inch) in the bottle. The bottles are capped with crown caps, preventing any loss of carbon dioxide, which dissolves back into the wine.

The choice of the yeast used to produce the second fermentation is very important. It is not the same yeast that fermented the grape juice into the still wine. First, the conditions in the bottle require a different strain. The yeast chosen now must be able to withstand high pressures of carbon dioxide, must exist in elevated alcoholic conditions, and must ferment at a lower temperature and sugar level. Another important consideration is what happens to the yeast after the fermentation is complete. The yeast must perform two functions after the fermentation. It must clump easily and not stick to the side of the bottle. It also must provide beneficial flavors as the yeast cells decompose.

The newly capped bottles are placed in the cellar to ferment a second time and also to age. The cellars are at 50–55°F (10–13°C), much cooler than the first fermentation. The second fermentation will take from fourteen days to four months, and the quality of the bubbles is directly related to the amount of time allowed for the second fermentation. The finer and more delicate the bubbles at the end of the second fermentation, the higher the quality of the wine.

Aging

The wine bottles are left stacked *sur lattes,* or horizontal, for a minimum of fifteen months in Champagne. (Other regions have different minimum times, which

Modern Riddling Innovations

In an effort to make the riddling process easier, several techniques have been tested to make not only riddling easier, but also removal of the yeast. The first is the development of a machine called a *gyropalette,* to riddle multiple bottles at a time. To use a gyropalette, the bottles are placed in a large crate that holds 500-plus bottles. The crate is then placed on a turning machine, which will spin and tilt the bottles three to four times daily. In effect, the gyropalette is a large centrifuge, but also does the work of an army of riddlers. The time to move bottles from horizontal to vertical is reduced from six to eight weeks down to three to seven days. The disadvantage of the machine is that it is expensive, and many producers cannot riddle all their bottles at the same time.

Less mechanical methods include additions to the bottle when the yeast and sugar are added. Inert substances like bentonite, isinglass, or commercial products can be added to give a more consistent substrate on which the lees will settle, and for ease of riddling. Small additions of oxygen (similar to the micro-oxygenation of red wine) may be introduced to give the yeast the added nutrients and prevent a poor second fermentation.

Finally, there have been experiments with impregnating alginate beads with yeast, or using gas-permeable cartridges filled with yeast, to eliminate riddling completely. The idea behind the beads is that the wine can permeate the alginate substrate and react with the yeast. The yeast will remain in the substrate during aging. Riddling would then consist of tipping the bottle from horizontal to vertical, and letting the beads settle in the neck of the bottle. Even easier is having a cartridge that would be attached to the crown cap. In this case, all the processes would happen in the cartridge while the bottles age, and removal is as simple as removing the cap and replacing it.

will be discussed later in the chapter.) During this time, the effects of the secondary fermentation are integrating into the wine. The carbon dioxide is dissolving into the wine, and the carbonic acid it produces helps with some of the aging reactions. Also during this time period, the yeast that died after fermentation begins to decompose. Cell walls burst open in a process called *autolysis,* releasing the contents of the yeast cell into the wine. Some of these components provide the signature "bready" character to Champagne. Others, such as amino acids and peptides, provide a structure for the bubbles. The amino acids allow the carbon dioxide to stay dissolved in the wine, and also to release it slowly when the bottle has been opened. Without these components, Champagne would fizz and go flat like ginger ale.

Removing the Yeast

A good bottle of bubbly has no trace of the yeast that caused the second fermentation. Because Champagne is sold in the same bottle as that second fermentation, the yeast has to be removed. This process is called *riddling* or *rémuage*. The process involves getting the lees to the neck of the bottle, or moving the bottles from *sur lattes* (horizontal) to *sur pointe* (vertical).

The traditional hand method takes anywhere from two to ten weeks, typically six weeks. There are lots of variables that determine the time, like how decomposed and fine the yeast has become, the structure of the glass inside the bottle, electrostatic charges in the bottle, and the like. The amount of time to riddle the bottles will vary with each batch.

The bottles are taken from their aging room, and are placed into large A-frame racks called *pupitres*, or riddling racks. These racks have a series of holes drilled into them, which will hold the bottles as they move from horizontal to vertical. As the bottles are moved, the yeast is loosened with a tap or a shake. Then, after resting in the riddling racks for about a week or so, the process begins again. Each bottle will be turned once a day, approximately one-eighth to one-quarter of a turn. The bottles may also be tapped or shaken slightly and tipped closer to vertical, to allow gravity to help move the lees toward the neck of the bottle. A good riddler will turn 30,000 to 50,000 bottles a day.

Disgorging

This process occurs after the lees have moved to the neck of the bottle. Called *dégorgement* in French, disgorging involves removal of the crown cap, and with it the plug of lees that have settled on the cap. The first step is chilling the bottles below freezing (typically 25°F or −4°C). This helps to retain the carbon dioxide in solution, but it also is cold stabilization of the wine, precipitating any tartrate crystals.

The neck of the bottle is then placed into a subfreezing bath (−15°F or −25°C) in order to freeze the contents of the bottle's neck. Once frozen, the bottle is angled up at a 45-degree angle, and the crown cap removed. If done quickly, the pressure in the bottle will force out the plug of frozen wine and lees, losing very little extra wine or pressure. Typically, the pressure in the bottle will decrease about one atmosphere (15 pounds per square inch), leaving the Champagne at around 6 atmospheres after corking. After the plug has been removed, the bottle is topped up with wine from the same blend and is corked. This whole process, from freezing to corking, can be done by hand, but is a mechanized process in many cellars.

Making nonvintage champagne

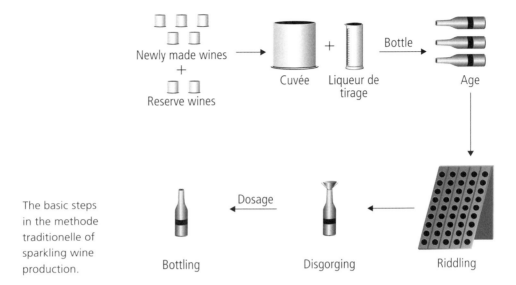

The basic steps in the methode traditionelle of sparkling wine production.

The wine that is added to replace what is lost when the frozen plug is expelled is called the *liqueur d'expedition* or *dosage*. This wine could be some reserved blend if the final product is to be completely devoid of sugar, but often a small amount of sugar is added to balance the high acidity of the wine. This is also the time to adjust the sweetness level, if an off-dry or sweet Champagne is the desired result. Besides sugar and wine, other additions could be made at this time. Those additions may include preservatives like ascorbic acid or citric acid, or alcohol boosters like brandy.

Final Steps

After addition of the dosage, the Champagne is sealed with a cork. The cork used is a modified agglomerate cork. The majority of the cork structure is agglomerated, but two thin slices of solid cork are placed at the end that will come into contact with the wine. The corks themselves are wider than the bottle's neck, and are straight plugs to start. Once they are placed in the bottle, the cork is wired in place with a cage, which also contains a *plaquette,* or metal button. The plaquette is on top of the cork to prevent the wire cutting into the cork, and also to identify the producer and prevent fraud. The pressure of the gas on the cork, and the presence of the cage, creates the iconic mushroom-shaped cork that is associated with Champagne.

The wine is not quite ready for market yet. It will typically be aged another three months before release. This additional aging is time for the dosage flavors to marry with the flavors of the wine. The three months is a minimum amount of time, and some producers will allow this period to last up to a year. This is not a typical "bottle aging" period. With the presence of higher pressure inside the bottle, no oxygen is migrating through the cork. The standard "bottle aging" flavors are not developing in this period.

Once released to the market, how long should a bottle be aged before it is consumed? Depending on the style and quality of the wine, most are ready to drink upon purchase. It is possible to hold on to a bottle for three to five years, and some of the best may be aged for a decade or more.

Other Sparkling Wine Production Methods

There are two aspects of methode traditionelle that makes it a difficult fit to create more inexpensive sparkling wines—aging and riddling. For some sparkling wines, shorter, easier methods have been devised to make wines that sparkle without some of the expense. Initially, the attempt was to maintain the quality of a methode traditionelle wine, but some of the new methods do not maintain the complexity.

TRANSFER METHOD

The *transfer method* was devised to save the time and expense of riddling. The transfer method is the same for methode traditionelle wine until the riddling step. Wines are blended to form the cuvée, the wine is inoculated with sugar and yeast, and then placed into bottles. The bottles undergo secondary fermentation and are allowed to age to develop flavors from autolysis. At this point, the process changes course.

The riddling process is replaced by a pressurized transfer of the wine into a large tank. All the bottles are emptied and the wine blended. The wine is then clarified by filtration. A dosage is added to the entire blend, and the wine is pumped, under pressure, back into clean bottles. The bottles are sealed with cork and readied for market.

Technically, the transfer method should have the same quality level as a methode traditionelle wine. It undergoes the same assemblage steps, it has a second fermentation in a bottle, and it rests on the lees for an extended period of time to gain the bready flavors from the lees. However, something in the transfer method process lowers the quality. It could almost be said that the use of pumps and filters removes some of the character of the wine.

Transfer method wines are on the decline in the marketplace. Wines made in this method are usually identified by "secondary fermentation in the bottle" or simply "bottle fermented" rather than methode traditionelle. Consumers may be mislead by these terms, but more and more producers realize that consumers see methode traditionelle wines as being of higher quality. With the advent of the gyropalette, it is also much easier and quicker to produce a methode traditionelle wine, and get the higher price, than to invest in pressurized tanks, filtering machines, and bottle-washing facilities.

TANK METHOD

The *tank method* was developed by a French chemist, Eugène Charmat, and is sometimes referred to as the *Charmat process*, in his honor, or as the *cuve-close* method. This method differs significantly from the methode traditionelle, not only in methodology, but also in the characteristics of the final product. This is a very inexpensive process, and makes very inexpensive sparkling wines.

The first difference is the types of grapes used to make a sparkling wine via the tank method. These grapes often have little varietal character and are often grown with large yields and harvested before peak ripeness. Typical grape varieties include Colombard, overcropped Chenin Blanc, and Sylvaner. Wine is made from these grapes and is then transferred to large tanks, where the secondary fermentation will occur.

The wine is inoculated with sugar and yeast and placed into small temperature- controlled tanks that can withstand high pressures. The fermentation is then conducted at 55°F (13°C) and the carbon dioxide is trapped in the wine. After fermentation the wine is quickly removed from the dead yeast cells. This is done because the thick layer of yeast in the tank may give off-flavors or sulfurous notes to the wine if it remains in contact for a long period of time. The wine will therefore not have the bread, yeast, or toast notes of a methode traditionelle wine, but rather remain fresh and lively tasting.

The now sparkling wine is cold stabilized, filtered, and given a dosage to adjust the sweetness. Sometimes the wines are treated with sulfur dioxide to prevent any stray yeast cells from fermenting the sugar in the dosage. The wine is then labeled and sent to market.

CARBONATION

The final method is simple, and not commonly used in wines for commercial release, but still needs mentioning. This method is direct carbonation, or for a French flair, *pompe bicyclette.* As is suggested by the name, there is no secondary fermentation in these wines. They are carbonated through the introduction of carbon dioxide into still wine. These wines seem like a soft drink, with large bubbles that will fizz and then go flat.

Single-Fermentation Sparkling Wines

Some wines do not get their sparkle from a secondary fermentation, but rather as part of capturing the carbon dioxide in the first fermentation. These are wines that were either produced before the advent of methode traditionelle, or are modified processes to create a specific style of wine.

METHODE ANCESTRALE

The *methode ancestrale* style of sparkling wine production is found in the south of France, in the regions of Limoux, Gaillac, and Savoie. The gist of the process is to bottle the young wine before all the sugar has been fermented. Fermentation continues in the bottle and creates sparkle by trapping the resulting carbon dioxide.

The usual style of this wine is lightly sparkling and medium sweet. The sweetness does not come from a dosage, but rather from residual sugar. In some cases, the wine may be transferred to a clean bottle to remove any sediment. The wine is also less fizzy because of the reduced amount of carbon dioxide that has dissolved into the wine.

ASTI PRODUCTION

Asti Spumante and Moscato d'Asti are sweet sparkling wines from the Piedmont regions of Italy that use a modified tank method of production. Part of the objective of a modified tank method of production is to retain the natural sweetness while creating carbonation. The standard tank method uses pressurized tanks for the secondary fermentation, while in Asti the tanks are used for the primary fermentation.

The juice of the Moscato grapes is placed into the pressurized tank and inoculated with yeast to begin the fermentation. The fermentation is monitored to determine when the process is complete. That stage depends on which wine is being made. In Asti Spumante, the fermentation must reach 7 percent alcohol and about 5 atmospheres of pressure. For Moscato d'Asti, the process is complete at 5.5 percent alcohol and 3 atmospheres of pressure. In both cases, the tank is quickly cooled to stop the fermentation. The wine is then filtered under pressure to remove the yeast cells, and placed into bottles. The result is a wine that has the natural sugar from the grapes, with light carbonation and low alcohol.

Sparkling Wine Styles

Many variables go into making sparkling wines. The variation creates different styles, some determined early in the process and others determined later. Each sparkling wine house will make different styles, creating a portfolio of wines that they hope will serve a wide segment of the market.

NONVINTAGE

About 80 percent of all sparkling wine produced does not possess a vintage date. This is the result of a choice at the assemblage stage. In order to make a wine that is consistent from year to year, and maintain the "house style," the blender will utilize *reserve wines,* or wines from previous vintages that have been held back from making sparkling wines. The use of reserve wines is more important in poor years, when body and flavor may need to be added to that year's crop. Good years may not need as much reserve wine added, but some will be saved to benefit wines in future years.

HOUSE STYLES

Champagne and sparkling wine houses create their basic style to be consistent from year to year. However, there can be big differences between the houses. Some houses, such as Perrier-Jouet and Taittinger, make light, elegant wines. These wines are usually made with a high proportion of Chardonnay. Other houses make more full-bodied and yeasty wines, such as Bollinger, Veuve Clicquot, and Krug. These wines will exhibit more nutty character compared to the lighter house styles. These houses tend to use a high proportion of Pinot Noir, providing extra body and structure to the wine.

VINTAGE

Vintage sparkling wine is made from the harvest of a single year, just as in table wine. No more than 80 percent of a year's harvest can become vintage wine, the rest must be saved for reserve wine. These vintage wines will not match the house style, but rather are indicative of that year's harvest. Vintage sparkling wines, especially in Champagne, are not made every year. In Champagne, it is typical to declare only three or four vintage years per decade. Because of the favorable conditions that year, these wines are often richer, fuller bodied, and more complex than the house style. Vintage wines in Champagne must be aged a minimum of three years before disgorging, and some houses age their wines longer. This provides these wines with much more character from the autolysis of the lees than nonvintage wines. After release, vintage sparklers can also age for longer periods than nonvintage wines.

CUVÉE DE PRESTIGE

Every sparkling wine house makes a top-of-the-line wine. These wines are made from the best grapes, from the best vineyards. They can be made in a nonvintage form, but are often the very best when they are vintage wines. The wines are made by traditional methods, with the wines fermented in wood barrels, sealed with corks for the second fermentation, and hand disgorged. Some of the most famous cuvée de prestiges are Cristal (produced by Roederer), Dom Perignon (Moet et Chandon), and la Grande Dame (Veuve Clicquot).

BLANC DE BLANCS

Translated as "white from white," *Blanc de Blancs* are wines made from 100 percent Chardonnay. They are considered the wines that have the greatest potential for aging, and often need aging to develop a full spectrum of flavors. Just-released Blanc de Blancs are often tight, lean wines without a lot of depth of flavor. After aging a few years, however, the wines exhibit more toasty and lemony flavors, making for a rich, delicious beverage.

BLANC DE NOIRS

Translated as "white from black," *Blanc de Noirs* possess no Chardonnay, but rather are made from the juice of Pinot Noir and Pinot Meunier alone. These wines may or may not have a slight tinge of color, depending upon how delicately the grapes were pressed. Blanc de Noirs is not a common style in Champagne, though it can be easily found made by California producers. The wine can be big and muscular, but more often than not it is a delicate wine similar to other styles, possibly only displaying hints of red fruit to give away its origins.

ROSÉ

Pink Champagne and sparkling wine are made by a method different than making still rosés. To make a rosé, sparkling wine houses make a small amount of red, still Pinot Noir. That wine is then used to color the blend that will become the rosé. Depending on the color desired, up to 15 percent of the final wine could come from the red Pinot Noir wine. Rosé sparkling wines are specialty items, not made by every house, though those that do make them often have *nonvintage*, *vintage*, and *cuvée de prestige* levels available.

Sweetness Levels

All sparkling wines receive a dosage before they are readied for market. Sometimes that dosage contains sugar, partially to balance the acidity of the wine, but also to create a sweeter version of wine. Historically, the wines drunk by the Russians were very sweet, while the English preferred very dry wines. In keeping with tradition, many houses make several sweetness levels. The sweeter wines now are promoted as dessert wines.

This is a measure of the residual sugar in the final sparkling wine. Dosage sweetness is not a good indicator, because it can be variable and is diluted into the final wine.

Sweetness Chart

Sparkling Wine Type	Grams of Sugar per Liter
Brut Nature	0–3
Extra Brut	0–6
Brut	0–15
Extra Sec or Extra Dry	12–20
Sec or Dry	17–35
Demi-sec*	33–50
Doux	50+

*In Europe, demi-sec is often labeled *rich*. Doux is the style of the Russian czars and is no longer commercially produced.

Bottle Sizes

Sparkling wines can be purchased in a wide range of bottles sizes. The more common sizes are smaller than a regular 750 milliliter bottle. Champagne served "by the glass" in restaurants and bars is really a split, or 187 mL bottle. Larger sizes are seen at special occasions, and are bottled in liter increments.

Sparkling Wine Bottle Sizes

Bottle Type	Bottle Amount
Split	187 mL
Half bottle	375 mL
Bottle	750 mL
Magnum	1.5 L (2 bottles)
Jeroboam	3 L (4 bottles)
Rehoboam	6 bottles
Methuselah	8 bottles
Salmanazar	12 bottles
Balthazar	16 bottles
Nebuchadnezzar	20 bottles

Sparkling wines in bottles smaller than 750 mL, and those Jeroboam and higher, are not made in the same bottle as they are sold. These bottles are filled by a process called *transversage*. In a modified form of transfer method, the disgorged bottles are then emptied into a pressurized tank, where the dosage is added. The wine is then bottled in the desired alternative-format-sized bottle.

Non-Champagne Sparkling Wines

Countries with wine making traditions around the world make some form of sparkling wine. Some countries try to emulate Champagne more than others, which may result in a more local style of sparkling wine.

FRANCE

Within France, every wine region makes sparkling wine. Most are called *crémant de* [region here], though occasionally the wines will be labeled *mousseux* (particularly in Saumur and Vouvray). These wines are required by law to be made by methode traditionelle. The regions that produce these wines also make some of the top wines in France. The grapes that go into making the crémant wines are not the top tier of grapes. They are often those that are too underripe or too overcropped to produce the signature wine of the region.

In the south of France, there are sparkling wines made via methode traditionelle. Examples of these wines include Clairette de Die Tradition and Blanchette de Limoux. Clairette de Die Tradition is made from minimum 50 percent Muscat (and the remainder Clairette) in the Rhône Valley. Do not confuse this with simply Clairette de Die, which is made in the methode traditionelle. Blanchette de Limoux comes from the Languedoc-Roussillon region of France. It is made primarily from Mauzac, and is treated very similarily to Champagne before the fermentation. Blanquette has been made since the sixteenth century in a sparkling style, a hundred years before Dom Perignon started his work in Hautvillers.

SPAIN

Spain began a deliberate effort to make "Champagne" in the late 1800s. Most of the production is centered around the town of San Sadurni in Penedes. Most of the grapes come from throughout the region of Cataluña, and therefore the wine does not possess a Denominacion de Origin (DO) label. To make a Champagne-like wine, the pioneering producers focused on vineyards at higher elevation. The grapes from these vineyards would retain the acidity needed to make a quality sparkling wine.

Some rules for Spanish sparkling wine production were set up to mimic Champagne. The amount of juice per tonnage of grapes was established as the quality benchmark. In Spain, no more than 100 liters of juice can be extracted from 160 kilograms of grapes and be used for sparkling wine.

While the Spanish producers were trying to mimic Champagne, they were forced to give their product another name. When Spain joined the European Union, it had to agree to the naming restrictions that protected Champagne. In searching for a name, the collection of producers decided that they would name the wine after the caves in which the wine was aged—*Cava*.

Cava has some significant differences with Champagne production. One of the most significant is the varieties of grapes that are used. Spanish Cava producers use the local white grape varieties Parellada, Macabeo (called Viura in Rioja), and Xarel-lo. Codorniu has been experimenting with adding a little Chardonnay to their blend. Very little experimentation has been done using black grapes.

Another significant difference can be found in how the wines are made. The secondary fermentation must occur at 66°F (18°C). The pressure in the bottle must reach a minimum of 4 atmospheres. Also, the aging required before disgorging is shorter than in Champagne. Cava producers are required to age their wines on the lees a minimum of nine months. Because of these differences, Cavas tend to be more herbal, tart, and lean on the palate, with less yeasty influence, and less nutty character and less body than Champagne.

ITALY

The Italians have three world-class sparkling wines, from three different regions. Two of these wines use the tank method of production, and one adheres fairly strictly to metodo classico.

The first wine is Asti Spumanti and Moscato d'Asti. As discussed above, both styles of Asti are made with a modified tank method. The wine has a single fermentation, which is stopped to retain the natural sweetness of the juice, and the carbonation is less intense. Both wines are made from Moscato Bianca grapes, the Italian name for Muscat Blanc à Petit Grains. The difference lies not only in the extent to which the wine is fermented, but also in the quality of the grapes used. Asti Spumante is an industrial process, making 250 million gallons a year. On the other hand, only about 18 million gallons of Moscato d'Asti are made annually. The growers of Moscato use their better grapes to make Moscato d'Asti, and sell their other grapes to the large makers of Asti Spumante.

The second wine made via the tank method is Prosecco. Prosecco is a light, dry wine made from the Prosecco grape in the Veneto region of Italy. A sweetish *frizzante,* or lightly sparkling wine, has always been the preferred style of the region, which is cool and has had issues with fermentations stopping during the winter. Once the tank method was introduced, a drier wine became the norm. The Prosecco grape is late ripening and not very aromatic. Its best region of production is near the communes of Conegliano and Valdobbiadene. The richer versions of Prosecco from these communes have a peachy quality, which may have led to Prosecco becoming the sparkling wine of choice to make Bellinis (Prosecco and white peach puree).

The Italian sparkler made in the metodo classico is Franciacorta. Though the region, in Lombardy northeast of Milan, has a wine making tradition stretching back centuries, the making of Franciacorta as a sparkling wine dates only to the 1970s. The wine is made from Chardonnay, Pinot Nero, and Pinot Bianco, though more Chardonnay is used than the other grapes. Much of the production mimics Champagne. The grape yield is kept low. The secondary fermentation must occur in the bottle. There is a definite nod to the French as well by using French terminology on the bottle, rather than Italian. It would not be unusual to see a wine labeled rosé or sec from Franciacorta.

There are some differences from the French process, however. A basic non-vintage *brut* will spend a minimum of eighteen months, more often twenty-five months, aging on the lees. A vintage brut will age a minimum of thirty months, and a reserve ages thirty-seven months. Two favorite styles have few counterparts in Champagne. One style, called Satén, is less carbonated and made from only white grapes. A Pas Dosé wine is bone dry, having no sugar added in the dosage before shipping.

GERMANY

German sparkling wines are called *Sekt*. They are made with the tank method, often from grapes or wines that are grown in other countries. It is not uncommon for Sicilian white wine to find its way into a bottle of Sekt. It is a light, easy drinking sparkling wine without much complexity. For better sparkling wine, the grapes need to be grown in Germany. If that is the case, the wine is labeled Deutscher Sekt. These can still be a blend of lesser grapes, like Muller-Thurgau, but the best wines will be made from Riesling. There are also occasional sparkling Rieslings made in the methode traditionelle.

UNITED STATES

A great deal of sparkling wine production comes from two states, New York and California. The sparklers from New York vary in their production. Some large producers make sparkling wines from a blend of native and vinifera varieties, blending

Chardonnay with Catawba and Aurore. Smaller boutique producers make classic Champagne-style wines, from a blend of Chardonnay and Pinot Noir.

The majority of sparkling wine in the United States comes from California, and in particular Carneros, at the north end of San Francisco Bay. Carneros is a cool region, getting morning fog from the bay, and remaining decidedly cooler than the rest of Napa or Sonoma counties. This combination of climatic factors has led many European winemakers to invest in production in the region. With French investment comes French ideology, and the sparkling wines from Carneros are made in the methode traditionelle.

A good deal of bulk sparkling wine comes from the Central Valley. Home to vast crops of grapes, the Central Valley is not only the home of jug and box wine, but also many sparkling wines made by the tank method. These wines have been made for years, and often are labeled as California Champagne, much to the upset of the French. Sparkling wines from the Central Valley labeled Champagne use the term in the generic sense, like Burgundy and Chablis on jug wines, rather than as a reference to the traditional method.

European Investors in California Sparkling Wine

California Winery	European Investor
Mumm Napa	Mumm
Domaine Chandon	Moet et Chandon
Piper Sonoma	Piper-Heidsieck
Gloria Ferrer	Freixenet
Roederer Estate	Roederer
Domaine Carneros	Taittinger

AUSTRALIA

The cooler regions of Australia are generating interest from international winemakers, much like California's Carneros region did several decades ago. Green Point in the cool Yarra Valley has investment from Moet et Chandon. Australia is a mirror to California, with good-quality producers making traditional method sparkling wines, while more industrial producers use the tank method to make cheap and cheerful bubbly.

A unique wine from Australia is sparkling Shiraz. This wine is a nontraditional-method wine, made in the tank method. The wines are very fruity without any yeast or oak influences. Good sparkling Shiraz will have soft tannins, otherwise the astringency is accentuated by the effervescence.

SUMMARY

Sparkling wine is a labor-intensive, specialty wine that has a special place in the world of wine. Wine with bubbles is a favorite for a romantic evening, or for a celebration. The best wines take their model from Champagne, and use the methode traditionelle to make wines that are yeasty, nutty, and delicately sparkling. These wines can come from France, Italy, Spain, the United States, or Australia. Other methods have been devised to reduce the time and expense of making sparkling wines. Some of these produce inexpensive sparklers from neutral grapes. No matter the expense, sparkling wine still carries the mystique of romance and luxury.

KEY TERMS

Methode traditionelle

Cuvée

Taille

Assemblage

Liqueur de tirage

Sur lattes

Autolysis

Riddling

Rémuage

Sur pointe

Pupitre

Gyropalette

Dégorgement

Liqueur d'expedition

Dosage

Plaquette

Transfer method

Tank method

Charmat process

Cuve-close

Pompe bicyclette

Methode ancestrale

Reserve wine

Blanc de Blancs

Blanc de Noirs

Nonvintage

Vintage

Cuvée de prestige

Transversage

Crémant

Mousseux

Cava

Frizzante

Brut

Sekt

QUESTIONS

1. Discuss the contributions of Dom Perignon and Veuve Clicquot to Champagne.

2. Outline the steps for methode traditionelle.

3. Discuss the pros and cons of the transfer method in relation to methode traditionelle.

4. Compare and contrast the two most common methods of riddling.

5. Why is gentle pressing of the grapes important for sparkling wine production?

6. Discuss the effect of aging on the flavor profile of Champagne.

7. How does Asti Spumante production differ from Champagne production?

8. Outline the styles of sparkling wines.

◀ The aromas and flavors characteristic of Merlot are chocolate, baking spices (cinnamon and nutmeg), plum, berry, and velvet tannins.

▶ Tangy sauce, creamy cheese, and a toasted crust are perfect matches for a California Merlot.

▲ The aromas and flavors characteristic of Sauvignon Blanc are grapefruit, lime, green apple, pear, and grass.

Steamed tofu and dumplings make a delicate match to a dry Mosel Riesling.

▼ The aromas and flavors characteristic of Syrah are plums and berries, anise, black pepper, and bacon.

▲ A meaty strip steak will tame a Northern Rhone Syrah's tannins and pair with the peppery and meaty character of the wine.

◀ The aromas and flavors characteristic of Grenache are high alcohol, white pepper, anise, berries, and plums.

▶ Rich game birds like this squab can handle red wine, in this case a Southern Rhone Grenache based blend.

▲ Spicy Thai Green Curry Shrimp with an off-dry Gewurztraminer to tame the heat and play up the exotic spices.

▶ Earthy rabbit and black beans match

◀ Soave Classico provides a tangy compliment to this simple pasta with sausage.

▼ Pan fried potstickers get a tangy contrast from Arneis.

▲ Carolina style barbeque, with its vinegary sauce, works well with fresh, tangy Barbera.

▼ A modern take on eggplant parmesan is accompanied by a tangy, earthy Chianti Classico.

▲ Roasting moves this simple chicken to red wine territory, here with a simple Valpolicella.

▶ Carmenere is a match in weight and intensity to these Asian-styled short ribs.

▼ Red cooked chicken, loaded with umami and flavored with star anise, matches with a Southern Italian Aglianico.

▲ Chicken braised with red peppers makes a hearty compliment to this Rioja.

▼ A classic English dessert: blue cheese, walnuts, and Port.

▲ This nutty, rich Sacher Torte is paired with a tangy, sweet Malmsey Madeira.

▲ This creamy strawberry soup is both complimented and contrasted by a Blanc de Noir sparkling wine.

▶ A sparkling wine is a delicious foil to the light, fresh sushi.

▼ The implied sweetness of a malty lager helps calm the heat of blackened catfish.

▲ The quintessential Ploughman's lunch: Cheddar, pickle, chutney, radish, and a cold Pale Ale.

◄ A rich, fatty, sweet ham is complimented by a malty, crisp Bock.

▲▲ A good German Pilsner accompanies soft pretzels, sausages, mustard, and radishes.

▲ Grilled salmon has the body and flavor intensity to pair with a good stout.

▼ Roasted pork with apples and potato dumpling gets paired with a cask conditioned amber ale.

▲ Oyster po'boy, with its toasty breading and rich shellfish is a hearty match of a Pale Ale.

▲ Classic schnitzel with lemon is a nice contrast to a fruity hefe-weizen.

▼ The rich flavor of a tortilla soup is balanced by a malty and hoppy bock.

chapter 23

Fortified Wines

*D*uring the long history of Europe, explorers traveled the world for trade and conquest, and brought their beloved wine with them. They found early on that their usual table wine did not fare well during the long sea voyages. What did travel well were wines that had higher alcohol content, and the category of fortified wines was born.

Upon completion of this chapter, the student should be able to:

> *Describe how fortified wines are made*
>
> *Discuss Port and how it is made*
>
> *Describe the different styles of Port*
>
> *Discuss Sherry and how it is made*
>
> *Describe the different styles of Sherry*
>
> *Distinguish between fortified wines made by the Port method and the Sherry method*
>
> *Describe the estufagem process for making Madeira*

What Are Fortified Wines?

Fortification of wine was developed to help preserve the product. It involves the addition of more alcohol to raise the percentage over 16 percent, sometimes as high as 20 percent. Standard table wine is typically between 9 and 14 percent alcohol by volume. The addition of extra alcohol preserves the wine by creating an environment in which yeast and bacteria cannot live. This will prevent a sweet wine from continuing to ferment, but also prevent any fortified wine from becoming infected with acetobacter and turning into vinegar.

The alcohol used to fortify a wine can come from a variety of places. Depending on the style of wine and the quality, the origin of the spirit is important. Top-quality wines use grape brandy, often made from the grapes that did not make it into the original wine. Other sources are neutral grain spirits or even alcohol derived from petroleum products. In many cases, because the additional alcohol is neutral in flavor, the source is not easily determined.

When the alcohol is added will influence the final product. If the alcohol is added before fermentation is complete, the wine will be naturally sweet. If fermentation is allowed to progress to completion, the addition of alcohol is strictly for preservation.

How Are Fortified Wines Made?

There are two methods for making any fortified wine. They differ in when the alcohol is added to the wine. They take their names from the major fortified wines that utilize a particular method. These are the *port method* and the *sherry method*.

The port method involves adding the fortification *during* the fermentation of the wine. This stops the fermentation by raising the alcohol level high enough that the yeast can no longer survive, and they die off. The result is a wine that has some of the natural sweetness from the grapes preserved because it has not been fermented.

The sherry method involves adding the fortification *after* the fermentation of the wine. The original base wine is fermented to dryness, and the additional alcohol is added. If a sweet version is desired, the sweet component is added after the fortification.

Port

Port wine is made around the world, in California, Australia, and Portugal. True Port or Porto can come only from Portugal. It is a product of the land, the grapes, the method of production, and aging. Porto has a long history that has influenced the evolution of the beverage and has created a number of different styles and levels.

HISTORY OF PORT

The first record of Port wine is found in the records of export from the city of Oporto in the late seventeenth century. The English had been driven to Portugal to find wine in order to replace the heavily taxed French wines they were used to. The English found a full-bodied, dark wine in the upper reaches of the Douro Valley. To ensure the wine survived the long voyage to England, extra alcohol was added to the wine. These wines were dry, as had been the wines from France.

On a tour of the Douro to find new growers, the sons of a Liverpool wine merchant stumbled across a monk who made his wine in a different way. Rather than add the alcohol after fermentation, this monk added brandy during the fermentation. This killed the yeast and created a sweet, dark, tannic wine, which was to become the model for all subsequent Port.

The English got more involved with Port at the outbreak of the War of Spanish Succession at the turn of the eighteenth century. In 1703, the Methuen treaty was signed, which gave Portuguese goods preferential tariff treatment in England. Within a couple of decades, however, fraud was rampant. Producers were making poor, thin wines and doctoring them with elderberry juice and sugar. Wines deemed to be Port were actually made in other areas of Portugal than the Douro region.

The complaints reached the Portuguese prime minister, the Marques de Pombal, who in 1756 began regulating the Port industry to place more control into Portuguese hands. Measures by the Marques included delimiting the Douro region as the only area of production and setting up the Port Wine Institute, which would control the actions of both growers and shippers. Many of the actions taken by the Marques, though modified with time, are still in place today.

THE DOURO VALLEY

Portugal's Douro Valley is the grape growing and wine making region for Port. Its boundaries correspond to outcroppings of *schist* and granite. On first glance, this area seems to be the most inhospitable region for grapes, let alone any other agriculture. The soils are thin and nutrient poor. There is little water and the topography is challenging at best.

It is important to understand schist and how it provides an advantage to the vines in the Douro. Schist is a metamorphic rock, having been transformed by heat and pressure into its current state from sedimentary rocks like slate and shale. Schist is high in minerals, like talc, mica, and graphite, all of which contribute to its lamellar structure. Schist is layered, and the different crystals of mica and other minerals flake off easily. In the Douro, the rock has been distorted, so that the layers are exposed at the surface. This allows water to seep between the layers. Water pockets can form deep in the cracks of the rock. If there is a freeze-thaw cycle, the water expansion will break apart the layers, forming crude topsoil.

Tilling schist involves the use of backhoes and bulldozers. If nature has not provided enough loose soil to plant grape vines, it is not uncommon to break the rock apart with heavy machinery to create some loose planting material. Occasionally, if the gradient is too steep for machines, small charges of dynamite will blast holes in the rock to accept small vine plantings. The roots of the vines can work their way through the layers of stone to find the water pockets that form, and therefore survive.

The Douro Valley is divided into three zones, mainly based on climate. In general, the Douro gets very little rainfall. It has a severe continental climate, with winter temperatures near freezing, and summer temperatures topping 95°F (35°C). The region closest to the coastline, just over the Serra do Marao mountains, is Baixo Corgo. This area, below the confluence of the Corgo river with the Douro, is the coolest and wettest region. It receives, on average, 39 inches (980 mm) of rain per year, mostly in the spring. The grapes grown here go into simple styles of Port rather than top-quality versions. The heart of the region is the Cima Corgo, or area around the Douro above the Corgo river. It is the home to most of the top producers. It receives less rainfall than the Baixo Corgo (28 in or 710 mm) and is a few degrees warmer. This is the region that provides the grapes for most of the top Port wines. The final region is the Douro Superior. It is the hottest and driest region (16 in or 400 mm), and becomes flatter as one approaches the Spanish border. It is still considered somewhat wild, but has great potential for quality production.

THE VINEYARDS

The vineyards in the Douro are in a precarious position, literally. The slope of the vineyards ranges from a somewhat manageable 30 percent incline up to 60 percent. Historically, to be able to grow grapes and control soil erosion, the land has been terraced. The historic terracing system is called *socalcos*. This style of terracing had very narrow terraces, often only two rows wide. The soil was held back by man-made stone walls, often 10 feet high between terraces. After phylloxera hit the vineyards, the socalcos were widened (now holding around six rows) and have shorter stone walls.

In the 1970s two new styles of vineyard layout appeared. The first eliminated expensive stone walls in favor of sloping natural soil held in place by groundcovers. This style is called *patamares*. These vineyards had greater spacing between vines, which would allow small tractors to work the soil. Another system developed planted the vines up and down the natural slope. This method is called *vinha ao alto*. The vines are trellised in rows that ascend the slope without retaining walls. These vineyards also allow for some limited mechanization, though erosion and access are difficult when the slope is greater than 30 degrees.

The vineyards are graded on a series of twelve characteristics, which are given points in a system called *cadastro*. Points can be added or deducted based on the vineyard. Once the total is determined, the vineyard is awarded a grading of A through F. This is known as the *beneficio*, which determines the annual authorization for port production. The maximum score is 1680, with anything total above 1200 receiving an A rating. This determines how much Port can be made that year, and how much it can be sold for.

Cadastro

The 12 areas of analysis (with some examples of point allotment) are:

1. Altitude: up to 150 m above sea level, 150 points, deductions for higher elevations

2. Productivity: 100 points if yield is less than 600 L per 1000 vines, more wine produced gets more deductions

3. Soil type: 100 points for schist, −500 points for granite

4. Locality: 84 sectors have point allocations (highest in Cima Corgo)

5. Vine training: 100 points for traditional low-trained vines

6. Grape varieties: classified as very good, good, regular, mediocre, or bad

7. Slope: up to 105 points if slope is greater than 35 degrees

8. Aspect: more points if vineyard faces south

9. Vine density: 50 points for widely spaced vines (<5700 per ha), deductions if vines are densely planted (>6900 per ha)

10. Stoniness of soil: more stones, more points

11. Age of vines: vines 25-plus years old get 50 points, vines 4–5 years old get 0

12. Shelter: 60 points if vineyard is sheltered, 0 if not

GRAPE VARIETIES

More than eighty varieties of grapes are authorized for Port production. This is partially forced by reality, where vineyards have multiple grape varieties planted, many of them unidentified. Modern research has led to the determination of the best grapes for Port production, which centers on six grape varietals:

Touriga Nacional	Considered the best grape, low yielding and small berries gives color, tannin, and aroma
Tinta Barroca	Early ripening provides high sugar levels
Touriga Franca	Similar to Touriga Nacional, provides lots of floral aromas
Tinta Roriz (Tempranillo)	Also called Aragonez in Portugal; provides finesse and acidity
Tinto Cao	High skin-to-pulp ratio gives color and tannin
Sousao	Red fleshed and low in acid

It seems Port originated as a field blend; that is, the blend is created simply by harvesting all the different grape varieties in the field at once. With the identification of the best varieties, it is now possible to plant the grapes in blocks, and harvest each variety at its absolute best.

PORT VINIFICATION

The production of Port requires a fast extraction of color and tannin before the sugars are fermented completely. A standard Port fermentation may take only two to three days, and if conducted in a way similar to red table wine, not enough maceration time would elapse to extract the color and tannin necessary. Several innovative methods have developed to get as much color and tannin out of the skins before fortification.

Traditionally, the grapes were placed in a *lagar* (plural *lagares*), a large, shallow stone trough made of granite. The grapes were then foot-trod to crush them and release the juice. Foot trodding continued for the first eight to twelve hours of the process. A lagar could hold enough grapes to make almost 2200 gallons of wine. This size requires thirty people to be in the lagar treading the grapes. Foot trodding is considered the best method for crushing the grapes, as it processes the skins while not crushing the seeds. The tannins in the wine, therefore, are only those from the skins, and not woody or unripe tannins from the seeds.

Fermentation begins while the grapes are being foot-trod, initiating from wild yeasts on the grapes and in the quinta or winery. Fermentation continues over two to three days. After about twelve hours, foot trodding is replaced by cap management. The skin and seeds begin to float in the fermenting juice, and the cap is punched down with the use of spiked planks that span the top of the lagar. After about twenty-four to thirty-six hours, the sugar level has decreased to about 90 grams per liter of juice. The alcohol content is between 6 and 8 percent by volume. At this time, the juice is drained out of the lagares and used to fill large, 550 liter barrels called *pipes*. The pipes have previously been filled with 110 liters of grape brandy. Therefore, each pipe can then be filled with 440 liters of wine. This 4:1 ratio of wine to brandy creates a final alcohol level of 19–20 percent by volume. This is high enough to kill any yeast and prevent any further fermentation or bacterial infection. The port is now ready for blending and aging.

The use of lagares has become less and less widespread. One main reason is a labor shortage in the Douro and surrounding regions. Many Portuguese have emigrated, depleting the labor supply. As a result, the producing wineries had to develop other methods of rapid extraction. At the time (the 1960s and 1970s) there was no electricity in the Douro, so the procedure developed had to run without electricity. The successful alternative was an *autovinifier*.

Autovinifiers use the energy of the fermentation itself to operate. The system involves a sealed tank with two release valves, one that allows wine to be pushed into a reservoir and one that is a water bubbler. As the fermentation progresses, the pressure builds in the tank, forcing wine into a reservoir. When the pressure gets high enough, the water bubbler releases the pressure in the tank. With some of the wine in a reservoir, a valve opens, pulling the wine from the reservoir back into the tank, spraying it over the cap of skins and seeds. When the process starts, this cycle may take a few minutes to occur, but as fermentation gets more vigorous, the cycle happens several times a minute. This allows for increased extraction of color and tannin during the short fermentation.

Once the Port has been fortified, it will age in the winery in the Douro until the spring. Before the Douro was dammed, the pipes would be loaded onto flat-bottomed boats called *barcos rabelos*, which would navigate the rapids of the Douro to bring the wine to Vila Nova de Gaia, the home of the Port houses across from the city of Oporto. The wine would be brought down to the coast because it was believed that the cooler temperatures and the higher humidity helped the wine to age more slowly. If the wine had remained in the Douro, it had a chance to develop *Douro bake,* or a sweetish, overaged, cooked taste. With the advent of electricity

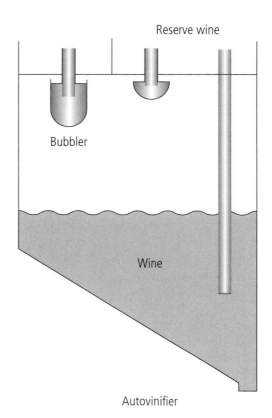

The autovinifier is a nonmotorized fermentation tank that allows rapid extraction of color and tannin.

in the Douro (generated from the dams), shippers either truck their wine to Vila Nova de Gaia, or use air-conditioned storage buildings on the winery property.

PORT STYLES

Port, for the most part, is a blended wine. Each vintage is different, and to maintain a house consistent style, several vintages are blended. This is supported by the Port Wine Institute, which does not allow more than one-third of a producer's stock to be sold in any given year. Thus, there is always a supply of reserve wine.

One separation of Port styles is based on how the wines are aged. The wines can be either predominantly wood (barrel) aged or they can be bottle aged. These create two different styles because barrel aging is oxidative, with small amounts of oxygen diffusing through the wood over time. Bottle aging is reductive, meaning that once the oxygen in the headspace is depleted, the aging occurs with no oxygen present. These two produce different flavor profiles, as they do in table wine.

Wood-Aged Ports

Wood-aged Ports are made to be consumed upon release. These wines undergo aging in wood to develop their flavors, then are fined, filtered, and stabilized before release. The wines in this category make up the majority of wine sold by the Port houses.

The simplest version of Port is *Ruby Port*. This is aged in large wood barrels for two or three years, and is then bottled. The wine retains its bright, ruby purple color, and has very simple flavors. A Ruby Port has simple fruit flavors, like berries, cherries, and raisins. Because the aging is only for a few years, the wine is still aggressive. It exhibits high alcohol and firm tannins, and is very sweet.

A better version of Ruby Port is the *Premium Ruby* or Reserve Port. For many producers, these are the signature Ports in their portfolio. Familiar Ports such as Fonseca's Bin 27, Graham's Six Grapes, and Warre's Warrior are excellent examples of this style. The difference between a Ruby and a Premium Ruby is in the depth of color and flavor. Premium Rubies have more complex flavor, often from a bit of older wine added to the blend. These wines used to be called Vintage Character but the name was deemed too misleading for consumers.

If Port is left to age longer in wood, the result is a *Tawny Port*. The name derives from the color obtained as the primarily purple anthocyanins disappear and the wine is left with an amber hue. There is a wide range of quality in Tawny Ports. Commercial, simple Tawnies are typically not the result of long-term aging. These wines, often at the same price point as a Ruby Port, are the result of winemaker intervention rather than extended aging. The grapes typically come from lesser vineyards, often in the Baixo Corgo. The wines are made with decreased color in mind, and are often left to age in the Douro. The bit of Douro bake they obtain tinges the rim brown and gives the appearance of extended aging.

A better-quality category is the *Aged Tawny Port*. These wines have been aged a minimum of seven years in barrels before they are released. They have lost the ruby color of a young wine, and have lost a large quantity of tannin as sediment. The result is a soft, silky wine with more developed flavors. These wines are more delicate, though they have been aged for a number of years. They start with good-quality wines, which have been left to age in Vila Nova de Gaia until the producer feels they have developed sufficient character. The wines are then blended and bottled to yield a "house-style" Tawny Port.

The next level of quality is a *Tawny Reserve*. These wines have some type of age indication on the label, such as ten-, twenty-, thirty-, or more than forty-year Tawny. The date is not an indication of the age of the wine, but rather is a reference to the flavor profile one would find in a wine of that age. There are older wines in these blends, but they are still blends, and have younger wines as part of the mix. Because these wines are very sensitive to oxygen, the labels will state the bottling date. Too much bottle age will reduce some of the more delicate fruit flavors in the wine. Once an aged tawny is opened, it is best consumed in a couple days before the oxygen in the atmosphere deteriorates the fruit flavors.

A special Tawny is the *Colheita,* the Portuguese term for "vintage" or "crop." These are Tawny Ports from a single year. They have aged at least seven years to achieve a Tawny designation, but they also express the character of a single year's harvest. Many Colheitas are aged longer than seven years, and the date of the harvest is on the label. The second date of the label is the bottling date, and wines in this category should be consumed within a year of their being bottled.

White Port is a style in which the extraction of color and tannin is minimal or nonexistent. The grapes used to make white port are commonly Codega, Malvasia Fina, and Rabigato. The wine is typically made in a medium-sweet style, though a drier style called leve seco (light dry) is made by some shippers. The wines are often aged in stainless steel or cement tanks, though some can be aged in oak barrels. A great deal of White Port is used to make cheaper Tawnies.

Bottle-Aged Port

The quintessential Port is *Vintage Port.* This is wine from a single, exceptional year. While these wines only make up 1 percent of all the production of a Port producer, they are highly anticipated. The British market especially desires Vintage Port, and has effectively made this wine into a "flagship" for the producers.

Vintage Ports are made from the grapes of a single year, from the best vineyards in Cima Corgo. The determination to release a wine as a vintage does not happen until the following year. The wine is assessed based on color, flavor, quantity of wine, and its character. The market is also factored into the equation. If all factors are right, a vintage is "declared." Typically, three to four vintages are declared in a decade. More years may create great wines, but the market determines whether the producers can sell another vintage lot based on the last release.

The wine is aged for two to three years in barrel, and then is bottled unfiltered and unfined. The wine itself will be extremely dark and intense. The reason is that the wine is intended to age in the bottle for twenty to thirty years. Many Vintage Ports, especially in the United States, get consumed earlier than that, and Vintage Port is thought of as the deepest, darkest Port on the market. These wines, even after a few years in bottle, will throw a great deal of sediment, so service must involve decanting.

A growing specialty within Vintage Port is the *Single Quinta Vintage Port.* A *quinta* is a vineyard in Portuguese, so Single Quinta Ports are made from single vineyards. These wines differ from Vintage Ports in two ways. First, they are made in good but not great years, and are undeclared. If the wines were from a great year, they would become part of the vintage blend. Second, they are released when they are ready to drink, often ten years after the vintage. The wines are still aged in wood for only two years, and the remainder in the bottle, so decanting is an important step in service.

Late-Bottled Vintage Ports are made in years that are good but not spectacular. They are aged for five to six years in barrels, and then bottled. Some are fined and filtered before bottling, while others in a "traditional" style are left untreated. The wines can continue to age in the bottle for another five to six years to improve their flavor. Those that are filtered and fined are considered ready to drink, but their character is often less intense than those untreated.

Crusted Ports are blended Ruby Ports that are not aged in wood, but rather in the bottle. They throw a great deal of sediment, or crust, hence the name. This is a recent creation of some Port makers, and is meant to be a more economical alternative to Vintage Port. While not from a single year, these wines still possess the full-bodied, dark, intense flavors expected from a bottle-aged port.

Port Styles

	Blends	Single Year
Wood Aged (<7 years)	Ruby, Premium Ruby, Commercial Tawny, White Port	Late-Bottled Vintage
Wood aged (>7 years)	Reserve, 10, 20, 30, over 40 years Tawny	Colheita
Bottle Aged	Crusted	Vintage

While each producer makes its own house styles, it is possible to categorize the producers by their common traits. British Port houses make wines that are full bodied and intense. They focus on Vintage Port, or styles that have a similar flavor profile. Portuguese Port houses, on the other hand, make lighter, more delicate wines. They often focus on aged Tawnies as their predominant wines.

Sherry

Sherry is a wine that has been known for centuries. It is written about in literature, and has graced tables around the world. The popularity of Sherry has also been its main detriment. Vineyards in poorer areas have produced low-quality Sherry to meet the demand, along with poor imitators around the world. The wine is experiencing a renaissance with its focus on quality and its discovery by a new generation of aperitif and cocktail drinkers.

HISTORY

Vines have been planted on the southern Atlantic coast of Spain for centuries. First planted by the Phoenicians, the vineyards were expanded by the Romans, and taxed heavily by the Moors. The English were drinking "sherris" in the 1300s and Sir Francis Drake took pride in angering the king of Spain by hijacking a Spanish trade vessel with 3000 barrels of "sack."

The name Sherry comes from the name of the town most associated with the wine production. The town name was originally Seris, which over time has been written as Xeres or Jerez. The official name of the village is Jerez de la Fronterra. Jerez, Sanlucar de Barrameda, and Puerto de Santa Maria are the official shipping villages for the export of Sherry. The Spanish have recognized the region with their top-quality designation, Demoninacion de Origin (DO) Jerez-Xeres-Sherry y Manzanilla-Sanlucar de Barrameda.

THE SHERRY REGION

The growing region around Jerez is a subtropical climate. The sun shines on average 300 days a year, with substantial rain during the late autumn and winter (25.6 in or 650 mm). Much of the rain comes off the Atlantic, brought in by the cool, wet *potente* wind. In the summer, the wind shifts and comes off the dry plains to the southeast. This is called the *levante*. The Atlantic also has an influence in the villages of the Sherry region. Puerto de Santa Maria and Sanlucar are on the water, and often are 18°F (10°C) cooler than Jerez just 12 miles inland.

The soils of the region have a distinct influence on the wines. There are three types of soils in Jerez. The most important is *albariza*. Albariza contains a high chalk content. There are some districts where grapes are not planted because of issues with chlorosis, but the majority of the region is planted with the best grapes to make Sherry. The soil consistency is unique. When the rain falls, the soil becomes very muddy and slippery. It is almost like wet plaster of paris. As the soil dries, a crust forms as a top layer to the soil. The crust allows for maneuvering in the vineyard, but it also serves as a "mulch" by preventing evaporation from the moist soil below. As the temperature rises, this prevention of evaporation is important so the vines have a steady supply of water.

The best albariza land has been subdivided into individual vineyards or *pagos*. Some are small (less than a hectare) while others are fairly large (over a thousand hectares). Those that are higher in elevation or are hotter make fuller-bodied wines. Those by the coast make lighter, more delicate wines.

The next soil is *arena*. This is a sandy type of soil, and the vines planted on this yield twice as much as vines on albariza. The quality of the juice is not as good as that coming from albariza soil, either. Finally, there are the *barro* soils. These are clay-based soils and yield wines that are fuller bodied than the other soils, and also coarser in flavor.

GRAPE VARIETIES

There are three main grape varieties that are important to Sherry production. The most important varietal is *Palomino*. It is a varietal that makes neutral, acidic wines of approximately 11 to 12 percent alcohol. It is thin skinned and therefore susceptible to rot and mildew. As with many varietals, there are two subvarieties: Palomino de Jerez and Palomino Fino. Both make up about 90 percent of all the plantings in Jerez, with the majority of the vineyards planted to Palomino Fino.

The second most important grape is *Pedro Ximenez* (or Pedro Jimenez), sometimes referred to as *PX*. Pedro Ximenez has lost vineyard ground to Palomino over the years, and now accounts for only about 5 percent of the vineyard area. It is most often planted on the barro and arena soils. The grapes are often raisinated before pressing and fermentation, leaving the resultant wine with significant residual sugar. This wine is then used to sweeten the base sherries for later shipping. Occasionally, producers will make a single-varietal Pedro Ximenez dessert sherry, labeled PX. Because of the low concentration of PX plantings, special dispensation has been granted to bring PX wine in from Montilla-Morilles to satisfy the need.

The final grape is Moscatel, or Muscat of Alexandria. This grape is planted on the worst barro and arena soils. It is an extremely small component of the plantings. The wine made from Moscatel is typically served in local bars and restaurants, though some may be used for sweetening purposes.

MAKING SHERRY

The first step in making Sherry is making the base wine. The grapes are harvested, and for Palomino they are immediately pressed. Press houses are set up near the fields, similar to Champagne. This keeps the juice as fresh as possible and limits the amount of oxidation. As stated earlier, the Pedro Ximenez grapes are dried in the sun. Traditionally the PX would be dried on straw mats, but now many growers dry them in plastic tunnels with fans.

Not all the juice makes the same style of Sherry. As with Champagne, the free-run juice and the earlier pressings is more delicate juice. This juice amounts to about 70 percent of all the juice and is used to make lighter styles of Sherry. The next 20 percent of the pressings makes fuller-bodied Sherries. The final 10 percent is made into wine that will be sent off for distillation into brandy.

Besides the distribution of the pressing fractions, there is a control over how much juice can be produced. While the vineyards are limited to 65 hl/ha yield, the pressings are restricted to 72.5 liters per 100 kilograms of grapes. That is only slightly more yield per 100 kg of grapes than is allowed in Champagne.

The juice is allowed to settle and clarify. It is often treated before fermentation to increase the acidity. The traditional method was the addition of gypsum sprinkled over the juice in a process known as plastering. This was done to encourage the precipitation of tartrates as well as increase the acidity. More producers are changing to the use of tartaric acid to increase the acidity of the juice.

Fermentation occurs in large, 600-liter vats made of stainless steel or old oak barrels called *butts*. The fermentation occurs at a very hot temperature for white wine: 77–86°F (25–30°C). Having the fermentation this warm changes some of the chemical reactions that occur. The alcohol formed gets oxidized by the yeasts to form aldehydes, which provide the classic, distinctive flavor of Sherry.

After the fermentation, the wine has achieved an alcohol level of 12–13 percent. Each fermentation batch is evaluated and those that are good-quality wines are fortified to 14.5 percent. Those that are fuller bodied or have coarser flavor profiles are fortified to 16.5 percent. The good-quality wines are placed into casks and set to age until spring, when they will be reevaluated.

In the spring, the barrels are evaluated. The winemaker, or *capataz,* is looking to determine if a specific species of yeast has begun to grow on the wine. This yeast is called *flor.* It is a special species of saccharomyces that does not need sugar to live, but rather, alcohol. It blooms in humid conditions and has very specific conditions for its survival. The wine it grows in must be dry (absence of fermentable sugars) and must contain little or no sulfur dioxide and little or no tannins. Flor will live only in wine with an alcohol content of 15.5 percent and at a temperature between 59–68°F (15–20°C). As flor grows, it decreases the glycerol content and volatile acidity of the wine, while increasing aldehydes and esters. Because it floats on top of the wine, it protects the liquid from oxygen, even though the barrels are not completely full. This keeps the wine pale and delicate in the barrel.

If a barrel has developed flor, it will be fortified to 15.5 percent alcohol. This will encourage flor growth, and the wine will follow a path to become a *Fino Sherry.* If there is no flor growth, the wine will be fortified to 17.5 percent alcohol and will follow a path to become an *Oloroso Sherry.* At this point, the wines are a year old, still single vintage, and are called the *añada.*

For a great deal of Sherry history, flor growth was a mystery. Eventually, the dependence on alcohol strength was determined. Also, the influence of where the juice originated was quantified. Now, it is common to see juice from grapes grown in albariza soils, or the first pressing of juice follow the path to become finos. The juice from grapes in lesser soils, or from later pressings, most likely will become Olorosos.

Fortification of the añada results from the addition of brandy to the wine. The brandy can come from the distillation of the wine made from the barro soils, or from the last 10 percent of the pressings. For the quality producers, the quality of the brandy is an important component of the Sherry.

THE SOLERA SYSTEM

With a rare exception or two, Sherry is not a vintage wine. For this reason it is important that the style of wine produced by the *bodega,* or winery, is consistent in flavor from year to year. The method of aging that has developed over the centuries ensures the consistency of the product. This method is called the *solera system.*

The solera system is designed to use fractional blending to maintain consistency. It consists of collections of barrels, with groupings based on the age of the wine. Imagine a collection of nine barrels, separated into three groups of three. One set contains the wine that will be fined, filtered, and bottled. This is also called the *solera,* and lends its name to the system in general. The other two groups of three barrels are called *criadera* (nursery). Our solera system is simplified while in reality, the distribution would have anywhere from six to fourteen levels of criaderas, each containing many barrels.

The wine removed from the three barrels in the solera will be blended and then prepared for bottling. No more than one-third of any barrel can be removed at one time, and the standard amount is 20 percent. Now the barrels in the solera need to be topped up. That wine comes from the first criadera, or the set of three barrels containing the oldest wine. Then, the first criadera needs to be filled. The wine for this comes from the second criadera. The second criadera now needs to be filled, and this is the job of the añada. This transfer is called *running the scales.*

The filling of each level is more intricate than just pouring off some wine and adding it to the next set of barrels. First, this process is slow. In a fino solera, the flor cannot be disturbed. The filling of each level occurs by having small amounts of wine drip into the barrel. This also means that the wine in the barrel is not homogenous, meaning it does not get blended together to make a uniform mix, but rather must diffuse together over time. Second, it is not a one-to-one transfer of wine. The wine from one barrel in the criadera is not filled by just one barrel in the criadera above it. Nor is the wine collected out of the criadera blended and added to the next level. Rather, a series of hoses connects one barrel with each barrel in the criadera below it. In the example above, each barrel in the first criadera is attached to each barrel in the solera by a hose. That means nine hoses connect the six barrels.

Solera system

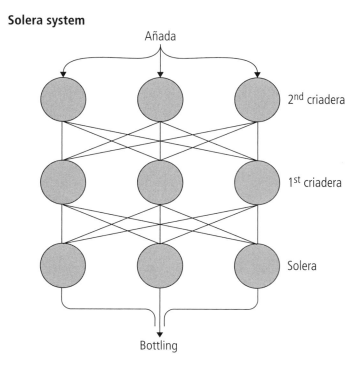

Añada

2nd criadera

1st criadera

Solera

A series of barrels comprises the solera system, and the transfer of wine from one level to the next is called "running the scales."

Bottling

With the slow infusion of younger wine into barrels containing older wine, two things occur. First, the older wine is refreshed by the younger wine, giving it more liveliness. Conversely, the young wine gains character from the older wine that it did not previously have. Because there is only 20–30 percent of the barrel emptied, one can envision that wine from the beginning of the system could still remain in the solera. For this reason, bottles of Sherry will display the date the solera was started rather than a vintage date.

STYLES OF SHERRY

At the first classification of the añada, the fate of a barrel of Sherry was determined to be a Fino or an Oloroso. These are the two families of Sherries, as well as the names of the classic examples of each family.

Fino Sherries

These wines have been fortified to 15.5 percent in order to encourage the growth of flor. While some evaporation occurs during the solera process, the wines are fortified back to their original 15.5 percent alcohol upon bottling.

Fino

The quintessential light, dry Sherry is called a Fino. It is made with the lightest wines, often from the free-run juice. During its development, a Fino is protected by flor, and therefore is light in color and delicate in flavor. Wines aged inland may have a hint of a deeper color and be more aromatic because the flor can die back in the heat of the summer.

Manzanilla

Manzanilla is a style of Fino whose solera is located in Sanlucar de Barrameda. The proximity to the ocean and the increased humidity makes the flor particularly active. The flor will be much thicker in a barrel that is to become Manzanilla than a regular Fino. Because the flor is more active, its effects are greater in a Manzanilla. This means it is often lighter bodied than a regular Fino and has more distinct flor character. If a Manzanilla is allowed to age in contact with oxygen, it will become a *Manzanilla Pasada*.

Amontillado

If a Fino remains in a solera for over fifteen years, the result is an *Amontillado* Sherry. After about eight years, the flor will die off, leaving a Fino to age oxidatively. A true Amontillado will be dry, and would exhibit not only the flor characteristics of a Fino Sherry, but also some of the oxidative aging expected in an Oloroso Sherry. The name means "in the style of Montilla," but it is no longer allowed to be used in Montilla as a descriptor.

Commercial Amontillado has very little in common with a true one. It is often sweetened and is the result of blending sweet wine with inferior Sherry called a *raya*. A commercial Amontillado will be medium bodied, rather than the light body of a true Amontillado.

Pale Cream

An uncommon style in the United States, a Pale Cream Sherry is the result of a Fino being sweetened. The sweetening does not come from PX or Moscatel, but rather by the addition of concentrated grape must, or juice concentrate, to increase the sugar level. Any color that may appear is removed by charcoal filtration.

Palo Cortado

This is a rare style of wine. It starts life as a Fino, but for some reason the flor dies off early. The result is extended oxygen contact. The wine will have a character similar to an Amontillado, but will also have strong Oloroso characteristics.

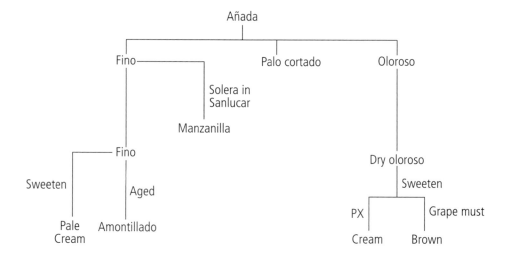

The families of Sherry and the relationship of styles within those families.

Oloroso Sherries

These wines are intended to age without flor. To that end, the wines are fortified to 18 percent alcohol. Again, this will decrease in the solera, but the wines will be refortified upon bottling.

Oloroso

The "flagship" of this family is also called *Oloroso,* which means "fragrant" in Spanish and refers to the intense aromaticity of the wine. They are dark, nutty, rich wines, which can often live up to a hundred years. They are dry by definition, and that dryness extends to the long finish of the wine.

Cream

A *Cream Sherry* is made by sweetening an Oloroso Sherry with PX. This is an *Oloroso Dulce.* The best Cream Sherries will be nutty and sweet. Sometimes the color is not deep enough and needs to be adjusted with *arrope* concentrate (boiled-down grape must). Arrope is sometimes referred to as *vino de color.*

Commercial Cream Sherries are called *Amoroso* or *Brown Sherry.* These are wines made from ordinary blends that have been sweetened and colored, or they are wines made from Palomino grapes that have been raisinated and fermented and fortified by the port method.

Specialty Sherry

Recently, new rules have allowed very old sherries to come to market. These wines are the pride and joy of a Sherry bodega, and were often only tasted by family, trusted workers, and visiting dignitaries. Two designations have been allowed to distinguish these wines. *V.O.S.* (Very Old Sherry or Vinum Optimum Signatum) is the designation for wines that are over twenty years old. *V.O.R.S.* (Very Old Rare Sherry or Vinum Optimum Rare Signatum) is the designation for wine more than thirty years old. These wines are often blended with very guarded wines from soleras that date back into the eighteenth or nineteenth centuries. The age of the wine must be confirmed by an independent panel, and the wines must also pass a taste test to confirm their exceptional quality.

Another category of specialty Sherry is the *Almacenista Sherries.* These started out as private soleras for stockholders. While they undergo the solera system, they are unblended. In other words, there is only one barrel per criadera. These were not available commercially until recently when Lustau began releasing some of their Almacenista wines. The size of the solera is often designated as a fraction on the bottle; for example, 1/10 would mean there were 10 criadera in the solera.

Madeira

Madeira is a wine that was accidentally discovered, found great popularity, was decimated, and has begun a revival. It is the only wine that will not deteriorate when exposed to oxygen, because of its method of production. It is a wine from an unlikely place, made in an unusual and unorthodox way.

HISTORY OF MADEIRA

The island of Madeira is approximately 600 miles (1000 km) from the Portuguese mainland, and 450 miles (750 km) off the coast of West Africa. It was not discovered until 1418 by Gonsalves Zarco, a Portuguese explorer. While exploring the coast of West Africa, he noticed a cloud on the horizon, and went to investigate. What he found was a garden island, covered in woods, which he named Madeira. A town, Funchal, grew around the natural harbor of the island.

Madeira is a volcanic island that juts dramatically out of the ocean. In order to prepare the island for agriculture, the forests were burned, and agriculture took hold by building terraces on the steep hillsides. First sugarcane was the main crop, but that gave way to wine. With a natural harbor and a position on the routes to South America, the Caribbean, and Africa, Madeira became a natural refueling station. One item that was brought on board was wine.

Initially, the wine of Madeira was simple table wine, but it was discovered that it was unstable and would not survive the sea voyages very well. This led to fortifying the wine to extend its lifespan. Sometimes the wine was drunk by the sailors for its vitamin C and scurvy prevention, but other ships used the wine as ballast. When the wine in the hold of the ship was tasted, it was found to be better than when it was loaded on the boat. This lead to the belief that the wine needed to cross the Equator or otherwise take long sea voyages (*vinhos da roda*) to gain the special flavor.

The popularity of Madeira increased in the American colonies. In the 1600s the British had imposed a ruling that no European products could be exported to the colonies unless they came on a British ship or from a British port. An exception was Madeira. Thus, Madeira became a layover for most trade going to the New World, and trade in Madeira increased.

By the 1900s, several things had happened. First, Madeira was plagued by mildew. Having a subtropical climate and constant cloud cover did not help prevent moisture-related diseases. Once the mildew issue was solved, phylloxera devastated the island. Many vines were pulled and replaced by sugarcane. The beginning of the downturn of Madeira had begun. Finally, those producers still making wine stopped using sea voyages to age the wine, and concentrated more on aging the wine on the island in heated rooms or tanks, called *estufa*.

CLIMATE

The island is tropical, but also has a large change in elevation. The vineyards are planted on tiny terraces called *poios*, which are watered using channels or *levadas* that redirect the island's rainfall. The vines are grown mainly on trellises, probably for two reasons. First, it keeps the grapes away from the soil and open to air circulation to prevent mildew diseases. Second, it is Portuguese tradition to have the vineyards as part of a polyculture. In other words, the vines were lifted off the ground to allow other crops to be grown alongside the vines; this is typical in northern Portugal.

The grapes are often grown at altitude, and the island rises 5,900 feet above sea level. The amount of rain at the highest point is 117 inches (3,000 mm), which is three times the amount found at Funchal. Mechanization is impossible due to the severity of the slopes, and many vineyard holdings are piecemeal.

GRAPE VARIETIES

Since phylloxera devastated the vineyards, the majority of grapes planted were American species or hybrids. These grapes have been outlawed from Madeira production. The main vinifera grape is called *Tinta Negro Mole,* and it constitutes the majority of the grape vines planted on the island. After Tinta Negro Mole are the "noble" grape varieties of the island. They are *Sercial, Verdelho, Bual,* and *Malmsey.*

Malmsey is the English name for Malvasia. There is another well-regarded grape, Terrantez, but it is on the verge of extinction.

The noble grapes are grown on different parts of the island. Sercial is grown at high altitude (2640 ft or 800 m). This is the region with the coolest vineyards, and Sercial will make a wine that is only 10 percent alcohol with searing acidity. Verdelho is grown on the northern side of the island, but ripens easier than Sercial does. Its higher sugar level lends itself to a medium-sweet wine. Bual is grown in warm locations on the south side of the island. It ripens to a higher sugar level and makes a rich, raisiny wine. Finally, Malmsey is grown in the warmest locations at the lowest altitudes on the south side. While Malmsey reaches the highest sugar level, it also retains a tangy acidity that prevents it from being cloying.

MADEIRA PRODUCTION

Madeira can be made as a simple commercial product, or as a more refined wine. The commercial brands of Madeira are made primarily with Tinta Negro Mole, and are simply labeled dry, medium dry, medium sweet, medium rich, or full rich. The wines that are of better quality must meet European Union guidelines for naming; that is, they must contain 85 percent of the grape named on the label. These wines are named after the noble grapes they contain: Sercial, Verdelho, Bual, and Malmsey.

The method of fortification for Madeira depends on the final outcome that is desired. For the drier styles (off-dry, medium sweet), the sherry method is used. For those that are sweeter (medium rich and full rich), the port method is used. Commerical bulk wines are almost always fermented to dryness and fortified after the wine has been aged, to prevent loss of alcohol.

Estufagem

The real key to Madeira production is the *estufagem* process. The wine must be heated to mimic the long sea voyages of the past. These are three methods by which the wine can be heated. First, for bulk, commercial wines, the wines are placed in concrete or stainless steel tanks that have heating coils attached. They may be immersion coils in the concrete tanks, or thermal wraps on the stainless tanks. In either case, the wine is heated to 104–122°F (40–50°C) for a minimum of three months. Better wines are placed in 600-liter pipes and placed into heated or naturally warm rooms. The temperature of these rooms is between 86–104°F (30–40°C), and aging takes at least six months to a year. The best wines are placed in the eaves of the bodegas to be heated naturally by the sun. These will age up to twenty years before they are ready. Some of the best wines may stay in barrel for a century before they are released as vintage wines.

SWEETNESS LEVELS

For wines made from the noble grape varieties, the name of the grape on the bottle is also indicative of a sweetness level. Sercial is considered the driest of the four wines. Verdelho would be classified as medium sweet and Bual as medium rich. The sweetest of the wines is Malmsey. The names actually stand for sugar ranges as well as the grape variety.

Madeira Grapes and Sugar Levels

Grape varietal	Sugar level
Sercial	8–25 g/L
Verdelho	25–40 g/L
Bual	40–60 g/L
Malmsey	60–120 g/L

QUALITY LEVELS

Madeira quality is often referenced by the grape varietal on the label. There are age designations as well that reference the quality in the bottle:

Three year old	Refers to blended wines that have experienced the estufagem in a tank. They are mainly made from Tinta Negro Mole.
Five-year-old Reserve	Blended Madeira in which some has been aged in tanks and some in barrels. It is commonly made with Tinta Negro Mole, unless a noble grape is noted on the label.
Ten-year-old Special Reserve	This wine has been aged a minimum of ten years, and experienced the estufagem in barrels. They are restricted to noble grape varietals.
Extra Reserve	A rare category referencing blended wines at least fifteen years old.
Solera wines	Some Madeiras have been aged in a solera fashion. This has been outlawed by the European Union, though some may still be available.
Colheita	Wines from a single year that have been aged in cask for at least five years.
Frasqueira	Top-quality vintage wines that have aged a minimum of twenty years in cask, and then some aging in bottles before release. These are restricted to the four best grape varietals.

Other Port Style Wines

MARSALA

This wine was invented in the late eighteenth century by John Woodhouse, who saw the wines around Marsala in Sicily and equated them to port and sherry. The wines are made from native Sicilian white grapes—Inzolia, Grillo, and the very productive Cataratto. The fortification, called *mutage,* involves the addition of 20–25 percent pure grape spirit to fermenting, overripe grape must.

There are many commercial styles of Marsala, most of which is made with poor-quality, overcropped grapes or is aged in decrepit equipment. These wines are often sweetened either with a *mistela,* or stop-fermented grape juice (that is, another port style fortified sweet wine) or by *mosto cotto* (boiled-down grape juice). Mosto cotto is only allowed to sweeten Ambra (amber) Marsala, and unfortunately gives the impression that this is a cask-aged wine, which it is not. Other colors of Marsala include Oro (gold), which is the natural color of the wine, or Rubino (red) made from red grapes. These wines may also be labeled secco (maximum 40 g/L sugar), semisecco (40–100 g/L), or sweet (over 100 g/L).

The Italian DOC wine laws allow for labeling cask aged Marsala with descriptors of the amount of time in cask. The simplest is Fino (one year), Superiore (two years), Superiore Riserva (four years), Vergine (five years), and Vergine Stravecchio (ten years). Superiore and Vergine are the only two with real historic connection to the original Marsalas of Woodhouse.

Marsala was once considered a great wine, but has fallen on poor times, with the proliferation of poorly made wines or the expansion of quality categories. The best examples of Marsala, the Vergine class, are practically extinct. Unfortunately, to the extent that the top-quality wines may disappear, the wine may be relegated to just a class of sweet cooking wine.

VINS DOUX NATURELS

This style of wine is common in the south of France. It involves stopping the fermentation of grape must by the addition of alcohol (mutage). While similar in the process to that of making Port, there are some distinctions. When the fermenting must reaches 6 percent alcohol, spirit that is 95 percent alcohol is added. The amount of the addition would only comprise 5–10 percent of the final volume (as opposed to Port's 20 percent). This translates to a final wine containing about 15 percent alcohol.

Commonly made from Muscat for white wines and Grenache for red wines, the flavor profile of these wines is very different than Port. The wines contain less alcohol and less water, but also retain much of the original grape flavors from the unfermented juice. There are also some fermented wine flavors in the *VDNs* because fermentation was allowed to commence. These wines are ready to drink upon release, and the additional alcohol preserves an open bottle for close to a week.

Well-known VDNs from Muscat include wines from the regions of Frontignan and Mireval in the Languedoc, and Beaumes-de-Venise in the Rhone. Grenache-based wines include Rivesaltes, Rasteau, and Maury, though the most famous is probably Banyuls. Banyuls can be made in an early drinking version, that is young and fresh, or the Grand Cru Banyuls, which must age in wood for thirty months.

Some of these wines are also made in a *rancio* style. This means the barrels are placed in the hot summer sun to age. This forces the wines to oxidize or maderize, plus they change color to a more tawny amber tone. These wines are an acquired taste, compared to the freshness of a Muscat Beaumes-de-Venise, for example.

VINS DE LIQUEUR

While technically not "wine," vins de liqueur are also known as *mistelles*. These are made by the addition of alcohol to grape must before fermentation begins. The final mistelle possesses an alcohol content of 16 to 22 percent, with very strong flavors of the natural grape juice and of spirit. The most famous of these wine are Pineau des Charentes from the Cognac region and Floc de Gascogne from the Armagnac region.

MÁLAGA

This wine from the south of Spain had its heyday in the Victorian period, when it was known as Mountain Wine. Málaga is made from dried Pedro Ximenez grapes, occasionally blended with Moscatel. Traditionally, the grapes are dried almost to a raisin, pressed, and fermented. The sweetness comes from having the fermentation arrested by the addition of alcohol, often to a final concentration of 23 percent. The wine then undergoes either static aging (kept in barrels) or more commonly dynamic aging (soleras). The wine must be aged in the city of Málaga to qualify for the legal designation.

The wine itself is extremely rich and raisiny. It often contains 600 g/L of unfermented sugar after fortification. There are versions of the wine that are not fortified, but allowed to ferment to 18 percent alcohol naturally. A less quality-oriented method uses arrope to increase the sugar content of the wine. The most common styles of the wine are Lagrima, which is extremely sweet and made from free run juice; Moscatel, made solely from that grape; Pedro Ximen, from PX; and Solera, from a dated solera aging process.

Australian Port and Others

The Australian wine industry was developed around making Port style wines. Several factors contributed to this path for the Australian wine industry, not the least of which was its British heritage and the need for a wine that could travel long distances for export.

AUSTRALIAN TAWNY PORT

The most commonly exported of all the Australian Port products, Australian Tawny is made with a local mixture of grapes, including Shiraz, Grenache, Cabernet Sauvignon, and Mataro (Australian term for Mourvèdre), besides Touriga Nacional. The wines are made by the same methodology used in Port production, and then aged in large oak barrels. A rancio style develops over time in the best wines. The final house style either comes from the blending of several barrels and vintages, or from the use of a solera system to maintain consistency.

AUSTRALIAN VINTAGE PORT

This is made in a similar fashion to Vintage Port. The grape of choice is Shiraz, because the color, tannin, and flavor is easily extracted. Once the wine is fortified, it is aged in oak barrels for about two years and then bottled. As with Vintage Port, this wine will continue to develop in the bottle.

LIQUEUR TOKAY AND LIQUEUR MUSCAT

These wines are unique to Australia. Liqueur Tokay is made from Muscadelle. Liqueur Muscat (also known as a *sticky*) is made from Brown Muscat, the Australian name for Muscat Blanc à Petit Grains. The fermenting wines are arrested with spirit early, leaving around 300 g/L of sugar in the finished product. The wines are then aged in large and small oak barrels. The regions of production, Rutherglen and Glenrowan, are hot, and the wine will evaporate while it ages. Typically 3–5 percent of the wine will evaporate per year, concentrating the wines flavors and sugars even more. To ensure consistency, many use a solera system as well. Quality labeling of the wines are a good indicator of what's in the bottle, even though following the rules is voluntary. The basic wine is a Rutherglen Muscat, followed by a Classic Muscat, a Grand Muscat, and finally, Rare Muscat. Rare Muscat lives up to its name, as little is produced from very old soleras.

Other Sherry-Style Wines

MONTILLA-MORILES

These wines come from the region in southern Spain of the same name. All the same styles of wine are made here as in Jerez. The main difference is that 90 percent of the grapes are Pedro Ximenez. The wine ferments to a naturally high level of alcohol, and additional alcohol is added as necessary.

The pressing of the grapes determines the style of the wine that will be produced. The free-run juice is used to make finos. The first pressing makes Olorosos. The second pressing is used for distillation. Just as in Jerez, the wines are made in stainless steel, then left to age over the winter and are classified in the spring. Some of the wine, called *joven afrutados,* is filtered and released for consumption. The remainder of the wine undergoes malolactic fermentation and is then placed either in large oak barrels or into concrete tanks called tinajas to await flor development. If flor develops, some ullage is left in the tank and the wines develop into finos. If no flor develops, the tanks are topped up with wine, and they will age to become Olorosos. The wines will then proceed through a solera system.

Modern Montillas will be classified one of three ways. First is the joven afrutados, which will be PX at 12 percent alcohol. Second are vinos crianzas, which are wines that have been cask or tank aged and are labeled dry, medium, or sweet. Finally are the generosos, or the solera-aged wines. Of these, Finos are often unfortified, though Amontillados and Olorosos are brought to 18 percent alcohol. Straight PX dessert wines are always fortified before release.

COMMANDERIA

This sweet wine from Cyprus probably has the longest running history of any wine. Its forebear was known by the ancient Greeks, and as a wine itself, Commanderia dates back to the tenth century. It is made from white (Xynisteri) and red (Mavro) grapes. The grapes must attain a minimum sugar level before harvest (212 g/L for Xynesteri and 258 g/L for Mavro). The grapes are dried before pressing and the juice must have from 390 to 450 g/L before fermentation. Because the sugar levels are so high, the wine will stop fermenting at about 10 percent alcohol, leaving some of the natural sugar behind. The wine can then be fortified, but the alcohol level cannot exceed 20 percent. Some producers use a three-tier solera system to age the wine as well.

Other Fortified Wines

Vermouth is the most common fortified wine that is not made by the port or sherry methods. It is a flavored wine as well as a fortified one. The original wine was developed in Germany and was called *wermuth,* after the wormwood that flavored the wine. Other styles were developed over time in both Italy and France, each with wormwood as a component.

Vermouth is made from bulk wine that is flavored with a mix of botanicals. The better wines still use real ingredients to flavor the wine, while large producers use concentrates to ensure a consistency of flavor. The definition of the botanicals has expanded over the years, so the definition of Vermouth is now very loose. The flavored wine is then fortified to 17 percent alcohol, and then fined, filtered, and stabilized before bottling.

Two generic styles have emerged over time. Italian Vermouth typically means the wine is red and sweet. French Vermouth means the wine is dry and white. There is a wide range of flavor profiles in the quality Vermouth category, from the bitter flavors of the Italian Punt e Mes to the delicate Lillet of Bordeaux.

SUMMARY

Fortified wines have a strong history in the wine community. It is fortified wines that have traveled the world or been developed to withstand long-distance export. These wines have kept sailors healthy at sea, and given a taste of the sun to drinkers in cold climates. To be made properly they involve many steps and much time, and yield nuanced and intricate beverages due to the time spent.

KEY TERMS

Port method

Sherry method

Schist

Socalcos

Patamares

Vinha ao alto

Cadastro

Beneficio

Lagares

Pipe

Autovinifier

Douro bake

Ruby Port

Premium Ruby Port

Tawny Port

Aged Tawny Port

Tawny Reserve

Colheita

White Port

Vintage Port

Quinta

Single Quinta Vintage Port

Late-Bottled Vintage Port

Crusted Port

Albariza

Pago

Arena

Barro

Palomino

Pedro Ximenez

PX

Butt

Capataz

Flor

Fino Sherry

Oloroso Sherry

Anada

Bodega

Solera system

Solera

Criadera

Running the scales

Manzanilla

Manzanilla Pasada

Amontillado

Raya

Oloroso

Cream Sherry

Oloroso Dulce

Arrope

Vino de color

Amoroso

Brown Sherry

V.O.S.

V.O.R.S.

Almacenista Sherries

Estufa

Tinta Negro Mole

Sercial

Verdelho

Bual

Malmsey

Estufagem

Mutage

Mistela

Mosto cotto

VDN

Rancio

Mistelles

Sticky

QUESTIONS

1. Outline the port method of making fortified wine.

2. How does the sherry method differ from the port method?

3. Where is true Porto made?

4. What are the key grapes for making Port?

5. Describe the different styles of wood-aged Port.

6. Discuss the styles of bottle-aged Port.

7. What is the solera system? Describe how it works.

8. What are the two families of Sherries and what styles are in each family?

9. Compare and contrast Madeira to Port and Sherry.

10. What are the four major styles of Madeira?

11. Describe the estufagem process in Madeira production.

12. What are vins doux naturels?

chapter 24

Sparkling and Fortified Wine Service

*S*pecialty wines deserve special treatment. The romance of sparkling wines practically demands special ceremony in their service. Fortified wines, with their high alcohol content, are not consumed the same way as table wines. Each has its own style of service, glassware requirements, and food pairings.

Upon completion of this chapter, the student should be able to:

> *Describe the ideal conditions for storing sparkling and fortified wine*
> *Discuss the proper service temperatures for sparkling and fortified wine*
> *Outline proper sparkling and fortified wine service*
> *Discuss proper food and wine pairings for sparking and fortified wines*

Sparkling Wine

Sparkling wines of all kinds are equated with celebration and romance. They are not, however, very amenable to spontaneity. These wines need special treatment in order to be at their optimum when it is time for service.

SPARKLING WINE STORAGE

The storage of sparkling wines is similar to that for table wines. For nonvintage sparkling wines, the wine is ready to be consumed upon release. The sparkling wine houses make these wines to be consistent in style and taste year after year. So there is no need to purchase and store wine until it is optimally ready to drink. Vintage wines, on the other hand, should be treated as many top-quality table wines. These expressions of a single year are consumable upon purchase, but often improve with age. When purchased, the vintage sparkling wine can be stored as a table wine; that is to say, on its side to maintain a moist cork and at a constant temperature, preferably 55°F (13°C).

SPARKLING WINE SERVICE TEMPERATURES

The temperature range for serving most sparkling wine is 40–45°F (5–8°C), effectively the temperature of a refrigerator. This is beneficial to the enjoyment of the wine for several reasons. First, the low temperature decreases the pressure of the carbon dioxide in the bottle. This makes the wine easier to open, and there is less chance of spillage from wine frothing out of the bottle. The cold temperature also makes pouring easier, restraining the frothing of the mousse so the wine does not lose too much carbonation. In the glass, the wine retains the carbonation longer. On the palate, the high acidity of the wine is mollified by the temperature. The wine is crisp and refreshing rather than acrid and strong as it would be at warmer temperatures.

There are times when sparkling wine can be served at a warmer temperature. Vintage Champagne that has aged for an extended period of time (say eight to ten years or more) can be served around 45–50°F (7–10°C). For these wines, the carbonation is secondary and the increased aromatic profile needs a slightly warmer temperature to fully appreciate it.

SPARKLING WINE SERVICE

The service of sparkling wine requires extra care compared to the service of a still table wine. With the contents of the bottle under as much as 6 atmospheres of pressure (about 100 pounds pushing on the end of the cork), caution is the primary concern in opening a bottle of bubbly.

The mise en place for sparkling wine service is:

The glassware (flutes)

The wine

A corkscrew

A serviette or napkin

A small side plate and a coaster

An ice bucket and stand

The following is a step-by-step procedure on sparkling wine service.

1. Approach the table with the appropriate glassware. From the guest's right side, place the glass on the right-hand side of the guest. The placement of glasses echoes the order of pouring the wine, with the host's glass placed last.

2. Place a small plate near the right side of the host, and a coaster in the center of the table.

3. Bring the wine to the table in a wine bucket draped with a napkin. Place it in view of the table, especially the host, but do not encroach the table.

4. Remove the wine from the bucket and wipe with the napkin.

5. Cradle the wine in the napkin and present to the host from the right-hand side. Confirm wine, vintage, and producer.

6. After receiving confirmation from the host, return the bottle to the ice bucket. Remove a portion of the foil capsule, cutting far enough down the neck with the knife on the corkscrew to expose the cage.

7. Remove the foil cap and inspect for mold or leakage. Place the cap on the small plate or in your pocket (depending on the policy of the restaurant).

   From this point forward, keep your thumb on the cork. Also, while removing the cage is described below, it is acceptable to leave the cage in place in order to have a better grip.

8. Untwist the hasp of the wire cage until the cage is loosened. This should be six turns. Pull the wire surrounding the neck away from the bottle. *Keep your thumb on the cork at all times. This, and subsequent steps, should be done with a napkin covering the cork to catch any forceful release of the cork.*

9. Shifting your thumb slightly, place the thumb under the cage on the cork, and remove the cage. Check the inside of the cage, or the plaquette, for mold or evidence of seepage. Place the cage on the small plate.

A variation of this step is to leave the cage on the cork to provide a better grip while trying to remove the cork.

10. Slowly twist the cork, all the while maintaining control over it. Once loosened, the cork may push strongly against your hand to release the pressure. You may feel more like you are holding the cork in than allowing it to quickly pop out.

11. Remove the cork with as little sound as possible. A hiss is best, but a small pop is acceptable. Check the mirror of the cork and place it on the small plate.

12. Wipe the neck of the bottle inside and out.

13. Remove the bottle from the bucket, wiping the excess moisture from the bottle. Hold the bottle in one hand, either by inserting your thumb in the punt (the depression in the bottom of the bottle), or by cradling the bottle with a napkin at its base. Hold the bottle so the label is visible to the host.

14. Pour a one-ounce taste for the host.

15. Receive confirmation that the wine is acceptable to be poured.

16. Proceed to pour the wine for the guests. Start with the first woman to the left of the host; proceed to serve all the women, then the men, then the host. Pour very slowly in one motion. If the wine foams too much, stop pouring and wait for the mousse to subside. Commence pouring wine to fill the glass between 60 and 70 percent full. Make sure to wipe the neck of the bottle between pours to collect drips.

17. Ask the host if the temperature of the wine is acceptable, and if he or she would like it back in the ice bucket or on the coaster to warm slightly.

18. Remove the small plate with the cork, cage, and foil as you leave the table.

Food and Sparkling Wine Pairing

Matching food to sparkling wines is something most people do not often consider. Sparkling wine is typically considered an aperitif wine, drunk before dinner begins or as a toast. However, many sparkling wines are great food wines, and entire menus may be paired just to sparkling wines.

CLASSIC PAIRINGS

The classic sparkling wine pairing is Champagne and caviar. There are many levels on which this pairing works. First, from the taste component perspective, there is

Turn the hasp six and a half times to release the hold of the cage. (The napkin has been removed here for illustration purposes.)

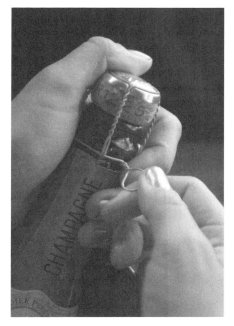

If removing the cage before extracting the cork, make sure a thumb is always on the cork to prevent accidental projection.

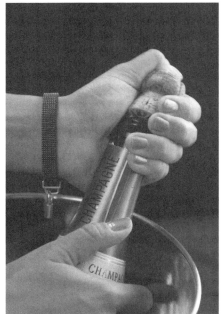

The bottle and cork are turned until the cork can be carefully removed and the pressure gently released.

Sparkling wine should be poured in a single motion to fill the glass three-quarters full. Allow the mousse to subside before topping off the glass.

the interplay of acid and salt. The saltiness of the caviar moderates the acidity of the Champagne. Caviar is also high in fat, which the acidity and the effervescence of the Champagne cuts through, encouraging another bite of caviar. Caviar's saltiness can be described as briny, which complements the minerality of the Champagne. Even the accompaniments in caviar service work well with Champagne. Egg, sour cream, and buckwheat blinis are typically served with caviar. Champagne can cut the richness of the egg and sour cream, while the wine's acidity matches that in the sour cream. The aging of Champagne provides a creaminess that is duplicated in the sour cream, but also a toastiness and earthiness that is matched in the blinis. This does not even take into consideration the textural matching (tiny bursting eggs with tiny bubbles) or luxury matching.

Another classic pair with Champagne is oysters. The briny character of the oyster matches the minerality found in the wine. Oysters are also very rich, and the acidity and the effervescence helps to cut that richness. Finally, there is the air of luxury that surrounds a platter of oysters on the half shell, which matches with the Champagne.

EVERYDAY PAIRING

Sparkling wines can be assessed as any other table wine. They have bright, crisp acidity and low alcohol. This makes them great wines for pairing with different dishes. As discussed in Chapter 4, high acidity in wine can pair with a variety of other tastes. Foods that are salty or have high fat content pair well with the crisp wine. Thus, sparkling wines are excellent matches for cream sauces, cheese, rich fish like salmon, and anything that is very buttery.

The addition of the bubbles allows for textural matches as well. The fizz is a great counterpoint to crisp foods. This could be something deep-fried, or wrapped in phyllo or puff pastry. Matching these foods is also enhanced by the toasty or biscuity flavors and aromas of a methode traditionelle wine.

More fruit-forward wines, such as sparklers from Australia or California, can be used just as fruit-forward still wines. Foods with natural sweetness, such as shellfish, or fresh produce-driven dishes are wonderful with a fruity sparkler.

Because of the low alcohol and lack of oak, sparkling wines fit with many ethnic cuisines. Champagne and other Old World sparkling wines can be served with Chinese, Thai, Vietnamese, or Japanese cuisine. The spiciness of these cuisines works with the low alcohol and the bubbles. Some wines with higher dosage, like a demi-sec, will also work well with more piquant dishes. The rules of food and sparkling wine pairing still are in play (that is, matching weight, intensity of flavor, and contrasting complexity). An example would be a pairing of Cochinita Pibil with Prosecco. Cochinita Pibil is a Yucatan preparation of braised pork, with the flavors of orange, achiote, and jalapeño. Prosecco cuts through the richness of the pork, while enhancing the flavors of orange and achiote. Because it is a light, low-alcohol wine, the piquancy of the jalapeño is moderated while the fruitiness of the chile is enhanced.

Of course, just because a wine is sparkling does not mean it is automatically a match. For example, if the course is nigiri sushi, made with tuna, yellowtail, and salmon, a big, yeasty Champagne would be out of place. The autolytic character would overpower the delicacy of the fish and rice. On the other hand, a Blanc de Blancs or a light, tank method wine like Prosecco may be a better match.

It is possible to match an entire menu to sparkling wines, based on their variation in styles. Early courses start light with Blanc de Blancs or another light style. This could build through the variety of house styles available as the dishes get weightier and more intense. Entrees may need a Blanc de Noirs, or a rosé as the pairing, depending on the protein and preparation. Dessert is an easy match, with something from Asti, or a demi-sec methode traditionelle wine.

Fortified Wines

Fortified wines were originally made to survive long voyages at sea. The increased alcohol content that stabilized the wine makes drinking an entire bottle difficult. It is the high alcohol content that drives the service of fortified wines.

FORTIFIED WINE STORAGE

The wide variety of fortified wines requires a range of approaches toward storage. Many fortified wines are bottled with the intention that they are consumed upon purchase. There are others, namely vintage port, which have special requirements for storage.

Sherry

All Sherries are bottled with the intention that they are ready to drink. Because they are the product of oxidative aging, no time is necessary for them to develop in the bottle before opening. This is reinforced by the type of cork used for the bottle closure. The T-stop is not meant to allow slow diffusion of oxygen through the cork portion; it is meant to be an aid in opening the bottle for consumption. Therefore, Sherries can be bought close to time of service, or if stored, can be considered short-term and kept upright on a shelf.

After opening, Sherries have a slightly longer shelf life than most table wines, but they are not indestructible. The Fino styles of Sherry have a shorter lifespan than Olorosos. Open Finos and Manzanillas can last for just shy of a week if kept sealed and cold when not being served. Olorosos can survive for a couple of weeks under the same conditions, and Amontillados last somewhere in between these times. Of course, these wines are best when first opened and will lose some freshness over this open period. Any wine not suitable for a casual sip can still be utilized for cooking.

Port

Most Port is bottled with its aging complete. Ruby, Tawny, and age-indicated Tawnies are all ready to drink. They are sealed with T-stop closures and can be stored standing upright, if not purchased immediately before service. Colheita styles, while vintage dated, have been aged in barrels long enough that further aging in the bottle is unnecessary. They also can be stored upright.

The two styles of Port that need long-term storage are crusted and vintage ports. Both of these wines are aged only two or three years in barrels, because the style dictates reductive, or bottle, aging. Vintage and Crusted Ports should be stored like any other wine intended for long-term aging: horizontally, at 55°F (13°F), with low light, no vibration, and 75 percent humidity. These wines are meant to age for ten to twenty years, so cork health is of utmost importance when storing.

As with Sherry, Ports have different shelf lives after opening depending upon their style. The wines that retain freshness and flavors for the shortest period of time are the crusted and vintage Ports. Because they have not been exposed to oxygen, and have many components of reductive aging that are susceptible to oxygen, these wines are at their peak for only a couple of days after opening. While they could be decanted and kept for future consumption, the quality and complexity of the wine will decrease quickly with time. Ruby Ports have the next shortest lifespan. They have had the least amount of barrel aging, and therefore are still susceptible to the effects of oxygen. These wines are at their peak for a week or two after opening, then degrade. Tawny Ports have the longest life after opening, probably close to a month. These wines have had the most extensive barrel aging, and therefore exposure to oxygen. They retain their flavor after opening the longest, and degradation of flavor begins when the oxygen begins to interact with the alcohol.

Madeira

Madeiras are wines that have had everything done to them. They have been oxidatively aged, and also subjected to slow heating. These are the world's indestructible wines. Once they are bottled, Madeiras will not change with further aging. Therefore, it is not necessary to purchase wines for storage. Madeiras are closed with T-stop closures, and may be stored upright. Even vintage Madeiras can be treated this way, because they will no longer age in bottle.

Once a bottle of Madeira is open, it can last for a long time. It is possible to transfer Madeira to decanters and keep them on the bar. Because the wine has already been oxidized and heated, there is not much that can happen to the wine after the bottle is opened.

Aromatized Wines

Wines such as Vermouth should be treated as Fino Sherries, if they are to be consumed on their own. The fresh quality of Vermouth will disappear within a few days of opening. If the Vermouth is used as a mixer, say in a martini, then the wine can be kept for several weeks.

FORTIFIED WINE SERVICE TEMPERATURES

Fortified wines are often considered decanter wines; that is, wines that are put into decanters and set upon the bar for consumption over a period of time. This presumes that room temperature is the correct temperature for consumption, and in many cases it is not.

Service temperature is important in fortified wines for several reasons. The higher alcohol level can seem out of proportion and harsh if the temperature is too warm. For some wines with higher acidity, too warm a temperature would also make the wine seem acrid rather than refreshing. Finally, wines like Port that may still contain tannins would be best at a warmer temperature, to prevent the astringency from dominating the palate.

See the fortified wine service temperature table for a list of fortified wines and their best service temperatures.

Fortified Wine Service Temperatures

Fortified Wine	Service Temperature
Fino Sherry	45–50°F (7–10°C)
Amontillado Sherry	55–60°F (13–15°C)
Oloroso Sherry	60–65°F (15–18°C)
Ruby Port	57–62°F (14–17°C)
Tawny Port	50–55°F (10–13°C)
Age-indicated Tawny	55–60°F (13–15°C)
Vintage Port	62–68°F (17–20°C)
Madeira	55–62°F (13–17°C)

FORTIFIED WINE SERVICE

The service of fortified wines differs from that of table wines. It is very uncommon for the whole bottle of wine to be served and consumed in one sitting. Opening most types, except Vintage Port, involves taking off the capsule and removing the T-stop closure.

Individual service of fortified wines necessitates smaller portions. Port or Sherry glasses typically hold only two to three ounces. Some Port glasses are larger, which allows for swirling the wine and enjoyment of the aromas.

Vintage Port Service

Vintage Port service is identical to red wine decantation (see Chapter 4) with two possible exceptions. First, if the bottle is very old, it may not be possible to use a corkscrew to remove the cork because it will fall apart. In this case, *port tongs* are necessary. To use port tongs, heat them until they are red hot. Place the tongs around the neck of the bottle below the bottom of the cork. Once the heat of the tongs has been transferred to the bottle, remove the tongs and wrap the neck with a towel or napkin that has been dampened with cold water. The bottle should crack smoothly where the tongs were applied. The decantation may now proceed. The second exception is an additional piece of equipment during the decantation. Some sommeliers prefer the use of a port filter during decantation. Place the filter in the decanter such that the base of the funnel is against the side wall of the decanter. Slowly decant through the funnel, and stop if a large amount of sediment begins to appear in the funnel. Remove the funnel before service. The funnel not only catches any sediment that escapes the bottle during pouring, but also helps to aerate the wine, making it more enjoyable.

Food and Fortified Wine Pairing

Just as white wine with white meat is not a meaningful recommendation for pairing food and table wine, there is not a single best pairing or generalization that can be made for fortified wines. Special considerations need to be made for the high alcohol content and for any sweetness that may be inherent to the specific fortified wine.

SHERRY

Different styles of Sherry match to different types of food, though there are some similarities. The oxidized character of all Sherries will make many of the pairings similar. Common items that work well with dry Sherries are almonds, hard cheeses, fried foods, seafood, cured ham, and olives. Sweeter-style Sherries, like Cream

Sherry, work best with blue cheeses, and dried fruits or nut desserts. Extremely sweet Sherry, like PX, is more of a dessert wine. It can be paired with chocolate, nut desserts, caramelized desserts, and even poured over ice cream.

PORT

Port is definitely a dessert wine. There are two classic pairings for Port. First is a savory pairing with Stilton or other blue cheese. The combination of sweet wine and salty cheese is a great contrasting combination. With Stilton, it is said that a third flavor appears that is not in the wine or cheese, that of butterscotch. The second combination for Port, especially Ruby Port, is chocolate. The trick with this pairing is to use semi- to bittersweet chocolate. Chocolate that is too sweet, like milk chocolate, will overpower the Port and accentuate its tannins. The usual accompaniment with cheese or chocolate is walnuts, which also match well to the port.

Individual styles of Port can pair with items that are mirrored in their flavor profile. Ruby Port is good for fruit desserts made from berries, cherries, or plums. Tawnies have less fruit flavor and more nuttiness, so nut-based desserts or fruit desserts made from apples or pears are more appropriate.

MADEIRA

Madeira spans a range of sweetness levels, and the drier versions can be served early in the meal with soup or rich savory items as well as dessert. For Madeira, it is often best to match the complex nutty, caramel, and dried fruit characteristics when pairing with food. As with Port and Cream Sherry, Madeira is great with blue cheese or some milder rind-ripened cheeses, like Taleggio. Dessert pairings can range from caramel and nut-based desserts to custard and dried fruit desserts to spiced items like pumpkin pie or coffee-flavored items.

QUESTIONS

1. How should sparkling wine be stored?

2. Outline the proper service temperatures for serving sparkling wine.

3. Outline proper sparkling wine service.

4. Describe a classic food and sparkling wine pairing and explain why it works.

5. What everyday foods are good pairings with sparkling wines?

6. How should fortified wine be stored?

7. Outline proper service temperatures for fortified wines.

8. What is a proper serving size for a fortified wine?

9. Describe the unique needs of vintage port service.

10. What are the food pairing possibilities for Port?

11. What are the food pairing possibilities for the different styles of Sherry?

PART SIX
beer, spirits, and liqueurs

A *beverage program in a hospitality setting is not complete without the other two most common alcoholic beverages: beer and spirits. Beer can be as complex as wine, with differences based on ingredients, water, and method of brewing. These differences are reflected in the flavor profiles, as well as the methods of pairing beer and wine. Spirits are influenced by their starting products and their methods of distillation. Each type of spirit has its own flavor profile and particular form of service when not used in a cocktail.*

Chapter 25 Beer

Chapter 26 How Spirits and Liqueurs Are Made

Chapter 27 Fruit-Based Spirits

Chapter 28 Grain-Based Spirits

Chapter 29 Vegetable-Based Spirits

chapter 25

Beer

*B*eer is one of the most popular alcoholic beverages on the planet. It can be made in regions that cannot grow grapes, and can be made as needed, as long as there is grain around.

It could be said that beer is too simple or too "blue collar" to be part of a sommelier's repertoire. That is too simple a view of beer. With almost as many styles as wine, beer is a complex, nuanced, versatile beverage that matches with food or can stand on its own.

Upon completion of this chapter, the student should be able to:

Discuss the ingredients necessary for making beer
Describe the process of beer brewing
Outline the styles of beer and the variations within those styles
Describe proper storage and service of beers
Discuss food and beer pairings

What Is Beer?

Beer is the result of using grain and water to make an alcoholic beverage. Styles vary depending on the type of grain used, the level of toasting of the grain, and the type of yeast used.

INGREDIENTS

Barley

The key ingredient to making any beer is barley. While other grains can be utilized in the process, barley has special properties that make it a necessary ingredient. Barley contains up to 80 percent starch reserves, and an enzyme called diastase that can convert those starch reserves into fermentable sugar.

Not all barley is created equal. There are two types of barley, two-row and six-row, named for how the kernels form on the stalks. Two-row barley is grown in cooler climates, and is softer barley than six-row. While two-row is the preferred barley of small brewers and traditionalists, six-row is the barley of choice for many commercial brewers.

Barley serves as the source of sugar for fermentation, but it must go through a conversion process for that sugar to be accessible. In the barley kernel, the main ingredient is starch, which yeast cannot digest. The conversion process is called *malting*.

The Malting Process

In order to get the barley starch converted to sugar, the grains must become *malt*. The first step involves steeping the grains in water. The grains absorb water until they reach about 40–45 percent moisture content, which allows the grain to begin germinating. The barley kernels are drained and brought to the malting floor, where they are allowed to sprout, which activates the enzyme *diastase*. The enzyme begins the conversion of starch into sugar, presumably so the new sprout can grow. After about five days, the germination process is arrested by drying the sprouting kernel before the starch can be consumed. Depending on the temperature at which the barley is dried, the diastase may or may not remain active.

Malt

Drying the malt at a lower temperature allows the enzymes to remain active while keeping any sugars from caramelizing. Higher temperatures create specialty malts, most of which have inactive enzymes and caramelized sugars. The base malt in any brewing process is called *pale malt*. It is dried at around 122°F (50°C). Specialty malts are made by either heating the barley before it is dry, or by roasting the dried malt.

Crystal malt is made by controlled heating of wet malted barley. As the temperature is increased, more sugar is produced inside the kernel. Eventually, the sugars that form in the malt will crystallize upon cooling. Crystal malt contains residual soluble starches and sweetness. Crystal malt, also known as *caramel malt,* also comes in a range of colors based on caramelization of the sugars.

Amber malt is made by heating the wet malt at slightly higher temperatures than crystal malt. The result is a reddish color and a crackerlike flavor profile. This is a British style of malt. The German version is called *Vienna malt,* and contains active enzymes. *Munich malt* is toasted even more than Vienna malt, and also contains active enzymes.

The darkest malts are *chocolate malt* and *black patent malt.* Chocolate malt is roasted to a dark brown. It is used to impart nutty and toasted flavors while retaining sweetness and aromatics. Black patent malt is heated to carbonization. It provides lots of color, and the burnt character of the malt will contribute coffee and bitter notes.

It should be noted that except for the large commercial breweries, the ingredient that is purchased by the brewer is malt, not raw barley. Many brewers do not have the means to sprout their own grain, but rather purchase whatever malt they will need for the beer recipe they will be making.

Hops

The main flavoring ingredient for beer is *hops*. Historically, many different items have been used to flavor and help preserve beer. Some items, such as ginger, wormwood, cinnamon, and others can be found in some specialty beers. However, these items have lost ground in the last couple of centuries because of the ease of cultivation and usage of hops.

Hops are used to add bitterness, tannin, and aroma to beer. These attributes come from the oils found inside the hop flowers. One set of insoluble oils provide bitterness to beer. More soluble oils provide aromatics. It is not uncommon for a brewer to use more than one type of hops in order to achieve the balance of aroma and bitterness that they desire. Cascade is an all-purpose hops variety from Washington State. Fuggles is used in British-style brews, along with Kent Goldings. Halltertauer and Saaz are Eastern European hops noted for their aromatics.

Yeast

Beer is brewed with one of two strains of *Saccharomyces.* The yeast strain with the longest history is *Saccharomyces cerevisiae.* This is the same yeast that is used in wine making. This yeast ferments best at warmer temperatures and forms a floating cap of foam on top of the fermentation vessel. The resulting style of beer that is produced is *ale.* Ales have a fruitier flavor profile and have creamy, soft carbonation.

Bavarian brewers noticed that beer stored in ice caves in the Alps produced a different style of beer. Once yeast was discovered by Louis Pasteur, a new strain of yeast was isolated that lived on the bottom of the fermentation vessel. The strain was isolated at the Carlsberg Brewery, and is called *Saccharomyces carlsbergensis*. The style of beer produced is *lager,* a name taken from *lagerung* or "storage" in German. Lagers are crisp and clean tasting, with more effervescent carbonation.

Water

Every brewery is proud of the source of their water. It is a major marketing point for even large commercial breweries. Water seems like it would just be a neutral base, and that would not have much of an effect on beer. However, the dissolved minerals in the water will affect the final taste. Soft water makes for softer mouthfeel in beers, and is typical for lager-style beers. More full-bodied ales use hard water, or high mineral content. Breweries may alter the mineral content of their water if it does not meet the requirements of the style of beer they are making. To make a Pale Ale similar to Bass Ale, breweries will add salts to their water to increase the mineral content close to what is in the water for Bass.

Adjuncts

Some styles of beer use other grains in addition to malted barley. Wheat is a common additive in Europe. In Germany, the wheat is malted before it is used, while in Belgium unmalted wheat is preferred. The use of wheat changes the flavor and the color of the beer.

Large-scale commercial breweries also use *adjuncts*, but for different reasons. The most common adjuncts are rice and corn. Both of these are cheaper than barley, and they do not provide any additional flavor to the beer. Instead, they are there to provide starch that will be converted to sugar. The use of adjuncts allows a beer to achieve the desired alcohol content, while keeping the flavor profile light. Corn and rice are merely steamed before use, not malted. This also keeps the flavor neutral.

How Beer Is Made

There are five major steps in the transformation of grain into beer. The first, *conversion,* is the malting process described above. While conversion is an important step in the process, most brewers start with grains that have already been malted.

Even if the malt contains plenty of sugars, it is not in a liquid form that makes a beverage. The process to get the sugars into water is called *extraction*. The malt is coarsely ground into what is known as *grist*. The grist and water are combined in a *mash tun,* a large copper vessel that will stir the mix and also control the temperature of the mix. Temperature control is important, typically starting around 120°F (49°F) and eventually ending at 160°F (71°C). The combination of temperature and agitation extracts the sugars and starches out of the grist. The temperature is also held in the range where diastase works quickly. Thus, as starch is extracted from the grist, the diastase quickly converts it to sugar.

After extraction, the liquid, now called *wort,* is transferred to a copper vessel where it will be boiled. The spent grist is sometimes washed to remove any remaining starch and sugar, in a process called *sparging.* The wash liquid is added to the wort, and the sweet liquid is then boiled for up to two hours. Boiling the wort deactivates the enzymes, and also help to precipitate proteins and other impurities that would cloud the final beer.

It is during this boiling period that the first addition of hops occurs. This is called *flavoring.* The hops added at this time provide bitterness to the final beer.

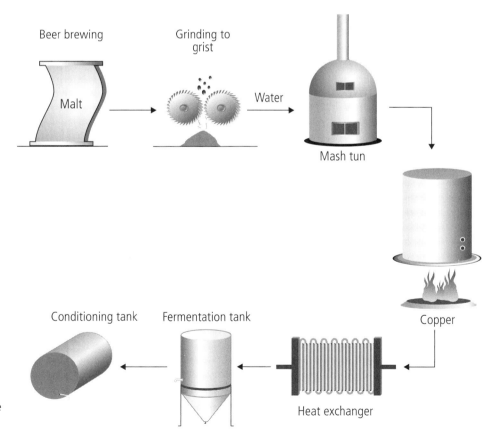

The basic procedure for brewing beer.

Any aromatics from the hops will boil away in the two-hour period; this will be added later.

The wort must be cooled before the next step, *fermentation*. The cooled wort is put into the fermentation vessel, and fermentation begins with *pitching the yeast,* or adding it to the wort. The fermentation of an ale will take three to seven days, depending on the temperature and the amount of sugar present. Lagers, fermented at lower temperatures, ferment for two weeks. Toward the end of the fermentation, the second addition of hops occurs. This is called *dry hopping,* and infuses the beer with the aromatic components of the hop flowers.

The last step, *conditioning,* varies between ales and lagers. Ales are placed into conditioning vessels or casks and sit for a few days. This allows the carbonation to develop and any remaining yeast to precipitate from the beer. Lagers are stored for two to four weeks at 32°F (0°C), which not only clarifies the beer, but also develops a crisp, sparkling carbonation.

Styles of Beer

As mentioned earlier, there are two major families of beers, ales and lagers, dependent on which strain of yeast is used. Within these families are many styles, based mainly on the use of malts to make the beer. There is also a unique style of ale made in Belgium that classifies as its own family of beers, the lambics.

ALES

The term "ale" is used to indicate a beer that is top-fermented, and that will have a fruity aroma and mild hops character. As a style, it is popular in the British Isles, where most of the beers made are ales. Within the category of ales there is a great deal of variation. The classic styles are described below.

Pale Ale

The name is not the best descriptor for this style of ale. The British-developed style is typically bronze to amber red in color, though clear. The term "pale ale" comes from the fact that the ale is not dark brown or black and opaque. Pale ale is made with amber malt, which imparts not only the color to the ale, but also a mild nuttiness. While the ale contains hops, the noteworthy character of the beer is the malty nuttiness on the finish, rather than a hoppy bitterness.

The style originated in Burton-on-Trent in England. The water of the area has a high calcium content, which makes the ale more full bodied, extends the length of the finish, and helps support the bitterness of the hops. In other areas of the world where a pale ale is the desired style, additional calcium salts are often added to the water in a process that has come to be known as *Burtonization*.

India Pale Ale

Burton exported much of its pale ale via river and ocean traffic. A great deal of that ale made its way to British colonies around the world, in particular to India. In order for the beer to survive the journey to India without being infected by bacteria or wild yeast, the ale was loaded with hops. India Pale Ales, or *IPAs*, are noted for extremely strong hop character. The ale is more full bodied than regular pale ale, with a distinct hop nose, and strong bitterness.

Brown Ale

Brown ales are northern England's answer to the pale ales of the Midlands. Brown ale is very malty in character, with very light hops. It is a reddish-brown ale, from amber and a dash of chocolate malt, and has both a fruitiness and a nutty character with a dry finish. Brown ales from southern England tend to be lower in alcohol, darker, and retain their malty sweetness.

Trappist Ale

The designation *Trappist ale* indicates a beer that has been made in a Trappist monastery. Six monasteries (Orval, Chimay, Rochefort, Westmalle, Sint Sixtus, and Schaapskooi) are the only Trappist breweries in the world. The name is not necessarily a designation of style, since many of the breweries make multiple styles. However, they do have a common pedigree. All the ales are top fermented and bottle conditioned (meaning a secondary fermentation in the bottle to produce carbonation). This means lots of yeast sediment, but also a very winey character—fruity and aromatic.

Stout and Porter

Most of the deep, dark ales on the market today are *stouts*. Stouts actually are a fuller-bodied version of the original Porter style. These dark beers developed as a dark, roasty, lightly fruity beer. Stout, originally stout porter, has come to embody the style, with both dry and sweet versions.

Dry stouts have a strong roasty, coffee flavor, strong hop bitterness, and a bit of fruity acidity. The quintessential dry stout is Guinness. Dry stout is not high in alcohol, yet seems satisfying due to the strong flavors and rich mouthfeel. The dryness acts like an aperitif, encouraging the appetite, though the beer seems filling.

Sweet stouts are made by the addition of sugar to the pasteurized beer before bottling. Pasteurization is necessary to prevent any stray yeast from fermenting the added sugar in the bottle. Cream or milk stouts derived their name from the addition of lactose to the brew before fermentation. Yeast cannot ferment lactose, so the sugar remains in the final ale, and provides a richness and sweetness to the brew. Oatmeal stout is a recent development, and oatmeal typically makes up a percentage of grain in the single digits. But even the use of that little amount of oatmeal produces a brew that is silky and sweet, to complement the chocolate and coffee flavors.

LAGERS

Lagers are the result of bottom fermentation at low temperatures and cold storage. This produces a beer that is foamy, clear, clean, crisp, and refreshing. The style originated in Bavaria, with the storage of beer in Alpine ice caves, but has since spread and is now equated with beers from Eastern Europe as well as Germany. As with ale, color is not an indicator of fermentation temperature, just of choice of malts.

Pilsner

Named for the city of Pilzn in the Czech Republic, *pilsner* is a golden lager that has taken over the beer world. The majority of the world's beer is made in a Pilsner style. Pilsner should have medium body and alcohol content, and is most noted for its light malt character and its distinctive hops bitterness and aroma. It is the aroma that distinguishes this beer. Every country has its dominant Pilsner style beer, from Budweiser to Stella Artois, Beck's, and Heineken.

Dortmunder Export

Often known just as export, this lager is not as aromatic as a Pilsner, and is more alcoholic. An export has more hops character, and is more bitter than a Pilsner, with less malty influences. It is lower in carbonation and therefore does not produce as foamy a head when poured. Exports are fuller bodied due to more unfermentable sugars in the wort.

Marzen or Vienna-Style Lagers

These beers are similar in color to a good pale ale. They are amber-red or bronze, and emphasize the malt character on the nose and the palate, giving it a certain sweetness. This beer gets its name from the month of March, typically the end of brewing season. This style is full bodied and higher in alcohol content, because it has to last through the summer until it is time to brew again. So the increased alcohol and body enables the beer to survive months of storage.

Bock

The darkest of the lagers is *Bock*. The name derives from Einbeck, a village in Germany whose local beer style is emulated. A Bock is a strong lager, often among the strongest beers. It was originally exported from Einbeck, which forced a stronger style to be made to survive the journey. It is a smooth beer, with strong malty character and a bit of sweetness. Even-stronger versions are called *doppelbocks.*

There are plenty of stories around the origin of Bock. It was made seasonally, and one legend states it is the beer made when the brewers clean their kettles at the end of the season. Sanitation aside, this is not true. Bock also translates to "billy goat," and some theories attribute the beer to being made during Capricorn, or having the kick of a goat. The seasonality of the style probably developed because the people of Eisbeck would brew a May bock (*Maibock*), whose release coincided with the end of the brewing season.

LAMBICS

This beer family is almost exclusive to Belgium, especially a small area around Brussels. The most striking distinction of *lambics* is their dependence on wild yeasts to do the fermentation. With the indigenous flora in the brewery, lambics have a distinct tartness and are often the base for fruit beers.

A lambic requires that a minimum of 30 percent, and sometimes up to 50 percent, unmalted wheat be used in the mash. This creates a beer that is lighter in color and flavor than one that is straight malt. True lambics are almost flat, with minimal carbonation and a distinct earthiness on the nose.

Lambic production differs from normal beer production in a few ways. First, the wheat and malt combine to create a milky white mash. The wort requires a boil of at least three hours, longer than normal. Hops are added, but not for flavor or aroma. In this style, hops are used as a preservative, meaning fresh hops are not used, but rather older, aged hops that have lost some of their aroma and bitterness. Finally, the cooled wort is placed in a shallow pan and placed in the fermentation room. That room, often the attic, has open windows and allows the wild yeasts to inoculate the brew.

There may be up to seventy different microorganisms that "ferment" the lambic. Two of the most important are from the genus *Brettanomyces,* a relative of brewer's yeast that yields aromas reminiscent of horse blanket or sweat (considered a fault in wine production). Other forms of yeast are similar to that of flor in Sherry making. The result is not only an alcoholic fermentation, but also a lactic one. This produces a beer with very vinous character, as well as a tartness from lactic acid. The lambic is then aged in wooden barrels for up to three years, during which more reactions and fermentations occur.

Gueuze

While true lambics are hard to find, a modification of the style is readily available. *Gueuze* is a blended lambic, combining old and new beers. The addition of new lambic (with its incomplete fermentation) to old lambic (with its host of micro-organisms) starts a secondary fermentation that carbonates the beer. The result is a Champagne-like beer. It has toastiness and acidity, it is complex and has carbonation reminiscent of Champagne, but with a longer lifespan. The final beer, depending on the brewer, may have a touch of sweetness or may be strictly dry.

Fruit Beers

Not all fruit beers are made from lambic. There are versions made from lagers and from dark ales. Here the discussion will be strictly about lambic-based fruit beers. The production of fruit-flavored lambics is a recollection of former flavoring components of beer before hops. Because lambics are wheat beers, hops are not the best flavoring ingredient. Instead, fruit such as cherries or raspberries complement the natural fruitiness of the lambic.

To make a fruit lambic, the brewer will add whole fruit to the barrels of fermenting beer. The beer is typically made in the spring, and the fruit from the fall harvest is added. After a month or two, the full flavor of the fruit has been extracted into the beer. Some producers may age their beers longer, but the beer will typically be bottled and released close to two years after it was initially brewed. The traditional styles are *kriek* (cherry) and *frambozen* (raspberry), though it is possible to find *pomme* (apple), *peche* (peach), and *cassis* (black currant) versions.

WHEAT BEER

There are two styles of wheat beers, one from northern Germany and one from southern Germany. The northern German beer is known as *Weisse*, or white beer. It is made with a small proportion of malted wheat added to the barley, and a minimal amount of hops. The fermentation occurs not only with yeast, but also with cultivated lactic bacteria. These bacterial perform the same function as they would during a wine's malolactic fermentation. They convert harsh acids to softer ones. The result is a beer with a distinct lactic tartness. Because of that tartness, weisse beer is often served with a shot of syrup, either an herbal woodruff syrup or raspberry.

The wheat beers of southern Germany are known as *Weizen* (wheat) beers. They are also made with malted wheat, but the emphasis on the lactic fermentation is not there. These are light, summery beers, meant to be refreshing. They can be served filtered or unfiltered, indicated by the hefe (yeast) added to the name, *Hefeweizen*. These beers have a distinct fruitiness, similar to apples, or even tropical fruits like banana and pineapple. They also have a clovelike character when extremely fresh. Hops do not play an important role in these beers. They are occasionally served with a slice of lemon, to highlight the refreshing quality and accentuate the acidity of the beer.

Storage and Service of Beer

Storage and service of beers, both ales and lagers, can significantly affect the overall flavor and enjoyment of the beverage. While many people consider it "just beer," the explosion of microbrews, craft beers, and imports suggests otherwise. Proper storage, glassware, and service of beer is important to its ultimate enjoyment.

STORAGE

All beers, whether they are ale or lager, have many of the same storage requirements. The two handling mistakes that are most destructive to beer flavor are light and temperature abuse.

Light, and in particular ultraviolet light, can significantly alter the taste and aroma of beer. This is because the aromatic oils from hops are extremely sensitive to ultraviolet light. If beer is exposed to sunlight for an extended period of time, the oils will become altered. The beer will take an aroma that is termed *skunky* because of its similarity to the aroma of that animal. In an attempt to prevent the beer becoming skunky, most beers are bottled in brown glass. The colored glass absorbs the ultraviolet light that alters the beer. Some beers are bottled in green or clear glass. Green glass offers some protection, but not as much as brown. Usually the beers bottled in clear glass either expect quick turnover of product or do not use significant levels of aromatic hops. Canned beer and *kegs* (large bulk barrels) do not have issues with light.

Temperature abuse can alter the flavor of beer. It is extremely important with beers that are unpasteurized. Keg beer is typically unpasteurized, and is more sensitive to temperature changes. Keg beer must be kept cold from the time the keg leaves the brewery until it is served. Beer that is allowed to warm and then cool again is often deemed *bruised* because of the loss of quality. Most bottled and canned beer is pasteurized to kill any bacteria or any yeast that may continue fermentation. These items can be held at room temperature for a short period of time without bruising, but anything above room temperature will alter the quality of the beer.

SERVICE

Packaging

Beer is shipped to market in one of two forms, either individually bottled or canned, or in bulk kegs. Bottles and cans are the most popular forms for consuming beer. The common size of cans or bottles is 12 ounces, though sizes can range from a 7-ounce "pony" to a 25-ounce "oilcan." It is also possible to buy bottles up to 40 ounces. Alternative packaging for individual consumption includes plastic bottles (used where glass would be dangerous) and newly introduced aluminum bottles (lined to prevent a metallic taste).

Kegs are used for draft beer, where individual servings are poured from a tap, connected to the keg by lines. A full-sized keg can hold 15.5 gallons, or about two hundred 16-ounce servings. Smaller versions are available, allowing for better use of storage space and a wider selection for the customer. A similar version of keg beer is *cask-conditioned beer.* These beers are served from the barrel in which the beer was brewed. The cask, called a *firkin,* is kept on the bar, and the beer is drawn by hand pumping.

Service Temperatures

Not all beer has the same flavor and aroma profile, and therefore not every beer should be served at the same temperature. The clean, crisp taste of a lager is enhanced by a cooler service temperature, while the fruity aromas of ale benefit from warmer temperatures. Serving beer at refrigerator temperature only serves to mute the flavors and aromas of any style all together. For some beers service in a chilled, frosty glass is even too cold for the flavors and aromas.

Below is a rough guide to service temperatures and beer style.

Beer Service Temperatures

Description	Temperature	Beer Style
Cold	39–45°F/4–7°C	Hefeweizen
		Pilsner
Cool	45–54°F/8–12°C	American Pale Ale
		Fruit and Gueuze Lambic
		Dry Stout
		Bohemian Pilsner
		Dortmunder
		Vienna
		Sweet Stout
Cellar	54–57°F/12–14°C	Brown Ale
		India Pale Ale
		English Pale Ale
		Bock

Glassware

Glassware is as important to beer as it is to wine. The cleanliness is important for a proper serving, but some styles have signature glasses that enhance the enjoyment of the contents.

A variety of special beer glasses (left to right): German Pilsner, tulip, chalice, stem, pint glass.

No matter what the style of glass, it should always be *beer-clean*. This means the glass is free of oil, grease, film, and lint. The basic three-compartment sink at a bar is essential for proper cleaning of glassware. Often the culprit of a not-so-fresh glass of beer is poor drying. The final step to washing a glass involves a sanitizing rinse, either by machine or by hand. If the glass is not allowed to drain and dry properly, that chemical remains behind in the glass, flattening the foam and giving an off-taste. A truly beer-clean glass can be identified by the rings of foam left on the side of the glass as the consumer drinks the beer.

Several beers have specialty glassware. It would be unusual to have a stout in a tulip-shaped glass rather than a standard, straight-walled pint glass. That standard glass is necessary for the beer to make enough foam on top. Pilsners look as good as they taste in their tall, flutelike glass. The tall glass allows the carbonation to delicately rise through the liquid, like Champagne. Belgian ales are often served in tulip-shaped, short-stemmed glasses, which allows for the aromas to be savored like wine aromas.

A PROPER POUR

Pouring beer is more than just getting the liquid into the glass. Part of beer's character is the head, or layer of foam, that makes up about one-quarter of the glass contents. It is the way for the beer to release excess carbonation, but also serves as a way to release the aromas of the beer. A good pour creates an inviting head without having just a glass of foam, or a loss of beer as it froths over the edge of the glass.

Beer service from a bottle should be similar to that of wine service.

1. Bring the beer and its glass to the table. Place the glass to the right of the customer, above the silverware.
2. Show the bottle to the customer, confirming the choice of beer.
3. Begin pouring the beer rapidly into the center of the glass, holding the bottle with the label facing the customer.
4. As the head begins to form, tilt the bottle base to a lower angle, filling the glass more slowly and not creating more foam.
5. When the head begins to rise over the rim of the glass, stop pouring.
6. Place the bottle to the side of the glass, label facing the customer.

Pouring from a keg tap takes a bit more practice to master in one movement.

1. Place the glass under the tap and open the lever.
2. Pour beer straight into the center of the glass, creating the head.
3. Tilt the glass and fill by pouring beer down the side of the glass. When the head begins to rise over the top of the glass, close the tap.

Food and Beer Pairing

Pairing beer to food is more than ordering a pitcher with a pizza, burger, or basket of wings. The same principles that govern food and wine pairing work for food and beer pairing. With an increase in craft and microbrewed beers, the demand for matching beer with food in increasing. More and more restaurants are offering beer dinners and beer pairings on the menu.

TASTE PROFILE

Just as wine can be analyzed in terms of its taste profiles (acid, sweetness, and so on), so can beer. For the most part, beer and wine differ in one key area. Beers have very little acidity (lambics aside). What they have to take its place, however, is bitterness.

The basic taste profile of a beer involves sweetness, acidity, and bitterness. Because acidity is a minor component of most beers, the interplay is really between sweetness and bitterness. In wine, the equivalent interplay of sweetness and acidity is all focused on the grape. Most grape varietals will give the same profile, unless climate has intervened. In the case of beer, the interplay is between sweetness and bitterness. The bitter component serves as a palate cleanser, especially to high malt sweetness. But for beer, these come from different sources (barley for sweetness and hops for bitterness). Thus, how true a beer is to its style is the important factor when determining flavor profiles.

As was seen in the discussion of styles, some styles have significant hops character. These styles, like Pilsner, dortmunder export, and IPA, have a strong bitter component. Others, like stouts, brown ales, and bocks, have a malty sweetness that dominates their tastes. This distinction will help in the pairing.

As with wine, weight and intensity of flavor is also a factor in pairing. Golden lagers tend to be light in flavor, while it is easy to see that a stout would be at the opposite end of the spectrum. Some lagers, like bocks, have more weight to them, and some ales, like an IPA, can be on the light-bodied side. With this in mind, it becomes apparent that simple style-to-food correlations will not work.

PAIRING GUIDELINES

The mechanics of food and beer pairing are similar to that for wine. First, get the taste components to match. Next, pair intensity of flavor and weight and finish with flavor matching. There are some basic rules to food and beer pairing:

- Crisp beers, like Pilsners, are the sparkling wine and white wine equivalents in beer. These can be paired with fatty, rich foods as a contrast, or with bright, acidic foods as a complement.
- Bitter beers, such as pale ales and some lagers, match well with rich foods and with meaty dishes. The bitterness helps to cleanse the palate and prepare it for another bite of food.
- Bitter beers are poor matches with spicy food. The synergy between the bitter and the piquant will increase both, making the items spicier and more bitter than individually.
- Beers with malty richness match well with spicy foods. The sweetness of the malt helps to tame the piquancy of the spices.
- Malt-driven beers are also good with acidic foods. The sweetness of the malt helps to tame the acidity of a dish. In fact, these beers often work better than wine.

CLASSIC FOOD AND BEER PAIRS

There are a few classic pairings that illustrate how well beer and food go together.

Fish and chips with pale ale. This combination demonstrates the pairing of fried food with a slightly bitter beer. The weight of each of these is on the lighter side, the fish having been increased in weight by frying and the beer being a light ale. The richness of the fried food is cut by the bitter hoppiness of the ale. The malt vinegar and lemon used to dress the food is balanced nicely by the malty richness of the beer.

Sausage and sauerkraut with German Pils. The food here has two main characteristics—fat and acid. The sausages are rich and meaty. The sauerkraut is quite tangy. Both of these attributes are complemented by the crisp effervescence of the Pilsner-style beer. The bitterness helps to cleans the palate of the fat in the sausage, while balancing the acidity and earthiness of the sauerkraut.

Roast ham with Bock beer. This pair demonstrates how well beer goes with salty food. The salty and meaty ham needs a contrast to balance its flavors. The Bock has a malty richness to balance the saltiness and just enough hops character to cut through the meatness. The natural sweetness of the pork is also complemented by the richness of the malt flavors.

SUMMARY

Beer is a beverage as complex and intriguing as wine. Beer has been more "accessible" to the everyday drinker, though not taken as seriously as wine. The method of making beer is more intricate than that for making wine, because of the need to convert starches into sugar and extract it into water before fermentation can occur. The styles of beer depend on the type of malts used, and also on the yeast strain chosen. Beer needs as much care in terms of storage and service as wine, and can pair to food equally well.

KEY TERMS

Malting

Malt

Diastase

Pale malt

Crystal malt

Caramel malt

Amber malt

Vienna malt

Munich malt

Chocolate malt

Black patent malt

Hops

Ale

Saccharomyces carlsbergensis

Lager

Adjunct

Conversion

Extraction

Grist

Mash tun

Wort

Sparging

Flavoring

Fermentation

Pitching the yeast

Dry hopping

Conditioning

Pale ale

Burtonization

IPA

Trappist ale

Stout

Pilsner

Bock

Doppelbock

Maibock

Lambic

Brettanomyces

Gueuze

Kriek

Frambozen

Weisse

Weizen

Hefeweizen

Skunky

Keg

Bruised

Cask-conditioned

Firkin

Beer-clean

QUESTIONS

1. Why is barley ideal for making beer?
2. Discuss the differences between the types of malt.
3. What characteristics does hops contribute to beer?
4. Outline the steps of beer brewing.
5. Compare and contrast ales and lagers.
6. How should beer be stored?
7. Outline the steps for a proper beer pour.
8. Discuss differences in service temperatures for different styles of beer.
9. How does pairing beer with food differ from pairing wine with food?

chapter 26

How Spirits and Liqueurs Are Made

*S*pirits and liqueurs were originally meant to be elixirs and medicines to aid the sick. The process by which they are made is thousands of years old, and the original intent has long fallen by the wayside, as spirits and liqueurs are consumed more for enjoyment rather than for their medicinal curative powers.

Upon completion of this chapter, the student should be able to:

> *Describe the process of distillation*
> *Explain the process of flavoring spirits*
> *Discuss the production of liqueurs*

Spirits

The discovery and development of spirits dates back to the Middle Ages. Alchemists who were concerned about the essence of matter looked at plain items and tried to find their true nature. During this time, the beverages that were consumed most were wine and beer, and their intoxicating nature was well known. The alchemists found that if they used an ancient technique employed by Arabs, it was possible to extract the "spirit" of the original beverage.

DISTILLATION

The process the alchemists used was *distillation*. This technique already had been known for centuries. The ancient Egyptians used distillation to create perfumes from flowers and other botanicals. The returning Crusaders brought the knowledge of distillation back to Europe, where the alchemists applied it to wine and beer.

Distillation is a process that takes advantage of liquids with different boiling points, and therefore the vaporization of one liquid before another. In the case of alcoholic beverages, the liquids in question are ethanol and water. Water boils at 212°F (100°C) and ethanol boils at 173°F (78.4°C). In a perfect world, it should be possible to heat a mixture of alcohol and water to 173°F (78.4°C), where the ethanol would boil away and the water would remain behind. Unfortunately, it's not that easy. The chemical structure of ethanol includes an oxygen atom bonded to a hydrogen atom, just as in water. When the two are combined, as they are in wine or beer, the ethanol molecules have an attraction to the water molecules. The result is that the actual boiling point of the combined liquids depends on the concentration of ethanol in the water. The mixture actually boils somewhere between 173°F (78.4°C) and 212°F (100°C). As the amount of ethanol in the boiling liquid decreases, the boiling point goes up, eventually reaching 212°F (100°C).

The actual separation does not take place in the boiling liquid, but rather, in the vapor above it. As the liquid boils, evaporating ethanol and water form a vapor. This vapor will consist mostly of ethanol when boiling commences, and the proportion will decrease as the temperature increases. In other words, it is possible to boil off the ethanol from the water mixture, though some water will evaporate with it.

If the vapor simply condenses and falls back into the boiling pot, then no separation occurs. The actual process of separating the ethanol occurs when the condensed vapors are not allowed to fall back into the pot, but are collected separately. The liquid that is collected will have a higher proportion of ethanol than was originally in the boiling pot.

Of course, it is still not that simple. During fermentation, not all the sugar is converted to ethanol. Other alcohols such as methanol and isopropanol are created. These are alcohols that one would not want to consume in a concentrated form.

Methanol cannot be processed by the body, and consumption of too much methanol will lead to death. Isopropanol and other alcohols heavier than ethanol have a fuel oil taste and should be avoided. Isopropanol is typically the alcohol of choice in denatured alcohol sold at drug stores.

As the liquid is boiling, the different alcohols will vaporize at different temperatures. They will also condense at those same temperatures, so if a thermometer is used to measure the temperature of the vapor, it is easy to determine when to start collecting the ethanol. In many systems, that is not the case. So the skill of the distiller is needed to determine when to start collecting the "spirit." The *distillate* (as the condensed vapor is called) is collected in three phases. First is the *heads,* known as the *foreshots* in England. This consists mainly of methanol and other light compounds. The transition between the heads and the *hearts* (spirits in England) is key, in order to avoid contaminating the spirit with methanol or losing ethanol to the heads. Once the hearts are collected, the remainder is called the *tails* or *feints* in England. Again, the transition here is important so as not to cut off the collection of the good hearts too early.

STILL STYLES

There are two styles of stills used in distilling spirits. The simplest is the *pot still* or *alembic still.* This is a very simple apparatus, with a boiling pot and a condensing coil. The upper part of the pot is called the swan's neck, and this area takes on different shapes, depending on the spirit being distilled. The shape of the swan's

Pot still

Swan's
neck

Condenser

Pot

Spirit

The simplest style of alembic still; note the pot, swan's neck, and condenser.

neck helps to separate the vapors and to allow some flavor compounds also to be distilled with the alcohol. The collection coil is a long tube that is wound into a coil, inside of which the vapors cool and condense, until they drip out the end and are collected.

The pot still is used for *batch distillation*. For a distillation to occur, the pot must be filled with liquid. It is heated and the heads, hearts, and tails are collected. The pot needs to be recharged before the next batch can be distilled. Because there is limited separation in a pot still, the alcohol removed is relatively low in strength. An 8 percent alcohol by volume wine may distill to 30 percent in a pot still. For this reason, many spirits distilled in alembic stills are often double or triple distilled. The other characteristic of a pot still is the similarity of the final distillate to the original product. With a pot still being fairly crude in its ability to separate vapors, many volatile oils and essences from the original liquid carry over to the spirit. These essences are called *congeners,* and provide some of the flavor of the final spirit.

The second style is the *column still,* also known as the *patent still, continuous still,* or *Coffey still* after its inventor Aeneas Coffey. The column still actually consists of two columns, and can produce high-strength alcohol that is also highly *rectified* or purified. In the first column, warmed liquid to be distilled is introduced at the top of the column. Rising from the bottom of the column is steam, which vaporizes

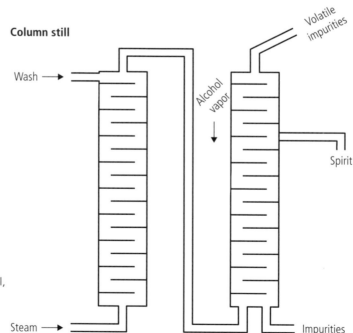

The column still does not use single batches of starting material, and can continuously produce distillate if the initial liquid is constantly introduced.

some of the liquid and carries the vapors over to the second column. As the vapor travels up the second column, it passes over plates. Inside these plates, more liquid to be distilled is being warmed on its way to the first column. The plates provide very minute temperature differences in the second column, allowing for more precision in which vapors are condensed. It is possible to select the plate where the highest concentration of alcohol can be obtained and collect the condensate there.

Because there is no single vessel to boil the liquid, there is no reason to stop a distillation to insert more. Liquid to be distilled is continuously introduced (hence one of the names) and alcohol is continuously collected. The alcoholic strength of the base liquid, say at 8 percent again, can be rectified to 96 percent alcohol if desired. There are few congeners collected from a column still, because of its ability to precisely separate the vapors.

FLAVORING

The flavor of a spirit is dependent on several factors. The method of distillation will have an influence on how the spirit will taste. If distilled in an alembic still, some of the flavor of the original liquid may be transferred to the final spirit. In a column still, this will rarely be the case.

The next major influence on flavor is method of aging. A large number of spirits are aged in oak barrels. Just as in wine, this imparts a certain flavor profile to the spirit. All spirits are colorless when they come off the still (alembic or column), and aging in oak imparts color to the spirit in the barrel. For spirits from pot stills, aging in wood allows for some of the heavier fusel oils and heavy alcohols to change over time. This decreases their influence on the final flavor profile. In column-distilled spirits, the caramel and vanilla flavors of toasted oak become predominant flavors.

Flavor may also come from additions to the spirit. Gin and flavored vodkas obtain their flavor through the influence of botanicals, or plant materials, that contain desirable essential oils. The botanicals are often soaked in the spirit. The essential oils, most of which are soluble in alcohol, dissolve into the spirit, thereby imparting flavor. This process is called *maceration*. Another, less common method places the botanicals above the distillation pot, in the path of the alcoholic vapor. The vapor then extracts the oils from the botanicals, and volatilizes only those that are in the lower temperature range of the vapor. This method is more tedious, but yields more delicate flavors.

STRENGTH

Spirits inherently have a higher concentration of alcohol than their fermented starting materials. It is possible to increase the concentration of alcohol at least a factor of 4, if not by a factor of 10, during the distillation process. The measurement of spirits does not typically follow the standard measurement of percent alcohol by volume that is used with fermented beverages. The measure of strength of spirits is called *proof*. Proof is calculated as double the alcohol by volume. For example, a spirit that is 40 percent alcohol by volume would be 80 proof. The term is derived from the method used to determine if there was enough alcohol in a liquid. The liquid was used to wet gunpowder, and if the powder still lit, that was proof the liquid contained alcohol. It wasn't until later that it was discovered that the mixture needed to be 50 percent or more alcohol in water for the gunpowder still to light.

Liqueurs

Liqueurs are a class of spirits made from a base spirit, flavoring, and sweetener. This class of spirits appeared as many alchemists tried to use spirits for medicinal and curative purposes. They had taken wine or beer and distilled it into *aqua vitae,* or water of life. The next logical step would be to infuse that water of life with items that were believed to possess curative or medicinal properties. To make the consumption easier, a little sweetness balanced any bitterness from the additives.

The first liqueurs to be produced on a wide-scale basis were made in monasteries. Benedictine is a liqueur made by Benedictine monks in France. The recipe, handed down through the centuries, is made up of a blend of herbs, based around angelica. The full recipe is known to only two monks, and while there have been many imitators, the recipe has not been copied. Another liqueur that originated in a monastery is Chartreuse.

BASE SPIRIT

Depending on where the liqueur originated, the base spirit may be the spirit of the region. The most common base spirits are cognac or brandy, whiskey, and vodka, more commonly referred to in this case as "neutral spirits." The herbal liqueurs, Benedictine and Chartreuse, start with brandy, which has herbs and spices infused into it. Liqueurs from Scotland, like Drambuie, and Ireland, such as Bailey's Irish Cream, use the local whiskey as a base. Many common liqueurs, such as schnapps or triple sec, use neutral spirits.

FLAVORING

Flavoring of the liqueur can encompass almost anything. The main categories are fruit, nut and seed, herb, and dairy. Fruit liqueurs encompass items like Chambord (raspberry), Kirsch (cherry), Cointreau and Grand Marnier (orange), and Midori (melon). Nut and seed liqueur flavors range from Amaretto (almond) and Frangelico (hazelnut) to Kahlua and Tia Maria (coffee) and de cacao (chocolate). Herb liqueurs make up a large group, with Drambuie, Irish Mist, Anisette, Sambuca, and Ouzo taking their place next to Benedictine and Chartreuse. Finally, though dairy is not thought of as a flavor for a liqueur too often, both Bailey's Irish Crème and the Dutch Avocaat (egg) use the products.

A subclass of herb liqueurs, known as *bitters,* remains true to its medicinal or digestive aid origin. These liqueurs fit the classic description, but are often more bitter than their counterparts. While some of these are used in drinks or alone, they are not drunk for pleasure but rather for their use as a digestive aid. Some examples are Angostora bitters, Punt y Mes, Campari, and Fernet Branca.

Below is a list of common liqueurs, along with their base spirits and main flavoring component.

Liqueurs, Their Base Spirits and Flavors

Liqueur	Spirit	Flavor
Amaretto	Neutral Spirit	Almond
Bailey's Irish Cream	Irish Whiskey	Cream and Chocolate
Chambord	Cognac	Raspberry
Cointreau	Neutral Spirit	Orange
Grand Marnier	Cognac	Orange
Kahlua	Neutral Spirit	Coffee
Ouzo	Brandy	Anise and Licorice
Southern Comfort	Bourbon	Bourbon
Tia Maria	Rum	Coffee

SWEETENERS

There is no set guideline as to what is used to sweeten liqueurs. Those with more traditional recipes may use honey, but they are also as likely to use sugar. In the case of fruit liqueurs, some of the sweetness may come from the fruit itself, only to be fortified with a little more sugar. The most common method is not actually straight cane sugar but rather, very concentrated simple syrup, making dilution and mixing easier.

MAKING LIQUEURS

The actual process for making a liqueur is very simple and can even be replicated at home. There are two key steps: getting the flavor in the spirit and then sweetening the mixture. To get the flavor into the spirit, a couple of methods can be used. The first method is *infusion*. Similar to maceration, the flavoring components are simply added to the spirit and allowed to infuse the alcohol with flavor. Another method is percolation. This method bubbles the spirit over the flavor components. Because the contact between the components and spirit is less intense, there is less chance of unwanted flavors or bitter components infusing the spirit.

After the flavor has been introduced into the spirit, the mixture is sweetened. The most common method is to use simple syrup, which allows for easy incorporation of sugar into the alcohol. Using syrup makes obtaining the correct proportion of sweetness to flavor easier. Some liqueurs use other natural sweeteners. For example, Drambuie uses honey as flavoring and sweetening. There is even a Canadian liqueur that is flavored and sweetened with maple syrup.

SUMMARY

The distillation of a fermented alcoholic beverage results in the production of a spirit. Distillation uses the differing boiling points of water and ethanol to separate the two liquids. Distillation of beer, wine, or any fermented alcoholic beverage can occur either in a pot still or a column still. In a pot still, the liquid is distilled in batches, and the flavor of the final spirit will have some resemblance to the starting point. A pot still will also produce a lower-strength distillate, and may require more than one distillation to achieve a high alcohol concentration. Column stills can run continuously, and create distillates with high concentrations of alcohol and little resemblance to the initial fermented beverage.

Liqueurs are a class of flavored and sweetened spirits. First developed for medicinal purposes, many contain herbs, spices, nuts, or fruit as their main flavorings. The items are sweetened to make consumption more pleasant, and the alcohol concentration is often lower than that of the base spirit. For many liqueurs, the base is a neutral spirit, while more traditional recipes may use brandy, whiskey, or rum.

KEY TERMS

Distillation

Distillate

Heads or foreshots

Hearts

Tails or feints

Pot still

Alembic still

Batch distillation

Congener

Column still

Patent still

Continuous still

Coffey still

Rectified

Maceration

Proof

Aqua vitae

Bitters

Infusion

QUESTIONS

1. Explain distillation.
2. Describe how each of the two types of stills work.
3. How is alcohol measured in distilled liquids?
4. What methods are used to flavor distilled spirits?
5. How is a spirit turned into a liqueur?
6. What distinguishes liqueurs from spirits?

chapter 27

Fruit-Based Spirits

*S*pirits can be made from any fermented beverage. With fruit providing
sweet juice for fermentation, it is not a stretch of the imagination to then distill
those beverages to make spirits. Every wine making region makes some form of
spirit from their wines, but this category of spirit is not restricted just to grapes as
the fruit of choice.

Upon completion of this chapter, the student should be able to:

> *Describe brandy making in terms of Cognac and Armagnac*
> *Explain the affect of maturation on Cognac and Armagnac*
> *Outline other brandy styles*
> *Discuss the use of other fruits to make brandies*

▊ Brandy

Brandy is a generic term for any spirit made from a fruit wine. It comes from the Dutch *brandewijn,* meaning "burnt wine." The Dutch used the distillation process to remove most of the water from wine to aid in shipping. It was then found that they enjoyed the taste. Brandy typically references wine-based spirits, and use of other fruits usually includes that fruit in the description (apple brandy, pear brandy, and so on).

COGNAC

The world's most famous brandy is *Cognac.* Named for the region in France where it originates, Cognac has served as the example of what brandy is for over five hundred years. Cognac and its popularity have been a benchmark for brandies in other parts of the world.

Region

The Cognac region is centered on the Charente River, north of Bordeaux. The land is farmed by a multitude of small farmers, who sell their grapes to the large distillation houses to become brandy. There are several subregions within Cognac, with a range of soils and therefore quality levels of the wines that they produce.

The best regions in Cognac are *Grande Champagne* and *Petit Champagne.* These two regions get their name not from any resemblance to sparkling wine, but rather from the extremely chalky soils in the area. The wines that are produced in these two areas are considered the finest, and Cognacs made from these wines are considered the most delicate and the most age worthy. If a Cognac is made from a blend of these two regions and at least 51 percent of the blend is from Grande Champagne, it is labeled *Fine Champagne.*

The next best region in Cognac is Borderies. This region has more clay in the soil, mixed with some chalk. The Cognac that comes from this area is mellower in style, and has a nuttier character. The last three regions are Fine Bois, Bon Bois, and Bois Ordinaire. These regions produce coarser wines and therefore cruder and coarser Cognacs.

The location of the river is a key factor in the success of Cognac. The Dutch were the first to utilize access to the river as a reason to invest in the area. The Dutch, followed by the English, set up large distilleries along the river. They purchased grapes from the local growers, made the wine, and distilled it, putting it on ships after distillation to be sent off to market. Cognac's reputation spread quickly because it was easily accessible to many markets.

Old cognac in the cellar. Once Cognac is placed in the bottle, it stops developing with age.

Courtesy Corbis Digital Stock

Viticulture and Vinification

The grapes that comprise the base wines for Cognac are not noted for their fine qualities. They are grown because they can make a light, acidic, low-alcohol wine. The major grape, responsible for about 90 percent of Cognac production, is *Ugni Blanc*. This grape is the same as Trebbiano in Italy. It is mainly blended with Colombard and Folle Blanche, though there are four other grapes allowed in the blend as well.

Low yields for quality base wine is not a priority in Cognac. The yields allowed are set at 102 hl/ha, much higher than for quality table wine. Yields at that level produce a large quantity of wine. On average, 11.25 kg (24.8 lb) of grapes will yield 9 liters of wine (9.5 quarts), which, after distillation, will yield 1 liter (1.06 quart) of Cognac. Yield is not the only thing that is different than quality table wine production. Harvesting is commonly done mechanically, as the typically underripe grapes do not need to be delicately handled.

The wine that is made as the base for distillation is a very simple one. The alcohol content is kept between 8 and 10 percent. Because a low alcohol level is required, chaptalization is not allowed. The wine is also fairly acidic, a result of early harvest. No sulfur is added to the wine during production, to prevent anything from carrying over in the distillation process.

Distillation

The rules for distillation of Cognac are very strict and traditional. The apparatus is a 30 hl copper pot still, known as a *Charentais still*. The copper is essential, as it is acid resistant, it is a great heat conductor, and it helps to remove any organic sulfur compounds. The shape of the still, and especially the swan's neck, is important because it allows for just the right amount of congeners to be retained. These congeners will provide the final spirit with its aromas and flavors.

Distillation occurs from November to March. During this time, the pot still is filled with 25 hl of wine. The pot is then heated to 176°F (80°C) with an open flame (required by the wine laws). The heart of this distillation is called the *brouillis.* It is approximately one-third of the original volume of wine, and is about 26–30 percent alcohol by volume.

This is not the final step. After three brouillis have been collected, they are recombined in the pot still, and distilled a second time. Again, the heart is collected (called the *bonne chauffe*), which is now at 70–72 percent alcohol by volume. Each of these distillations takes about one working day, so the entire sequence can take a week.

Maturation

Cognac straight off the still is like any other distilled spirit. It is the maturation process that makes Cognac special. Aging occurs in oak barrels. These barrels must come from either the Limousin or Troncais forests, both of which are near the Cognac region. Wherever the wood originates, the trees must be at least fifty years old before they can be made into barrels. The new barrels are often seasoned with lesser-quality Cognac until they have mellowed somewhat. Limousin wood is the most popular, and is considered the best for quality Cognac. It has a very open grain, which allows more oxygen and also more tannin into the spirit. Troncais wood, with its tighter grain, is used for Cognacs that require less aging.

The spirit must be aged a minimum of two years. The age of the spirit is guaranteed by the authorities for its first six years, and tracked by the *Compte system.* The system dates the spirit on an anniversary of April 1. After distillation and before April 1 of the following spring, the spirit is designated Compte 00. After April 1, it is Compte 0, and each year the number increases until the spirit reaches Compte 6.

The Compte designation is not used on labels of Cognac for purchase. Age designation is indicated by a collection of letters, whose combination indicates the age of the spirit in the bottle. The designation for a two-year-old Cognac is ★★★ or VS (very superior). At four years, the designation becomes VSOP (very superior old pale). At six years, Cognac get the XO (extra old) label.

Aging changes the Cognac in several ways. First, the spirit begins to extract flavor and color out of the wood barrels as they age. Sometimes enough color is extracted into the spirit, but addition of caramel is allowed when bottling if the color is not strong enough.

The second effect of aging occurs with the evaporation of the barrel contents. Over time, the spirit mellows and decreases in strength to around 60 percent alcohol by volume. Evaporation accounts for about a half of a percent in the loss of strength, but also accounts for big changes in flavor. The amount of evaporation will depend on the humidity of the cellars, but on average the annual loss is 3–6 percent of the total volume of Cognac. That can translate to 20 million bottles of Cognac lost to evaporation each year. The spirit lost to evaporation is called the angel's share.

Manipulating the rate of evaporation can change the flavor of the spirit. In England, a distinction is made between these two styles. *Early-landed Cognac* is brandy that has been shipped to England before it is six years old. Continued cask aging then occurs in English warehouses, with decidedly different humidity than in the Charente. The slower evaporation affects the ultimate flavor of the Cognac. Brandy that arrives in England after having aged in the Charente is called *Late-landed Cognac.*

Before bottling, the Cognac is blended to create the house style of the shipper. This is the time when color may be corrected with caramel. Finally, the strength of the Cognac is reduced by cutting the spirit with distilled water. This typically put the bottled spirit at 40 percent alcohol by volume, or 80 proof.

Vintage Cognac is very rare. It was common for many years, but with fraud becoming rampant, it was outlawed in 1963. Some vintage Cognac has been allowed to be produced since then, but under extremely strict conditions and constant monitoring by the French wine authorities.

ARMAGNAC

The other great French brandy is Armagnac. Armagnac has a longer history than Cognac, but not the recognition. If Cognac is the equivalent to Bordeaux, Armagnac is Burgundy. Poor access to markets outside the local area kept this spirit a secret, or at least underappreciated, for many years.

Region

Armagnac is the spirit of Gascony, in southwest France. Gascony is southeast of Bordeaux, in the mountains between the Atlantic and the Mediterranean. It is a warmer region than Cognac, and produces riper grapes. Gascony is secluded, in that it has no major rivers on which commerce is conducted. It is a quiet, rural area that only opened to trade with the building of canals and rail lines.

Gascony has a greater mix of agriculture than Cognac. Grapes are merely one of the crops that are grown. There are three main subregions that grow grapes for Armagnac. Bas Armagnac is considered the best region. Its combination of rich topsoil over sand and clay yields wines that are low in alcohol and high in acidity. The next best region is Tenareze. More chalk in the soil here yields wines that are more full bodied and flavorful than in Bas Armagnac. The third region of production is Haut Armagnac. This region has the highest chalk content in the soil, and makes the poorest wine for Armagnac. Much of the production from Haut Armagnac is not even labeled as Armagnac.

Viticulture and Vinification

The grape varieties used to make Armagnac are similar to those used to make Cognac. The major grape is Ugni Blanc, and it is often combined with Colombard and Folle Blanche (locally called Picpoul). Armagnac is the only region in France that is allowed to use a hybrid grape, Baco 22A. This hybrid is being phased out in favor of local vinifera varieties.

Making the base wine for Armagnac is the same as it is for making Cognac. The goal is to have a low-alcohol, high-acid wine to distill. The grapes are slightly riper at harvest than in Cognac, but the goal is still to keep the wine in the 8–10 percent alcohol by volume range.

Distillation and Maturation

Distillation of Armagnac differs from the method in Cognac. The primary difference is that Armagnac is only distilled once. While there are a lot of winemakers, the region's economy did not allow everyone to own a still. The still, a kind of modified continuous still, was brought to the wine, instead of the other way around as in Cognac. The cart with the still would pull up to a farmhouse, and the owner would pour his wine into the still. After the hearts were removed, the still moved on to the next farmhouse.

Because the still was mobile, it was smaller in capacity than a Cognac still. The spirit would come out of the still at a higher concentration of alcohol than Cognac (around 60 percent alcohol by volume) after the first distillation. Since 1972, the legal regulations have allowed the use of pot stills in Armagnac production.

Maturation of Armagnac takes place in barrels made from the local oak. This oak is very resinous, and influences the flavor of the final product. The spirit tends to age faster than in Cognac, and the designations indicate the youngest spirit in the blend, with ★★★ being two years old, followed by VSOP at five years, and XO at six years. The designation *Hors d'age* indicates an Armagnac that has aged at least ten years. Vintage Armagnac is common, with not only the date of the vintage on the label but also the date of bottling, which must be at least ten years after the vintage.

Bottling of Armagnac is often at barrel strength. Because the spirit was only around 60 percent alcohol by volume initially, after offering the angel's share with aging, the spirit is between 40 and 48 percent alcohol. Often caramel is added to enhance the color.

SPANISH BRANDY

The Spanish are the second largest producers of brandy, which use unique aging methods. The two most familiar brandies from Spain are Brandy de Penedes and Brandy de Jerez. In each case, most of the wine used for brandy making comes from the region of La Mancha, though excess wine in each region is also used.

Brandy de Jerez is a unique product. It must age in American oak barrels, which are organized in a solera system. Solera aging allows the brandy to mature faster. Aging can only occur in the three main villages of the Jerez region: Sanlucar de Barrameda, Santa Maria de Puerto, and Jerez de la Fronterra. After six months of aging, the brandy can be labeled Solera. Reserva is the designation for brandy that is one year old, and Gran Reserva is used for those that are at least three years old.

POMACE BRANDY

Not all brandies are made from wine. Some are made from the skin and pulp that remains after the wine has been pressed. What remains after pressing is called the *pomace,* and these brandies are therefore pomace brandies. At one time these brandies were made simply to make sure nothing went to waste. Now they are made in their own right.

Grappa

The most well-known pomace brandy is *grappa*. This Italian brandy is typically unaged, though some producers now age their grappa for one to two years in oak. Grappa's reputation is that of fire water, about as close to moonshine as possible. Some grappas still fit this description, having been distilled from any leftovers of wine making. Cheap grappa will be a mix of pomace from red and white grapes, with no distinction as to varietal or origin.

The better grappas come from pomace that is treated as gently as the juice that will make the wine. The pomace is kept as fresh as possible, with little chance for oxidation. Better grappa is actually varietal based, and the bottle designated by what grape the distillate came from. Common sources of grappa are Nebbiolo, Barbera, Sangiovese, Chardonnay, and Dolcetto. Grappa that is varietally based is not typically aged in wood, in order to retain the aroma and varietal character.

Marc

Marc is a French pomace brandy. It is made in many regions around France, including the major quality wine regions of Bordeaux, Burgundy, Alsace, and

Champagne. Very similar to grappa, marc is a clear brandy that is not typically aged in wood. It is distilled in pot stills, though the style may vary from region to region. In Burgundy, marc is distilled in a Charentais still. In Champagne, the pomace is combined with the degorgement extractions and distilled in pot stills that move from village to village.

Pisco

Pisco is a South American brandy that is made from Muscatel or Pais grapes. In Chile, the main grape used is Pais, and the majority is produced in the wine regions farthest to the north. In Peru, the best pisco is made from Muscatel grapes. Peruvian pisco is aged in barrels lined with wax to prevent wood influence and keep the spirit clear.

FRUIT EAU-DE-VIE

The term *eau-de-vie* is French for water of life. It is the generic term used for brandy that is made from fruit other than grapes. Fruits commonly used to make eau-de-vie are apples, pears, cherries, plums, and berries.

Calvados

The most famous eau-de-vie is *Calvados*. The name and the manufacture are strictly controlled by the French government. It is made from apples in the Normandy region of France, and for Calvados du Pays d'Auge the apples can only come from that subregion.

There are up to thirty kinds of apples used to make Calvados. The first picking of the season is not used because the temperature is too warm to properly ferment the juice into cider. Of the remaining apples, a combination of sweet, bittersweet, bitter, and tart apples are used to make the cider that will be distilled. For the best Calvados, the cider must ferment naturally, which should take at least a month.

The distillation method may determine the style of Calvados produced. The top Pays d'Auge Calvados must be double distilled in a Charentais pot still. After distillation, the spirit must be submitted to a tasting panel. The spirit is aged at least two years in Limousin oak barrels, though old Port or Sherry barrels are allowed. Cider that is fermented in a column still is called eau-de-vie de cidre, and is commonly not aged.

Other Fruit Eau-de-Vie

Almost every fruit-producing region in the world makes an eau-de-vie. The process is the same as it would be for grapes or apples: picking, crushing, fermentation, and distillation. Typically, eau-de-vies are distilled in pot stills and the resulting spirit is not aged. It takes almost 25 pounds of fruit to make one liter of eau-de-vie. Below are fruits, and the eau-de-vie they produce.

Fruit Eau-de-Vie

Fruit	Eau-de-vie
Pear	Poire Williams
Yellow Plum	Mirabelle
Raspberry	Framboise
Cherry	Kirsch
Black Plum	Slivovitz
Black Currant	Cassis

Service of Fruit Spirits

Fruit spirits are typically served *neat,* or without ice at room temperature. The preferred glassware for brandy and other eau-de-vie is a snifter. This glass is shaped such that the bowl of the glass containing the spirit can be held in the palm of the hand, slightly warming the spirit. This allows the more aromatic compounds to evaporate and fill the glass. The snifter then narrows at the rim, to contain the aromas and allow the drinker to enjoy them with each sip. While there are some devices that allow for even greater warming of brandy and other eau-de vie, often this just results in increased alcohol evaporation, masking the aromas.

SUMMARY

Fruits have often been the source for eau-de-vie and brandies. The wine making regions of the world utilize their leftovers to make pomace brandies such as marc and grappa. Other regions that cannot make fine wine have concentrated on brandy, like Cognac and Armagnac. Aging of these products mellows the alcohol and adds flavor from years in barrels. Regions that are not amenable to grape growing can make brandy and eau-de-vie from other fruits. The most famous, Calvados, is a brandy made from apples in the Normandy region of France. Other types of eau-de-vie, such as Poire Williams and Cassis, come from fruits common to their region of origin.

KEY TERMS

Brandewijn

Cognac

Grande Champagne

Petit Champagne

Fine Champagne

Ugni Blanc

Charentais still

Brouillis

Bonne chauffe

Compte system

Early-landed Cognac

Late-landed Cognac

Armagnac

Brandy de Jerez

Pomace

Grappa

Marc

Pisco

Eau-de-vie

Calvados

Neat

QUESTIONS

1. What is brandy distilled from?
2. Outline the top regions in Cognac.
3. What grape varieties are used to make Cognac?
4. Discuss the distillation process in Cognac.
5. How does maturation influence the flavor of Cognac?
6. Compare and contrast Cognac and Armagnac.
7. What is a pomace brandy?
8. How does brandy differ from eau-de-vie?
9. Discuss the proper service of brandy and eau-de-vie.

chapter 28

Grain-Based Spirits

The most common alcoholic beverage around the world, beer, is grain based. Once the starch has been converted to sugar and fermented, beer is just another alcoholic beverage to distill. Hops are no longer the flavoring component after distillation, rather the flavor comes from the treatment of the grain before fermentation and distillation, and the treatment of the spirit after distillation.

Upon completion of this chapter, the student should be able to:

    Explain the process for making whiskey
    Discuss the influence of peat on Scotch whiskey
    Outline the differences between styles of whiskey
    Explain the making of vodka and gin
    Discuss the method of flavoring gin

Whiskey

When considering grain-based spirits, the one category that encompasses the most styles is whiskey. The name derives from the Gaelic words for "water of life," *uisge beatha*. That became "uiske" and eventually "whiskie" by the 1700s. Modern spellings can either be whiskey (U.S. and Ireland) or whisky (Canada and Scotland).

INGREDIENTS

The essential ingredient for whiskey is grain. Depending on the region, that grain could be barley, rye, corn, or an assortment of other grains. Barley will always be present to some extent in a grain spirit. The diastase that it provides before fermentation converts not only the barley starch to sugar, but also the starch from any other grain.

If a whiskey is made with only barley, it is called a *malt whiskey*. Those that are made from barley plus other grains are labeled *grain whiskey* or *blended whiskey*. If one of those grains accounts for at least 51 percent of the blend of grains, then it is a *straight whiskey*.

Yeast is a key ingredient in whiskey making. As with wine, choice of yeast will influence the flavor profile. Some yeast strains make more esters, aldehydes, and other congeners that can influence the final flavor profile of the spirit.

The most important ingredient after the grain is the water. Unlike fruit distillates, whose liquid comes from the fruit itself, grain distillates must start with the sugar from the grain getting extracted into water. Water will leach minerals and salts from the earth, which in turn will make the water more acidic or alkaline. That may influence what gets extracted from the grain, as well as the congeners the yeast produces. The water source is often touted as part of the marketing of a fine whiskey.

Types of Whiskey

There are several significant styles of whiskey made around the world. Because it is mainly a British product, the major producers around the world are regions of historic British influence: Scotland, Ireland, the United States, and Canada. Each area makes its own style of whiskey, based on local conditions and easily accessible grains.

SCOTCH

The most famous, and probably the first, of all whiskeys is *Scotch*. The name Scotch Whisky is protected by law, and is also legally defined. Scotch must be a spirit distilled from a mash of grains, saccharified by the diastase of malt, fermented by yeast, distilled, and matured in oak casks in Scotland for no less than three years. This definition is generic, but the methods used in Scotland, and the specific conditions for aging there, make Scotch a unique beverage.

Regions

Scotland is divided up into four major Scotch making areas, each with a distinct style. These regions are *Highland, Lowland, Campbeltown,* and *Isley.* Within Highland is a concentrated area of distilleries called *Speyside,* along the river Spey. Each of these regions has a distinct style, based on the water sources and on the location of the distilleries and their aging warehouses.

Highland Scotch is the most familiar, yet the hardest to categorize. The area is fairly large, and the highest concentration of distilleries is in Speyside. Speyside Scotch is a delicate spirit. It is created from the soft water that comes from granite-lined streams and springs. The Scotch gains a honey and heather note upon aging, and a slight smokiness at the finish.

The most distinctive Scotch comes from Isley and the islands. These spirits have a lot of smokiness and also a distinctive iodine or seaweed-like character. This comes from aging the Scotch on the shore, literally. Many of the distilleries in Isley have their aging warehouses where the sea laps against the foundation.

Campbeltown only has one operating distillery. Its style is smoky, without the strong medicinal character of Isley. Finally, Lowlands Scotch is the lightest in style. It is often used for blending with other styles.

Making Scotch

The first step in making Scotch is the malting process. This process is very similar to the one described in beer making (see Chapter 26). But the Scottish have a distinct twist that influences how the malt dries, and the final taste. That twist is the use of *peat.*

Peat is naturally composted vegetal matter. It forms from the decay of heather and grasses in wetland areas in Scotland. Because there are little to no trees in Scotland, peat is the source of fuel for building fires. The peat must be dug out of the ground, using long square shovels. The process creates blocks of peat, which are left out to dry. The blocks are then broken into smaller chunks and used as fuel. Peat has one major characteristic: it gives off a lot of smoke. When the malt is ready to be dried, peat is used in the kilns to fuel the fire. Not only is the malt then dried, but it is also smoked, as the smoke from the peat in the kiln fills the malting room. The smoke gives Scotch its distinctive smoky character. Peat also influences the Scotch via the water. Most of the water used to make Scotch comes from streams or lochs. Much of this water has filtered through the peat bogs, picking up some of the flavors of peat along the way.

The peat influence varies by distillery and by region. In some areas of Scotland, peat is more of a nuance and in others it is a predominant flavor. In Highland Scotch, peat is used in a ratio of 1:100, which is one pound of peat used in the kiln for every 100 pounds of malt. In Isley, by contrast, the ratio is closer to 1:8. With that ratio, Isley Scotch has a much higher peat influence and will taste much smokier than its Highland counterpart.

After the malt is dried, a low-alcohol beverage is made in a method that resembles beer brewing. The liquid, called the *wash,* is then distilled to make Scotch. The choice of still depends on the style of Scotch that is being made. Ultimately, the distillate is placed into barrels and aged the minimum of three years, though often much longer than that.

Maturation is the key step in making Scotch. First, flavor is imparted into the spirit from the barrels, whether they are oak barrels made just for Scotch or old Port or Sherry barrels being recycled. As the spirit ages, some evaporation occurs. This concentrates the flavors and also takes the burning, alcoholic edge off the spirit. Additionally, the local climate and conditions affect the flavor. There is no temperature regulation in the warehouses, so with each summer and winter the barrels expand and contract, allowing the locale to influence the flavor. The porosity of the barrels also allows for a slow oxidation of the spirit, again influencing flavor. Once the spirit is bottled, aging stops.

When the Scotch is to be sold, it is often blended between different batches and different years to produce a consistent style. The blend will be diluted to 80 or 100 proof with distilled water and will be filtered before bottling. The age that is stated on the bottle is the age of the youngest batch in the blend. There are some producers that make vintage Scotch, though it is rare.

STYLES OF SCOTCH

One division of style in Scotch would be by region. It is easy to see that a Highlands Scotch is very different from an Islay. Islay is said to be the ultimate Scotch, even if it is an acquired taste. However, even within these regions, there are categories of Scotch based on the grains used in their manufacture and if any blending occurs.

Malt Whiskey

When whiskey is made with just barley and no other grains, it is called *malt whiskey.* The top of the line is a *single malt Scotch.* This is a malt whiskey that is made in a single distillery. These whiskies are the best any distillery can produce, and utilize the most traditional methods.

Single malt whiskies are double distilled. The first distillation of the wash is done in a copper pot still called a *wash-still*. The hearts, or *low-wines,* are collected and are sent to be redistilled. The low-wines are typically around 30 percent alcohol by volume. The second distillation occurs in the *spirit still,* also a copper pot still, and the hearts, or *British Plain Spirits,* are collected in a *spirit safe,* because they are now taxable. These spirits are close to 70 percent alcohol. The foreshots and the feints from the spirit still are added to the next batch before distillation.

Different distilleries have different shapes of swan necks in their spirit stills. Some are simply conical, while others have a bulb in the swan neck, called a Balvenie ball. Shorter swan's necks give stronger, fuller-flavored spirits. Spirit stills with longer swan's necks or a Balvenie ball yield more delicate spirits.

A *pure malt whiskey,* also known as a *vatted malt whiskey,* is a blend of malt whiskies. The whiskey could be a blend of malts of different ages from a single distillery, or it could be a blend of malts from different regions. The blend is more approachable than the unique single malts, and will have a consistent flavor profile.

Cask strength malts are bottled straight from the cask. They will be between 45 and 60 percent alcohol and are not filtered before bottling. These whiskies are very strong and fuller flavored due to the lack of filtration.

Grain Whiskey

Any whiskey that is made with barley plus another grain is called a *grain whiskey.* Because of their lighter quality and less intense flavor, these whiskies are usually not distilled in a pot still, but rather in column stills. The other grains that are commonly used are oats, rye, unmalted wheat, and corn. There is typically a little malt in the grain mix, primarily to provide the diastase to convert the starch to sugar. The whiskey is distilled to a higher strength, and ages faster than malt whiskey. There are some single-grain whiskies, but they are very rare.

Blended Whiskey

Blended whiskies are composed from a dozen to fifty different grain and malt whiskies. The typical ratio is 60 percent malt whiskey to 40 percent grain whiskey. That ratio can change based on the style desired, with cheaper brands using more grain whiskey. The whiskies chosen to be blended are at least five years old, but for better brands, many can be older than that. The blender has to know when each individual whiskey is ready for blending. Once the blend is made, it is often aged for several months, so the flavors have a chance to marry. The blended whiskey category produces the lightest and easiest drinking Scotch. Blended whiskey makes up approximately 95 percent of the market for Scotch.

IRISH WHISKEY

Irish whiskey has its origin in the same monastic tradition as Scotch whisky. However, there are distinct differences between Irish whiskey and Scotch. Irish whiskey can be single malt, blended, or single grain. There is also a uniquely Irish style called a pot still whiskey. This is made from 100 percent barley, but only some of it has been malted. The unmalted barley gives a spicier note to the whiskey.

The next distinction is how the malt is dried for Irish whiskey. First, the malt is dried without the influence of smoke. Some distillers use peat to dry the malt, but it is kept in a closed oven and the smoke is not allowed to interact with the malt. Many distillers have changed from peat to coal as their fuel of choice, which removes smoke from the drying process.

Finally, Irish whiskey is triple distilled, rather than double distilled like Scotch. The first distillation yields the low-wines. These are distilled and collected as strong and weak feints. It is the strong feints that are distilled a third time to produce the final product.

Irish whiskey is aged for a minimum of four years before it can be sold. In most cases it is aged seven or eight years before bottling. The result is a mild, smooth whiskey that is medium bodied with a unique flavor.

BOURBON

The Scottish and Irish immigrants to the American colonies brought with them the knowledge of distillation. As they emigrated west of the Appalachian Mountains, they resorted to using corn as a starting material for distillation. Much of the resulting whiskey was shipped down the Ohio and Mississippi Rivers to New Orleans, from Bourbon County, Kentucky. Soon the whiskey was known as *Bourbon*.

Bourbon is a straight whiskey, made from a minimum 51 percent corn. Producers use about 10 percent malt, and the remainder is typically rye. Some distillers, looking to make a smoother whiskey, use wheat rather than rye in the grain mix.

One distinction of bourbon is the use of *sour mash*. Sour mash refers to the leftovers of the fermentation or distilling process. In making bourbon, fresh yeast along with up to 25 percent sour mash is added to the next batch of wort. Sour mash improves the yeast growth while inhibiting bacterial growth and adding a continuity of flavor. Bourbon can then either be double distilled in copper pot stills or made in a column still. The better-quality Bourbons are double distilled.

Legally, bourbon must be aged a minimum of two years in brand-new charred-oak barrels. Once the whiskey is put into the barrels, it is loaded into the barrel house. Some producers leave the barrels alone once they enter the barrel house. This means that there will be a variation among the barrels depending on where they spent their time in the barrel house. Other producers, to keep consistency among the barrels, will rotate them throughout the barrel house over their two-year aging period. Unlike Scotland, where the humid environment causes loss of strength with evaporation, the dry air in Kentucky leads to increased alcoholic strength during aging. Those barrels at the top of the barrel house get the most heat and will age faster and gain strength faster.

Two specialty Bourbons have developed from the aging process. *Single barrel Bourbon* is just that, the bourbon from a single barrel. Each barrel will have a different flavor, and the barrel number is placed on the label. *Small batch Bourbon* is a collection of several barrels that are blended together to make a pleasant blend. Different small batches will taste slightly different. The barrels that make the batch are often from different parts of the barrel house, to ensure a mix of the best flavors.

Very similar to Bourbon is Tennessee whiskey, made famous by Jack Daniel's. The process to make Tennessee whiskey is the same for making Bourbon, with one additional step. Tennessee whiskey is filtered through maple charcoal before bottling. This removes some of the coarser flavors from the whiskey and makes a lighter spirit.

CANADIAN WHISKY

Canadian whisky is a blended grain whisky. It is light in flavor and body. Whiskies made in Canada must be made from cereal grains and be aged a minimum of three years. The grains used are a combination of corn, rye, malt, and wheat, though each brand uses different proportions.

Vodka

Vodka is included in the grain spirits category because that is what the majority of distillers use for production. Vodka originated in Poland and Russia as a way to use excess agricultural product. The original starting material was grain, but the Polish eventually used potatoes. In fact, vodka can be made from many things, and its starting material now ranges from wheat to barley, potatoes to grapes. Vodka is not so much about the starting material as it is the quality and style of the end product.

Vodka was originally a grain distillate that was unaged—similar to any whiskey without the barrel aging. It was often flavored with herbs to mask the rough taste. Eventually, it was discovered that running the spirit through charcoal filters removed the congeners. This is vodka as we know it today. The Tobacco and Trade

Bureau (TTB) defines the *standard of identity* of vodka as "neutral spirits so distilled, or so treated after distillation with charcoal or other materials, as to be without distinctive character, aroma, taste, or color."

In order to get as pure a vodka as possible, the distillation occurs in a column still. This allows the distillate to be remove as high as 95 percent alcohol. Therefore, vodka is often described as being highly rectified. Some producers don't even distill their own vodka; they purchase neutral spirits (the term for 95 percent alcohol), treat it, and then dilute it to the desired proof. Some producers tout that their vodka is triple, quadruple, or even five times distilled. This is one method to improve the flavor of neutral spirits. The spirit is placed in the still again and "washed" with water. Any impurities that are attracted to water are removed, and the spirit comes out cleaner tasting. Other methods to improve the taste are to bubble oxygen through the vodka, or to place it in a centrifuge and separate the impurities that way. Finally, the vodka passes through the charcoal filter to remove any last impurities.

After the vodka is filtered, it is diluted with water. That water will have a small influence on the subsequent taste of the vodka. If spring water is used, then the minerals from the spring will be noticeable in the flavor. Distilled water will give a more neutral-flavored product. The vodka is diluted down to 80 to 100 proof before it is bottled.

FLAVORED VODKA

Vodka is no longer solely a colorless, tasteless beverage. Many producers have a line of flavored vodkas that are intended for use in specialty drinks. The flavor comes from infusion of the flavoring agent into the vodka. Flavors include various citrus fruits, berries, vanilla, coffee, chocolate, even hot peppers. In the United States, flavored vodkas are required to have the name of the flavoring on the bottle.

Gin

Gin could be considered the original flavored vodka. Even though it is a Dutch invention rather than a Russian one, both spirits start the same. Gin is basically a neutral spirit with the predominant flavor of juniper berries. The spirit was named *Genever,* after the juniper berry that flavored it. The English shortened the name to gin.

The method of flavoring is slightly different than that for flavored vodka. First, the flavoring in gin is not just juniper, but a combination of *botanicals* (roots, seeds, leaves, stems, and the like). Each distiller has its own recipe. Common ingredients include citrus peel, angelica, cassia, coriander, fennel, and caraway. These botanicals do not just infuse the spirit with flavor; they are involved in a distillation. There are two methods of infusing the botanicals into the spirit. In the first case, the botanicals are added to the spirit, and the combination is then distilled in a pot still. The spirit evaporates and condenses, but so do the essential oils of the botanicals. The second method produces a more delicate and nuanced flavor. Here, the botanicals are placed in a basket in the pot still above the boiling spirit. Now only the vapors will extract the flavor out of the botanicals. This method prevents heavier, harsher oils from being extracted and allows only the most delicate flavoring.

Gin also has differences in style of the spirit itself. The original style, Genever, begins with a mash of malt, corn, and rye, which after fermentation is distilled in a pot still. It is then redistilled with the botanicals. This spirit still has the flavor of malt as well as the juniper. It is full bodied and even a bit oily on the palate. This is not mixing gin; this spirit is meant to be drunk cold and straight.

The English developed a lighter, drier style of gin called *London Dry*. It is distilled in a column still and reduced to 120 proof before being redistilled with the botanicals. This is the mixing gin, used for martinis and gin and tonics. A unique version is Plymouth gin, which is made exclusively from soft water and wheat. Only seven botanicals flavor Plymouth gin, which is lighter and smoother than regular London dry.

The final style is really flavored vodka. *Compounded gin* adds an extract of botanical flavors to neutral spirits. No second distillation occurs. These gins will not specify compounded on the label; they more than likely will just say distilled gin.

Service of Grain Spirits

Grain spirits can be served in a variety of ways. The first is alone or with water. Whiskey and vodka are the two spirits that are most likely to be served alone. Whiskey is served neat, or *on the rocks,* that is, over ice. It is recommended that a few drops of water be added to any neat whiskey, particularly single malt scotch. The small amount of water, about a quarter teaspoon per 1.5 ounces of whiskey, actually enhances the aromatic character of the spirit. The water seems to tame the harshness of the alcohol, opening the way for more aromatics to be observed. Vodka is traditionally served in small 1- to 1.5-ounce glasses, ice cold. Vodka served in this way is best stored in a freezer until service. The enhanced chill on the spirit also counters the harshness of the alcohol. Dutch gin, Genever, is also served as vodka is.

The next most common service of these spirits is in mixed drinks. Whiskey is usually relegated to being mixed with soda, water, or mixers that enhance the aromatics or sweetness of the spirit. Gin is mixed the same way, with less variety due to the unique character of the juniper. Vodka is the quintessential spirit for mixed drinks. It is neutral in flavor, and basically adds alcohol to whatever it is mixed with. This provides a wide range of possibilities for mixed drinks.

SUMMARY

Spirits are not restricted to distillates of fermented juice. The grain-based spirits use a beerlike base for distillation. Grains are malted, ground, and the sugars extracted into water. That wort is then fermented and the subsequent wash is distilled. Differences between the grain spirits include the type of grain used, distillation methods, and aging methods (if any).

Whiskey is a malt-based beverage, though it can be made with corn or rye. Better whiskies are distilled in pot stills, while more commercial spirits are made in column stills. All whiskies are aged in wood, which gives them their color and influences their flavor. Vodka is a highly refined spirit, getting distilled in column stills and filtered through charcoal. Vodka is the most neutral spirit, but many producers have begun to create specialty flavored vodkas. Gin may be the original flavored vodka. Using juniper as the main flavoring, gin uses a variety of botanicals to create its unique profile.

KEY TERMS

Malt whiskey

Grain whiskey

Blended whiskey

Straight whiskey

Scotch

Highland

Lowland

Campbeltown

Isley

Speyside

Peat

Wash

Malt whiskey

Single malt Scotch

Wash-still

Low-wines

Spirit still

British Plain Spirits

Spirit safe

Pure malt whiskey

Vatted malt whiskey

Cask strength malts

Grain whiskey

Irish whiskey

Bourbon

Sour mash

Single barrel Bourbon

Small batch Bourbon

Standard of identity

Genever

Botanicals

London Dry

Compounded gin

On the rocks

QUESTIONS

1. Outline the different styles of whiskey.

2. What are the different regions of Scotch production?

3. Discuss the influence of peat on the flavor of Scotch.

4. How does a malt whiskey differ from a grain whiskey?

5. Compare and contrast Scotch and Irish whiskey.

6. What are the unique characteristics of Bourbon?

7. Discuss the standard of identity of vodka. What steps are taken to meet the standard?

8. How does gin get its flavor?

9. What are the service standards for grain spirits?

chapter 29

Vegetable-Based Spirits

*T*he sugar for fermentation can come from any source. Fruit, which produces sugar naturally, and grain, which stores sugar as starch, are easy choices. There are other plants that have natural sweetness and sugars that can make a fermented beverage. The most common plants with natural sweetness are from hot weather and tropical regions, and whose spirit reflects the heat and flavor of the tropics.

Upon completion of this chapter, the student should be able to:

> *Discuss the use of vegetable matter to make spirits*
> *Explain the differences in rums*
> *Explain the method of Tequila production*
> *Describe the styles of Tequila*
> *Outline the service of vegetable-based spirits*

Rum

Rum is a by product of the sugar industry. It is the result of fermenting sugarcane juice, molasses, and other by products of sugar refining to make a spirit. Depending on the refinement of the juice and the still, different styles of rum have emerged. Because sugarcane can be grown in a multitude of tropical regions, each has its own rum. The most diverse area for rum production is the Caribbean.

STYLES OF RUM

"Spanish" Rum

The most familiar rum could be termed a Spanish style. It is the rum of Cuba, and currently Puerto Rico. This rum is made from molasses, in order to obtain all the sugar from the cane. The sugarcane is harvested and pressed. The juice is boiled to concentrate the sugar, and then it is placed in large high-speed centrifuges, which collect the crystallized sugar. What remains is molasses and up to 5 percent sugar that cannot be extracted. Rather than discard this material, it is diluted with water and fermented. Fermentation will take about two to four days. The wash, at 7 percent alcohol, is distilled in a column still and collected at at least 160 proof. Because it is highly rectified, there is little flavor, a light body, and few congeners. Then the rum is blended with batches from other stills or different ages to create the manufacturer's style.

The rum is aged only two or three months in vats before it is sold as *white rum* or *silver rum*. By Puerto Rican law, that aging must be one year, though the rum is still colorless and light bodied. If aging lasts three years, often in charred wood barrels, these will be sold as *amber* or *gold* rum. Often, to have consistency of color, these rums have caramel added to enhance the flavor. A few producers make a *Red Label rum,* which is more full bodied and darker in color.

French Rhum

Rum (Rhum is the French spelling) in the French style comes from the island of Martinique, a French protectorate. Two types of rum are made on the island. Rhum industiel is made from fermented molasses and distilled in a column still. When the sugarcane industry slowed and molasses was not as prevalent, the *rhum agricole* style emerged. This rhum is made from sugarcane juice. All aging and blending for the French market takes place in France. French rhum has been given legal AOC status by the French government.

Jamaican Rum

Jamaican rum is more full-bodied than the other rums of the Caribbean. This is the result of a unique method of production. Jamaican rum starts with the molasses left from sugar refining. To the molasses is added the leftovers from previous distillations. The vat is left open, so that wild yeast can start a natural fermentation. This fermentation takes longer than fermentation with cultured yeast, on the order of one to three weeks. During this time, more congeners are produced, which will end up in the final product. Jamaican rum is double distilled in pot stills, and is aged in oak barrels for between five and seven years. The final product is blended and often colored with caramel to give a deep dark color to match the flavor.

Cachaça

The Brazilian cousin to rum is *cachaça*. The main difference between rum and cachaça is that rum is made from molasses and cachaça is made from sugarcane juice. The sugarcane "wine" is distilled in pot or column stills. Artisan producers use pot stills to create unique bottlings, while industrial producers use column stills to make a generic spirit that is then altered by bottlers who buy it as raw material. Cachaça has a distinct, strong sugarcane aroma, and is often not aged before bottling. Some producers have begun to age cachaça, though they use a large array of local woods to make the barrels, again imparting unique flavors to their bottling.

Tequila

Tequila is a Mexican distillate that utilizes the agave plant as the source of the fermentable sugars. Tequila is also a protected name and region, with the production of the spirit restricted to the state of Jalisco, and in particular to the area surrounding the village of Tequila.

TEQUILA PRODUCTION

Tequila is produced from a special variety of agave. The *blue agave* or *Agave tequileana Weber, var. azul,* is the only species and variety of agave allowed to be used in tequila production. While agaves are usually lumped into the category of cactus, this plant is really a member of the lily family.

Blue agaves take eight to ten years to reach maturity. In this time, they spawn pups, or small mini-plants that will become the next generation of agave. Once the agave has reached maturity, the harvesters, or *jimadors,* cut the plant at the root. The leaves are then stripped, leaving a large central stem. This stem is called the *piña,* because of its resemblance to a large pineapple.

The piñas are taken to the factory, where they are halved or quartered. Traditional producers place the pieces in an oven (*horno*), where they are roasted over twelve to twenty-four hours. Actually, the pinas are so packed into the ovens, they steam in their own moisture. Some larger producers have changed to giant auto-claves to steam the piñas in less than nine hours. The steamed piñas produce *agua miel,* or honey water. Full extraction of the agua miel comes from processing the steamed piñas in juicers or shredders and presses.

The finest tequila comes from fermenting the agua miel with yeast that has been cultivated from the agave plant. Lesser tequilas will use cultivated yeasts and add sugar to aid in the fermentation process. This is called *pulque.* The pulque is then distilled twice. The first distillation produces *ordinarios,* which are redistilled to yield tequila. If the pulque has been made with the addition of sugar, the second distillation will create a spirit close to 55 percent alcohol, which will then be diluted before bottling.

Types of Tequila

Tequila can be classified on the amount of aging it has had. If the spirit is bottled straight off the still, it is called *blanco* or silver. This style has the most agave taste, which has not been influenced by any aging. A version of silver is *oro* or gold. How can gold be a version of silver? In reality, this style of tequila is really just silver with the addition of caramel coloring. It is often sold as "young and smooth."

If the tequila is aged in barrels it gets one of two designations based on time. The first is *reposado* (resting). Tequila that has been aged for between two and eleven months is designated a reposado. These are highly popular tequilas, whose color comes from the barrel aging. The other aged tequila category is *añejo.* An añejo tequila has been aged a minimum of one year. Because of the warm climate in Jalisco, tequila ages very quickly, and the best añejos are less than four years old. A new category is developing, though the name is not definitive. Labeled *ultra-añejo, muy añejo,* or *tres añejo,* these are tequilas that are over four years of age. These spirits have lost much of their agave character at this point, and approach more of a whiskeylike character.

In the 1970s, the Mexican government lifted the restriction that all tequila must be made from 100 percent blue agave. This allowed the addition of neutral spirits, corn, or sugar into the fermentation. Blue agave still had to account for at least 51 percent of the sugars. Any tequila made with these adjuncts is labeled *mixto.* Mixtos can be aged the same way as 100 percent agave tequila, but the flavor of the agave itself will be muted.

Mescal

Some describe *mescal* as the poor cousin of tequila; others feel it deserves the same recognition. Mescal is made from agave plants (not necessarily blue agave) outside the Tequila region. The main center for mescal production is Oaxaca.

Mescal production is a bit different than tequila production. First, the piñas are slow-roasted for three days in clay ovens or in pits. This imparts a smoky character to the agua miel. The cooked piñas are not crushed but rather allowed to ferment naturally. This will take up to a full month. The piñas are then crushed and distilled. Depending on the producer, that distillation could be single or double, and in copper or clay pot stills. All mescal is 100 percent agave.

Aquavit

Aquavit is the Scandinavian version of vodka. Typically, aquavit is produced from potatoes. The potatoes are cooked and then grain malt is added to convert the starch to sugar. The combination is fermented and then it is distilled to a high alcohol percentage (95 percent). It is flavored by redistilling with flavoring, like gin. The common flavoring for aquavit is caraway seed, though cardamom, coriander, clove, and dill are also found. It is occasionally aged in oak sherry casks before bottling

Service of Vegetable-Based Spirits

Rum is typically the base for a variety of mixed drinks. The spirit is usually mixed with something that enhances or utilizes the inherent sweetness of the spirit. Examples are rum and cola, or any of the "island" drinks like piña colada, daiquiri, or mai tai. Older rums or rhum agricole can be served neat, often in snifters to appreciate their aged complexity.

Tequila is notorious as the "shot" spirit. The requisite lime and salt are also included in this service. There is a purpose to the lime and salt. As with wine, the added acidity and salt change the flavor of the tequila, enhancing its agave character. The more traditional service of tequila is with *sangrita,* a tomato and citrus juice combination served alongside the tequila. To enjoy a tequila and sangrita, the two should be sipped alternately. Tequila is also the base for some mixed drinks, the most famous of which is the Margarita. Añejo tequilas are meant to be drunk straight, as would a single malt Scotch or Cognac.

Aquavit is the Scandinavian equivalent of vodka, and is served in a similar manner. It is usually served in small glasses, ice cold, and drunk quickly. Aquavit is not a good base for mixed drinks, as its own flavorings get smothered by the mixer.

SUMMARY

Even plant material can be used to make a spirit. The juice from the grass that gives us sugar, the sweet nectar of a lily relative, or the starch of a tuber all can be turned into a spirit. In each case, the starting material influences the flavors of the final product. Each spirit—rum, tequila, or aquavit—are indicative of the area of origin. Rum is reminiscent of the tropics, tequila reminds the drinker of the agave from which it comes, and the caraway-flavored aquavit is as bracing as a Swedish winter.

KEY TERMS

White rum

Silver rum

Amber rum

Gold rum

Red label rum

Rhum agricole

Jamaican rum

Cachaça

Tequila

Blue agave

Jimador

Piña

Horno

Agua miel

Pulque

Ordinarios

Blanco

Oro

Reposado

Añejo

Mixto

Sangrita

Mescal

Aquavit

QUESTIONS

1. What is the source material for making rum?

2. Outline the different styles for rum.

3. How does Cachaça differ from rum?

4. Compare and contrast Tequila and Mescal.

5. How is Tequila made?

6. Describe the different types of tequila.

7. Describe aquavit.

8. What are some of the service standards for vegetable-based spirits?

PART SEVEN

the **role** of the
sommelier

The job of the sommelier is not restricted just to serving wine. The sommelier will be responsible for all the beverage-related items in the venue. A sommelier will sell wine, serve, recommend pairings, and take care of all the tools necessary for proper service. The sommelier will also be responsible for purchasing, inventory, and wine list creation, especially with the idea of matching the wine list to the menu. Sommeliers are constantly upgrading and sharing their knowledge, and determining whether wines are faulty or flawed and need to be removed from service.

chapter

30

In the Dining Room

*F*or most nonindustry people, the image of a sommelier is someone whose job is to take care of your wine service when having dinner. While that is true, the job in the dining room goes beyond just walking around, taking orders, and opening bottles. Depending on the restaurant, the sommelier may be a floor manager, diplomat, flavor guide, and more.

Upon completion of this chapter, the student should be able to:

> *Describe the types of guests who order wine*
>
> *Discuss methods for working the floor during service*
>
> *Discuss the balance between education and sales in the sommelier position*
>
> *Describe the behind-the-scenes tasks of the sommelier*

On the Floor

Someone in every restaurant is responsible for wine and beverage service. Depending on the style of restaurant, that person may be your server or it may be a person whose sole job is wine and beverage service. This person is the sommelier. Because that title has certain connotations, many restaurants use the term wine manager or beverage manager to make the person seem more approachable.

As the alternate titles suggest, one of the jobs of the sommelier is to be a manager. As a manager, the person will have to plan and control how the product (wine and spirits) is purchased, stored, and sold. Those aspects of the job will be discussed in later chapters. The other aspects of management are the training and performance of people.

A fine-dining restaurant will often have a dedicated wine person or persons working the floor during service. This style of service can be expected in places where the wine list boasts very expensive and/or rare bottles of wine. The investment in these top-quality wines requires a person who is knowledgeable and skilled in their service, and that is what the customer expects.

Most restaurants do not have a dedicated sommelier working the floor every evening, if at all. These restaurants rely on the waitstaff to handle wine sales. Depending on the volume and size of the restaurant, wine sales may or may not be a priority for the waitstaff. These restaurants do have a manager who handles issues with wine service, staff training, and maintaining approved standards for wine service.

What does a sommelier do during service? First, it should be understood that the sommelier has a much larger station than any waiter. There may be ten waiters working tables that evening, but maybe only one or two sommeliers. The reason is that they do not have to be as active at a table as a waiter does. The sommelier is there for wine sales and service. Once the wine is chosen, it is opened, poured, and occasionally replenished. A sommelier can cover many tables while a waiter has to time items from the kitchen, replace silverware, clear plates, and so on, on several tables at a time.

UNDERSTANDING THE GUEST

It is easy to assume that the type of guest who dines out frequently is also an avid wine drinker. For the majority of wine consumers, that is not the case. In 2007, Constellation Wines US conducted a study of wine consumers called Project Genome. This study looked at consumer attitudes and behavior in retail wine buying venues. The data that resulted will be used to help market wines for retail, but the information is also of interest to sommeliers and anyone who sells wine in restaurants.

Project Genome determined that there were six categories of wine buyers:

1. Overwhelmed
2. The Image Seeker
3. The Traditionalist
4. The Savvy Shopper
5. The Satisfied Sipper
6. The Enthusiast

The Overwhelmed category is the largest group of consumers at 23 percent. These consumers are overwhelmed by the selection options and process and are looking for guidance on what to buy. They are often frustrated because that guidance is often not there for them. If they get too confused, they don't buy anything.

The Image Seeker views wine as a status symbol, and will choose wines for its packaging or its uniqueness. This group is also media savvy, and will cross reference a restaurant's wine list to a wine magazine's scores. This group is 20 percent of the population. On the other hand, the Traditionalist likes wines from established brands and wineries and feels having wine with dinner makes the occasion more formal. Traditionalists account for 16 percent of the populace.

The last three groups are similar in their approach to wine. Savvy Shoppers (15 percent of consumers) are proud of their research into wine and will try new things to find a great buy. They often purchase wine in restaurants based on value. Satisfied Sippers (14 percent) know what they like, even if they are not well educated about wine in general. Wine is a beverage to them, with a favorite brand that is drunk everyday. Wine as an enhancement to a dining experience is not a priority; rather, a simple glass of their favorite wine with dinner suffices. Finally, Enthusiasts (12 percent) consider themselves well informed about wine and will tend to buy better wines for weekends and events over their everyday wine. These consumers are influenced by wine reviews and will browse for wine to try.

How can a sommelier apply the information from this study in a restaurant setting? Understanding the mindset of the consumer can help the sommelier in wine list design (see Chapter 31) and with sales at the table. The most striking information is that the majority of consumers are confused about wine. This is the opportunity for the sommelier to shine, to share knowledge, and to help educate the guest to make an informed choice. The world of restaurant sales is not the place for a dissertation on the Grand Crus of Burgundy, yet it is a place to learn what the consumers like and try to steer them to something they will enjoy, and can use in the future.

While the Overwhelmed make up the majority of consumers, they only purchase 13 percent of all sales. The real wine buyers are the Enthusiasts and Image Seekers, who comprise 49 percent of all sales. Having an Enthusiast at the table is a great opportunity for the sommelier to sell some of the more unique offerings on the menu. The same holds true for Image Seekers, as long as the wine is notable and unique.

APPROACHING THE TABLE

Every restaurant has its own procedures as to how the guest should be greeted at the table. In most instances, the wine list is presented at the same time as the menus. Wine-savvy restaurants will not attempt to sell a bottle of wine until the meal has been ordered. They understand that wine is meant to complement the dinner, and therefore it is a secondary order after the meal has been decided upon. The majority of restaurants take the wine order first, treating it as a beverage and also as a "distraction" for the guest until the appetizer arrives. By taking and serving the wine before food arrives, the guest is entertained by the service and then has something to enjoy as they wait for their meal. Neither is technically wrong; it is just a matter of service philosophy.

In either case, when the sommelier approaches the table, he or she is "reading the guest." The sommelier may have received some information from the host or from the server regarding the "state of the guest." What needs to be determined is why the guest is there that evening. Is it a celebration or special occasion? Is it a business event? Is the guest hurried to get to a show or other event? Is the guest there to relax and "dine" as the evening's entertainment? Is the guest looking to be pampered? All of this needs to be assessed early in the service encounter so that appropriate actions can be taken to meet the guest's expectations. If it is possible to determine what category of wine consumer the guest falls into, the sommelier can then tailor the approach accordingly. These assessments will determine how to approach wine sales at the table.

There are three guest moods in relation to wine service. The dream guests are those who care as much for the wine as for the food. They want to have the ultimate experience, whether with a wine they always order and enjoy, or with a great food and wine pairing experience. These guests are probably Enthusiasts, Image Seekers, or Traditionalists. Second are the guests who normally would not purchase wine, but feel that because it is a special occasion or celebration, or because they are dining in an exclusive restaurant, that wine must be part of the meal. Some Traditionalists fall into this mood, along with Satisfied Sippers and Savvy Shoppers. The third person is the one who loves wine and will frequent restaurants not for the cuisine, but because they have a great wine list and great bargains of things they can-not get themselves. This is classic Savvy Shopper, but also includes Image Seekers.

Often, the state of the guest may be easy to assess, but not what mood they are in with relation to wine. This is the focus of the initial observations at the table. Through some questioning, it is possible to confirm what has been observed prior approaching the table, and to explain what type of wine service would be best for the guest. This is also the time to determine how much the guest would like to spend on wine.

Initial inquiries at the table could confirm what may already be known. Asking if this is a celebration, when the host has told you it is someone's birthday, is a way to communicate that the guest's needs are being taken into consideration and not taken for granted. If there is no prior information, it is the job of the sommelier to assess what type of wine guest they are serving. Direct questions may be off-putting to the guest, but a warm, welcoming approach will often elicit information as to the style of service the guest expects.

The next job is to assess who is the wine host. The wine host and the host of the party may be the same person, but sometimes the party host may defer to another guest to make the wine selections. This is the person who should receive the wine list. The proper way to determine this is to ask who will make the wine selections for the evening. Never ask a yes or no question like, "Will you be having wine with dinner?" That gives the guest the opportunity to say no, and all wine sales are lost.

MAKING RECOMMENDATIONS

The second major job of the sommelier is to make recommendations to the guest. This can be approached in two different ways, often depending upon when the wine is to be ordered. Let's take the scenario where the meal has already been ordered. Ideally, before the sommelier approaches the table, he or she should have looked at what the food choices are. As the guest is deciding which wine to order, the som-melier can make recommendations as to what the best pairing options may be.

What if food has not been ordered yet? Then a bit more work is required. Because the main goal is guest satisfaction, determining what type of wine the guest likes is the best avenue of approach. This is often accomplished by asking the guest what types of wine have been enjoyed in the past. This can be tricky, because a guest may say that he or she enjoys French wine, but there is a big dif-ference between fruity Beaujolais and a Médoc Cabernet Sauvignon. It is best to determine a style the guest has enjoyed—fruity, rich, tannic, etc. From that point of reference, a sampling of wines can be suggested that the guest might enjoy.

In either scenario, the proper method of recommending wine should include at least three choices. These choices should cover three different price points. One suggestion should be the economy version. This would be a wine on the list that meets the desires of the guest and is a great bargain. The second suggestion should fall in the middle of the price range of the wine list. The final wine may be a bit more expensive, possibly a splurge wine. Why three recommendations at different price points? Because no matter how well sommeliers read a guest, they can never fully know the motivations behind a wine selection. Maybe this guest is willing to pay top dollar for a special bottle this one evening. Maybe tonight the focus is the food, and a nice simple, inexpensive wine is all that is desired. Three price points allows the guest to make the decision based on cost, without it looking like the decision was based on cost. Saving the guest embarrassment or even the threat of embarrassment is the sign of a good waiter or sommelier.

Do the three wines have to be from the same category? Not necessarily. If a guest states that he or she loves red Burgundy, then it is pretty easy to recommend three red Burgundies. To include an Oregon Pinot Noir or a Rioja would be foolish. The guest has stated a preference and by including wines that are not in that category, no wine has been effectively suggested. Should the guest choose the Rioja, for example, and then decide it is not what was wanted or expected, it is possible that the bottle will be returned, leading to other complications.

On the other hand, if the guest likes fruity white wines, that opens a realm of possibility. It is always safe to recommend the usual suspects when given a broad category, though with the right guests it is possible to try to expand their wine horizons. Most guests may be adventurous, but with some fiscal caution (in other words, they don't want to waste their money on something they may not like). Therefore, the more daring recommendations may occur at the lower price points. With the fruity white wine example, suggesting an Arneis from northwestern Italy may seem like a stretch for some consumers, yet at the right price point it may be a fun experiment.

EDUCATION

The final major job of a sommelier on the floor is education. That education is two-fold. The sommelier is responsible for training assistants and other waitstaff about the wine list. But the education may also extend to the customer.

The role as educator within the staff involves multiple tasks for the sommelier. The most frequent training opportunity will happen at a preservice meeting. These meetings are held for the waitstaff to cover what the plan of action for the evening will be, make announcements, and ensure proper treatment of VIP guests. This is also the time that the kitchen makes announcements to the waiters, and often describes the specials that will be offered that evening. Samples are typically provided so the staff knows what they are selling. This is a perfect time to include wine in the announcements.

The wine education provided during a preservice meeting will more than likely not be an in-depth tasting, or a review of a major wine region. It may be a sampling of a wine that pairs best with the special that evening. It may simply be a sampling of a wine on the list. This type of short teaching moment keeps the wines fresh in the minds of the staff, and allows them to feel more confident about the wine list as a whole because they have more than one opportunity to sample the offerings.

More structured wine training may happen on a recurring basis. That may be annually or quarterly, depending on when the wine list is changed. These tasting lessons could be general education seminars or specific tastings. It is common for new waitstaff to get a basic wine training session that educates them about the wine list. During this time, depending on the size of the list, wines are sampled so that the waitstaff can speak to the guest intelligently and with first-hand knowledge of the product. As the wine list changes, the entire staff may come in for refresher training on the new wines and their styles.

Finally, a sommelier is a mentor to those who work as his assistants. The job of mentor will change from person to person, but the sommelier really is responsible for the development and expansion of knowledge of the assistants. The sommelier should provide tasting opportunities to assistants to increase their tasting skills, as well as guide them in acquiring the academic understanding of the wine world that is required by the profession.

How does the sommelier educate the guest, without turning the sale into a boring lecture? Very carefully. Not every sale is a teaching opportunity. The best opportunities are when the chance to sell the guest on a wine outside of his or her usual choice comes into play. Let's return to the guest who likes fruity white wines. This is an excellent teaching moment, which can encourage a sale. In offering an Arneis as a possible choice, the sommelier has the opportunity to talk about the style of the grape, its history in Italy, and about the producer. Education does not have to be a dissertation on the balance of acid and sugar or other technical aspects of wine making. It is most successful when it is a story that serves as a connection between the guest and the wine. If the story can open the mind of the guest to try a wine, even that little experimentation is education.

In the Back

Unlike the food side of the restaurant industry, there is not a distinction between the producers of the product and the sales of the product when it comes to wine. In the case of the sommelier, the job is not restricted just to selling wine and refilling glasses for the evening. The sommelier is also responsible for all the preparation needed to provide successful wine service for the evening.

TEMPERATURE

One of the most critical unseen aspects of the sommelier's job is to maintain the proper temperature of wines for service. The temperature of the wine can enhance or detract from the enjoyment of the wine. In Chapter 5, the proper service temperatures for most wines were presented. It is essential for all wines to be presented at the proper temperature. A white wine that is too cool will taste flat, because the aromatic compounds are not being released. On the other hand, if it is too warm the wine will taste acidic and thin. For red wines, too cool a temperature will result in the wine seemingly overly tannic. Too warm a service temperature and a red wine will appear thin and alcoholic. Therefore, it is important that wine is served at the proper temperature. Unfortunately, most white wine served is too cold and most red wine is served too warm.

What can the sommelier do to control service temperature? In many cases, the wines are kept in short-term storage units, often reach-in refrigerators or storage cabinets. The temperature within those storage units is critical. It is also possible to chill a wine by a quick dunk in an ice bucket to drop the temperature. It may be worthwhile to invest in a rapid cooling unit, which circulates chilled water around a bottle and can drop its temperature in minutes. To regulate the temperature at the table, a combination of an ice bucket and a coaster is usually all that is necessary to keep the wine in the proper temperature range.

EQUIPMENT

The setup and maintenance of the proper service equipment also falls under the sommelier job. The primary piece of equipment is glassware. Whether the property has several styles of glassware for its wine service or a basic set for red and white wine, the proper care and cleaning of the glasses are important. Glassware should never be washed with soap and certainly not with any rinse agent in the dishwasher. Often crystal stemware is too delicate to be washed in a dish machine, so these glasses are washed by hand simply with hot water. Other properties have dedicated dish machines that are solely for the cleaning of stemware.

Polishing stemware is a custom for many restaurants. Local health department laws may restrict the polishing of glassware with linen napkins, so research of the local laws is appropriate before beginning such a practice. If allowed, polishing of glassware is not just wiping the bowl with a napkin. Steam is utilized, usually in the form of a bowl of hot water, to lightly moisten the glass before it is polished with a lint-free cloth. The entire glass is polished, including the stem and base. It is important to care for the glassware, as it shows the guests the level of detail the restaurant focuses on, as well as the increased enjoyment the guests have from crystal-clear glassware to enjoy their wine.

Other items that need care and attention include decanters and the equipment required for decantation, ice buckets and stands, and coasters for the table. Decanters should be treated as glassware, though there are specialized tools for eliminating the sediment or excess water in a decanter. Ice buckets and stands should be polished, and coasters and napkins readied for service. If older bottles are common on the wine list, the apparatus for decantation should be ready if needed. This means there should be baskets to carry the wine in the cellar, as well as carts or other specialized areas prepared with the tools for decanting—candles, decanters, and so on.

The final aspect of the sommelier's job in the back of the house is inventory. This is not the inventory to make sure the shelves are full and more product is ordered from the supplier. This is a nightly inventory of all the wines that will be needed for service. No matter how large or small the wine list is at a restaurant, there are always some wines that are more popular than others. Based on sales histories, it is easy to determine how much of any particular wine will probably be sold in an evening. It is the job of the sommelier to make sure that amount of stock is available for easy access during service. This will not necessarily guarantee that it is the correct amount for that particular evening, but the majority of the time sales history is a good indicator of future sales volume.

SUMMARY

The job of sommelier is more than opening and serving wine. The aspects of the job that affect the customer directly are service; recommendations based on taste, price, or food; and education. The education aspect may involve giving the guest a short story about a grape or producer, or it may be more intensive via staff training. Much of the job also occurs behind the scenes. These aspects include preparing glassware and equipment for service as well as making sure the wine is in adequate supply and at the proper temperature for service.

QUESTIONS

1. How do the different types of consumers influence the sales method of the sommelier?

2. What is meant by "reading the guest," and how does it influence the sales method chosen?

3. Why should three recommendations be given for any wine sale?

4. Why is education an important role of the sommelier?

5. What are the behind-the-scenes duties of the sommelier?

chapter 31

Wine List Creation and Menu Matching

*S*ommeliers are not simply glorified wine stewards or servers. Rather, they are the wine equivalent of an executive chef. They must create a menu of wines that will appeal to their clientele, price them to make the restaurant a profit, and make sure the choices are in alignment with the other items offered in the restaurant—that is, the menu and the decor.

Upon completion of this chapter, the student should be able to:

Outline the different aspects of a beverage program
Discuss the importance of flights as a sales tool
Outline a wine list based on different organization styles
Explain the importance of bin numbers on the list and in the cellar
Describe the hot zone and its importance in writing a wine list
Explain the various methods for using markups to price wine
Describe the philosophy behind matching the wine list to the menu

The Beverage Program

Restaurants have two major sources of income: food and beverages. It is the job of the sommelier (or the manager in charge of wine and spirits) to develop a set of offerings that are congruent with the offerings of food and decor. This is called the beverage program, or because most restaurants focus on wine, a wine program.

The first controlling factor in developing a wine program is the concept of the restaurant. Who is the restaurant going to serve? In what area of town is the restaurant located? What is the style of the service? Is the food refined, rustic, or some other style? Is there an ethnic theme to the restaurant? All of these considerations and more need to be taken into account when developing the program.

BY THE BOTTLE

The most common offerings in the wine program are bottles of wine. The bottle is the icon of wine sales. This is the format that most consumers are used to seeing in a restaurant. It is also the most common method of purchasing wine wholesale. It is a convenient, self-contained unit that can be priced simply based on cost. The standard wine bottle is 750 mL or 25.5 ounces, and can serve five 5-ounce portions.

How many different bottles should a restaurant carry? Again, that goes back to concept. The restaurant trying to be a destination place, with offerings of the best items available, will likely have a larger selection of wines than a small corner bistro. Space is also a consideration. A large selection of wines requires a large area for storage, though off-site storage may be an option in some cases.

What wines should be selected? That depends on both the food and the concept. Two considerations need to be addressed. First is the style of food. If the restaurant highlights California cuisine and promotes its artisanal producers, the wine list should reflect that. The wines should be small producers, focused mainly in California, to help maintain the concept. Does that mean that Cru Classe Bordeaux is out of place? Not necessarily. That takes us to the second consideration, price point. The wines must also fit in the pricing structure of the restaurant. For most restaurants, the wine pricing has to be in line with that of the other offerings.

BY THE GLASS

An avenue of wine sales that is becoming more and more popular in restaurants is wine by the glass. The popularity of wine by the glass has grown with the advent of stricter drinking and driving laws as well as more savvy wine consumers. With the right equipment, wines by the glass can potentially equal sales of wine by the bottle.

The history of wine by the glass sales in restaurants has not been amazing. The old wine by the glass mentality was to serve a house wine in red or white. It was assumed that the wine was a special selection from the management to complement the dining experience. In more cases than not, it was an innocuous jug wine that was very inexpensive and sold for a large profit. This curtailed sales and gave the concept of wine by the glass a poor image. Innovations in storage and service have allowed wine by the glass to become a more integral part of a beverage program.

Any program that includes wine by the glass must incorporate somewhat disparate offerings. First, one must include the popular items. This is for the customer who wants wine with dinner, but may not want to consume a whole bottle. This style of service has developed as house wine has evolved and as concern over drinking and driving has increased. The wines offered in this service are commonly available, and familiar to the customer. The choices are driven by consumer demand and wine popularity.

The other style of wine by the glass is the esoteric. Some restaurants use the idea of serving wine by the glass to offer their customers wines that they normally might not be able to afford by the bottle. A customer is more likely to splurge on one glass of fine Napa Cabernet Sauvignon at $25 per glass than drop $125 on a bottle they may not finish.

Where the sale of wine by the glass has been very effective is on the dessert menu. For years, restaurants have offered single glasses of Ports, Sherries, and Madeiras, along with Cognac and Armagnac on their dessert lists. The same philosophy applies for dessert wines as it does for table wines. The wines should fit the concept of the restaurant and should match the desserts to which they may be paired.

Flights

Serving wines by the glass allows for a new twist in wine education sales and enjoyment. It is possible to serve more than one type of wine at a time. This style of sales is called a flight. The wines can be sequenced in different ways, depending on what is to be highlighted. Overall, the amount of wine remains the same as for a single glass. If the flight comprises three wines, each would be about a 2-ounce pour.

A typical version may be a vertical flight. This involves pouring the exact same wine from a winery with the vintage as the only variable, such as pouring three glasses of Cambria Julia's Vineyard Pinot Noir from 2003, 2002, and 2001. The years do not have to be consecutive, but they are often chosen to illustrate great vintages, how the wine evolves over time, or variations in style based on the weather during each vintage year.

Another version is the horizontal flight. This is a combination of wines from the same year, but from different producers, vineyards, or regions. This style of flight shows the variation within a given year based on the producer. A comparison of 2006 Chardonnays from Napa, Burgundy, and Australia would be a horizontal flight.

Finally, there is the theme flight. This encompasses pretty much any other combination of wines. There does not have to be any consistency of producer, vintage, or region. It is merely a collection of wines that are showcased in relation to each other. Comparing samples of the wines mentioned in any single chapter would constitute a flight. For example, Viognier, Muscat, and Albarino (Chapter 15) served as a flight would compare aromatic grapes.

ALTERNATIVE FORMATS

A well-rounded wine program will offer wine in more than one size. One way to do that is to offer wine by the glass alongside wines by the standard bottle size. Another method is to offer alternative-format bottlings. These are wines that are bottled in sizes other than the standard 750 mL. The two most common alternative formats are half bottles and magnums.

Half bottles are exactly what they sound like—half the size of a normal bottle, or 375 mL. This is enough for a glass for two people, and a little to spare. Wines sold in this format are not as plentiful as they are in standard bottles, yet more and more wineries are beginning to sell wines in this size package.

Half bottles present a great opportunity for the sommelier. Because the wine is bottled, it is possible to have a wider variety of wines available than by the glass. The fear of oxidation of an unsold bottle is no longer applicable. Second, half bottles offer the ability to pair wine with food better. In most cases, a table of two will order one bottle of wine. That will give them each two glasses plus some extra. It is very rare that a couple will order an appetizer and an entrée that would match with the same wine for both courses. With half bottles, it is possible to sell a couple a bottle of white wine to go with their appetizers, followed by a bottle of red for their entrées.

Magnums are bottles that hold 1.5 liters of wine, or two standard bottles. For restaurants that serve large parties, these are an excellent addition to the wine list. Magnums are slightly more cost effective than two standard bottles of the same wine. Thus, purchasing a single magnum of a wine can be less expensive for the guest. As we have seen in previous chapters, magnums age more slowly than regular bottles, and often older vintages unavailable in standard bottles are still young and drinkable in magnums.

OTHER BEVERAGES

Most restaurants focus a great deal of attention on the wine program, leaving other beverages as a second thought. However, more and more customers are looking for nonalcoholic beverages or inventive cocktails. These can bring as much profit to the restaurant as wine, and demonstrate a commitment to guest satisfaction.

Operations that target a non-wine savvy section of the population (the Overwhelmed) often turn to what the consumer does understand: beer. Beer sommeliers have appeared in many restaurants. The idea of having someone to guide the customer through the craft and microbrew choices has been received very well. Many consumers understand beer and beer terminology. Having someone who can "talk beer" with them and guide them to a beer that will pair well with their meal is less intimidating than delving into an area like wine. If a restaurant does not have a beer sommelier, it is often easy to train the staff to explain the choices on the menu.

Decisions about other beverages will be made by the entire management staff, including the chef and sommelier. Tastings and cost analysis should be conducted for coffee and teas, as well as spirit choices for the bar. Finally, nonalcoholic beverages (iced tea, sodas, and the like) and bottled waters round out the beverage program.

Wine List Creation

The wine list is an organized method of informing the guest about the wines that are for sale in the restaurant. There are many types of organizational systems for a wine list, some traditional and others more contemporary. Aside from how the list organized for the guest, there needs to be organization in the storage area in order to find the wine a customer orders.

WINE LIST ORGANIZATION: FORMAT

Regional

The most traditional organization of a wine list is by region. This places wines on the list according to their place of origin. First, the wines are organized by country, then wine region within that country. Further organization may include subregions, districts, and, ultimately, vineyards. This is the style that wine lists have followed for years. Wine connoisseurs understand geography in relation to wine, and know what grape varietals and what wines are best in each region.

This style of the wine list is not easily understood by the common wine consumer. While consumers may know what countries make wine and which country's wine they like, they are not as informed on the details of wine regions. In fact, the style of organization can be partly to blame for the stereotype of the snobbish sommelier. Customers who were not informed as to great wine regions, along with sommeliers who did not think education or customer service was part of their job, converged to create a stereotype of a sommelier who only appreciated educated (and often wealthy) customers, while looking down on the novices.

LES VINS BLANCS
WHITE WINES

BIN		
	CHAMPAGNE & SPARKLING	
	VARIETALS: CHARDONNAY, PINOT NOIR, PINOT MEUNIER	
01	SIMONNET-FEBVRE – CRÉMANT DE BOURGOGNE, MV	42
02	BAILLEY-LAPIERRE – CRÉMANT DE BOURGOGNE ROSÉ, 04	45
03	PERRIER-JOUËT – GRAND BRUT, MV	75
04	PIPER HEIDSIECK – ROSÉ SAUVAGE, MV	85
05	A. MARGAINE – CUVÉE TRADITIONELLE, MV	90
06	PIERRE GIMONNET – 1ER CRU BRUT, MV	95
07	GASTON CHIQUET – BLANC DE BLANCS D'AY, MV	99
08	PIERRE PETERS – CUVÉE DE RÉSERVE, MV	105
09	L. AUBRY FILS – ROSÉ, MV	110
10	RENÉ GEOFFROY – CUVÉE EMPREINTE, MV	119
	BOURGOGNE	
	VARIETAL: CHARDONNAY	
20	MÂCON VILLAGES – BOUCHARD AÎNÉ, 06	32
21	SAINT VERAN – DOMAINE DES MAILLETTES, 06	38
22	BOURGOGNE BLANC – ALBERT BICHOT, 05	45
23	CHABLIS – DOMAINE LAROCHE, 04	48
24	RULLY – JOSEPH DROUHIN, 05	50
25	POUILLY-FUISSÉ – DOMAINE SOUFRANDISE, 05	52
26	BOUZERON – A&P DE VILLAINE, 05	59
27	CHABLIS 1ER CRU MONTMAINS – J. DUBOIS, 06	62
28	MONTAGNY – FAIVELEY, 05	65
29	MEURSAULT – LOUIS LATOUR, 05	70
30	HAUTES-CÔTES DE NUITS – JAYER-GILLES, 05	80
31	PULIGNY-MONTRACHET – OLIVIER LEFLAIVE, 05	95
32	CHASSAGNE-MONTRACHET – BADER-MIMEUR, 02	120
33	CORTON-CHARLEMAGNE GRAND CRU – LOUIS LATOUR, 04	165
	BORDEAUX	
	VARIETAL: SAUVIGNON BLANC, SÉMILLON	
40	BORDEAUX BLANC – CHÂTEAU LA MOULINIÈRE, 06	29
41	ENTRE-DEUX-MERS – CHÂTEAU LES ARROMANS, 06	36
42	GRAVES – CHÂTEAU CHANTEGRIVE, 05	45
43	BORDEAUX BLANC – CHÂTEAU DOISY DAËNE, 05	50
	RHÔNE & SOUTHERN FRANCE	
	VARIETALS: VIOGNIER, MARSANNE, ROUSSANNE	
50	CÔTES DU RHÔNE – PERRIN RÉSERVE, 06	30
51	VDP D'OC – VIOGNIER, DOMAINE DE COUSSERGUES, 07	32
52	CORBIÈRES – CHÂTEAU LA BARONNE, 06	36
53	CROZES-HERMITAGE BLANC – DOMAINE LES BRUYÈRES, 04	50
	ALSACE	
60	RIESLING – RENÉ MURÉ, 06	36
61	PINOT GRIS – PIERRE SPARR RÉSERVE, 06	42
62	GEWÜRZTRAMINER – LOUIS SIPP, 04	48
63	PINOT BLANC – MARCEL DEISS, 03	55
64	RIESLING GRAND CRU – LOUIS SIPP, 00	60
	LOIRE	
	VARIETALS: SAUVIGNON BLANC, CHENIN BLANC, MELON DE BOURGOGNE, CHARDONNAY	
70	JARDIN DE LA FRANCE – DOMAINE DE BERNIER, 06	27
71	MUSCADET – DOMAINE DES DORICES, 06	30
72	CHEVERNY – DOMAINE DE SALVARD, 07	35
73	VOUVRAY – DOMAINE PICHOT, 06	38
74	SANCERRE – LES CHAILLOUX, CHERRIER, 06	48
75	SANCERRE – CELESTIN BLONDEAU, 06	50
76	SAVENNIÈRES – CHÂTEAU D'ÉPIRÉ, 05	55
77	POUILLY FUMÉ – DOMAINE BERTHIERS, 05	58
78	SAVENNIERES-LES CLOS SACRES – NICOLAS JOLY, 04	65

WINES BY THE GLASS
=====::: OFFERED ON OUR :::=====
ROLLING CART

LES VINS ROUGES
RED WINES

BIN		
	BORDEAUX	
	VARIETALS: MERLOT, CABERNET SAUVIGNON, CABERNET FRANC, PETIT VERDOT	
100	CÔTES DE FRANCS – CHÂTEAU BOIS DE NAUD, 05	32
101	BORDEAUX SUPÉRIEUR – CHÂTEAU CADILLAC, 04	34
102	BORDEAUX – CHÂTEAU LARROQUE, 05	36
103	BORDEAUX – CUVÉE PRESTIGE, CHÂTEAU LES ARROMANS, 05	40
104	GRAVES – CHÂTEAU LE BONNAT, 03	42
105	PESSAC-LEOGNAN – CHÂTEAU BOIS-MARTIN, 05	48
106	HAUT-MÉDOC – CHÂTEAU D'ARVIGNY, 00	52
107	CÔTES DE FRANCS – PÉLAN, 98	55
108	MARGAUX – CHÂTEAU PAVEIL DE LUZE, 03/04	62
109	ST. EMILION GRAND CRU – CH. LA ROCHE MANGOT, 00	64
110	LALANDE DE POMEROL – CH. MOULIN DE LAVAUD, 05	68
111	MARGAUX – CHÂTEAU D'ANGLUDET, 04	90
112	ST. EMILION GRAND CRU – CH. QUINAULT L'ENCLOS, 03	95
113	POMEROL – VRAY CROIX DE GAY, 00	120
114	MARGAUX – CHÂTEAU PRIEURÉ-LICHINE, 03	145
	BEAUJOLAIS	
	VARIETAL: GAMAY	
200	BEAUJOLAIS – DUPEUBLE, 06	33
201	BEAUJOLAIS-VILLAGES – ALBERT BICHOT, 06	35
202	BROUILLY – LAURENT MARTRAY, 05/06	38
203	MOULIN-A-VENT – POTEL-AVIRON, 04	40
204	FLEURIE – JP CHAMPAGNON, 04	45
205	MORGON – MARCEL LAPIERRE, 06	52
	LOIRE	
	VARIETAL: CABERNET FRANC, PINOT NOIR	
300	SAUMUR CHAMPIGNY – CAVE DU ROCHER, 05	32
301	CHINON – CHARLES JOGUET, 05	45
302	SANCERRE – DOMAINE SAUTEREAU, 05	47
	BOURGOGNE	
	VARIETAL: PINOT NOIR	
400	BOURGOGNE – DOMAINE PARENT, 05	38
401	GIVRY – LOUIS LATOUR, 02	55
402	CHASSAGNE-MONTRACHET – BADER-MIMEUR, 02	62
403	BOURGOGNE – DOMAINE LEROY, 99	75
404	POMMARD – DOMAINE PARENT, 04	90
405	MERCUREY – A&P DE VILLAINE, 05	99
406	MOREY ST. DENIS – MICHEL MAGNIEN, 05	105
407	VOLNAY 1ER CRU – LOUIS LATOUR, 05	110
408	GEVREY CHAMBERTIN – MICHEL MAGNIEN, 05	115
409	CORTON GRAND CRU – DOMAINE PARENT, 01	160
	LANGUEDOC, PROVENCE & SOUTHWEST	
	VARIETALS: SYRAH, GRENACHE, MALBEC, MOURVÈDRE, CARIGNAN, CINSAULT, CABERNET	
500	CAHOR – LE GOULEYANT, 06	29
501	MINERVOIS – CHÂTEAU CABEZAC, 03	32
502	VDP DU GARD – CABERNET/SYRAH, MAS DE GUIOT, 05	36
503	CORBIÈRES – CASTELMAURÉ, 05	38
504	CABARDÈS – CHÂTEAU SALITIS, 04	40
505	CAHORS – CLOS LA COUTALE, 05/06	42
506	FITOU – CHÂTEAU DES ERLES, 04	45
507	LES BAUX DE PROVENCE – MAS DE GOURGONNIER, 05	46
508	LANGUEDOC – DOMAINE GRANDES COSTES, 05	48
509	CORBIÈRES – DOMAINE LIGNERES, 03	52
	RHÔNE	
	VARIETALS: SYRAH, GRENACHE, MOURVÈDRE	
600	CÔTES DU RHÔNE – CHAPPELLE NOTRE DAME D'AUBUNE, 05	32
601	COTES DU RHONE – PERRIN, 06	35
602	RASTEAU – CAVE DE RASTEAU, 05	38
603	VACQUEYRAS – DOMAINE MAS DU BOUQUET, 04	42
604	CAIRANNE – DOMAINE BERTHET-RAYNE, 06	45
605	GIGONDAS – NECTAR DU TERROIR, 05	50
606	CROZES-HERMITAGE – LES JALETS, JABOULET, 05	54
607	ST JOSEPH – OFFERUS, J.L. CHAVE, 05	62
608	CHÂTEAUNEUF DU PÂPE – DOMAINE DU PÈRE CABOCHE, 05	65
609	CHÂTEAUNEUF DU PÂPE – PATRICK LESEC, 04	75

VINTAGES SUBJECT TO AVAILABILITY

This wine list from Mon Ami Gabi is a fine example of a broad, regionally organized French wine list.

Courtesy of Lettuce Entertain You Enterprises.

The regional wine list does have its benefits. For restaurants with large lists that offer multiple vintages, the comparison of wines from the same place and producer based on vintage is easier. This system is one of the methods that the restaurant may use to categorize its own storage system in the cellar. That makes it easier for wines to be found and brought to the table.

Varietal

The varietal wine list is currently the most popular version used in restaurants. Since the 1970s when varietal labeling became popularized by Frank Schoonmaker, most wine lists have moved to the same practice.

The idea of a varietally driven wine list is very in tune with customers today. When perusing their local wine shop, most of the wines are divided by variety. Old World wine regions are often still categorized by country and region, yet New World areas are broken down by country and then varietal. Consumers are used to looking for the varietal name on a wine, and have their allegiances to a particular varietal.

Because a list is organized by varietal does not mean it cannot have regions or other methods as a secondary tool. In fact, most varietal lists are then broken down by country or region. This allows for the determination of style or flavor profile, but still based on the varietal of choice.

The downside to a wine list organized in this manner comes into play if there is not a large selection of wines. It is difficult to create a category for Grenache, and then only have one or two wines to offer of that varietal. The result is usually a general grouping of red wines and white wines, which looks as if there is no organization to the list at all. For those wines that do not or cannot make a separate category, many restaurants use a clever title to designate a broad category of unique wines.

Style

The latest trend in wine lists is to organize the wines by style. Just as some of the chapters earlier in this book were categorized by style, so too can a wine list. This is a very modern approach to selling wine, and may take some education and instruction on the part of the sommelier for those who are unfamiliar with the style.

The simplest method of categorizing by style is to use it as a secondary approach. This would involve categorizing the wines initially by varietal, but within the varietal labeling, listing the wines from lightest to fullest in body. That method can even be taken a step further by listing the varietals in such a way that they are listed from lightest to fullest in body.

The most modern method of listing by style is similar to looking for music on a file-sharing site. It assumes that if you like one particular item in a category, you may enjoy the others. In terms of wine, it means that Chardonnay is not restricted

WINES BY THE BOTTLE

BIN #	CAVA	BTL
	The grand sparkling wine of Spain	
100.	segura viudas, brut reserva, nv	25
101.	freixenet "cordon negro", extra dry, nv	29
102.	cristalino vintage 2001, brut nature	32
103.	codorníu "pinot noir" rosé, brut, nv	35
104.	juve y camps, brut reserva, nv	35
105.	l'hereu de raventós i blanc, brut, nv	48
106.	segura viudas "heredad", brut reserva, nv	49

CONTEMPORARY WHITES

BIN #		BTL
	new grapes, new styles	
200.	viña esmeralda, **moscatel/gewurztraminer**, cataluyna, 04	26
201.	hada, **verdejo**, rueda, 05	26
202.	can feixes blanc sélecció, **parellada**, penedés, 02	29
203.	gran viña sol, **chardonnay**, torres, 02	47
204.	aura, **verdejo**, rueda, 04	47
205.	fillaboa **albariño**, rias baixas, 03	55
206.	fransola, **sauvignon blanc**, torres, 04	64
207.	la conreria d'scala dei, **les brugueres**, priorat, 05	69
208.	mas d'en compte blanc, **white grenache**, priorat, 04	70
209.	absum, **chardonnay**, somontano, 04	75
210.	masia serra, **ctònia**, empordà-costa brava, 01	85

TRADITIONAL WHITES

BIN #		BTL
	spain's noble grapes	
300.	naia, **verdejo**, rueda, 05	31
301.	burga'ns, **albariño**, m. codax, rias baixas, 04	33
302.	viña godeval, **godello**, valdeorras, 02	37
303.	segura viudas creu de lavit, **xarel-lo**, penedés, 04	40
304.	txomin etxaniz, **hondarribi zuri**, txakolina, 03	45
305.	morgadío, **albariño**, rias baixas, 05	49
306.	viña mein, **treixadura**, ribeiro, 02	50

CLASSIC REDS

BIN #		BTL
	traditional grapes	
400.	viña honda, silvano garcia, **monastrell/temp.**, jumilla, 03	25
401.	mayoral, bodegas 1890, **syrah**, jumilla, 02	29
402.	vila vilano, **tinto fino**, ribera del duero, 04	29
403.	montebuena, **tempranillo**, rioja, 03	29
404.	marques de arienzo crianza, **tempranillo**, rioja, 02	33
405.	altos de luzón, **monastrell/syrah**, jumilla, 04	35
406.	marqués de cáceres crianza, **tempranillo**, rioja, 03	35
407.	villacampa del marques, **tinta del pais**, 02	36
408.	bodegas juan gil, **monastrell**, jumilla, 04	40
409.	altico, **monastrell**, jumilla, 03	49
410.	montecillo reserva, **tempranillo**, rioja, 98	49
411.	faustino V reserva, **tempranillo**, rioja, 01	55
412.	sierra cantabria cuvée especial, **tempranillo**, rioja, 02	56
413.	condado de haza, **tinto fino**, **ribera del duero**, 03	57
414.	torres celeste, **tinto fino**, ribera del duero, 03	59
415.	tarsus, **tinta del pais**, ribera del duero, 99	62
416.	gondomar del reino roble, **tempranillo**, ribera del duero, 03	65
417.	campillo reserva, **tempranillo**, rioja	68
418.	pesquera crianza, **tempranillo**, ribera del duero, 02	72

This list from Café Baba Reeba is based on traditional versus modern styles, and then by varietal.

Courtesy of Lettuce Entertain You Enterprises.

to one single category. Chablis and unoaked Chardonnays may be found alongside Sauvignon Blancs, Pinot Grigio, and Pinot Blanc as light, crisp white wine. Oaked Chardonnays may appear along with Viognier, Semillon, and Pinot Gris as full-bodied whites. This style takes a minute to get used to, but once the guest is no longer looking for the Chardonnay section, they can find the wine they want, or get adventurous and order the one it is listed next to.

Other Considerations

One final method of organizing a wine list is very simple, but not used frequently. That method is to organize by price. Many sommeliers avoid listing by price because they fear it will focus the guest on less expensive wines, and therefore decrease the amount of profit from the list. Also, the wines that are at the low end of the price scale are often those the customer sees everyday in their favorite wine store. Seeing the price the restaurant is charging for a bottle they can usually get cheaper at the store may convince some guests to save their money and not order wine at all.

Other restaurateurs have a different view. The Spaghetti Western Restaurant Group in Scottsdale, Arizona, lists its wines by price. What makes this unique is that it has over 3000 wines in the cellar, many of them small or unique producers, and all are included in the list. The guests merely have to decide what price they are willing to pay and start looking. Even at the inexpensive end of the spectrum, the wine list has a large selection of wines and varietals to satisfy any palate.

Whatever method is chosen to organize the wine list is often based on the style of the sommelier. Many are trained by studying the wine regions of the world. Because wine region focused lists are not popular with customers, they change to varietal lists. Sommeliers understand the varietal characteristics of wines, and can list and explain them fairly simply. The style-based list is more work for a sommelier. As evidenced by the example above, it is not always obvious what the style of the wine is without tasting it. That takes a lot of work (not necessary hard work, as far as a sommelier is concerned), and good organizational and tasting skills on the part of the sommelier.

Bin Numbers

Cellar organization, both short term and long term, is often accomplished through the use of bin numbers. These are the numbers of the slots in the cellar where the wine is being stored. Many wine lists also list the bin number on the list. This aids the server in trying to find the wine, and also aids the guests, who can order by number if they cannot pronounce the name of the wine or its producer.

VINO ROJO continued (hey, we're just getting our third wind!)

'03 Domaine Louis Bernard grenache blend, Côtes du Rhône Villages, France............................22
'05 Cantine Sant' Agata barbera, Baby Barb, Asti, Piedmont, Italy..22
'05 Crios de Susana Balbo syrah/bonarda, Rivadavia, Argentina..22
'05 Felsina sangiovese blend, Berendenga, Chianti Classico, Tuscany, *half bottle*..............22
'04 Abundance zinfandel, Mencarini Vineyard, Lodi..22
'06 Palacios Remondo tempranillo blend, La Vendimia, Rioja, Spain..22
'00 Odak kadarka, Mostar Vineyard, Blatina, Herzegovina..22
'04 Paul Achs zweigelt blend, Gols, Burgenland, Austria..22
'05 Moillard gamay, Domaine des Reyssieres, Beaujolais-Villages, France................................22
'02 Alderbrook zinfandel, old vines, Dry Creek..22
'05 Falesco tuscan blend, Vitiano, Umbria, Italy..22
    the house label of winemaker extraordinaire Riccardo Cotarella; the Vitiano is equal parts sangiovese, merlot and
    cabernet sauvignon, never filtered or fined; medium bodied, lush, delicious, quality/price ratio heavy on quality
'05 Castell del Remei tempranillo/cabernet/merlot, Gotim Bru, Costers del Segre, Spain.........22
'05 Plantaže vranac, Lake Skadar Valley, Montenegro..22
'04 Parróne syrah, Colchagua Valley, Chile..23
'04 Pedroncelli zinfandel, Mother Clone, Dry Creek Valley..23
'03 Bonny Doon mourvèdre/syrah/grenache, Le Cigare Volant, Santa Cruz, *half bottle*...........23
'06 Francis Berwyn zinfandel, Paso Robles..24
'05 Gimenez Riili malbec, Mendoza, Argentina..24
'05 Hahn bordeaux blend, Santa Lucia Highlands..24
    Adam Lazarre is a Wildman, climbing on stacks of barrels in grape-stained sneakers with no regard for life or limb,
    blasting Led Zep in the background, blending on a whim, and racheting Hahn's quality up higher than ever before
                                    °°°*SPOTLIGHT* °°°
'05 Enzo Boglietti dolcetto d'Alba, Piedmont, Italy..24
'05 Enzo Boglietti dolcetto, Tiglineri, Alba, Piedmont, Italy..37
'01 Enzo Boglietti nebbiolo, Fossati Vineyard, Barolo, Piedmont, Italy....................................111
'01 Enzo Boglietti nebbiolo, Brunate Vineyard, Barolo, Piedmont, Italy..................................112
'01 Enzo Boglietti nebbiolo, Case Nere, Barolo, Piedmont, Italy..113
    Boglietti is one of Italy's newer hot shot producers who burst on the scene in the early 90s and challenged the
    staid establishment with fresh techniques, including the liberal usage of new small toasted barrels and an insistence
    on cultivation that results in very low environmental impact...impressive, elegant, aromatic, finesse-laden wines

'04 Luna Beberide mencia, Bierzo, Spain..24
'04 Guigal grenache blend, Côtes du Rhône, France..24
'03 Flor de Guadalupe zinfandel, Baja California, Mexico..24
    finally, quality beverages from Mexico that don't require you to lick salt off your hand (unless you really want to)
'05 Chateau Recougne bordeaux blend, Supérieur, France..24
'06 Le Rocche Malatestiane refosco, Adesso, Cagnina, Emilia-Romagna, Italy..........................24
'04 Domaine Jordan Valley cabernet sauvignon, King Ruby, Jordan..24
'03 Peterson carignane blend, Zero Manipulation, Mendocino/Sonoma......................................24
                        look, a wine inspired by the ballot boxes in Florida
'04 Recanati cabernet sauvignon, kosher, Galilee, Israel..24
'98 Castello di Neive barbera, Alba, Piedmont, Italy..24
'05 Marquis-Philips shiraz/cabernet sauvignon, Roogle Red, South Eastern Australia..............24
'06 Casa Silva carmenere, classic, Colchagua, Chile..24
    originally grown in Bordeaux before phylloxera wiped it out, carmenere is now grown only in Chile and was just
    recently recognized by the BATF as a grape varietal (they used to ship it to the US market as merlot); the
    distinctive cumin-scented spice profile of this wine is not for everyone, but it is wondrous with the stuffed pork chop

This list shows playfulness, with varieties organized by price. It also highlights a producer and offers its products together.

Courtesy Spaghetti Western Productions.

Bin numbers should be organized with plenty of room to add new wines as needed. It may be simple to think that the list should not change that much and only a few numbers would be necessary for the extra space. That is not true. Not only may the sommelier decide to place new wines on the list; every year the entire list will change when the new vintages come out. Just with vintage changes alone, it is important to provide plenty of room for expansion.

For the purposes of demonstration, let's say that white wines would have bin numbers between 100 and 1000. Chardonnay would fall from 100 to 400, Riesling from 400 to 500, Sauvignon Blanc from 500 to 700 and interesting whites from 700 to 1000. The proper number of the wines would not be in strict numerical sequence (100, 101, 102, and so on). Instead, space would be made between each wine for changes in vintage. Thus, the first Chardonnay might be 100, but the next bin number would be 105 or 110. This allows not only for changes in vintage, but also for the addition of new Chardonnays to the list.

The cellar does not have to have a lot of empty spaces to accommodate the unused numbers. Rather, one or two spaces may be all that is needed in case a new wine is added to the list. By the time a second vintage change occurs, most of the initial vintage will be gone, and its bin available for the newest release. Only in restaurants where a series of vintages is to be kept on the list would more than one or two empty slots be reserved.

What Wines Should Be Represented?

In constructing a wine list it is typically believed that all major grapes should be represented along with aligning to the concept. The issue of how much of each varietal is often based on popularity. The typical wine list will have more Chardonnay and Cabernet Sauvignon offerings than most of the other varietals. Those may be followed by more red varietals than white wines. Also, at least in the United States, California wines will typically dominate the list over European wines.

The varietal representation is not a hard and fast rule. Imagine being an Italian restaurant trying to find Italian Rieslings and Sauvignon Blancs to round out the list. In this case, having a more regionally representative list is important, though California may still be strongly represented because of the clientele.

The philosophy really determines whether the list will have breadth and/or depth. Breadth in a wine list refers to the wide range of wines that are represented. In the Italian wine list example, a broad wine list may have wines represented from every region of Italy, as well as many of the native grape varietals. A deep wine list, on the other hand, has increased representation in some specific areas. A list may focus on offering multiple vintages of several producers, or it may offer many small producers from one single area. In the Italian list example, a deep list might have most of the Barolo producers represented, or have multiple vintages from a couple of the top producers to offer.

PRICING THE WINE LIST

Part of the construction of the wine list is determining the pricing of the wines to be sold. Depending on the concept and the prices charged on the menu, the range of wines may be limited or boundless.

The best approach to pricing a wine list is to first determine what pricing is appropriate for the restaurant. This is determined by focusing on what the hot zone of the wine list will be. The hot zone is the range of prices within which between 30 and 50 percent of the wines offered will fall. To calculate the edges of the zone, one needs to know the average entrée price. For example, the average entrée price at a restaurant is $25. The low end of the zone would be double the entrée price, or $50. The upper end would be triple the price, or $75. While a good portion of the wines will fall in this range, there should be wines both above and below these prices.

Sample Hot Zone Ranges

Average Entrée Price	Hot Zone Range
$15	$30 to $45
$25	$50 to $75
$35	$70 to $105

The distribution above and below the range is not equal. If 50 percent of the list is in the hot zone, then the distribution above and below is not 25 percent each. Instead, more emphasis should be given to the pricing above the hot zone. This allows for the inclusion of kickers. These are wines that are the highest priced on the list. They provide a splurge or a celebration wine for those who desire one, but it also provides a psychological advantage to the restaurant.

Many people will calculate the median price of the wine list by looking for the highest-priced wines. They divide this in half, and feel if they order a wine slightly lower than the average price, they do not look too cheap. By having kickers on the list, it makes the average price of the wines seem higher than it really is. If the hot zone is between $50 and $75, the average price for a bottle will most likely fall around $62. By having wines close to $200 per bottle, the customer may feel comfortable ordering a bottle near $75 though it is the top of the hot zone.

HOW TO SPLIT UP THE WINES

The next step is determining how many red wines and how many white wines should be on the list. Currently, red wine is more popular with consumers than white wine. Therefore, red wines should make up a substantial portion of the wine list. How much of a portion depends on the concept of the restaurant, and possibly its locale. If the restaurant is a beachfront seafood restaurant, there is the likelihood that more white wine would be desired by the guests, and therefore more white wine options should be on the list. If it is a grill, there will be more call for red wines. The same may be true for cooler regions, where red wine is seen as a hearty beverage to stand up to the cold.

The wines can be distributed based on the percentages in and around the hot zone. Because Chardonnay or Cabernet Sauvignon are the most popular varietals, there will probably be at least one in each cost bracket. When figuring white wines, some restaurants include their sparkling wines in the calculation (they are white wines, after all). Once the number of wines has been determined for each cost bracket, it is time to make the selections.

Markups

Most chefs understand the concept of food cost and how to convert the cost of the product on the plate to a sale price that will cover their expenses. The same holds true for wine, yet there are some differences in how the sale price is calculated.

The first concept is that wine pricing often refers to markup. This is the percentage by which the wholesale price is increased to create the sale price. A wine whose wholesale price is doubled will have a markup of 200 percent. The standard in the industry has been between a 250 percent and 350 percent markup on wine. That means a bottle that was purchased for $5 can sell between $12.50 and $17.50. Because wine can range widely in price, various methods of markup have been devised.

STRAIGHT MARKUP

This markup method is as simple as it sounds. A markup percentage is determined, and all wines are treated the same. This means that if a 300 percent markup is used, a wine costing $10 would sell for $30 and a wine costing $100 would sell for $300.

This method has its advantages and disadvantages. It allows for consistent pricing of all wines when they are purchased. It also guarantees that, if the markup has been chosen correctly, all costs are covered and a profit realized. On the other hand, this method disfavors the high end of the wine list. Because the higher priced wines are increased by the same percentage, the sale price is disproportionately high. Wine buyers who would like to purchase these wines at the restaurant may see them on the list as being expensive, relative to retail or to other restaurants. This will lower the number of sales of these wines, and restrict cash flow and profit from their sale.

FLEXIBLE MARKUP

This method attempts to resolve the problem at the high end of the wine list. It creates more than one markup, depending on the wholesale cost of the wine. Those wines with a high wholesale cost would have a lower percentage markup. The wine at $10 may still have a 300 percent markup and would still sell for $30. The wine at $100 may only have a 200 percent markup, and sell for $200. Technically, it may seem like the restaurant is losing money on the higher-priced wine. In effect, it is probably making more money, because sales of all high-priced wines are increased. The lower-priced wines still make their overhead, and profit is made through volume. The higher-priced wines, now that they are priced more moderately, may see increased sales, and therefore increase cash flow and profit. Also, restaurants that use this method tend to be favorites of wine aficionados who become regulars as much for the wine list as for the food.

COST PLUS

The third pricing method takes the flexible markup one step further. Rather than have a set percentage by which wines are priced, a set amount is added to the wholesale cost of the wine. This amount would be the contribution to the overhead and a small profit. If that amount is determined to be $18, the $10 bottle above would be $28, and the $100 bottle would sell for only $118. This is a true wine lovers' pricing scale. It is not often used for the majority of the list, but could be used for certain items on sale or as a feature on the list.

THE RESERVE LIST

For some restaurants, the hot zone and the concept of it may curtail the types of wines that may be attractive to the clientele. If the restaurant is in a wine-savvy city, or the types of wines the restaurant would like to offer are out of step with the standard pricing, a reserve list can be created. This list is often the most expensive wines the restaurant has to offer. If these wines were placed on the regular list, it would make that list seem expensive, and possibly scare guests away from ordering wine. Instead, the most special bottles are placed on the reserve list, and the sommelier can offer it to those who may be wine connoisseurs or out to splurge or celebrate.

PRICING WINE BY THE GLASS

There are two approaches to pricing wine by the glass. First, remember that a bottle of wine contains 25.5 ounces, yielding five 5-ounce portions. The sale price of the bottle is then divided by 5 to yield the price per glass. Some restaurants leave that calculation alone, so that purchasing five glasses of the same wine would cost the same as a bottle. Others increase the price per glass slightly, making it more cost effective for a group to order a bottle rather than spend the extra money on a per-glass basis.

The second method leaves room for error in pouring the wine. The price of the bottle is divided by 4, and that becomes the price per glass. This can be used two ways. The house can decide to pour more than 5 ounces per glass, making the difference a true cost per glass. The house could also still pour 5 ounce portions, and the final pour from the bottle is extra profit. This is a way for the bottle to be paid for with the first glass sold, and all subsequent sales are profit.

One way to increase the profit from by the glass sales is to calculate the prices based on 750 mL bottles, but pour from 1.5 L magnums. Typically magnums will cost slightly less than two standard bottles. This small cost savings, when translated to the per-glass price, helps increase profit slightly, and often covers any spillage or mistaken pours.

Menu Matching

The wine list should not be created in a vacuum. In other words, the sommelier should have a sense of the menu and the style of food created by the chef in order to make good decisions regarding what wines to place on the list. This is not a solitary project and should include not only the sommelier and chef, but also key members of their staff and the management team. Menu matching is also a process that occurs continuously, as vintages change, dishes change, and consumer demand changes.

BASIC MENU MATCHING

Matching wines to the menu can take many forms, depending on how much the sommelier, manager, and chef wish to incorporate wine into the dining experience. The most basic matching should involve choosing wines to match the restaurant's style of cuisine.

Determining the best wines to match with the menu items cannot be successful with just a list of dishes. Each menu item should be prepared by the chef as it would be served in the restaurant and then analyzed to see how it would interact with wine (for a discussion of the interaction of tastes between food and wine, see Chapter 5). From this point of reference, the tasting panel or just the sommelier can choose wines that fit the required profiles for the menu.

In this basic attempt at menu matching, it is not the goal to find one single wine that would pair with each dish. Rather, it is to find a trend or a style to the wines that would form the backbone of the wines on the list. The sommelier is trying to create a menu of wines that is complementary to the food. Creating a list in broad strokes allows guests to choose wines to their liking, while still having any wine complement the food.

CHOOSING WINES

In some instances, finding wines to pair has a starting point. Wines produced in the same region as the food will most likely work well together, as least as far as European food and wine matches are concerned. Even indirect associations to European cuisines can help guide initial wine choices for matching. For example, California cuisine is heavily influenced by French and Italian cuisine. Therefore, French and Italian wines as well as native varietals to those countries make a good starting point.

What about ethnic cuisines? The Slanted Door, a Vietnamese restaurant in San Francisco, shows that wine can pair with diverse, unique ingredients. The wines on their list are specifically chosen to complement the food. Looking at their wine list reveals a large number of whites, some dry and some off-dry, and a small quantity of reds. What makes the red wine section noteworthy is that all the reds are low in alcohol and tannin, which would detract from the food and make the wine taste poor.

DETAILED MENU MATCHING

In restaurants that focus on good food and good wine, it is common to see recommendations for food and wine pairings. These suggestions could be on the menu or they could be on the wine list. Most often they are seen on the menu. It is not uncommon to see a menu listing with a wine selection underneath. Is this the only wine match for the dish? No. It is merely the recommendation by the sommelier of what may be the best pairing. An approach like this is very demanding, needing exacting understanding of the food and a wide knowledge of wine tastes and flavors. This is a much more time-consuming process, and definitely should include more palates than just that of the sommelier. It is possible in basic menu matching to taste only a few dishes and have only one taster to get a feel for the style of the food. In this case, exact matches are being suggested, and consideration needs to be made for diverse palates. Therefore, the sommelier, chef, and manager/owner or another trusted palate should be the minimum present when trying to decided detailed matches.

There is a rough method that forms the starting point for helping determine good, detailed wine matches. If the food is a classic dish or based on a classic, it is easiest to start with an Old World wine. If the dish is more ethnic, a fusion of cuisines, or contains nontraditional ingredients in the preparation, a New World style of wine is often a better starting point. From there, wines can be specified.

THE WINE DINNER

The ultimate menu matching is for a wine dinner. Depending on the restaurant, the sommelier may do the majority of the work, or very little. If the dinner is one in which there is a focus on the food, the sommelier has a great deal of work to find the right match for each course. Basic wine drinking rules apply as well, with light-bodied wines preceding full-bodied ones, and dry wines before sweet. More often than not, there is a curve ball thrown in by the chef that makes pairing a challenge. The use of foie gras as an early course is a good example. While foie gras is an excellent starter, it is often paired with Sauternes, which is a sweet wine. This pairing would throw off the sequence of wines. The sommelier should work with the chef to create a menu progression that will allow for the best pairings as well as the best showcase for the food.

Another style of wine dinner is one hosted by a winery. In this case, the winery will decide which wines are to be showcased. For this type of wine dinner, the sommelier has little work to do. More work rests with the chef, who must either find a dish on the menu that matches the wine, or in most cases, create special dishes just for this purpose. The sommelier can be a guide to the winery due to his or her understanding of the menu and the chef's style of cooking. In this case, it is imperative that the chef and sommelier taste the wines before the menu planning begins, in order to create the best match.

SUMMARY

Creating a wine list is the beverage equivalent of developing a menu. The most important facet of the wine list is that the wines work well with the food. Choosing the wines is dependent on the concept of the restaurant, the food style, and the clientele. There are multiple methods of organizing the list for the customer, as well as pricing the list for sales. Wines do not need to be sold in only standard-sized bottles, but also by the glass and in alternative formats. Ultimately, the wine list must work with the menu for the entire dining experience to flow together and make a pleasant experience for the guest.

QUESTIONS

1. Describe the different components of a complete beverage program.

2. What opportunities are available when offering wines by the glass?

3. Give an example of each kind of flight.

4. Why are alternative formats important to a beverage program?

5. What are the pros and cons of formatting a wine list by region? By grape? By style?

6. How do bin numbers help the consumer order wine?

7. How is the hot zone calculated? What percentage of wines should fall in the hot zone?

8. Describe the different types of markups.

9. Why is menu matching important when designing a wine list?

chapter 32

Cellar Management and Product Research

*T*he visible job of the sommelier is on the floor serving guests. The most invisible job involves determining what will be in the restaurant's wine cellar and how to keep it fresh and drinkable. Managing the cellar and sourcing new wines is an integral part of the sommelier's job, and of crucial importance for the success of any beverage program.

Upon completion of this chapter, the student should be able to:

Discuss the importance of purchasing and inventory control in the wine cellar

Explain the difference between a perpetual inventory and a physical inventory

Describe the different avenues for product research.

Cellar Management

A beverage program in any restaurant or resort can only be successful with the proper choice of product, and its proper storage and control in relation to its access and sale. These are the main jobs of the sommelier in the cellar. If the operation is large enough, like a large hotel or resort, the job of cellar master may be conducted by someone other than the sommelier.

PURCHASING

The crucial job of the cellar manager is the proper maintenance of wine and spirit inventory. Sales cannot be made if product is not available, and excess product ties up the cash flow of the restaurant and limits the amount of other items that can be purchased.

Proper purchasing procedures are necessary to maintain the balance between having too much wine and having too little. It is a good practice for the cellar master to have set scheduled delivery days for product. This allows a routine to be created in checking stock levels as well as ordering and receiving of product. In the case of popular wines, it is beneficial to develop a par stock, or a set amount of wine to have on hand that will cover the sales between deliveries. Par stock level is determined by analyzing the sales of a particular wine over a set time, say four days between deliveries. The amount of wine that must be on hand should be enough to cover the average number of sales over that four-day period as well as a little extra as a safety measure. Ordering then entails determining the amount of wine needed to bring what is on hand back up to the par level.

Distributors prefer to sell product by the case. It is possible to purchase single bottles or quantities less than a case. These are called broken cases, and often entail an additional charge per bottle. Flexibility with the par stock levels is needed to maintain proper wine costs. Ordering nine bottles to maintain the par stock level may make the par appropriate, but those nine bottles technically cost more per bottle, and therefore the markup would be different or the cost percentage would be changed. It would be more appropriate to order the full case, maintaining the cost of the bottle, and adjusting the overage on the next order.

Some wines have limited availability. These are allocated wines, in which the winery controls who gets to purchase the wine and how much they get. Allocated wines are often limited in production or are in extremely high demand. To purchase the wine, the property must be on an approved list of purchasers. There are even waiting lists to get onto an allocation list. Once allocations are allowed, the purchasing privilege is continued yearly. If for some reason the property does not purchase its allocation, it can lose the privilege. The allocations are typically small;

they are on the order of two cases to as little as six bottles. There is no reordering when the stock runs low.

INVENTORY

The management of the wines in the cellar and their sales on the floor is done through inventory. In the case of alcoholic beverages, the most common method of tracking is a perpetual inventory. A perpetual inventory is the constant tracking of product as it enters and leaves the cellar. At any given moment, the amount of wine or spirit on the shelf can be determined by looking at the perpetual inventory.

To establish a perpetual inventory, a system of bin cards and requisitions must be created. A bin card is a sheet that tracks the addition or subtraction of product in a particular bin. Each time a wine is ordered and received, the amount is added to the inventory. Decreases to that inventory are made with requisitions. The bartender or front-line sommelier must fill out a requisition form to obtain product from the cellar. If three bottles of a wine are needed, the requisition reflects the request for the three bottles, and the bin card tracks that three bottles left inventory. In very strictly controlled operations, a triple check on the system is to compare sales to quantities on the requisition. Ideally, only bottles that were sold will need to be replaced with a requisition.

A perpetual inventory should not be the sole method of tracking wine. At least once a month, preferably twice, a physical inventory should be taken. Physical inventory is the actual counting of product on the shelf. Physical inventories are needed to determine the amount of wine on hand (and therefore the amount of money tied up in the inventory), and to determine the accuracy of the perpetual inventory. The physical inventory should not deviate from the perpetual inventory. Of course, the perpetual inventory has to be accurate for this to occur. If the perpetual inventory is accurate and is in dispute with the physical inventory, there should be a record of breakage, comp sale, or other removal from the cellar. If there is no record of the wine leaving the cellar, theft is the only possibility.

STORAGE

Storage of wine, whether it is short-term storage or long-term, is discussed in detail in Chapter 4. Proper storage procedures are important not only for the quality of wine but also for the accessibility and ease of inventory. The cellar needs an organizational model, often similar to the organization of the wine list. At the least, wines should be organized by bin numbers, as discussed in Chapter 31.

Stock rotation is an important component of a wine cellar. In the case of food, rotation is important because it maintains the freshness of the product. For wine,

An example of a perpetual inventory tracking system.

Item	AP unit	cost	count unit	Par	Date	Mon	Tue	Wed	Thu	Fri	Sat	Sun
La Villa Vitae Pinot Noir North Coast	case	$100 / $8.33	ea	24	open	13	21	18	15	23	17	
					in	12			12			
					out	4	3	3	4	6		
La Villa Vitae Pinot Noir Cornell Cuvee	case	$250 / $20.83	ea	12	open	9	18	14	11	7	3	
					in	12						
					out	3	4	3	4	4		
La Villa Vitae Pinot Noir Josephine's Vineyard	ea	$45.00	ea	4	open	2	6	4	4	4	2	
					in	4			4			
					out		2	2	2	2		

The requisition form required to replenish product at the bar.

Date: _____

Bartender: _____

Bar Requisition Form

WELL

item	count	quantity
Vodka	btl	_____
Bourbon	btl	_____
Gin	btl	_____
Scotch	btl	_____
Rum	btl	_____
Tequila	btl	_____

WINE

item	count	quantity
Pinot Noir	ea	_____
Sauv Blanc	ea	_____
Riesling	ea	_____
Cal. Chard	ea	_____
Chablis	ea	_____
Chianti	ea	_____
Napa Cab	ea	_____

LIQUEUR

item	count	quantity
Amaretto	btl	_____
Coffee Liqueur	btl	_____
Schnapps	btl	_____
Triple Sec	btl	_____
Grenadine	btl	_____
Sloe Gin	btl	_____
Brandy	btl	_____
Irish Cream	btl	_____
Vanilla Liqueur	btl	_____
Crème de Cacao	btl	_____
Crème de Menthe	btl	_____
Crème de Cassis	btl	_____

BEER

item	count	quantity
Pils	6 pk	_____
Pale Ale	6 pk	_____
Bock	6 pk	_____
Stout	6 pk	_____
Brown Ale	6 pk	_____
Lambic	6 pk	_____
Wheat	6 pk	_____

ADDITIONAL NEEDS

_____   _____
_____   _____
_____   _____
_____   _____
_____   _____
_____   _____
_____

freshness is not as important. However, the conditions in the wine cellar are different from those in the wholesaler's warehouse, or from the long-term storage facility. Those wines that have been in the cellar longest should be the first sold. This is the same First In, First Out principle seen in food storage.

Product Research

The role of continued education in the life of a sommelier cannot be underestimated. Each year creates the opportunity for a natural learning progression as the new vintages are released. Even without vintage changes there are thousands of producers, each creating several bottlings and varietals. The list seems endless. But the job of the sommelier is to determine which of these wines is the right fit for their concept.

DISTRIBUTORS

The distributors that provide the wines are a major source of product knowledge. Keep in mind that in many states, distributors are monopoly holders for particular brands. This means that if you desire a particular Washington State Syrah, you have to find the distributor who carries that label. The sommelier will deal with multiple distributors so that their list is well represented. However, the knowledge any one distributor can provide is restricted to the products that they sell.

TRADE SHOWS

Wine and liquor distributors conduct trade shows once or twice a year. These are open only to buyers of wine and spirits for restaurants and resorts, and this is a time to taste new vintages and new styles, or to sample wines not currently on the wine list but in the warehouse of the distributor. These trade shows often have the marketing directors of the wineries present, and sometimes the winemakers themselves. This gives the sommelier a chance to get more in-depth knowledge of the wine making process and the philosophy of the winery.

Trade shows can be a wealth of information or an overwhelming effort for organization. As with any critical tasting, it is important to take notes. This allows the sommelier to focus on one wine at a time, and to have a detailed recollection when deciding on what to bring in house to sample with the menu. Organization is critical. So is planning a strategy. There are hundreds of wines to sample at a trade show. Without any preplanning, it is easy to simply walk table to table and sample wine. While that is a great plan for exploration, it is not conducive to finding a new Merlot or Riesling to add to the list. If the sommelier is looking for particular wines, it is best to walk the show several times, first looking at what is available, then planning an approach to sampling potential wine list items.

THE SALES REPRESENTATIVE

Sales representatives should act as a partner with the restaurant. They should understand what the price points, clientele, and style of the restaurant are in order to help the restaurateur serve the customer. Good sales reps will bring samples to the restaurant because they feel the wine may be a fit for that property. The sales reps can be a great source of knowledge and of guidance when looking for a particular wine or a particular style of wine.

Sales representatives often travel with winemakers or marketing personnel from wineries. They bring them to restaurants to sample their wines, or as a thank-you to the restaurant for using that winery's products. It is the sales rep who can help coordinate winemaker dinners at the restaurant or travel to the winery to taste and sample other wines.

TRAVEL

A great opportunity to source new wines is through travel. The location does not necessarily have to be a wine growing region. Any type of travel provides opportunities to see new products and to source new items.

Travel to a wine growing region is an excellent way to source new items. It could be merely an educational trip, in which the sommelier has the opportunity to taste the wines of the region and get a feel for the food and the style behind the wines. This type of experience will translate to better understanding of the wines and how they work with the food in the sommelier's restaurant.

These regions may also be sourcing trips. This is an opportunity to travel to particular wineries and taste all their products. Not all wineries travel with all their items to trade shows, and not all distributors carry all the wines of a winery. Going to the source is a great opportunity to find wines that are not currently available in the local market or to discover new wineries that are developing and have not gotten distribution rights secured. If the sommelier finds a wine that is not currently carried by its distributor, he or she can request that the wine be placed into stock for the restaurant.

Another benefit of visiting wineries is the opportunity to taste wines before they are ready for sale. These are called barrel tastings, because the wines are tasted while they are still aging in the barrel. This is often done for wines that must age several years in the barrel before release, yet are able to be purchased now at a reduced price. This style of purchasing wine is called the futures market, and it is common for wines from Bordeaux.

Travel does not have to be to where the wine is made, however, to find new and different wines. Traveling to other markets outside that of the restaurant exposes the sommelier to wines that are available from distributors in that area. This is an opportunity to taste and experience wine that is not available locally. It is also a chance to see how others interpret wine lists and form food and wine pairings. These trips can be inspirational as well as educational and encourage experimentation that keeps the wine list fresh and relevant as the cuisine develops.

TRADE MAGAZINES

Finally, trade magazines are an excellent source for new products. Wine magazines are constantly offering tasting notes and comparisons of new products (often with price information included), and current trends in the industry. Other industry publications include both educational articles as well as trend articles for the industry. When travel is not in the restaurant or time budget, reading about what other restaurants and resorts are doing and serving can help inspire a sommelier to research new product lines and new wineries to offer on the list.

SUMMARY

The job of the sommelier includes continued education and a continuing search for new wines. Education is extremely important to understanding new wines, new wine regions, and the new vintages as they are released. The quest to serve the best requires finding items that fit the style of the restaurant. This is commonly done with the help of distributors, who conduct trade shows or send sales representatives to pour potential wines for the restaurant. The distributors are the connection to the wine makers and to the marketing branch of the wineries, which can help secure new wines for the restaurant. Travel to the wineries themselves can help find wines that are not carried by the distributor, or find new wineries whose whole line is not represented. When travel is not an option, reading trade magazines and industry trends keeps the sommelier current as to the trends in the industry, the ideas of other restaurateurs, and the release of new and interesting products.

QUESTIONS

1. Why is proper purchasing of wine and spirits important for a restaurant?
2. What is a perpetual inventory, and what is needed to implement its usage?
3. How do distributors aid in product research?
4. What other methods does the sommelier have for doing product research?

chapter **33**

Understanding Wine Faults

*T*he sommelier must not only be able to store and serve wine, but also be able to determine whether a wine is healthy or not. A full understanding of what makes a wine unhealthy can be used to make purchasing and/or storage decisions that will affect wine sales.

Upon completion of this chapter, the student should be able to:

> *Discuss the importance of determining faulty wine*
> *Describe the procedure for handling a guest sending back wine*
> *Describe single bottle faults*
> *Describe wine flaws and their difference from faults*

Wine Faults

Aromas and flavors in wine come from many places. They could be natural to the grape varietal, or they could be transmitted from terroir. They could be the result of fermentation and other aspects of wine making or from aging wine in barrels. In most cases, these aromas and flavors are pleasant and give the wine its enjoyable character. However, in some cases, the aromas and flavors are not enjoyable. They actually denote that something is wrong with the wine. These are termed wine faults.

In Chapter 3 the process of tasting wine was discussed. At several key stages in an analytical wine tasting, the wine's health is assessed. This is where a fault in the wine can be determined. Faults will first be noted on the nose, and if the taster is brave enough, confirmed on the palate.

Faults are not random occurrences if proper wine making and wine storage procedures are followed. Faults are the result of mistakes, errors, accidents, or mishandling of wine. Some of these faults may affect single bottles, but others may be inherent in an entire batch or vintage. Understanding the fault, its origin, and its implications will help to determine the course of action for resolving the situation.

WINE FAULTS AND THE GUEST

A guest orders a bottle of wine. The bottle is presented, and the producer, vintage, and varietal are confirmed. The bottle is opened and a sample is poured for the host. The host grimaces and states there is something wrong with the wine. What does the sommelier do?

The immediate response is to remove the offending bottle and ask if the host would like to choose something else. This is a fairly safe approach to the situation, but does leave a window for more bottles to be rejected. Upon removing the bottle from the table, the sommelier should check out the wine himself or herself. There are several reasons why a guest may return a bottle, not the least of which is that they just don't like it. However, if the wine is faulty, it is important to determine quickly what the extent of the fault may be before offering another bottle of the same wine. If there was a flaw in wine making, that will show up in every bottle of that wine from that vintage. Bringing a "fresh" bottle of the same wine will more than likely result in the same course of events. If the fault is confined to the bottle, there is a good chance that the next bottle will be fine and the guest will be happy.

If there was no fault with the wine, it is never in good taste or good manners to question the guest or force them to have something they do not like. The recourse one has for an open bottle of wine that cannot be sold by the bottle any more is to sell it by the glass, provide tastings to some of the restaurant's more loyal customers, or use it for staff tasting. Even faulted wines, when returned, can be used as a teaching lesson during a preservice or staff meeting. Faulted wines can also be returned to the distributor for a credit to the account, so there is not a complete loss.

SINGLE-BOTTLE FAULTS

Single-bottle faults are the result of poor handling of the wine, poor storage, or possibly a failure in packaging. The reason these are categorized as single-bottle faults is that the conditions that caused the fault may have occurred only to the single bottle or maybe to a case. However, the wine produced was actually healthy. The error occurred somewhere outside the winery or as part of the packaging process. Correcting the service of a faulted wine is often as simple as opening the next bottle on the shelf.

Cork

Corked wines, corkiness, and cork taint are all terms used for a wine that has been contaminated with TCA, or 1,3,5-trichloroanisole. This compound, and its cousin TBA or tribromoanisole, is a packaging fault. The TCA contaminates the wine from the cork used to close the bottle. The TCA is not natural to cork. It develops when the cork, a natural product, needs to be sterilized before use. Some cork is infected with a mold when it is removed from the trees. Treating the cork with chlorine or bromine kills the mold, and sterilizes the cork for use with wine. However, the chlorine reacts with the mold, creating TCA. The compound is not detectable by looking at or even smelling a cork. It is only noticeable when the cork has come into contact with wine and contaminated it.

What does cork taint smell and taste like? Cork taint has been described as the smell of a damp basement, wet cardboard, or musty old books. It is a smell that increases in strength as the opened wine is exposed to oxygen. Different people have different thresholds for corked wine, with some drinkers just thinking they have an especially earthy bottle of wine. Often consumers may judge corked wine as earthiness, and often will decide they are not a fan of the wine and will not order it again. If unclear, a determination can be made on the palate. If the wine also tastes like wet cardboard, or has a complete lack of fruit components, or has a bitter, harsh aftertaste, the wine is probably corked.

As noted earlier, this is typically a single-bottle fault. The cork in one particular bottle was tainted and it contaminated the wine that was in the bottle. It is a safe bet that the next bottle will be fine. However, there have been instances where there is an increased propensity for corked wines from a producer of a specific vintage. In a sampling of one Rioja producer, two out of three wines tested from a single vintage were corked. This goes to a higher level, where the quality of cork chosen by the producer may be in question. That is not obvious from a single bottle of wine. A wider quality issue such as that can only be determined from finding several corked bottles of wine in the cellar.

Reductive Faults

Reductive faults are a generic term used for wines that smell of sulfur. This fault actually falls into both single-bottle and systemic faults. The most common occurrence of a single-bottle reductive fault is with a screw-capped wine. Because screw caps are tighter than corks and do not allow oxygen to seep into the ullage of the bottle, the sulfur dioxide used to preserve the wine reacts with some of the components rather than eliminating oxygen. The result is a wine that smells of burnt matches or of rubber. Fortunately, this is a reversible fault. Once the bottle is opened and the wine is exposed to oxygen, the rubber smell will dissipate. It will probably not dissipate fast enough for the benefit of the guest, but the wine is useable for service as a by-the-glass offering, as samples, or in cooking.

Volatile Acidity

Volatile acidity is a term used to cover two related aromas in wine. The first is acetic acid or vinegar. This fault is the result of the wine becoming infected with *Acetobacter,* the bacterium that converts wine into red wine vinegar. Complicit in this fault is oxygen. Somewhere along the line, after becoming infected with Acetobacter, the wine was exposed to oxygen. Oxygen is necessary for the bacteria to convert ethanol into acetic acid. Many wine drinkers assume if the bottle has been open to oxygen it will become vinegar, but that cannot happen without the bacteria. Opening a bottle of wine and having it be vinegar is almost always the result of poor handling of the wine.

The second and probably more common expression of volatile acidity is ethyl acetate. This is the combination of a small amount of acetic acid, which may have developed during fermentation, and ethanol to create ethyl acetate. This is the smell of nail polish and some nail polish remover. A very strong chemical smell is the hallmark of volatile acidity. The expression of ethyl acetate is more of a systemic fault, because the acetic acid developed in the wine making process.

Oxidation

When wine is exposed to oxygen, it becomes oxidized. This occurs when the closure is compromised (a dry shrunken cork, for example). Oxygen in the air reacts with the ethanol to create aldehydes. These compounds give the wine a stale, almost nutty aroma and taste. Interestingly, in Sherry, these are the compounds responsible for the flavor of the wine and are considered good qualities. In table wines, the stale character from the aldehydes is a fault. This is a single-bottle fault because of poor storage of the wine (letting the cork dry out).

Oxidation usually can be observed before it is detected on the nose or the palate. Oxidation in white wine will make it darker than it should be. It will give a brownish tint to whatever color is already present. In red wines, the brownish character will lighten the color and give a brick or mahogany color to the rim.

Maderization

One step beyond oxidation is maderization. In this fault, the wine has been treated like Madeira—it has been oxidized and heated. This is a single-bottle fault, though it may affect more than one bottle in the case. It depends when the mishandling occurred. Maderization is a danger in areas where there is hot weather, when delivery trucks are not refrigerated, or if storage of the wine is not properly observed. Maderized wine is not only oxidized, as described above, but also tastes cooked. The fruit flavors are not fresh and lively, but taste as if they have been stewed or boiled.

SYSTEMIC FLAWS

These flaws are usually the result of a bad decision or error in the wine making process. They are called flaws rather than faults because there is something inherently incorrect or unbalanced about the wine. These flaws will more than likely be found in all bottles from the same producer for that vintage. Some producers make their wine in batches, so there is a chance that a new case would be clean. In the case of some other errors, though, waiting until the next vintage release may be required.

Is it possible to avoid flaws, if they are systemic to a single vintage of wine from a specific producer? The answer is yes, if the sommelier is diligent. It is often an easy decision simply to accept the new vintage of a wine currently being sold without thinking about it. However, good product research should always take precedent, and a tasting of any wine that aspires to be on the sommelier's wine list should be conducted.

Vegetative Wines

This fault is a judgment call for the sommelier and guest. In many cases, grapes have strong vegetal expressions. It may be the grass of a Sauvignon Blanc, the mint of a red Bordeaux, or the dill of an Oregon Pinot Noir. Those are not faults, but rather expressions of the grape. However, a Chardonnay that tastes like a can of creamed corn could be considered a flaw. Wines that are too vegetative are flawed because the grapes were picked too early or the canopy was not managed properly to allow full ripening of the grapes. The flaw lies with the grapes themselves, rather than the wine making. The wine-maker can only do the best with what is available.

Unbalanced Alcohol

This flaw could be considered the opposite of vegetative wines. Unbalanced alcohol occurs when the grapes have gotten very ripe. This increase in sugar level will result in high alcohol levels after fermentation. In some cases, like a big Napa Cabernet Sauvignon or Sierra Foothills Zinfandel, the alcohol is balanced by all the other components in the wine. If the other components are not as intensely concentrated, the alcohol will seem unbalanced and the wine will taste "hot."

Brett

The final systemic flaw could be a fault, because it happens in wine making. It is the infection of the wine with *Brettanomyces,* a type of yeast that can ferment wines, creating off flavors. The most pleasant description of the effect of "Brett" is fresh horse manure. For years, Brett infection was actually considered a positive trait for Pinot Noir. Over time, the hallmark of Pinot became less about the barnyard and more about a general earthiness. Most Brett infections occur in the oak barrels that are used to age wine. The barrels, with their open wood grain and microscopic pores, are hard to sterilize. Once Brett has infected a barrel, its influence will be smelled and tasted on all the wine that passes through it.

Sulfur

As stated above, sulfur can be seen as a single-bottle flaw when too much sulfur dioxide is used in the bottling process. Sulfur can also be a systemic flaw, when too much sulfur has been used earlier in the wine making process and its effects are noted in the subsequent wine. If too much sulfur is used early in the wine making process, either on the grapes after picking or during maceration or fermentation, the sulfur can interact with the yeast and create some noxious compounds. Another reason sulfur compounds arise is a poor choice of fermenting yeast strain and poor yeast nutrition.

The most obvious one is hydrogen sulfide, the smell of rotten eggs. Hydrogen sulfide develops when yeast does not have enough nitrogen and oxygen to survive. Sulfur compounds in the must, whether from added sulfur or amino acids, are attacked by the yeast, which releases the hydrogen sulfide. If the hydrogen sulfide is not removed, it can react with alcohol and other by products to create mercaptans. These compounds present as the aromas of boiled cabbage or garlic.

Not all sulfur compounds are flaws or faults. Much of what is responsible for minerality in a wine is due to sulfur compounds, as are some of the minor vegetal qualities of some grapes. It is only when the wine is dominated by the smell of rotten eggs or boiled cabbage that the wine is considered flawed.

SUMMARY

Understanding the flaws and faults of wine is important for providing the proper service for the guest, as well as managing the cellar correctly. Faults, usually the result of poor handling or storage or a faulty closure, are often found in single bottles, rather than through a whole production lot of wine. The remedy for a single bottle fault is to open a new bottle. Flaws, on the other hand, are systemic. That means the flaw is inherent in a particular vintage of wine from a specific producer. Flawed wines should never make it to the cellar if the sommelier is conducting proper product research in order to stock the wine list.

QUESTIONS

1. What is a wine fault?

2. What are the most common wine faults?

3. Which faults can be prevented by the sommelier and which may be the responsibility of others?

4. Describe a flawed wine.

5. Is it possible to fix a flawed wine?

Maps

*T*he following maps of the wine regions of Australia, California, France, Germany, Italy, South Africa, Chile and Argentina, and Spain and Portugal represent approximate locations of wine regions. They are not to scale; nor do they represent the actual borders of the wine regions.

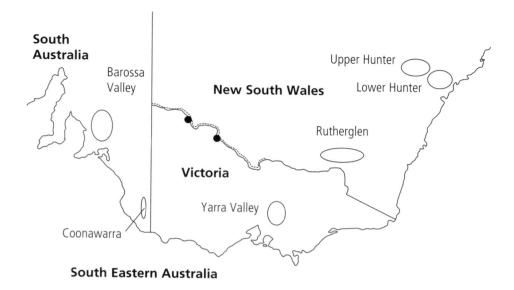

France

Champagne

Alsace

Loire Valley

Burgundy

Beaujolais

Cognac

Rhone

Bordeaux

Armagnac

Languedoc

Roussillon

Italy

Piedmont

Lombardy

Veneto

Tuscany

Marche

Abruzzo

Puglia

Sardinia

Campania

Sicily

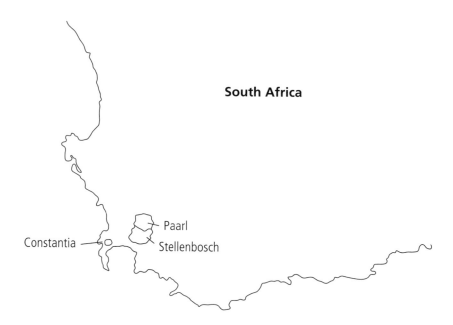

Rias Baixes

Vinho Verde

Douro

Rueda

Rioja

Ribera del Duero

Penedes

Priorato

Montilla

Jerez

Malaga

**Spain &
Portugal**

Appendix B

Label Terminology

How to Read an Australian Label

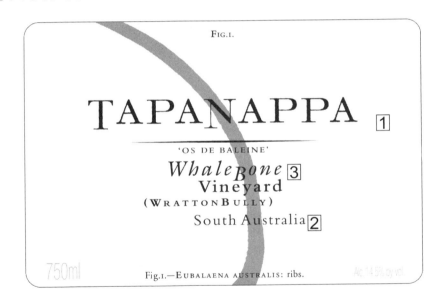

Courtesy Palm Bay Imports

Australian labels are some of the easiest to read. Because of the government-prescribed Label Integrity Program, the consumer is provided with explicit information about what is in the bottle.

1. Producer: The company that made and bottled the wine

2. Region of origin: Geographic indicator of origin. Because one locale is mentioned, at least 85 percent of the grapes have been sourced from this area.

3. Vineyard: A vineyard can be named on the label if it has unique characteristics and at least 85 percent of the grapes making the wine came from that vineyard.

4. Grape varieties: The grapes are listed in descending order of their makeup in the blend.

5. Vintage: The date of the vintage can be listed if at least 85 percent of the grapes were harvested in the stated year.

How to Read a German Label

Courtesy Palm Bay Imports

1. Producer: The company that made and bottled the wine.

2. Region of origin: On German labels this is the village or *bereich* where the grapes are sourced (in this case, Wehlen).

3. Vineyard: The vineyard or *einzellage* in the bereich where the grapes are grown.

4. Grape: German wines are labeled by varietal. The varietal mentioned is 100 percent of the content of the bottle.

5. Grape quality level: The *pradikat* level describing the ripeness of the grapes when harvested.

6. Vintage: The year of harvest.

7. Production quality: Estate bottled refers to the wine being produced at the facility of the producer that owns the vineyard.

Other German Label Terminology

Weingut: Winery, bodega.

Weinkellerei: Wine cellar, chai.

Winzergenossenschaft: Cooperative-type association.

Erzeugerabfullung: Producer-bottled.

Gutsabfullung: Estate bottled.

Trocken: Dry.

Halb-trocken: Half-dry.

Amtliche Prufungnummer: AP number.

The AP number is placed either on the front or the back label. It appears as:

AP 2 583 063 14 08

The numbers each indicate a particular fact about the wine, which allows that single bottle to be tracked back to the source.

2: The testing center, where the wine was approved

583: The village in which the producer is located

063: The code number for the producer

14: The producer's application number

08: The year in which the producer filed the application

A producer may have multiple applications in a single year, since each time a batch of wine is bottled for sale, it must have an application on file. Thus, individual batches of wine can be tracked from the same producer in a year.

How to Read a Spanish Label

Courtesy Kobrand

1. Producer: Producer of the wine.

2. Region of origin: Place of origin of the wine, often suggesting style as well.

3. Quality level: government-determined level of quality of the region.

4. Age designation: Legally defined term that reflects how wine has been aged; see legislation appendix for description of terms.

5. Alcohol: Alcohol content in percent by volume.

6. Volume: Volume of bottle contents.

7. Local seal of inspection: Local *consejo regulador* stamp showing the wine has been approved for sale.

Also on most labels is vintage, which can only be stated if 85 percent of the grapes that made the wine are harvested in that year.

How to Read a U.S. Label

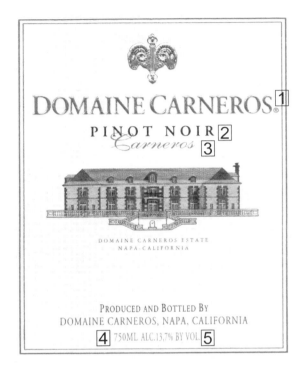

Courtesy Kobrand

1. **Producer:** Name of the wine producer.
2. **Grape variety:** Varietal that makes up 85 percent of the wine contents.
3. **Region of origin:** AVA of grape origin.
4. **Volume:** Volume content of the bottle.
5. **Alcohol content:** Alcohol content of the bottle.

Also on most labels is vintage, which can only be stated if 85 percent of the grapes that made the wine are harvested in that year.

How to Read a Vintage Port Label

Courtesy Kobrand

1. **Producer:** Company that produced the wine.
2. **Vineyard designation:** In special cases, such as this, single vineyards are allowed to be added to the label. All the grapes must come from this vineyard.
3. **Vintage designation:** Statement that wine is a vintage port. Year of harvest will be included, often with year of bottling as well.
4. **Volume:** Volume of the bottle.
5. **Alcohol level:** Alcohol level indicated as percent by volume.

How to Read French Labels

BASIC AOC: GEVREY-CHAMBERTIN

Courtesy Kobrand

1. Producer: Producer of the wine.

2. Region of origin: AOC recognized area of production.

3. Quality level: Indication that wine is AOC level.

4. Volume: Volume of the bottle.

5. Alcohol level: Alcohol content as percentage by volume.

6. Production responsibility: Indicates the wine was aged and bottled by the producer, although it may have been made by someone else.

Also on most labels is vintage, which can only be stated if the grapes that made the wine are harvested in that year.

PREMIER CRU LEVEL: GEVREY-CHAMBERTIN CLOS SAINT-JACQUES

FONDÉE EN 1859

GEVREY-CHAMBERTIN [2]
CLOS SAINT-JACQUES [3]
Appellation Gevrey-Chambertin 1er Cru Contrôlée [4]

Récolté, vinifié, élevé et mis en bouteilles par [7]
750 ML   LOUIS JADOT [1]   ALC. BY VOL. 13.5 %
[5]   F 21200 - FRANCE   [6]

Domaine Louis Jadot
PRODUCE OF FRANCE

Courtesy Kobrand

1. Producer: Again, Jadot is the producer.

2. Region of origin: AOC in which the stated vineyard is located.

3. Vineyard: Single vineyard that serves as origin of the grapes.

4. Quality level: Indicates the vineyard has Premier Cru recognition in AOC scheme.

5. Volume: Volume of the bottle.

6. Alcohol level: Alcohol level as percentage by volume.

7. Production responsibility: Indicates Jadot was responsible for growing the grapes (récolté), making (vinifié), aging (élevé), and bottling the wine.

Also on labels is vintage, which can only be stated if the grapes that made the wine are harvested in that year.

GRAND CRU WINE: LE CHAMBERTIN

FONDÉE EN 1859

Le Chambertin 2

GRAND CRU 3
Appellation Contrôlée

Élevé et Mis en bouteilles par 6
LOUIS JADOT 1
Beaune - France

IMPORTED BY
KOBRAND N.Y.
ALC. BY VOL. 13.5% 5

RED TABLE WINE 4
750 ml
PRODUCE OF FRANCE

Courtesy Kobrand

1. Producer: Final producer of the wine.
2. Vineyard: Vineyard alone is noted, as it is the recognized AOC region of production.
3. Quality level: Indicates this is a Grand Cru wine.
4. Volume: Volume of the bottle.
5. Alcohol level: Amount of alcohol in the wine as percentage of volume.
6. Production responsibility: Indicates the wine was aged and bottled by producer; the wine was probably made by someone else and purchased by the producer.

Other French Wine Terminology

Proprietaires-Recoltants: Individual growers who make their own wine.

Negociants-Eleveurs: Middlemen who purchase and age wine before release.

Monopole: Wine produced from one single negociant; negociant solely owns vineyard.

Grand Cru Classé: Designation in Bordeaux of a wine that has been classified by its AOC region of origin as a top wine.

Cru Bourgeois: Classification of wine from Bordeaux that indicates good wines superior to the majority of wine produced.

Moelleux: Sweet.

Mousseaux: Sparkling.

Supériéur: Containing 0.5 percent higher alcohol than standard bottling.

Domaine: Vineyard holding winery that produces its own wine in Burgundy.

Chateau: Winery in Bordeaux.

How to Read Italian Labels

REGIONAL WINE: BAROLO

Courtesy Kobrand

1. Producer: Wine producer and bottler.

2. Region of origin: Accepted legal name for area of wine production and style.

3. Vineyard: Single vineyard within region of origin.

4. Quality level: Indication of legally defined quality level of region.

5. Volume: Volume of the bottle.

6. Alcohol level: Alcohol content by volume.

GRAPE VARIETAL WINE: BARBERA

Courtesy Kobrand

1. Producer: Wine producer.

2. Region of origin: Village where grapes are grown.

3. Grape: Varietal of grape that made the wine.

   Combined, these also form a regional label for a wine. It is possible to label by varietal without tagging the region of production onto the title; the region would then be referenced elsewhere on the bottle.

4. Quality level: Legally recognized quality level of the wine.

5. Volume: Bottle volume.

6. Alcohol level: Alcohol level as percentage of volume.

7. Proprietary name: Name given by producer to designate this blend of sites, style, or unique characteristics. Also may just be an effort to distinguish the wine with a name, but with no actual meaning behind it.

PROPRIETARY NAMED WINE: SASSICAIA

Courtesy Kobrand

1. Producer: Name of the producer.

2. Region of origin: Region name as legally recognized. Some proprietary wines may have provincial names rather than specific local names, such as this.

3. Quality level: Legally recognized quality level of the wine; some proprietary labeled wine may be designated as IGT wines.

4. Volume: Bottle volume.

5. Alcohol level: Alcohol level as percent of volume.

6. Proprietary name: Name given; probably has no inherent meaning except to producer.

Other Italian Label Terminology

Abboccato: Slightly sweet.

Amabile: Sweeter than abboccato.

Amaro: Bitter or very dry.

Ascuitto: Bone dry.

Azienda: Estate winery.

Bianco: White.

Cantina Sociale: Cooperative winery.

Classico: The best or most famous part of a DOC zone; traditional heartland.

Consorzio: Group of producers who produce and control wine; usually about higher standards.

Dolce: Very sweet.

Fattoria: Farm.

Frizzante: Semi-sparkling (petillant).

Frizzantino: Very lightly sparkling.

Imbottigliano all'Origina: Estate bottled.

Rosso: Red.

Rosato: Rosé.

Spumante: Sparkling.

Riserva: Special wines aged for longer than standard; extent varies from region to region.

Tenuta: Winery.

Appendix C

Legislation

*E*ach country has laws that regulate the way in which wine is labeled and sold. Those of the Old World (Europe) have a common system, even though there are differences from country to country. In the New World, the regulations are less strict than in Europe, and vary greatly from country to country. Understanding the legislation behind the wine can help the sommelier determine quality as well as authenticity.

European Wine Regulations

European wine laws are based on the system developed by the French, but with some variations by country. One could assume the laws are aligned because of the overarching political entity of the European Union, but the countries' similar wine making philosophy, focusing on terroir, is the real driving force.

HISTORY

Regulating wines and their origin has occurred over the centuries. The ancient world was the first to recognize their wine origins. The Egyptians had regulated wine labeling by the time of King Tut in 1550 B.C.E. The Romans were thought to be the first to stamp the vintage and the origin of a wine on the amphora that held it. The Romans also knew that the best wine came from a single region south of the city, which was called Falernum.

After Charlemagne was crowned Holy Roman Emperor in the year 800, he instituted some of the first wine laws in what would become Burgundy. He decreed that the emperor's wine could come only from specific vineyards. Those vineyards, skirting the Hill of Corton in Aloxe-Corton, Burgundy, would get the names Corton-Charlemagne and Le Charlemagne. This type of recognition of special places continued through history, notably in the eighteenth century, when the areas of Chianti, the Douro, and Châteauneuf-du-Pape were all delimited for their production.

The modern development of laws relating to the production and labeling of wine is based on a series of events over a half a century, starting in the mid-1800s. The initial event was in Bordeaux in the early 1850s. The vines experienced a disease that they had never seen before in powdery mildew. It took a couple of years, but eventually the right mix of chemicals was found to spray on the vines, which would prevent the mildew from taking hold. The years between the initial infection and the treatment produced small vintages, with less wine than normal.

Soon after, the invasion of phylloxera occurred. While the invasion of phylloxera was slow—starting in the south of France in the 1860s and not reaching Champagne until after 1900—its effect on wine production was great. When a vineyard succumbed to phylloxera, the whole vineyard succumbed. That meant in many places the wine production fell to zero. Even after the "cure" of grafting vines was common practice, there was often a three- to six-year gap in wine production as the new grapevines matured enough to be able to bear quality fruit.

The dearth of wine available for sale did not diminish the demand. That demand began to be supplied in some unscrupulous ways. It became common that grapes were imported from areas that had not been affected by the louse. The sources were often Spain, southern Italy, or Sicily. As more areas became affected, the wine making would be conducted with raisins. Another method was piquette, the addition of water, sugar, and yeast to spent must so that another batch of wine could be made.

Desperate producers did not just defraud the public by making poor wine. Included in the fraudulent activities was the misrepresentation of famous-name wines. For example, an empty bottle of Chateau Latour would be filled with poor wine, recorked, and sold as the real thing.

Those producers who were trying to stay alive by making legitimate wines began to protest. In 1905 and 1907 the farmers demanded government intervention. Riots occurred in Champagne in 1911, when more Champagne was sold the year before than could have been produced in the region. The French government responded by setting up the *Service de la Repression des Fraudes et du Controle de la Qualite*. The government responded to the two main concerns of the time: the preservation of quality and the respect of established names.

One of the first steps the government took was to define wine. Defining wine as the fermented product of grape juice or fresh grape must eliminated the use of raisins and the piquette method. The government was not the only group taking steps to protect wine. In 1924, Chateau Mouton-Rothschild in Bordeaux decided to abandon the age-old practice of allowing the negociants to age and bottle their wine, and began to bottle it themselves. It was also around this time that producers began to imprint their label and vintage on the corks. The authenticity of the wine could be guaranteed if the imprint on the cork repeated what was on the label.

In 1923, Baron le Roy of Châteauneuf-du-Pape petitioned the government to legally recognize the area and the techniques used in that region. The government went one step further. In 1927, they took what had been locally controlled in Châteauneuf-du-Pape and used it as an outline for the rest of the country. This began the first delimitation of the quality wine regions throughout France. In 1935, the French government established the *Comité National des Appellation d'Origine,* which would take over the administration of delimiting wine regions.

STRUCTURE

In 1963, the remainder of the countries in the Common Market aligned their laws regarding wine growing and production with those of France. The basic structure of the European wine laws divides wine into two categories. The first and simplest category is table wine. This is wine that is meant to be easy drinking, simple refreshment. The second category is Vin de Qualité Produits dans des Régions Déterminées (VQPRD, or quality wine produced from designated regions), commonly referred to as quality wine.

Most European governments created these two levels in 1963. Some created divisions within each category at the same time, while others ultimately did so at a later date. The quality wine level is usually separated into the top-quality wines and those that strive to become quality wines. The table wine category typically contains both table wines and country or land wines, which are wines more indicative of a large regional area.

The rules covered not only where the wines came from, but also how they could be labeled. For all European Union wines (and those entering the EU from other countries) there is the 85 percent rule. This rule states that if a vintage is declared on the label, at least 85 percent of the wine must derive from grapes grown that year. If a varietal is noted on the label, at least 85 percent of the wine must be from that varietal. The laws of some regions, such as most of France and Brunello di Montalcino in Italy, actually require 100 percent of their legal varietal.

French Wine Law

French wine is split into four classes. Two classes, *vin du table* and *vin du pays,* are considered table wines. The quality wine classes are *vin délimitée de qualité supérieure* (VDQS) and *appellation d'originé contrôlée* (AOC or AC). The levels are regulated by different governmental bodies. ONIVINS (*Office National Interprofessionel des Vins de Table)* is the controlling body for vin du table. For the quality wine level, the controlling body is the INOQ (Institut National de l'Originé et de la Qualité, formerly the INAO). Under the INOQ, all the legislation regarding what areas can use the AOC designation is enforced. A separate body, the Service de Répréssion des Fraudes, is the managing department. This department is responsible for the paper trail that shows the INOQ laws are being followed.

VIN DU TABLE

The vin du table (table wine) category is the most basic of all French wines. It is a declining category, representing less than 18 percent of all wine production. The rules for a vin du table are very simple. The wine can be produced anywhere in France, with no restrictions on what grape varieties are used, though the varietal is not allowed on the label. If grapes are used from elsewhere in the European Union, that must be noted on the label. No chaptalization is allowed in the making of vin du table. There is also no restriction on the amount of wine a vineyard can produce. The amount of wine produced per vineyard is measured in hectoliters per hectare (hl/ha). While there is no restriction in the amount that can be produced, anything over 100 hl/ha must be sent off for distillation into industrial solvent or ethanol. There is no quality tasting assessment of the wine before sale. Finally, there is no vintage on the label.

VIN DU PAYS

The vin du pays (country wine) category was created in 1979. Its purpose was to give recognition to some vin du table that had some distinction. With the recognition came restrictions as to what would be accepted as a vin du pays. Currently, this category makes up 29 percent of French wine production, and is growing.

The first stipulation in making a vin du pays concerns the region of origin of the wine. There are four designated regions that can produce vin du pays. The largest region is Jardin de la France, which covers the Loire Valley. Comtés Rhodaniens is the region that covers the Rhone Valley, Beaujolais, Jura, and Savoie. Comté Tolosan covers the southwest of France, with the exception of Bordeaux, and the Oc covers Languedoc and Roussillon.

Each region is further subdivided into departments and zones. A wine is designated by where the grapes are sourced. If they come from a single zone, the wines can be labeled with just that zonal name. If the grapes are sourced from two or more zones within the same department, the wine can have a departmental designation. Similarly, if the grapes are from more than one department, the wine must be designated by region.

Some distinct regions in France are not covered by the vin du pays regions. These are Alsace, Bordeaux, and Burgundy. In these three areas, if a winemaker needs to declassify their wine from the quality level, it would have to be a vin du table.

The next stipulations on vin du pays wines involve viticulture. The grape varieties that can be grown are restricted to better-quality vinifera grapes. This allows Chardonnay to be a vin du pays d'Oc or Merlot to be a vin du pays de la Jardin de la France. Yields are somewhat restricted, depending on the region.

Finally, all wines must undergo analytical testing. The test for minimum alcohol level is really a test that the grapes were ripe enough when the wine was made, and that the wine was fully fermented. Another test is with a tasting panel, who check for quality and consistency.

VDQS (VIN DELIMITÉE DE QUALITÉ SUPÉRIEURE)

The VDQS level is the entry level for quality wine. The VDQS wines only account for 1 percent of all French wine production. The level is meant to be a temporary one, in which regions that wish to be recognized at the highest level can demonstrate their readiness. The rules for this level often are developed to mimic the rules the region will follow when they are elevated to AOC.

Rules at this level include regulation of approved grape varieties, maximum yield allowed, minimum alcohol of the finished wine, and the wine making techniques employed. Producers need to demonstrate that they can meet the requirements for a minimum of five years before they are elevated to the next level. Most producers voluntarily follow stricter guidelines, ones more closely aligned to the future AOC requirements, to demonstrate the ability to comply in the future.

AOC (APPELLATION D'ORIGINE CONTRÔLÉE)

The top-quality level of French wine is designated AOC. There are over 470 different appellations in the AOC level, which comprise around 52 percent of all the wine made in France. Some appellations may have better name recognition or better perceived quality than others, but on the legal front they all are equivalent.

Six areas are regulated by the AOC rules. The primary distinction is the region of origin. The region of production is delimited by soil composition. Next, the rules control certain viticultural practices. The INOQ regulates what grape varieties can be grown in the region. It also controls the methods of planting and vine training, and the maximum yield per hectare. On the vinification side, the regulations control the methods of wine making as well as the minimum alcohol percentage.

The regulations are not consistent from area to area, but rather are unique to each individual location. Comparing some areas will help to illustrate the rules. Burgundy is a top-quality region in the eastern area of France. It has two white grapes that are allowed, and two red grapes. The white grapes are Chardonnay and Aligoté. Chardonnay is allowed wherever white grapes are approved, but Aligoté is only seen in Bouzeron and in the Hautes Côtes region of Burgundy. The same is true for the red grapes. Pinot Noir is the main red grape, which is grown throughout Burgundy. Gamay is grown mainly in Beaujolais, with a little grown in the Maçon.

In contrast, in Bordeaux, there are fourteen permitted varietals, both red and white. The most common red varietals are Cabernet Sauvignon, Merlot, Cabernet Franc, Petit Verdot, and Malbec. The common white varietals are Sauvignon Blanc, Semillon, and Muscadelle. The wines are blends of all these grapes, as opposed to the single-varietal vines of Burgundy.

The AOC rules allow for more and more specific designations of place. The breakdown can be viewed as a series of concentric circles. An AOC could be a large region, like Bordeaux. Within Bordeaux could be smaller AOCs, known as districts. For example, in Bordeaux is the Médoc. Within a district could be communes. In the Médoc are the communes of Pauillac, Saint Julien, Margaux, and Saint Estephe. This is fairly common throughout the AOC system; however, not every region has districts or communes.

In Burgundy, there are additional designations based on vineyards. Some vineyards are designated Premier Cru. These are exceptional vineyards in prime spots in the communes of Burgundy. Even better than the Premier Cru vineyards are those designated as Grand Cru. The Grand Cru vineyards, thirty-three of them, have the best soil, the best drainage, and the best aspect to the sun. The wines made from these vineyards are often labeled with just the vineyard name (see Appendix B, Label Terminology).

Italian Wine Law

Italy aligned its wine laws with the rest of the Common Market in 1963. The original law created two levels. The table wine level was called *vino da tavola*. The quality wine level was called Denominazione d'Origine Controllata (DOC). While the quality level appears to be similar to the French AOC, there is one significant difference. The Italians did not designate small, easily identified regions. Many designated regions overlapped one another, allowing a village to create many different DOC wines. In addition, the Italian government used the DOC designation as an attempt to regain a reputation for high-quality wines. The legislation as it was written, however, gave preference to high-yielding grapes and large production of wines. What had been classic quality wine producing regions, like Chianti, were increased in size. The additional area was also the vineyards that had the highest production.

In 1971, the Italian government added a level to the quality wine designation. The new level, Denominazione d'Origine Controllata e Garnatita (DOCG), was designed to give special recognition to the best wines. The requirements to achieve elevation to DOCG included submission to a tasting panel and a contribution of economic or historic significance to Italian wine. Even with these rules in place, wines that were not considered to be top-tier Italian wines received the designation. To illustrate, in the very first elevation of wines, Barolo was elevated. The first white wine elevated was not Prosecco or Soave or any other more famous Italian white, it was Albana di Romagna. The general consensus upon seeing Albana as the first white elevated was that this level would have many of the same issues that were levied against the DOC level.

The rules implemented by the DOC and DOCG levels were very strict. For example, Chianti would be made by the recipe developed by Marquese Ricasoli. That recipe allowed for up to 30 percent of white grapes in the blend, and a blend of five different grapes. Any variation outside that allowed by the recipe and the law meant the wine could not be classified as Chianti.

In the 1970s, a new style of wine began to develop in Tuscany. First termed Predicato and then Capitolare, these wines used international varietals rather than native Italian grapes. More commonly, these wines are known as Super Tuscans. Because they did not fit into the governmental quality schema, the wines were often declassified and sold as vino da tavola. They had to follow the vino da tavola rules of no vintage labeling and simply the designation of rosso or bianco. Yet these wines cost hundreds of dollars a bottle.

In response to the growing trend of proprietary wines, the interior minister Giovanni Goria revised the law in 1992. He created a new table wine level, Indicazione Tipica Geografica (IGT). This new level allowed wines that did not fit the DOC or DOCG mold still to be recognized for their unique qualities. Similar to the French vin du pays, this is a wine typical of a region, but also one that can be made outside the strict rules of the quality wine levels.

Spanish Wine Law

The Spanish also developed differentiation within their quality wine level and their table wine level. In the table wine level, the simplest wine was *vino de mesa*. Like other simple table wines, this wine could not designate vintage or location of origin. It is often the blend of wines from several different regions. It often simply stated *rosso* or *blanco*. To placate winemakers who were trying new grapes, new methods, and/or new regions, a level called vino de mesa de (region) was created. This suggested that the wine was a table wine from a particular region, yet often meant that the grapes, the wine making techniques, or the region of production were new and not yet recognized by the authorities.

Slightly better than the vinos de mesas, yet still table wines as far as quality, are *vino comarcal* and *vino de la tierra*. Vino comarcal allows a producer to post the vintage date and the region of origin. There are currently twenty-one recognized regions for producing vino comarcal. This level is often used for producers who wish to make wine outside the quality wine system in Spain. Vino de la tierra are local, regional wines. They have a distinct character relating to their location of origin. There are twenty-five recognized regions for vino de la tierra. Vinos de la tierra are the equivalent to the French vin du pays. These wines could apply for acceptance into the quality wine level if they desired.

At the quality wine level, the original single designation was Denominacion de Origen (DO). These wines are the equivalent of the French AOC and have similar restrictions on grape varieties, viticulture, and vinification techniques. The Spanish also decided to recognize the best regions. These receive the designation DOCa or Denominacion de Origen Calificada. This is a very rare designation, which has been given to only two regions in Spain. Those regions are Rioja and Priorato.

The wines that are designated DO or DOCa are regulated on a local level. The grape variety restrictions, viticultural practices, and vinification techniques are monitored by a local group, the consejo regulador. The consejo is made up of local grape growers and bodegas. If the wines pass the requirements enforced by the consejo regulador, they receive the local stamp of acceptance and can be sold under the DO or DOCa label.

In 2003, new quality wine levels were allowed by the Spanish government. The first was DO Pago. A Pago is a specific single vineyard. Thus, the DO Pago is effectively the equivalent of the French cru system. A top-quality wine made from grapes from a single vineyard could be designated a DO Pago. Because the wine must be of top quality, this level is considered on par with the DO and DOCa levels.

The rule changes implemented in 2003 also created a new level below the DO levels. Termed Vinos de Calidad con Indicación Geográfica (VCIG), these wines are those that are attempting to become recognized as DOs. The equivalent is the French VDQS level of wines.

LABELING RULES

In Spain, there are specific rules regarding terms that can be placed on a label. For wines that have not seen any wood aging, the terms *sin crianza* or *vino joven* are allowed. Both indicate young wines that have not been aged in wood and are meant to be drunk soon after the vintage release.

For wines that have been aged, there are several terms, each indicating a different length of time. *Crianza* wines are the youngest of the aged wines. Translated as "wine of breeding," these wines must spend two years aging, with a minimum of six months of that aging being in an oak barrel. *Reserva* wines can only be made in very good years. Reserva red wines must spend three years aging before release, with a minimum of one year in oak and one year in bottle. For white and rosé wines, the aging time is lower. White and rosé reserve wines age for a minimum of two years, with at least six months in a barrel. Finally, the best years can produce *Gran Reserva* wines. Red Gran Reserva wines must age a minimum of five years, with at least two in barrel and two in bottle. White and Rosé gran reserve wines must age four years, with at least six months in barrel.

Along with the quality level changes in 2003, new aging terminology was released. Noble, añejo, and viejo are the new terms, representing twelve, twenty-four, and thirty-six months of aging in barrel or bottle. Viejo wines must also show classic signs of oxidation as well.

German Wine Law

German wine laws went through a range of changes in the twentieth century. In 1930, two major laws were implemented. First, hybrids were outlawed—not only their use in wine making but even the planting of hybrids. Second, the blending of red and white grapes was forbidden, as was the blending of domestic wine with foreign wine.

In 1971, as a way to align German wine law to the requirements of the European Community, agricultural reform was required. The Germanic inheritance laws were based on Napoleonic law, meaning a farmer's holdings had to be split among all the children. This resulted in vineyards with multiple owners, and owners possessing land that was spread out and not contiguous. The government instituted a policy of *flurbereinigung,* or land exchange. This allowed farmers to exchange land so that they would have contiguous fields rather than far flung areas to farm. This policy also saw the beginning of planting wine grapes on the flat, fertile land. The result was greatly increased production. Where Germany had been known for quality, it quickly became known for mass-produced, sweet, fruity wines.

The land reorganization changed the way vineyards were organized. Legally, a recognized vineyard now had to be at least 5 hectares. This reduced the number of recognized vineyards, called *einzellage,* from 30,000 to 2600. A new category, *grosslage,* was created that was a collection of einzellagen. A grosslage comprised 17 of the new einzellagen (what would have been 197 einzellagen before 1971).

Unfortunately, the requirement of a 5-hectare minimum for each einzellage eliminated the special terroir attributes of smaller vineyards. The best vineyard in Germany, Bernkasteler Doktor, was recognized as being only 1.35 hectares, yet after 1971 it had to be 5 hectares.

LAND ORGANIZATION

German wine areas are known as *anbaugebiet*. There are thirteen designated anbaugebiete, most of which are in the southwestern portion of the country. Each anbaugebiete is comprised of *bereiche,* of which there are a total of thirty-nine. Within the bereiche are the grosslagen (a total of 160) which, in turn are comprised of einzellagen (2632 total).

QUALITY DESIGNATIONS

German wine is broken into the standard table wine and quality wine categories of the European Union. There is also a third designation, known simply as *wein*. This level is especially for wines that have been made from grapes sourced outside the European Union. As for the table wine and quality wine categories, table wine accounts for only 2 percent of all German wine production. Table wines are broken into three categories. The simplest is *tafelwein*. This is wine made from grapes sourced anywhere in the European Union. If the grapes are sourced in Germany, the category is called *Deutscher Tafelwein*. The grapes must be sourced from one of the four *tafelweingebiete*. The grapes must also meet a minimum must weight before fermentation to be in this category.

The highest table wine category is Landwein. A landwein is the equivalent of a French vin du pays. One difference is that this is not a category that prepares a wine for a higher quality designation. The grapes must be sourced from the seventeen *landwiengebiete*.

Quality wines have two major categories. The simplest is *qualitatswein bestimmte anbaugebiete* (QbA). These wines must be sourced from one of the thirteen anbaugebiete. There are minimum must weight requirements, which vary depending upon the anbaugebiete. The minimum potential alcohol strength is 5.9 percent and chaptalization is allowed to make the wines reach the minimum alcohol level acceptable. Wines are usually sweetened slightly, through the use of sussreserve.

There is a type of QbA that is special because it is indicative of a particular locale. This is a *Quälitatswien Garantierten Unsprungs* (QgU). These wines are officially QbA level, yet have a consistent flavor profile that is associated with their village or district of origin.

The best wines are in the category *Qualitatswein mit Pradikat* (QmP), or quality wine with special characteristics. These wines are from a specific anbaugebiete and are sourced from a single bereich. Chaptalization is not allowed, because the wines are categorized into six levels based on how ripe the grapes were at harvest. The ripeness is determined by testing the juice on a refractometer and registering the sugar concentration in degrees Oechsle (Oe).

The levels of ripeness, which are displayed on the label, are Kabinett, Spatlese, Auslese, Beerenauslese (BA), Eiswein, and Trockenbeerenauslese (TBA). Kabinett wines are the most delicate of German wines. The grapes are picked from 67–85° Oe, which is barely ripe at the normal harvest time. Some grapes will be riper if they are on preferred sites with good exposure to the sun. The minimum must weight is also higher than what it would be if the wines were to be designated QbA.

Spatlese wines are picked with a sugar content of 76–95° Oe. While the literal translation means "late harvest," the grapes are really what most other growers would consider ripe. Harvest for Spatlese wines is at least one week later than it is for Kabinett. That extra hang time allows the grapes to get more flavor and more sugar to develop.

Auslese wines are harvested when the sugar content reaches 83–105° Oe. Harvesting the grapes that make Auslese wines involves individual selection of the bunches. Only the extra ripe bunches are picked, often with occasional botrytis (called *edelfaule*) infection present. Auslese is often defined by the term "bunch selection."

These initial three levels have some overlap between their technical required sugar levels. This allows producers to wait for the proper time to pick at the higher quality level, yet declassify to the lower level. This makes the wine richer and fuller flavored than would normally be expected at that level.

Beerenauslese is even riper than Auslese, being picked with the grapes at 110–128° Oe. The sugar level does not overlap with that of Auslese, forcing grapes to be picked at this level to be used for making wine at this level. The difference, besides sugar level, is indicated in the name. *Beeren* means "berry" in German, and this level requires the individual selection of grape berries that meet the ripeness requirements. The grapes that are chosen are very ripe, often being affected by botrytis. The grapes have an extremely high sugar content and would taste like honeyed raisins.

Eiswein is a special category that requires the same sugar content as a BA wine (110–128° Oe). Besides the proper sugar level, the grapes can only be picked at 18°F (−8°C). Once the grapes are picked, they must be pressed immediately. The grapes must meet all the quality requirements of a BA, not just sugar level. Harvesting must occur while the temperature is at or below the required 18°F (−8°C), which means harvest is usually in the dark of the early morning and is completed by 10 A.M.

The final level is Trockenbeerenauslese. As the name suggests, only individual dried berries are selected. Each berry is fully dried from botrytis infection. The resulting sugar content must be 150–154°Oe. These are the rarest, ripest grapes and are only available in the absolute best vintages.

The last three categories are not produced every year. The conditions need to be right for a BA and especially a TBA to be produced. In order to get full sugar development and botrytis infection, the season must extend past its normal time-frame and be cool and dry. Obviously, it would take longer to achieve TBA status, rather than BA. For that reason, a BA is more common than a TBA, whose conditions may only occur two or three times a decade. For Eiswein, the decision to save some grapes means leaving them on the vine until December or January, with the threat of birds or rot. Then there is still no guarantee that the temperature over the winter will cooperate. That makes Eiswein a gamble, and increases its rarity.

RECENT CHANGES

In 1994, the wine laws were revamped again. Not all the issues that had arisen since 1971 were corrected, yet some significant advancements were made. In general, the yield calculations were restructured so that yield was calculated by the area in production, as opposed to the previous calculation, which used the area under ownership (whether currently yielding grapes or not). Must levels for some of the pradikat levels in specific anbaugebiete were increased as well.

June 2002 saw the creation of the Verband Deutscher Pradikatsweinguter (VDP), the Association of German Pradikat Wine Estates. This voluntary association created rules to which a producer must adhere to be a member of the group. The basic requirements stated that grapes must be harvested at least at the Spatlese ripeness level and that the wine must be dry. A second category was created for what were termed lusciously sweet wines.

The VDP wines were separated into three categories: Grosses Gewachs, Klassi-fizierte Langenwein, and Gutswein. Grosses Gewachs are "Great Growth Wines," which are super-premium dry wines from top vineyard sites. They are made by the region's top producers and are sold in distinctive packaging. These wines are meant to correlate to Burgundian or Alsatian Grand Cru wines.

Klassifizierte langenwein are wines from a classified site. They are meant to be terroir-driven wines, from vineyard sites that have been analyzed for years. The wines are allowed to carry a special VDP capsule and state the single vineyard on the label.

Gutswein are simply house wines. They are either proprietary wines from producer, or designated by a broad region of origin. The quality is guaranteed by the fact that the estate who produced it is a member of the VDP.

Two anbaugebiete modified the rules set by the VDP. In the Mosel, many of the best wines would be excluded because of the Spatlese ripeness requirement. The Mosel producers are allowed to list their vineyards as *Erstes lage* or first vineyards, and create wines that could be Kabinett, Spatlese, or Auslese. In the Nahe, the ten leading producers agreed to additional requirements for their VDP wines. The requirements stipulate only handpicked Riesling grapes from only classified sites. The yields must be below 48 hl/ha, and the must weights at least 0.5 degrees of potential alcohol higher than the allowed minimum. Finally, the wines must be approved by a blind tasting panel, and cannot be released until April 1.

New World Wine Regulations

The New World wine regions have a distinct disadvantage when compared to the Old World. They just haven't been around for very long. That means that instead of having a long history of wine making and analysis of specific vineyard sites, everything is new and undiscovered. While that may be exciting, it does not give a lot of background when trying to develop wine legislation.

The other difference between New World and Old World legislation is in regard to viticultural and vinification practices.

AUSTRALIA

The Australians have developed a system that recognizes where the wine grapes are sourced as well as informing the customer about what is in the bottle. The Label Integrity Program was instituted to relay to the customer exactly what is contained in the bottle. The result is seen on every Australian wine bottle. Every varietal that is in a wine is listed on the label, by decreasing amount. For instance, a bottle of Cabernet Shiraz would have more Cabernet in the blend than Shiraz. Another component of the Label Integrity Program is the 85 percent rule. If anything is stated on the label—location, vintage, or varietal—the contents must be made from 85 percent of the stated item. Therefore, a 2001 Barossa Shiraz must have 85 percent of the grapes be Shiraz, 85 percent from Barossa, and 85 percent from 2001.

The Australians added Geographical indicators as the identification of origin for the wines. Following the European model, the areas of production are broken into smaller and smaller areas. The superzone of S.E. Australia encompasses the states of New South Wales, Victoria, Tasmania, and parts of South Australia. The next level is the states themselves, followed by zones, regions, and subregions. A zone is an area of land with no particular attributes. A region must be a single tract of land that is made up of at least five independently owned vineyards of five hectares each. These vineyards must produce at least five hundred tonnes of grapes. The area must have some homogeneity in grape production, yet be distinct from surrounding regions. A subregion has the same requirements as a region, yet is even more distinct from the region in which it resides. In every case, the 85 percent rule is followed.

NEW ZEALAND

The laws in New Zealand are relatively underdeveloped compared to the rest of the world. The major regions for wine production were first established in 1974. In 1994, a Wine of Certified Origin program was introduced, though it is still not fully enforced. Varietally labeled wines produced in New Zealand cannot contain more than 25 percent of any other varietals.

SOUTH AFRICA

The Wine of Origin system was instituted in 1973. This system set up rules that controlled point of origin, quality, and truth in labeling. Wines labeled under the WO system must be made from grapes solely from the location on the label. The varietals on the label, however, only need to make up 75 percent of the wine (85 percent if exported to Europe). Even the vintage reported only needs to make up 75 percent of the wine. All wines that wish to label under the WO system must undergo tasting by an independent panel before receiving their certification seal.

In 1993, the WO system was amended to define the geographical units. Two units were defined: Northern Cape and Western Cape. These are then broken down into regions, districts, wards, and units. The most productive regions are the Coastal region, Boberg region, and Breede River Valley region. The commonly recognized locations on wine bottles, like Stellenbosch, Paarl, or Constantia, are districts. In 2004, special designated estates were eliminated to make way for estate wines. These wines have to be made from contiguous vineyard land and must have facilities on site to take the grapes from vineyard to bottle.

SOUTH AMERICA

Chilean wine legislation was instituted in 1995. The basic wine law is a 75 percent rule. If a vintage, location, or varietal is stated on the label, 75 percent of what is in the bottle must be from that year, place, or grape. Terms to designate special wines, such as Reserva, Gran Reserva, and Reserva Especial, have no real legal definition. If these terms are used on a label, a place of origin must be indicated.

As for Argentina, there are very few laws regarding location, use of varietals, or claiming vintage. While there is an Instituto Nacionale de Vitivinicultura, the institute currently just oversees grape production and exportation. There are no quality regulations except what the producers impose upon themselves. The one rule in effect is an 80 percent rule regarding varietal claims on the label.

CANADA

The Canadian quality control system is called the Vintners Quality Alliance (VQA). Membership in the VQA is mandatory for producers in Ontario, but is still voluntary for producers in British Columbia. The VQA was established to guarantee consumers that they were drinking wines made from 100 percent Canadian grapes. Other regulations require that stated locations of origin must provide at least 95 percent of the grapes used in making the wine. The stated vintage must also make up 95 percent of the wine. Any wine designated as estate bottled must have the grapes grown on winery-owned land and be processed completely at the winery. Finally, all VQA wines undergo testing by an independent panel, which must taste and approve each wine.

USA

The United States has a variety of national wine and liquor regulations, as well as regulations by state. The national regulations are determined by the Tobacco and Trade Bureau (TTB). The TTB regulates the definition of wine and other alcoholic beverages, as well as determining locations of origin used on labels.

Geographic Identification Rules

The simplest type of wine has an American or United States appellation. The grapes might come from anywhere in the country and the wine is not allowed to carry a vintage. If a group of contiguous states produce the grapes for a wine, it could receive a multistate appellation. In this case, all the states that have contributed grapes to the wine must be indicated.

Probably the most common large appellation is an indication by state. The rules set by the TTB state that for a wine to receive a state appellation, the grapes that produced the wine must make up 75 percent of the contents. Some states, however, have increased the requirement. For Texas, the grapes must make up 85 percent of the content. In California, the requirement is 100 percent California-grown grapes.

Within each state, wines may be labeled by the county from which the wines are sourced. Single-county wines must provide 75 percent of the grapes that make the wine. If more than one county provides grapes, there is a multicounty designation. The counties must be contiguous and the percentage of grapes from each county must be indicated. The North Coast and Central Coast designations are examples of a multicounty appellation.

The ultimate designation of origin is the American Viticultural Area, or AVA. The TTB will approve an AVA if it is a defined grape growing region, with distinct geographical features and distinct boundaries. The downside to AVA designation is that it is merely a set of boundaries. There are no rules regarding choice of grapes planted, yields, or viticultural practices. There are rules about what can be in the bottle if the AVA is on the label. At least 85 percent of the grapes must come from the AVA used on the label. If the wines are labeled by varietal, 75 percent of the wine must be made from that varietal. If the vintage is stated, 95 percent of the grapes must be from that vintage, and if the grapes are from a single vineyard, 95 percent of them must be from that vineyard.

The states have a great influence on the wines produced in their jurisdiction. Some stay with the rules set by the TTB, while others set requirements either stricter than the TTB or in areas not covered by the TTB rules.

Washington

The Washington Wine Commission created the Washington Wine Quality Alliance (WWQA). Almost all the wineries in the state of Washington have joined the alliance. The members agree to discontinue use of generic names for wines, such as Burgundy, Champagne, and Chablis. Alliance members agree to use only vitis vinifera grapes grown in Washington State. The WWQA also defines the term "reserve" when used on a Washington wine. For a wine to be designated as a reserve wine, it must be of higher quality than the winery's usual output. The wine can only account for 10 percent or 3000 cases of the winery's total production, whichever is smaller. Finally, the wineries agree to adopt Best Management Practices, which are designed to grow the best possible grapes while addressing sustainable viticulture, environmental quality, and economic viability.

Oregon

In Oregon, the grapes used in a wine must all come from their stated location of origin. The majority of wines must meet a 90 percent minimum to be labeled by varietal. Several varietals have an exception to that rule, mainly Bordeaux and Rhône varietals and those varietals that are typically blended in Europe, like Tempranillo and Sangiovese. The eighteen exempt varietals can constitute a minimum of 75 percent on any blend.

Distribution Law

After the repeal of Prohibition with the 21st Amendment, the states gained control of how alcohol was distributed in their jurisdiction. In every state, and in Canada, a three-tier system of distribution was established. The three tiers are the producers, distributors, and retailers. It is illegal in most cases for a producer to sell directly to the public. Exceptions are made for wine sales at the winery and, in some states, over the Internet.

In some states, and all provinces of Canada except Alberta, the distributor is actually the government. In the other states, it is private wholesalers who serve as the middlemen. In most cases, there are multiple distributors in a state. Each has a monopoly on the products they distribute. The retailers are forced to purchase their product from the distributor who carries it. If a consumer wishes to purchase a wine that is not represented by a distributor, the producer must find a wholesaler who will act as the middleman in the transaction.

Glossary

Acidity

characteristic of wine that references the pH level of the wine, but more often is used to describe tanginess of a wine when tasted.

Adjunct

a non-barley grain used in beer brewing to provide sugars without contributing to flavor.

Aerobic fermentation

yeast fermentation in the presence of oxygen. The type of fermentation yields water and carbon dioxide as byproducts.

Agglo cork

a semi-synthetic cork that is made of pieces of cork bonded together with an epoxy, then sandwiched between two slivers of whole cork. Also called a one+one cork.

Aglianico

a Southern Italian red grape that makes rich, tannic wines. The name may be derived from hellenico, the Roman term for something of Greek origin.

Agua miel

literally "honey water", the juice from an agave plant after roasting. This liquid will be fermented to form the base for distilling tequila.

Ah-so

a two-pronged cork removal tool. The prongs fit between the cork and the bottle neck, pinching the cork and allowing for removal by twisting and pulling the cork out.

Albariño

vinifera grape grown in Galicia and Northern Portugal. Made as a varietal wine in Spain, or as high quality Vinho Verde in Portugal.

Albariza

the chalky soil in Jerez, Spain that is considered to be the best soil for growing Palomino grapes for Sherry production

Ale

a style of beer made using Saccharomyces cerevesiae. Ales are top fermented at warm temperatures, which produces beers with fruity aromas.

Alembic still

another term for a pot still. It is comprised of a pot, swan's neck and condenser. Distillation in this still must be conducted in batches.

Almacenista sherries

originally private stockholder sherry. Solera systems of almacenista sherries consisted of only one barrel per criadera.

Alsace

an AOC recognized region in North Eastern France. Its best grapes are Riesling, Pinot Gris, Muscat and Gewurztraminer. It is the only region which allows AOC wines to use varietal labeling.

Altec cork

a semi-synthetic cork made from fine cork pieces held together with epoxy.

Amber malt

toasted malt which has a reddish color and a cracker-like flavor

Amontillado

an aged fino sherry. An Amontillado develops through a fino solera system, then is aged in the presence of oxygen to yield a darker, nuttier flavored sherry.

Amoroso

term used for commercial sweetened oloroso Sherry. Typically not top quality.

Añada

the term for the latest vintage of wine used to refresh the solera in Sherry making.

Anaerobic fermentation

yeast fermentation in the absence of oxygen. The byproducts of anaerobic fermentation are ethanol and carbon dioxide.

Añejo

aged tequila, which has been kept in oak barrels for at least 12 months.

Aqua vitae

translated as "water of life", the original term for the product of distillation.

Aquavit

Scandanavian distillate similar to vodka made from potatoes. Often flavored with caraway.

Arena

a type of sandy soil in Jerez. Vines planted on arena had almost twice the yield of vines planted on the best soil, albariza.

Armagnac

a grape based brandy from Gascony in France. The product of single distillation of a Ugni Blanc based wine that is aged in local oak. It is considered more rustic than its cousin, Cognac.

Arneis

white grape found in Northwest Italy. Originally planted to be eaten by the birds, makes a fruity wine with a hint of almond.

Aroma

the term for the primary smells of a wine. Aroma refers to a young wine, meaning the smells are from the varietal character and from fermentation.

Aromatized wine

wine that is fortified and flavored with herbs and spices

Arrope

grape must that has been cooked down by two-thirds and used to sweeten and color fortified wine, especially Malaga and oloroso dulce.

Assemblage

blending of wines to create a certain style. The term is typically used to describe forming the base wine in Methode Traditionelle.

Astringency

the drying action felt on the palate that is a characteristic of tannins.

Autolysis

the decomposition of dead yeast cells by the action of its own internal enzymes. Autolysis provided a toasty, bready component to the wine.

Autovinifier

a self-contained, self-propelled fermentation tank which uses the energy of fermentation to pump wine over the cap in order to quickly extract color and tannin.

Barbera

red grape native to Northwest Italy. Noted for low tannin and high acidity.

Barrel fermentation

description of the use of oak barrels as the vessel for initial fermentation of grape juice or must into wine. Typical in Chardonnay production.

Barro

the poorest soil for growing grapes for Sherry production. Grapes in barro soils yield the coarsest juice. Often planted with Pedro Ximenez grapes that will be used for sweetening oloroso sherries.

Basket press

the traditional press in wine making. Made of wooden staves with gaps between each stave, the press has a flat bottom and a screw press on top. The name derives from its appearance as a wooden basket holding grapes before pressing.

Batch distillation

distillation that must be conducted in small quantities. Conducted in alembic or pot stills, the initial liquid boiled and the vapors collected. When the pot starts to dry out, the process is stopped, the pot is cleaned and recharged with more liquid.

Baumé

French measurement scale of sugar content. Used in determining ripeness at harvest and for determining potential alcohol

Beer–clean

a description of properly cleaned beverage glasses for serving beer. A beer clean glass has no chemical residue and is characterized by rings of foam left clinging to the glass after a sip is taken.

Beneficio

the grading of Douro vineyards from A to F. Determined by the cadestro point system, and resulting grade determines quality of wine that can be made from the harvested grapes

Bentonite

a powdery clay used as a fining agent for wine.

Bin numbers

system of organization for a wine cellar and/or wine list. Allows sommelier to find wines in the cellar, as well as giving customers a method of ordering wines they may not be able to pronounce.

Bitters

a type of liqueur that is flavored with bitter orange and herbs. Named because the bitter taste is predominant.

Black patent malt

malt that has been roasted to the point of carbonization. The burnt character translates to coffee and bitter notes in the beer.

Blanc de blancs

sparkling wine that is made in the Methode Traditionelle, but only with Chardonnay juice.

Blanc de noirs

sparkling wine that is made in the Methode Traditionelle, but with the juice of Pinot Noir and/or Pinot Meunier only.

Blanco

Spanish for "white." Used to describe white wine, or used to describe Tequila that has not been aged.

Blended whiskey

whiskey which is made from barley and a combination of other grains, such as rye, corn, wheat or rice.

Blind tasting

a tasting in which the participants do not know what the wine is before tasting it. A blind tasting is often employed for comparing quality or for analyzing wine for its origin.

Blue agave

species of agave that is used in the production of tequila

Bock

style of lager which dark in color, with noticeable malty sweetness.

Bodega

the Spanish term for winery or wine cellar

Bonne chauffe

the term in Cognac for the hearts of the second distillation of spirits. The bonne chauffe is placed into barrels for aging.

Bordeaux

the largest wine producing region in France, found in the southwest of the country, straddling the Gironde estuary. Its red wines are blends based on Cabernet Sauvignon or Merlot, and its white wines are blends of Semillon and Sauvignon Blanc. It is the home of the Grand Cru Classé chateaux.

Botanicals

the term for vegetal material like seeds, leaves, roots and stems used for flavoring gin and liqueurs.

Bouquet

term used for developed smells in a wine. Bouquet develops with bottle aging.

Bourbon

straight corn whiskey that originated in Kentucky and is aged two years in heavily charred oak barrels.

Brandewijn

original Dutch term meaning "burnt wine" which evolved to become Brandy.

Brandy de Jerez

distilled spirit from the region known for sherry making. Uses the same base wine for sherry, often utilized in the fortification process or sold on its own.

Brettanomyces

strain of yeast which produces barnyard aromas during fermentation. Once considered essential for red Burgundy, now typically considered a fault.

British Plain Spirits

technically the final collected distillate when making Scotch. Collected in a spirit safe, to allow for tax collection, it is then aged before being called Scotch.

Brix

the measurement scale used to check the grapes' sugar level in the United States and other New World countries

Brouillis

the hearts of the first distillation of wine in Cognac. Typically 26–30% alcohol.

Brown sherry

name for commercial sweetened oloroso sherry

Bruised beer

beer which has been warmed from a chilled state, resulting in off flavors.

Brut
the most common level of dosage in Champagne. Represents a sugar content of 0–15 grams per liter of wine.

Bual
a wine grape and a quality level of Madeira. Bual is made by the port method, is medium rich and has 40–60 grams of residual sugar per liter.

Burgundy
a wine region in Eastern France. Noted for top quality Pinot Noir and Chardonnay wines. Also, contains the district of Beaujolais, which is known for wines from Gamay.

Burtonization
the practice of adding mineral salts to water in order to mimic the mineral content of the Burton river and to yield the correct flavor profile for pale ale.

Butt
a large cask commonly used in Sherry production. Holds 132 gallons.

Cabernet Franc
red grape used to make single varietal wines in the Loire Valley and the New World, or as a component of Bordeaux blended wines. One of the parent grapes of Cabernet Sauvignon.

Cabernet Sauvignon
one of the major red wine grapes. Makes ageworthy wines around the world, but most notably in Bordeaux, Napa and Chile. Known for deep color, and high tannin content.

Cachaça
spirit produced from the fermentation and distillation of sugar cane. Cachaça is the national drink of Brazil.

Cadastro
the grading system which ranks the vineyards of the Douro on twelve factors. Results in the beneficio classification.

Calvados
brandy made from apples in Normandy, France.

Campbeltown
small region and style of Scotch production.

Cane
the growing portion of a grape vine. The growing cane is where the fruit will form.

Canopy
the combination of canes and leaves that shade the grapes

Canopy management
a system of managing cane placement, amount of leaf growth and trellising to promote healthy grapes in challenging environments.

Cap

the skins and pulp which float to the top during red wine fermentation

Cap management

treatment of the cap to extract the most color and tannin.

Capataz

the winemaker in Sherry who evaluates the wine and assigns it to a solera.

Caramel malt

also known as crystal malt, this type of malt contains residual starch and sugar crystals. It can have different levels of toast.

Carbonic maceration

the method of fermentation used to make Beaujolais Nouveau, and found in some other wines. Fermentation takes place in a carbon dioxide rich environment, and whole grapes initially ferment by the action of enzymes inside the pulp, before bursting and allowing yeast to continue the fermentation.

Carmenére

the lost grape of Bordeaux, found in Chile where it was misidentified as Merlot. Makes a soft and juicy red wine with a hint of spice.

Cask strength malts

malt whiskey that is bottled at cask strength, typically around 126 proof.

Cask-conditioned

beer that develops carbonation while held in a barrel

Cava

Spanish term for sparkling wine made in the traditional method. Aging is typically 9 months before disgorging.

Cellar temperature

the temperature at which wine is stored. The ideal cellar temperature is 55°F (12.8°C)

Chaptalization

also known as enrichment, it is the addition of sugar to increase the potential alcohol of the must.

Chardonnay

one of the top white wine grapes. Grown and made all over the world, but noteworthy examples come from Burgundy, Napa and Australia. Neutral grape which can be made in a style of the winemaker's choosing.

Charentais still

a version of a pot still found in Cognac. The characteristic of a Charentais still is the shape of the swan's neck

Charmat method

method of sparkling wine production which occurs completely in a tank.

Chenin Blanc

a classic wine grape, which can make high quality wines as well as bulk wines. Makes wines in the Loire in styles ranging from light and dry to sweet to sparkling.

Chocolate malt

dark roasted malt which provides deep brown color to the brew as well as chocolate flavor components.

Clarity

the characteristic of a wine's appearance that describes the absence of haze, cloudiness or foreign matter.

Clean nose

general description of wine smells that do not contain faults.

Clone

a single vine with special characteristics that is propagated through leaf cuttings.

Coffey still

see column still

Cognac

brandy made along the Charentes river, north of Bordeaux. Considered the finest example of a grape based spirit.

Cold soak

the technique of allowing the pressed grapes to sit in their own juice. This allows extraction of tannin in red wine, as well as color and aromatic compounds.

Cold stabilization

chilling wine for 8 days at close to freezing in an attempt to precipitate tartrate crystals before bottling.

Colheita

a vintage tawny port.

Column still

a continuous still, it allows distillation to be conducted constantly, producing very pure distillate.

Compounded gin

inexpensive gin which has been flavored with concentrates rather than botanicals.

Compte system

the method of tracking the age of a Cognac.

Conditioning

the final stage of brewing beer. Conditioning is the stage when final carbonation takes place.

Congener

a flavor compound which distills along with the ethanol, typically found in products of a pot distillation

Continuous still

see column still

Conversion

an initial step of beer brewing or whiskey making. Conversion is the action of diastase on the malt starches in order to convert them to fermentable sugars.

Core to rim variation

change in color from the deepest section in a glass of wine to the thin rim. Observing the core to rim variation can indicate grape varietal or age.

Cork taint

a wine fault. Cork taint is the result of TCA (trichloroanisole) from a bad cork contaminating a wine.

Corkscrew

the instrument used to remove a cork from a bottle. Several styles have been developed

Corvina

grape varietal from Northeast Italy that serves as the main component of Valpolicella, Ripasso and Amarone della Valpolicella.

Coulure

a failure of pollination during vine flowering. Grape vines which experience coulure have some grape flower clusters fail to form fruit.

Cream sherry

Oloroso sherry which has been sweetened with Pedro Ximenez wine.

Crémant

the French wine term for sparkling wine that is not made in the Champagne region.

Criadera

a "nursery" of the solera system. The levels between the top of the system and the solera level, this is where most of the sherry aging occurs.

Cross

the botanical term for taking two vitis vinifera varietals and cross-pollinating to create a new, third varietal which is also known as a cross.

Crusher-destemmer

machine in which whole clusters of grapes are introduced, and in which stems are removed and the grape berries are burst to release juice.

Crusted port

a blended port which has been aged predominantly in the bottle.

Crystal malt

type of malt which contain sugar crystals and soluble starches.

Cultured yeast

any yeast strain which is grown in a lab for consistent results

Cuve-close

alternative French term for charmat or tank method of producing sparkling wine

Cuvée

term for blend, often used in reference to Champagne, but could be used for any wine that is a blend of grapes. Also the name for the juice that comes from the second pressing of the grapes for making Champagne.

Cuvée de prestige

the top quality blend of a Champagne house. Made from the best grapes from the best vineyards.

Dealcoholization

removal of alcohol from a wine after fermentation is complete. Dealcoholization could be complete, removing all the alcohol, or partial, intended to balance the alcohol content while retaining flavor

Dégorgement

process by which yeast is expelled from sparkling wine made in the traditional method. The neck of the bottles containing the yeast is frozen and the cap removed. Pressure inside the bottle pushes the frozen wine and yeast out of the bottle.

Degree days

a measurement of heat developed by UC-Davis. It is designed to categorize the climate of a region and aid in grape selection. Degree days are the summation of the difference between the average daily temperature and 50°F. The difference is summed from April 1 to October 30.

Demi-sec

meaning half-dry, it is a term that describes the sweetness level of some sparkling wines. Demi-sec on a Champagne bottle means the wine contains between 33 and 50 grams of sugar per liter.

Diastase

an amylase enzyme responsible for converting starch to sugar in grain for beer brewing or whiskey making

Disgorging

see dégorgement

Distillate

the condensed vapor of a heated fermented liquid.

Distillation

the process of boiling a liquid and collecting the vapors, thereby concentrating the starting liquids components.

Diurnal variation

the variation in daily temperature between the daytime high and the nighttime low.

Dolcetto

red grape native to Northwest Italy. The name translates to "little sweet one" and the grape makes a fruity, low tannin, easy drinking red wine.

Doppelbock

the strongest and darkest lager. Similar to bock, but with more alcohol, a dobbelbock has a malty sweetness to balance the alcohol.

Dosage

the wine used in sparkling wine production to replace that lost during disgorging. The dosage may or may not contain sugar to adjust the final sweetness level of the wine.

Douro bake

a term used to describe the cooked taste of Port aged in warehouses in the Douro Valley before the arrival of electricity and warehouse refrigeration.

Dry

the absence of sugar in wine.

Dry hopping

addition of hops during fermentation to add hoppy aroma to the beer.

Dual-wing opener

a common household corkscrew. Screwing the worm into the cork raises two handles on either side of the corkscrew. Pressing down on the handles, which resemble wings, pulls the cork out of the bottle.

Early-landed Cognac

a Cognac which was sent to England before its aging was completed in France. Aging is finished in warehouses in England, and the flavor differs from Cognac aged in France.

Eau-de-vie

French term meaning "water of life". The term is used for most fruit brandies other than those made from grapes.

Elévage

translates as "raising" as in raising a child. References the aging of a wine until it is mature enough for bottling and release.

Enrichment

see chaptalization

Estufa

the warm room in which Madeira is heated and aged.

Estufagem

the process by which Madeira is slowly heated while aging. The heating could be conducted mechanically or in naturally hot rooms.

Extraction

the step in the beer brewing process when the soluble sugars and starches are extracted from the grains and dissolved into water.

Extruded plastic cork

a synthetic cork characterized by a spongy cellular structure as the interior and surrounded by a smooth plastic shell. The corks are extruded and sliced, exposing the cellular interior.

Filtration

the process of mechanically removing impurities from a liquid. Filtration can be through a paper filter (similar to a coffee filter) or a membrane filter which has specifically sized openings.

Fine Champagne

label terminology for Cognac made from a blend of base wine from Grande Champagne and Petit Champagne. The blend must contain at least 51% of wine from Grande Champagne.

Fining

the process of adding an agent to clarify a wine. Choices include egg whites, bentonite or isinglass, which help precipitate insoluble proteins and tannins.

Fino sherry

a family of sherries as well as a style. A Fino is characterized by aging under a layer of flor. This provides protection from contact with oxygen, as well as unique flavors from the flor converting alcohol into aldehydes.

Firkin

the cask in which a beer is conditioned and also then from which it is served.

Flavoring

addition of flavor to an alcoholic beverage. Examples of flavoring are adding hops to beer, fruit to lambics, botanicals to make gin and the flavorings to make liqueurs.

Flight

a series of small samples of one kind of beverage to compare and contrast side by side. Fights could be of wine, beer or spirits.

Flor

a special yeast that requires 15.5% alcohol and no fermentable sugar to survive. Flor ferments alcohol into aldehydes and is responsible for the distinct flavors of fino sherry.

Fortified wine

a wine which has had additional alcohol added to it. Added alcohol can be neutral spirits or brandy.

Frasqueira

a vintage Madeira that has been aged a minimum of 20 years in barrel and additional in bottle

Frizzante

lightly carbonated. The term is used for Italian sparkling wines with around 3–4 atmospheres of pressure.

Gamay

the main grape of Beaujolais, Gamay makes light, low tannin, high acid wines.

Garganega

the white grape of Northeastern Italy responsible for Soave DOC wine.

Garnacha

Spanish name of Grenache

Genever

Dutch style gin. Genever has a malty character as well as strong juniper flavor. It is thick and is drunk cold and straight.

Gewurztraminer

a white wine grape which originated in Northern Italy. It is a noble grape in Alsace and is also grown in Washington State and Germany. Gewurztraminer is noted for its low acidity, brassy color and exotic tropical fruit and sweet spice aromas

Gold rum

barrel aged rum that has spent at least three years in charred barrels

Grain whiskey

another term for blended whiskey. This type of whiskey is made with a variety of grains

Grande Champagne

the best region in Cognac for growing grapes, its soil is made of chalk with a composition similar to that in Champagne

Grappa

a pomace brandy, made from the pressed must of finished red wine. many grappas are labeled with the name of the wine from which they have been made.

Green harvest

the removal of excess grape clusters before ripening in order to concentrate the energy of the vine in the remaining clusters

Grenache

a red grape widely planted in Spain and Southern France. It is thin skinned, oxidizes easily and ripens to a high sugar content. It is the grape that forms the basis of Châteauneuf-du-Pape and vins doux naturales, as well as being a part of the blend in Rioja. It makes rosé wines in Provence and dark, tannic wines in Priorato.

Grist

ground malt before addition to water in a mash tun

Gueuze

an unflavored lambic from Belgium. It is fermented with wild yeast and lactic bacteria.

Gyropalette

a very large machine which serves as a replacement for riddling. The centrifugal force moves the yeast from the side of the bottle to the neck in as little as three days, rather than six weeks.

Heads/foreshots

the first collected distillate in a pot distillation. This consists of light, volatile compounds such as methanol, and is discarded.

Hearts

the main distillate in a pot distillation. It is made up of ethanol and is the desired product of distillation

Hectare

a unit of land measure in Europe. It is equivalent to 10,000 square meters or 2.47 acres.

Hectoliter

a unit of volume in the Metric system. It is the equivalent to 100 liters or 26.4 gallons.

Hefeweizen

a wheat beer from Bavaria. It is made from 50% wheat, and is served unfiltered. When young, it has aromas of clove, banana and pineapple.

Highland

the largest region of Scotch production, it is the area which makes the most familiar style of Scotch. Most Scotch producers are located in the Highlands

Hops

the seed cone of a vine, whose oils are used to flavor beer. Hops adds bitterness, aroma and preservative qualities to beer.

Horizontal flight

a flight of wine in which one characteristic is held constant. It may be producers, region, varietal or a trait of the sommelier's choice.

Horizontal screw press

a double screw press in which both ends move, pressing the grapes in the center. The ends are connected by chains, which break up the cake of grape skins when the press is unscrewed.

Horno

Spanish for oven. Piñas are roasted in an horno before being processed for tequila production.

House style

the style in which a producer maintains their product. Champagne houses blend new wine and reserve wine to create the same flavor as they have previously made. The same can be said for blended whiskeys and liqueurs.

Hybrid

a hybrid is the result of breeding a vitis vinifera varietal with another vitis species. Hybrids were first developed in an attempt to maintain vinifera character while adding native American grape resistance to phylloxera.

Hydrometer

a measuring device which measures specific gravity of a liquid. Hydrometers are used to monitor the progress of fermentation.

Inflorescence

the botanical term for grape vine flowering.

Infusion

a method of flavoring a spirit. Botanicals or other flavorings are soaked in the spirit and the flavors are transferred to the spirit by infusion.

IPA

short for India Pale Ale. IPAs have higher hops content, resulting in more bitterness and hops character. The additional hops were added to aid in preserving the beer on its sea voyage to India from England.

Irish whiskey

a malt whiskey which is triple distilled and has no peat influence.

Isinglass

a protein derived from the swim bladder of a sturgeon. It is ground and used as a fining agent.

Isley

a small region in the islands off Scotland which produces a characteristic Scotch. Isley Scotch is noted for its strong peat and iodine flavors and aromas.

ISO

International Standards Organization, the group which creates world standards for products.

Jamaican rum

a full-bodied rum which is fermented using wild yeasts. It is double distilled and aged in oak barrels for three to five years. It is often colored with caramel.

Jimador

the name of the farmer who harvests blue agave, trims the plant down to the piña and prepares the piñas for roasting.

Keg

a metal tank which is used to transport and serve beer.

Kimmeridgean

a type of soil first identified in Kimmeridge England. It is a chalk soil, composed of fossilized oyster shells. The soil extends throughout England, Champagne, Chablis and into Sancerre.

Kriek

a Belgian lambic flavored with black cherries.

Lagares

the shallow stone trough used to crush and ferment grapes in Port production.

Lager

a bottom fermented beer, using saccharomyces carlsbergensis. Lagers are placed in cold storage to condition. They possess a crisp flavor profile with notable carbonation.

Lambic

a Belgian style of beer that is fermented with wild yeast. Lambics are made with 50% wheat, and also are naturally tangy from the action of lactic bacteria.

Late bottled vintage port

also known as an LBV. Late bottled vintage are single vintage ports from very good (but not declared) vintage years. LBV ports are aged for 6 years before release. They are ready to drink and have little sediment in the bottle.

Late-landed Cognac

Cognac sold in England that was aged in France. The difference in climate of the aging site affects the flavor of the Cognac.

Lees stirring

stirring the yeast that settles in the bottom of barrels during fermentation and aging. Called battonage in French. Lees stirring increases the creamy and toasty character of a wine, Chardonnay in particular.

Length

the term which describes how long the flavor of a wine lasts on the palate after spitting or swallowing

Liqueur d'expedition

the French term for dosage. A mix of wine, and possibly sugar that tops off a sparkling wine after disgorging, and determines the final sweetness level of the wine.

Liqueur de tirage

the blend of base wine, yeast and sugar which causes the second fermentation of a sparkling wine.

Loire valley

the longest river in France, it is the backdrop to a vin du pays region as well as four major AOC regions.

London Dry

a style of gin developed in England. London Dry gin has cleaner, less malty character and is designed for mixing.

Lowland

a region of Scotch production, and also the term for the style made there. It is the lightest in style, and is often used for blending.

Low-wines

the Scottish term for the hearts of the first distillation of wash. The low-wines are collected, combined with other low-wines and redistilled.

Maceration

this terms refers to soaking to extract flavor and color. Maceration occurs in red wines after fermentation, when the must remains in contact with the wine before pressing. Maceration is also a process with botanicals to flavor gin and in liqueurs.

Macroclimate

the climate of a large region. Two approaches to macroclimate exist. One views the geographical region as the macroclimate, while another views the climate of the vineyard as the macroclimate.

Maderization

the change in a wine when it is exposed to oxygen and heat. Considered a fault, the wine takes on some characteristics of Madeira.

Magnum

the equivalent of two bottles of wine, or 1.5 liters

Maibock

a special lager made in Einbock. It was made and released to celebrate the end of the brewing season in May.

Malbec

a red wine grape that was used as a blending grape in Bordeaux or as a primary grape in Cahors. Malbec has found a home as a single varietal wine in Argentina.

Malmsey

the sweetest of all Madeiras. It is also the name of one of the grapes which makes Madeira. It is the English name for Malvasia. Malmsey contains between 60 and 120 grams of sugar per liter.

Malo-lactic fermentation

a secondary fermentation in still wine making. Also known as ML or the malo. It uses lactic bacteria to convert the malic acid in a wine to lactic acid. This has the effect of softening the perceived acidity of a wine.

Malt

sprouted and dried barley. Malt has activated diastase to convert starch into sugar, and provides maltose for fermentation.

Malt whiskey

whiskey that is made with only malted barley. Single malts are whiskeys that made by one distiller.

Malting

the process of germinating barley in order activate diastase and start the conversion of starch into sugar.

Malvasia

a group of grapes found throughout the Mediterranean. It is most known for making sweet dessert wines, like Malmsey in Madeira, or as a component to Marsala.

Manzanilla

a special fino sherry whose solera is located in Sanlucar de Barrameda. The humidity of the coastal city allows the flor to become very vigorous, and the final sherry has more flor influenced flavors.

Manzanilla Pasada

a manzanilla sherry that has had some aging in the presence of oxygen

Marc

a pomace brandy in France. Each region makes its own marc, from the pressed grapes, or from other byproducts of winemaking.

Markup

how much the price of a wine is increased from the wholesale cost. Doubling the price is a 200% markup. Typical markups for wine lists range from 250% to 400%.

Mash tun

the apparatus in the beer brewhouse where conversion and extraction occur. The mash tun is filled with water and grist, and a paddle mixes the two to prevent caking.

Melon de Bourgogne

the grape responsible for making Muscadet AOC. It makes a light, crisp wine. It is often vinified sur lie (on the lees), to increase the body of the final wine.

Merlot

a major red wine grape. It is noted for its texture of silky tannins. It is the most widely planted grape in Bordeaux, and comprises the majority of the blend on the right bank. It is a single varietal wine in the United States and Chile.

Mescal

a spirit made in Mexico. It can be made from a variety of agaves, and roasting the piñas in hornos gives the spirit a smoky character.

Mesoclimate

the 'middle" climate. Depending on the definition, mesoclimate may be the climate surrounding the vineyard, or it may be the climate around the row of vines.

Methode ancestrale

a single step sparkling wine vinification technique. The wine is placed into the bottle while it is still fermenting. The wine is typically lightly carbonated and medium sweet.

Methode traditionelle

formerly known as Methode Champenoise. It is the classic sparkling wine making technique. Base wine is inoculated with sugar and yeast, this is bottled and aged for a specific length of time. The yeast sediment is disgorged and the bottle is then ready for sale.

Metodo classico

Italian term for Methode Traditionelle

Metodo tradicional

Spanish for Method Traditionelle

Microclimate

the smallest area of climate categorization. One definition of microclimate is the climate around the vine, another is the climate within the canopy.

Micro-oxygenation (MOX)

a process of slow, microscopic introduction of oxygen to aging wine. The effect of MOX plus wood is to reduce the number of years a wine needs to age before it can be released.

Millerandage

a failure of grape development after pollination. Millerandage is the formation of seedless grapes along with seeded on the same cluster. Seedless grapes do not develop and ripen as do seeded grapes and disturbs the balance of the grapes at harvest.

Mise en place

"everything in its place". The term, typically used by chefs, of having everything necessary to complete a task. For a sommelier, the proper mise en place is all the tools needed to properly open a bottle of wine.

Mistela

Italian for a stop fermented grape juice (like port) that is used to sweeten Marsala

Mistelles

the category of beverage that contains vins de liqueur, or juice that has been fortified with alcohol.

Mixto

a tequila that is not made with 100% blue agave, but includes other agave species.

Molded plastic cork

a synthetic cork substitute. The plastic is molded to look like a complete cork, with smooth plastic encapsulating the sides and the ends of the cork.

Monastrell

Spanish name for Mourvèdre. It is grown in the southeastern portion of the country and is the grape of choice in the developing regions of that area.

Mosto cotto

translated from Italian as "cooked must". It is boiled down grape juice used to sweeten Marsala.

Mourvèdre

a red grape commonly found in Southern France and Spain. It makes dense, tannic wine with a meaty, animal-like character. It is commonly used as a blending grape, but is becoming a varietal in emerging wine regions.

Mousseux

the term which signifies that a wine is sparkling, used commonly in the Loire valley.

Munich malt

a highly toasted amber malt, typically produced in Germany. It produces beer with dark reddish color.

Muscadet

an AOC region located at the junction of the Loire River and the Atlantic. Often used to describe the grape, Melon de Bourgogne, which makes Muscadet wine.

Muscat

a versatile white grape. Used for both wine production as well as table grapes. Commonly used to make sweet wines, such as Asti or Beaumes-de-Venise. Also makes a dry wine in Alsace, where it is considered a noble grape.

Must

the juice of freshly crushed grapes before fermentation. Must may also contain skin, seeds and pulp.

Mutage

the French term for the addition of alcohol to stop the fermentation of a wine. Mutage is often utilized to create a sweet dessert wine.

Napa

the premier wine region in California. It is most known for its Cabernet Sauvignon and Chardonnay, though other grapes are also grown there.

Neat

the term used for serving a spirit without any accompaniment, including ice.

Nebbiolo

the king of the red grapes from the Piedmont region of Italy. It is responsible for Barolo and Barbaresco. Its name is derived from nebbia which means fog in Italian. Nebbiolo makes a light colored, but high acid, high tannin wine.

Negroamaro

a red grape variety from Southeastern Italy. Its name translates to "black bitter". The wine is floral as well as a little medicinal and animal-like.

Nero d'Avola

The native red grape of Sicily. It is a late ripening grape that makes dark, tannic, rich wines.

Nonvintage

the term used to describe wines that are a blend of grapes or wines from different harvest years. Wines that are non-vintage may also be labeled NV.

Oechsle

German measurement scale for evaluating the sugar content of grapes or juice.

Off-dry

the term used for wines that have a little residual sugar and are slightly sweet on the palate.

Oloroso dulce

the Spanish term for a sweet oloroso sherry. Also known as a cream sherry.

Oloroso sherry

a sherry family as well as a style. An oloroso sherry is aged in the presence of oxygen, created a dark, nutty style of sherry. It can be dry or sweetened with PX.

On the rocks

the term for serving a spirit or cocktail over cubes of ice.

Ordinarios

The first distillate in tequila production. Ordinarios are collected and redistilled to make tequila.

Oxidation

the term used for the reaction of oxygen with wine. It can be a fault, as with still wines that have been exposed to air, or a positive characteristic, as in Sherry and Madeira.

Oxidative aging

aging in the presence of oxygen. Aging in barrels, which allows slow transfer of oxygen, is an example of oxidative aging.

Pago

a single vineyard in Spain.

Palate

term used for the flavor profile of a wine. Also, the parts of the body that contain taste buds and perceive tastes.

Pale ale

the classic ale of Northern England. Made with amber malt, the beer has a noticeable nuttiness on the finish.

Pale malt

the lightest toasted malt. It is toasted at the lowest temperature, and pale malt forms the basis of all beers

Palomino

the main white grape for making Sherry. It makes a light, low alcohol, high acid wine before aging.

Patamares

the terracing system in the Douro valley which uses broad swaths of soil held in place by groundcovers to separate the rows of grapevines.

Patent still

see column still

Peat

decomposed vegetal matter that is used as fuel in Scotland. Peat is used to dry malt in making Scotch and can impart a smoky flavor to the malt.

Pedro Ximenez

the second most important grape in making Sherry. Commonly written as PX, the grapes are often dried in the sun before being made into wine. Occasionally a sherry will be made solely of PX, but more often the PX is used to sweeten oloroso sherry to make oloroso dulce or cream sherry.

Petit Champagne

one of the top regions in Cognac. The name refers to the chalky soil of the region, similar to that in Champagne. Petit Champagne is special enough that the grapes can make single region Cognacs.

Phenolic ripeness

the proper development of tannins before harvest. Phenolic ripeness is important for tannins to be able to soften with age.

Phylloxera vastatrix

a microscopic louse which has a complex lifecycle. The louse feeds on the roots of grape vines. Grapes native to North America have developed a resistance to the damage done by phylloxera, but the louse will kill vinifera vines.

Physiological ripeness

the point where the fruit is technically ripe. The sugars have reached a level for the grapes to be sweet and the acid had decreased to the level to become palatable.

Pigeage

French term for punching down. This is a cap management technique which pushes the cap back under the wine during fermentation.

Pilsner

a style of lager that originated in Pilsn in the Czech Republic. Light, crisp, carbonated and with a significant hops flavor and aroma.

Piña

the "stem" of the blue agave. The leaves of the agave are removed leaving the fleshy core of the piña. The piña is roasted and pressed to provide the juice for fermentation to form tequila.

Pinot Blanc

a white grape used for winemaking in France, Germany and Italy. Often confused with Chardonnay, Pinot Blanc makes light, fresh wines.

Pinot Grigio

Italian name and style of white wine grape. The Italian style is harvested early, yielding high acidity and minerality on the palate.

Pinot Gris

the French name and style of the same white wine grape as Pinot Grigio. The style is low in acidity, high in extract and a lanolin like character.

Pinot Noir

a top red wine grape which makes top quality wine in Burgundy, Oregon and California. Pinot Noir makes a light bodied wine with low to medium acidity and tannin and has an earthy character

Pinotage

a cross between Pinot Noir and Cinsault, developed in South Africa. Pinotage has a smoky, almost burnt rubber aroma. It makes a fresh and juicy wine.

Pipe

the 660 liter barrel used for aging and transporting Port

Pisco

a brandy from South America. Different grapes are used to make pisco, depending upon the country of origin.

Pitching the yeast

the term used for describing adding yeast to wort to start beer fermentation.

Plaquette

the small metal tab between the cage and the cork on a sparkling wine bottle. The plaquette is a place to denote the winery on the bottle.

Pneumatic press

an enclosed press which utilizes a rubber bladder which is inflated to press the grapes. The bladder is filled pneumatically, either with liquid or air.

Pneumotage

a new technique of cap management in which pulses of air are released at the bottom of the fermenting tank, and their eruption through the cap disrupts the cap and mixes it back into the wine.

Pomace

the name for the pressed skins, seeds and pulp after fermentation.

Pompe bicyclette method

the "bicycle pump" method of making sparkling wine, basically referring to the direct injection of carbon dioxide into the wine.

Port method

the method of fortification where the addition of the alcohol occurs before the wine has finished fermenting. The result is a wine which retains some residual sugar.

Port tongs

a special tool needed to open vintage ports when the cork is too delicate to be removed by a cork screw.

Port Wine Institute

the Portuguese body which controls the export of Port wine. The declaration of a vintage year is determined by the Port Wine Institute.

Pot still

a still made from a single pot, swans neck, and condenser. It is a batch still, meaning each distillation is uses a separate batch of wine placed into the pot.

Premium Ruby Port

a high quality, young Port. It is either top quality ruby port or a ruby port which has had some tawny port added for increased character.

Primary aroma

aromas in a wine that are inherent to the grape varietal itself.

Primitivo

Italian wine grape that is a sibling to the American Zinfandel. Primitivo makes a spicy, rich wine.

Proof

the designation of alcohol content. Proof is the equivalent to double the percentage of alcohol by volume.

Pulltap

also known as the waiter's friend, it is the most common type of cork screw used by sommeliers. It consists of a lever, knife and worm.

Pulque

the fermented liquid from roasted piñas which is then distilled to make tequila

Pupitre

an A-framed rack which contains of multiple holes. Sparkling wines undergoing riddling or remuage are placed in a pupitre and regularly turned to move the sediment to the neck of the bottle.

Pure malt whiskey

a blend of malt whiskeys. The blend could be of different years from the same distillery or a blend of different regions.

PX

shorthand for Pedro Ximenez. This is either a sherry solely made from Pedro Ximenez, or it is the wine used to sweeten oloroso sherry.

Quinta

a single vineyard or estate in the Douro valley

Racking

the process of siphoning clean wine off of sediment into a fresh barrel

Rain-shadow effect

the influence of a mountain range on the land downwind from it. The clouds meet the mountains and must go up in elevation to pass over the range. When the clouds move up in elevation, they lose their moisture on the windward side of the range, and once they have passed to the leeward side, there is less moisture available for rain.

Rancio

an oxidized style of wine, particularly for vin doux naturale

Raya

a lower quality sherry which is often sweetened and sold as commercial amontillado

Rectified

refined, or separated into finer distinctions

Red label rum

a full bodied dark rum that has been aged in charred wood barrels

Reductive aging

aging in the absence of oxygen. Reductive aging occurs in the bottle.

Refractometer

a tool which uses light and a prism to determine specific gravity. A drop of grape juice is placed on the prism and aimed at the light. Looking into the refractometer shows a scale which indicates the sugar content of the juice

Remontage

French term for pumping over. Wine is siphoned from the bottom of the fermentation tank and sprayed over the cap to extract color and tannin.

Rémuage

French for riddling. This is the process of removing the sediment of the second fermentation by moving the bottles from being horizontal to vertical.

Reposado

meaning "rested". The term placed on tequila that has aged in wood barrels for 2 to 11 months

Reserve list

a separate wine list of special wines, typically more expensive than the majority of the list.

Reserve wine

wine that is kept in storage to be used later in blending. Commonly used in sparkling wine making.

Residual sugar

sugar that remains in the wine after fermentation. Residual sugar is sometimes stated on a bottle as a percentage by volume, or it is measured as grams per liter.

Resveratrol

a compound found in grapes that is an antioxidant. Resveratrol is found in higher levels in grapes from cool climates. It is believed to be responsible for many of the health benefits derived from drinking wine.

Rhône

a river valley in the southeast of France. Separated into two regions, the northern Rhône is a narrow valley while the southern is more wide open.

Rhum agricole

French rums from the Caribbean. The result of fermented sugarcane juice, aging of the rhum occurs in France.

Riddling

English translation of rémuage.

Riesling

a great white wine grape. It is known to make dry, off-dry, sweet and sparkling wines. It is grown in Alsace, where it is a noble grape and is considered the best grape in Germany. It is also grown in Washington state and New York state.

Rotary fermenter

a fermenting vessel that resembles a cement mixer. A fin inside mixes the cap under the fermenting juice. When fermentation is over and the wine drained from the fermenter, the direction of spin is reversed and the pomace is expelled out the end.

Ruby Port

a young, barrel aged Port. Ruby ports are aged in wood for less than seven years. Ruby ports retain their color, tannin and fruitiness.

Running the scales

the term used to describe the movement of wine through the solera system

Saccharomyces carlsbergensis
a species of yeast which ferments wort at low temperature to produce lager

Saccharomyces cerevisiae
species of yeast that is responsible for most fermentation. This species is used to make ales and also to ferment grape juice to wine.

Sangiovese
the main grape of Tuscany, it is the grape that makes Chianti, Brunello and Vino Nobile de Montepulciano.

Sangrita
the combination of tomato and orange juice that is served alongside a shot of tequila

Sauvignon Blanc
a classic white grape, it is known for its high acidity and vegetal aroma and palate notes. Sauvignon Blanc is the grape of Sancerre, Pouilly-Fumé and New Zealand, is used as a blending grape in Bordeaux and makes Fumé blanc in California

Schist
a type of metamorphic rock which originally was mica, which give it a layered quality. It is the main soil of the Douro valley.

Scotch
a whiskey that is the product of grains saccharified by diastase, fermented by yeast, double distilled in pot stills and aged in barrels in Scotland for three years.

Screwpull
a type of corkscrew. A screwpull uses the constant twisting of the worm while the corkscrew is wedged against the bottle to twist the cork from the neck of the bottle.

Secondary aroma
this aroma is characteristic of fermentation and vinification procedures. The aroma of oak in a wine is a secondary aroma.

Sediment
the fine solids that settle to the bottom of a bottle of wine. The sediment typically consists of tannins and color compounds that have become insoluble over time.

Sekt
sparkling German wine.

Semillon
a white wine grape that make fat, full wines. It is blended with Sauvignon Blanc in Bordeaux and is the base wine for making Sauternes.

Sercial
a noble wine grape for making Madeira. It is also the style of wine made from the grape. Sercial is made using the sherry method and is the driest style of wine, containing 8 to 25 grams per liter of residual sugar

Shatter

see coulure.

Sherry method

the method of fortifying wine that adds the neutral spirits or brandy after the wine has completed fermentation.

Shiraz

the Australian name for Syrah. The name also suggests a style of wine which is fruity, rich and full bodied.

Single barrel Bourbon

Bourbon which as been aged in one barrel and then directly bottled.

Single malt Scotch

a malt whiskey made from only malt at a single distillery. It is the best Scotch a distillery can produce.

Single pump corkscrew

known commonly by the brand name The Rabbit™, two handles grip the bottle while a third works the worm. One pump of that handle drives the worm into the cork and pulls it from the bottle.

Single quinta port

a special port made at a single estate or from a single vineyard. Often made as vintage port as well.

Small batch Bourbon

Bourbon which is bottled after several barrels are blended to create a pleasant flavor. Different small batches of Bourbon may taste differently.

Smell

the sense of perception that picks up on odors. It is registered at the olfactory bulb in the sinuses.

Socalcos

the oldest style of terracing in the Douro valley. Its greatest characteristic is tall stone retaining walls which create the terraces holding the grape vines.

Solera

the final level of the solera system. The wine from the solera barrels is blended and bottled for sale.

Solera system

a system of fractional blending to ensure consistency. Wines slowly trickle through the solera system gaining character along the way.

Sommelier

the cellar master. The person in a restaurant who is responsible for the purchase, storage and sale of wine and other alcoholic beverages.

Sonoma

a county in California known for its high quality wines. It has a cooler climate and more diversity of grape varieties than its neighboring county of Napa.

Sour mash

the leftovers from fermentation or distillation. It is added to the next fermentation to nourish the fresh yeast and to inhibit bacterial growth.

Sous bois

French term meaning undergrowth, used to describe earthiness in red Burgundy or other Pinot Noir wines

Sparging

the rinsing of the extracted grist to extract the most sugars before fermentation.

Sparkling wine

wine which contains dissolved carbon dioxide, which is released upon opening and pouring the wine

Speyside

a small region within the Highlands where a majority of Scotch distillers are located. Speyside is a sub-style of Highlands Scotch.

Spirit safe

the collection point for the final Scotch distillation. The spirit is contained in a locked case so taxes could be collected on the amount distilled.

Spirit still

the pot still which is charged with the low-wines and is used for the final distillation of Scotch.

Split

a small bottle which holds 187 mL.

Standard of identity

the definition of an alcoholic beverage as set by the TTB. The beverage must meet the standard of identity in order to be able to label the beverage with the name.

Stelvin™ closure

trademarked name for the screw cap closure.

Sticky

the Australian nickname for a Liqueur Muscat. The name comes from the syrupy character of the Liqueur Muscat, which make the wine sticky.

Still table wine

a wine which possesses between 7 and 14 percent alcohol and is not carbonated.

Stout

a deep, rich form of ale. It often has slightly more alcohol than normal ales, and is made with chocolate or black patent malt.

Straight whiskey

a whiskey made from at least 51% of one type of grain

Stuck fermentation

a fermentation which slows or stops. It is often due to lack of yeast nutrients or from too low a temperature.

Sulfur dioxide

a wine additive which is an antiseptic and an antioxidant. It is used at many points in the wine making process.

Sur lattes

French term for laying wine on its side

Sur pointe

French term for describing sparkling wine that is resting on its neck, i.e. upside down.

Syrah

a main red grape of the Rhône Valley. It is the dominant red grape in the Northern Rhône, and a major contributor to the blended wines of the Southern Rhône.

Taille

the name for the juice that is collected as the third pressing of the grapes harvested for Champagne.

Tails/feints

the last distillate collected, it contains fusel oils and higher weight alcohols. This distillate often has a bad flavor and is discarded.

Tank method

also known as Charmat or Cuve Close. It is the method of making a sparkling wine completely in a sealed tank.

Tannat

highly tannic grape grown mainly in Southwest France and Uruguay.

Tannin

the complex phenolic compounds that derive from wood portions of plant material. Tannin is astringent on the palate, and provides antioxidant protection for red wines.

Tartrates

insoluble salts of tartaric acid which precipitate upon cold stabilization of a wine. If found in a bottle, they are often termed "wine diamonds".

Taste

the sense of perception that is picked up on the palate. There are only five recognized tastes: sweet, sour, salt, bitter and umami.

Tastevin

a shallow silver cup with small depressions used by a sommelier to analyze the color of a wine.

Tawny Port

a Port which has been aged in barrel for at least 7 years.

Tawny reserve

a top quality tawny port. Often a blend of tawny ports and labeled with the style that would be exhibited based on age (10 year, 20, 30 or over 40 year)

TCA

tricholoroanisole. The byproduct of treating a mold tainted cork with chlorine to sterilize it. TCA is responsible for the wine fault known as cork taint or corked wine.

Tempranillo

the main grape of Rioja. It makes a juicy, fresh wine which resembles Pinot Noir to an extent.

Tequila

a spirit made from the fermented juice of blue agave. It can only be produced in the five villages designated by the Mexican government in the state of Jalisco.

Terroir

a sense of place translated into a wine. Terroir is a combination of grape, soil, climate, aspect, drainage and all things that make that one place unique.

Tertiary aroma

also called bouquet. The smells that develop from reductive aging of a wine in a bottle.

Tinta Negro Mole

the most common grape for making Madeira. It was planted after the infestation of phylloxera. If Tinta Negro Mole is the main grape in the blend, the Madeira cannot use any of the four noble grape names to describe the sweetness level.

Torrontes

a white grape found in Argentina which makes aromatic white wines.

Touriga Nacional

the main grape in the blend for Port. It is now also used to make tannic, full bodied red wines from the Douro.

T-pull

the simplest corkscrew. It is simply a worm attached to a handle in the shape of the letter T. It is often the corkscrew that requires the opener to place the wine between their knees to get the leverage to remove the cork.

Transfer method

a method of making sparkling wine that eliminated riddling and disgorgement by emptying the now sparkling wine into a tank, where it is filtered and placed into a fresh bottle under pressure.

Transversage

the process by which sparkling wines of uncommon sizes are filled. It is a modified form of the transfer method.

Trappist ale

an ale that is less a statement of style than of a place of origin. Only six monasteries in Belgium make Trappist ale.

Trebbiano

a white wine grape from Italy. In Italy it makes simple, light wines. It is also known as Ugni Blanc in France.

Trie

a pass through the vineyard during harvest. Grapes picked in tries will not all be picked at the same time, but when the cluster is ripe. This causes several passes through the vineyard.

T-stop

the closure for Port and Sherry. It is a plastic disk which holds a small cork which is in the neck of the bottle. Once the capsule is removed, the disk is turned and the cork can be removed. The T-stop is easy to replace in the bottle.

Ugni Blanc

the main grape in making Cognac and Armagnac. It is the Trebbiano of Italy.

V.O.R.S.

Very Old Rare Sherry or Vinum Optimum Rare Signatum. This is a special sherry that is over 30 years old.

V.O.S.

Very Old Sherry or Vinum Optimum Signatum. This is a special sherry that is over 20 years old.

Vatted malt whiskey

also known as a pure malt whiskey. It is a blend of malt whiskeys from different regions or different distilleries.

VDN

short for vin doux naturale, this is a stop fermented dessert wine made by the port method. They can be red or white wines.

Veraison

French for ripening, this is the time in the life cycle when the grape berries begin to plump and change color.

Verdejo

a white grape in Spain that make light, crisp wines

Verdelho

one of the noble grapes that makes Madeira, as well as a style of Madeira. Verdelho contains 25 to 40 grams of sugar per liter.

Verdicchio

a white wine grape native to Italy. It makes light, crisp wines.

Vertical flight

a flight of wine whose only variable is the vintage. All other aspects of the wine must stay the same. A vertical flight is a way to experience a wine over a multi-year span.

Vienna malt

the German version of amber malt. It has a reddish color and a cracker like flavor profile.

Vinha ao alto

a new style of vine growing in the Douro valley. Vinha ao alto trellised vines run up and down the slope and do not have any retaining walls.

Vinification

the process of turning grape juice into wine.

Vino de color

also called arrope, vino de color is boiled down grape must that gives color and a little sweetness to oloroso dulce sherry.

Vintage

the year in which the grapes are harvested. The term is also used to describe the harvest itself.

Vintage Port

a port made in a single, exceptional year. It is aged for two years in barrels before being bottled where aging should continue for up to 20 years. The Port Wine Institute is the only body which can declare a year a vintage.

Viognier

a white wine grape from the Northern Rhône. It is the grape in Condrieu AOC, but also is made in Australia. It is an aromatic grape, which is full flavored and peachy when fully ripe.

Viticulture

the activities involved in grape growing

Vitis vinifera

the genus and species of wine grapes. The varietals that are familiar as wines are all vitis vinifera. This species originated in the Middle East.

Volatile acidity

also seen as VA. Volatile acidity is considered a fault, and is the result of oxidation or bacterial action on a wine. It is experienced as acetic acid or as ethyl acetate, which is nail polish remover.

Wash

the name for the alcoholic liquid that results from primary fermentation in whiskey production

Wash-still

the first still used in the production of Scotch. This still distills the low alcohol wash into the low wines.

White Port

a Port that is made from white grapes. It is aged in stainless steel, and is made in an off dry or medium sweet style.

White rum

rum which has not been aged, but is bottled immediately after distillation.

Wild ferment

fermentation which occurs as the result of ambient yeasts inoculating the mash or must

Wine Aroma Wheel

The creation of Dr Ann Noble, the wine aroma wheel categorizes the basic aromas found in wine and develops the progression of aromas and flavors in wine.

Wine fault

a flavor or aroma which identifies a problem with the wine. A fault may be the result of poor winemaking or of poor storage of the wine

Winterkill

the death of grape vines from extreme cold. Winterkill is seen in regions with hard winters or in varietals which do not have good cold resistance.

Worm

the screw portion of a corkscrew. It is inserted into the cork and grips it for removal.

Wort

the sugary liquid that results from extraction of sugars from grist into water. Yeast is then added to wort to make beer, or wash if that liquid is to be distilled.

Zinfandel

the "American vinifera grape". Zinfandel is related to Primitivo in Italy. It was originally imported to be a table grape, was used to make raisins and bulk wine and is now the basis for several styles of table and dessert wines.

Bibliography

Baldy, Marion W., PhD. *The University Wine Course*. San Francisco: Wine Appreciation Guild, 2005.

Bastianich, Joseph, and David Lynch. *Vino Italiano*. New York: Clarkson Potter, 2005.

Bird, David. *Understanding Wine Technology*. San Francisco: Wine Appreciation Guild, 2004.

Broadbent, Michael. *The Simon and Schuster Pocket Guide to Wine Tasting*. New York: Simon & Schuster, 1990.

Clarke, Oz. *Oz Clarke's Encyclopedia of Grapes*. New York: Harcourt. 2001.

Delos, Gilbert. *The World of Cognac*. Edison, N.J.: Chartwell Books, 1999.

Dias Blue, Anthony. *The Complete Book of Spirits*. New York: HarperCollins, 2002.

Dominé, André. *Wine*. Cologne: Könemann. 2000.

Fielden, Christopher. *Exploring the World of Wines and Spirits*. London: Wine and Spirits Education Trust, 2005.

Galet, Pierre. *Grape Varieties*. London: Cassell Illustrated, 2002.

Goode, Jaime. *The Science of Wine*. Los Angeles: University of California Press, Berkeley, 2005.

Grossman, Harold. *Grossman's Guide to Wines, Beers and Spirits*, 7th ed. New York: Scribners, 1983.

Herbst, Ron, and Sharon Tyler Herbst. *Wine Lover's Companion*. New York: Barrons, 1995.

Immer, Andrea. *Great Tastes Made Simple*. New York: Broadway Books, 2002.

Jackson, Michael. *Michael Jackson's Beer Companion*. Philadelphia: Running Press, 1994.

———.*Ultimate Beer Companion* London: DK Publishing, 1998.

Johnson, Hugh. *Vintage: The Story of Wine*. New York: Simon & Schuster, 1989.

Johnson, Hugh, and Jancis Robinson. *The World Atlas of Wine*, 5th ed. London: Mitchell Beazley, 2002.

Kramer, Matt. *Making Sense of Italian Wine*. Philadelphia: Running Press, 2006.

Maclean, Charles. *Scotch Whisky: A Liquid History*. London: Cassell Illustrated, 2003.

MacNeil, Karen. *The Wine Bible*. New York: Workman Press, 2001.

Papazian, Charlie. *The New Complete Joy of Home Brewing*. New York: Avon Press, 1993.

Pigott, Stuart. *Planet Wine*. London: Mitchell Beazley, 2003.

Priewe, Jens. *Wine: From Grape to Glass*. New York: Abbeville Press, 2006.

Robinson, Jancis. *The Oxford Companion to Wine*. Oxford, U.K.: Oxford University Press, 2006.

———. *Vines, Grapes and Wines.* London: Mitchell Beazley, 2002.

Rosengarten, David, and Joshua Wesson. *Red Wine with Fish.* New York: Simon & Schuster. 1989.

Sharp, Andrew. *Winetaster's Secrets.* Toronto: Warwick Publishing, 2005.

Stevenson, Tom. *The Sotheby's Wine Encyclopedia,* 4th ed. London: DK Publishing, 2005.

Wine and Spirits Education Trust. *Wine and Spirits: Looking Behind the Label.* London: Wine and Spirits Education Trust, 2005.

Index